# Rape, Sexual Violence and Transitional Justice Challenges



It is estimated that 20,000 people were subjected to rape and other forms of sexual violence during the 1992–1995 Bosnian war. Today, these men and women have been largely forgotten. Where are they now? To what extent do their experiences continue to affect and influence their lives, and the lives of those around them? What are the principal problems that these individuals face? Such questions remain largely unanswered. More broadly, the long-term consequences of conflict-related rape and sexual violence are often overlooked. Based on extensive interviews with male and female survivors from all ethnic groups in Bosnia-Herzegovina (BiH), this interdisciplinary book addresses a critical gap in the current literature on rape and sexual violence in conflict situations. In so doing, it uniquely situates and explores the legacy of these crimes within a transitional justice framework. Demonstrating that transitional justice processes in BiH have neglected the long-term effects of rape and sexual violence, it develops and operationalizes a new holistic approach to transitional justice that is based on an expanded conception of 'legacy' and has a wider application beyond BiH.

**Janine Natalya Clark** is a Reader in Gender, International Criminal Law and Transitional Justice at the University of Birmingham, UK.

## Transitional Justice

Series Editor: Kieran McEvoy

*Queen's University Belfast*

The study of justice in transition has emerged as one of the most diverse and intellectually exciting developments in the social sciences. From its origins in human rights activism and comparative political science, the field is increasingly characterised by its geographic and disciplinary breadth. This series aims to publish the most innovative scholarship from a range of disciplines working on transitional justice related topics, including law, sociology, criminology, psychology, anthropology, political science, development studies and international relations.

**Titles in this series:**

**After Violence**
Transitional Justice, Peace and Democracy
*Elin Skaar, Camila Gianella Malca and Trine Eide (2015)*

**Transitional Justice and Reconciliation**
Lessons from the Balkans
*Edited by Martina Fischer and Olivera Simic (2016)*

**Transitional Justice in Latin America**
The Uneven Road from Impunity towards Accountability
*Elin Skaar, Jemima Garcia-Godos and Cath Collins (2016)*

**Violence, Law and the Impossibility of Transitional Justice**
*Catherine Turner (2017)*

**Resistance and Transitional Justice**
*Edited by Briony Jones and Julie Bernath (2017)*

**Amnesties, Pardons and Transitional Justice**
Spain's Pact of Forgetting
*Roldán Jimeno (2017)*

**Transitional Justice and the Politics of Inscription**
Memory, Space and Narrative in Northern Ireland
*Joseph Robinson (2018)*

**The Reparative Effects of Human Rights Trials**
Lessons from Argentina
*Rosario Figari Layus (2018)*

**Rape, Sexual Violence and Transitional Justice Challenges**
Lessons from Bosnia-Herzegovina
*Janine Natalya Clark (2018)*

# Rape, Sexual Violence and Transitional Justice Challenges

## Lessons from Bosnia-Herzegovina

Janine Natalya Clark

Routledge
Taylor & Francis Group
LONDON AND NEW YORK

First published 2018 by Routledge

2 Park Square, Milton Park, Abingdon, Oxfordshire OX14 4RN
52 Vanderbilt Avenue, New York, NY 10017

*Routledge is an imprint of the Taylor & Francis Group, an informa business*

First issued in paperback 2018



*British Library Cataloguing in Publication Data*
A catalogue record for this book is available from the British Library

*Library of Congress Cataloging in Publication Data*
A catalog record for this book has been requested

ISBN: 978-1-138-74898-9 (hbk)
ISBN: 978-0-367-19178-8 (pbk)

Typeset in Galliard
by Out of House Publishing

In loving memory of Professor Mike Foley

# Contents

*List of figures* *viii*
*Acknowledgements* *ix*
*Abbreviations* *xi*

Introduction: setting the foundations 1

1 Rape and sexual violence in conflict: a historical overview 24

2 The long-term effects of rape and sexual violence: a legacy gap 51

3 Survivors of war rape and sexual violence in Bosnia-Herzegovina: long-term psychological effects and contributory contextual stressors 75

4 The wider impact of war rape and sexual violence in Bosnia-Herzegovina: survivors and their families 101

5 Prosecuting crimes of rape and sexual violence: macro developments, micro realities 124

6 Reparations, rape and sexual violence: developments and setbacks in Bosnia-Herzegovina 155

7 Transitional justice and survivors' long-term needs: mapping and operationalizing a new holistic approach 185

Conclusion: final reflections 219

*Index* *235*

# List of figures


| | | |
|---|---|---|
| 3.1 | A mother's fears | 88 |
| 3.2 | An interviewee's tiny one-room living accommodation | 96 |
| 3.3 | A former factory in central BiH | 99 |
| 7.1 | Rural Bosnia | 203 |
| 7.2 | Macerated oils made by an interviewee | 203 |
| 7.3 | Soaps and lavender gifts made by an interviewee | 204 |
| 7.4 | Knitting and sewing work by survivors in Tuzla | 209 |
| 7.5 | An interviewee's artwork | 210 |

# Acknowledgements

The research underpinning this book was made possible as a result of a Leverhulme Research Fellowship. I would like to thank the Leverhulme Trust for supporting my work (for a second time) and for giving me the opportunity to spend an extended period of time in the field.

Conducting the research for this book was immensely challenging, on a number of levels, and at times the pace of progress was extremely slow. Yet, the whole process was also an incredible journey and one that I would never have completed without the extensive help and support that I received along the way. First and foremost, I would like to thank the 79 male and female survivors of war rape and sexual violence who participated in this research and who gave up their time to speak to me. They demonstrated not only great courage, but also sincere warmth and generosity. Working with them was a truly humbling experience. Despite the fact that some of them had already told their stories on previous occasions, they were nevertheless able to see the value of this research project. I hope that I have done justice to their stories and experiences. My special thanks go to L and her family, who welcomed me into their home and shared with me their everyday lives.

A number of non-governmental organizations (NGOs) fundamentally facilitated this research and to them I extend my heartfelt gratitude. I would especially like to thank Dr Branka Antić-Štauber, the head of *Snaga Žene* in Tuzla, and her wonderful team. While some NGOs were sceptical of my research and questioned my motives, Branka believed in me and the project from the outset and did everything that she could to help me. She made me feel part of *Snaga Žene* and provided me with numerous opportunities to meet survivors and to travel with her and her team. My time in the field would undoubtedly have been very different and far less fulfilling without this collaboration. Branka and her family also made me very welcome in their home and I spent many happy weekends with them.

I would additionally like to thank Sabiha Husić, the head of *Medica Zenica*, who took time out of her extremely busy schedule to speak to me and to listen to my ideas. Thank you also to Irma Šiljak from *Medica Zenica*.

During several visits to Zagreb, I had lengthy conversations with Marijana Senjak, one of the founders of *Medica Zenica* and a superb psychologist-psychotherapist with years of experience of working with survivors of war rape and sexual violence in both Bosnia-Herzegovina (BiH) and Croatia. I learnt so much from talking to Marijana and her sense of humour always lifted me. My discussions with Teufika Ibrahimefendić and Mira Vilušić, psychologists at the Tuzla-based NGOs *Vive Žene* and *Horizonti* respectively, were also of great use and opened my eyes in new ways.

Thank you to Adrijana Hanušić and Selma Korjenić from TRIAL International. Adrijana provided me with valuable insights into the complexities of the Bosnian legal system, particularly in relation to reparations, and Selma spoke to me in depth about civilian victim of war status. I further extend my thanks to Saliha Đuderija, BiH's Assistant Minister of Human Rights and Refugees and a tireless advocate for the rights of survivors of rape and sexual violence; to Mirsad Tokača from the Research and Documentation Centre in Sarajevo; to Amila Džinalija from the State Court of BiH; to Almir Alić, the outreach representative of the International Criminal Tribunal for the former Yugoslavia; and to the extremely talented journalist Denis Džidić.

Several organizations for former camp detainees also aided my research journey in numerous ways. Particular thanks must go to Alija Feriz in Velika Kladuša, Vukan Kovač in Trebinje, Jasmin Mešković in Sarajevo, Džafer Radončić in Brčko District and Saja Ćorić in Mostar. I hit many stumbling blocks along the way, and these individuals offered invaluable support. Thank you also to Vukan for showing me some of the sights of beautiful Trebinje.

I extend my sincerest thanks to my editorial team at Routledge, notably Dr Colin Perrin and Hannah Lovelock. They have always patiently and promptly responded to my questions.

Finally, I would like to thank my Mother for all her love and support throughout the process of writing this book, and for continually reassuring me that I would successfully deliver the manuscript on time.

# Abbreviations

| | |
|---|---|
| ABiH | Army of Bosnia-Herzegovina |
| AFRC | Armed Forces Revolutionary Council |
| APWB | Autonomous Province of Western Bosnia |
| BiH | Bosnia-Herzegovina |
| CDF | Civil Defence Forces |
| DRC | Democratic Republic of Congo |
| EC | European Commission |
| HOS | Croatian Defence Forces |
| HPV | Human papilloma virus |
| HVO | Croatian Defence Council |
| IASC | Inter-Agency Standing Committee |
| ICC | International Criminal Court |
| ICRC | International Committee of the Red Cross |
| ICTJ | International Center for Transitional Justice |
| ICTR | International Criminal Tribunal for Rwanda |
| ICTY | International Criminal Tribunal for the former Yugoslavia |
| JNA | Yugoslav National Army |
| KM | Bosnian Convertible Mark |
| LRA | Lord's Resistance Army |
| MLC | Mouvement de libération du Congo |
| NGO | non-governmental organization |
| OHR | Office of the High Representative |
| OTP | Office of the Prosecutor |
| PTSD | Post-traumatic stress disorder |
| RPE | Rules of Procedure and Evidence |
| RS | Republika Srpska |
| RSCSL | Residual Special Court for Sierra Leone |
| RUF | Revolutionary United Front |
| SCSL | Special Court for Sierra Leone |
| SFRY | Socialist Federal Republic of Yugoslavia |
| SIPA | State Investigation and Protection Agency |

| | |
|---|---|
| STI | sexually transmitted infection |
| TJS | Transitional Justice Strategy |
| TFV | Trust Fund for Victims |
| TRC | truth and reconciliation commission |
| UN | United Nations |
| UNDP | United Nations Development Programme |
| VRS | Army of Republika Srpska |
| VWS | Victims and Witnesses Section |
| VWU | Victims and Witnesses Unit |
| WISP | Witness Support and Protection Unit |
| WSO | Witness Support Office |
| WSS | Witness Support Section |
| ŽŽR | Žena Žrtva Rata |

# Introduction

## Setting the foundations

The air was thick with cigarette smoke. Marija[1] pushed her ashtray around the table, unsure of how or where to begin her story. She had forgotten some of the details. It was a long time ago. Twenty years ago. 1994. She had been at home when a neighbour and cousin knocked at her door, saying that they needed to question her. She was subsequently taken to a camp in Velika Kladuša, in the far north-west corner of Bosnia-Herzegovina (BiH), and from there to a second camp. One night, a soldier came for her. He had a torch and took her into an office. He proceeded to rape her, orally and vaginally. He looked about 50 years old. She was 20 and a virgin. He said he was a colonel. She did not tell any of the other women in the camp what had happened to her. With difficulty, she lit another cigarette. Her hands were shaking as she told her story. She often asks herself why it happened to her. She never hurt anyone. With the exception of her parents and husband, nobody knows that she was raped. She will never tell her children; she feels ashamed. After the war ended, she saw some television footage of the marriage of Željko Ražnatović (Arkan), a notorious Serbian paramilitary leader.[2] In the background, she recognized one of the guests – the colonel who had raped her. He has never been brought to justice. Sometimes she wishes that he had killed her.[3]

During and immediately after the 1992–1995 Bosnian war, there was huge interest in 'raped women'. Journalists, health workers and human rights activists wanted to speak to them and to document their stories.[4] What had they experienced? Who had raped them? What had they seen? Today, in contrast, BiH and its war victims are old news. Time has moved on, and new conflicts and victims are now at the centre of international affairs. The simple passage of time, however,

1 Not her real name.

2 Arkan married the folk singer Ceca (Svetlana Ražnatović) in February 1995. He was assassinated five years later. See Christopher S. Stewart, *Hunting the Tiger: The Fast Life and Violent Death of the Balkans' Most Dangerous Man* (New York: Thomas Dunne Books, 2007).

3 Author interview, 2 December 2014.

4 Karen Engle, 'Feminism and Its (Dis)Contents: Criminalizing Wartime Rape in Bosnia and Herzegovina', *American Journal of International Law* 99 (2005): 778–816, at 794.

does not mean that Marija, and the thousands of men and women who suffered rape and sexual violence during the Bosnian war, have themselves 'moved on'. Many survivors continue to live with, and to be affected by, their war trauma. As the United Nations (UN) Secretary-General underlined in a recent report, 'The social imprint of conflict-related sexual violence remains profound more than 20 years since the end of the war, with slow progress towards the establishment of a comprehensive support system for survivors'.[5] What is striking is that in BiH, and indeed more broadly, the long-term 'social imprint' of conflict-related rape and sexual violence remains seriously under-researched.

This book addresses that gap. Based on semi-structured qualitative interviews with male and female survivors across BiH, it constitutes a novel and in-depth study of the multi-layered long-term consequences of the mass rapes and sexual violence committed during the Bosnian war. Survivors in BiH are frequently referred to as mere statistics: 20,000, 50,000, 60,000. Their suffering is thus collectivized, their identities subsumed within the meta category of 'rape victims'. This research, in contrast, is about *individuals*. Using a narrative approach in the form of interwoven vignettes, it examines some of the myriad ways in which male and female survivors are still affected by their war trauma today. The aim is not to depict these men and women as broken and destroyed, but rather to convey the reality of their everyday lives as they themselves described them. Few interviewees had happy stories to tell, and their pain, sadness and disappointment are integral parts of this book.

As a note on terminology, reference is consistently made throughout this book to both rape and sexual violence. While the latter broadly encompasses the former, rape and sexual violence are distinct crimes. Rape is fundamentally an unwanted and non-consensual act of vaginal, anal or oral penetration that may or may not include the use of force. Sexual violence is a wider and more diverse category. According to the Rome Statute of the International Criminal Court (ICC), it includes – in addition to rape – sexual slavery, enforced prostitution, forced pregnancy and enforced sterilization.[6] All of the female interviewees who participated in this research had been raped. Some of them had also experienced sexual violence, including forced pregnancy. Few of the male interviewees disclosed what had happened to them during the war. At least one of them, however, had been raped. The others had suffered various forms of sexual violence, including genital beatings and being made to perform sexual acts on other men.

5 UN Security Council, *Report of the Secretary-General on Conflict-Related Sexual Violence*, S/2016/361 (20 April 2016), § 74, available at: www.securitycouncilreport.org/atf/cf/%7B65BFCF9B-6D27-4E9C-8CD3-CF6E4FF96FF9%7D/s_2016_361.pdf (accessed 7 May 2016).

6 See, for example, ICC, *Rome Statute* (17 July 1998), Article 8(2)(e)(vi), available at: www.icc-cpi.int/nr/rdonlyres/ea9aeff7-5752-4f84-be94-0a655eb30e16/0/rome_statute_english.pdf (accessed 10 July 2016).

## Approaching rape and sexual violence

Feminist scholars have been at the forefront of research on rape and sexual violence. Feminism, broadly defined, has thus become the dominant lens through which the subject is examined and explored. Feminists such as Rhonda Copelon and Catharine MacKinnon were among the first to write about the use of rape and sexual violence during the Bosnian war.[7] Ultimately, however, the attention given to these crimes, both in BiH and in Rwanda during the 1994 genocide, triggered a feminist backlash. Some scholars, for example, have expressed concern that a heavy focus on rape and sexual violence essentializes women as vulnerable and passive victims. According to Žarkov, 'if women are already defined as rapable, then rape defines femininity as violability and becomes a female mode of being, and simultaneously ascribes propensity to rape as an essential prerogative of maleness'.[8] In her view, therefore, such definitions[9] 'reinforce the greatest of all gender distinctions, assuming, once again, the omnipotence of men and the absolute powerlessness of women'.[10] For her part, Simić has drawn attention to the fact that some consensual sex took place between soldiers and civilians during the Bosnian war. In so doing, she has sought to challenge the dominant rape narrative, wherein 'the body of a Bosnian woman is exclusively constructed as victimized, precarious, unstable and pained'.[11]

The purpose of this book is not to portray survivors of rape and sexual violence as individuals without agency. Indeed, it deliberately uses the more empowering term 'survivors' rather than 'victims'. Born as a result of war rape, a young Bosniak woman underlined that 'When you use the word "survivor", you know that these women are still here. They are present and alive. When you use the word "victim", it's as if these women are dead and gone'.[12] In BiH, men and women who

7 See, for example, Catharine A. MacKinnon, 'Rape, Genocide and Women's Human Rights', *Harvard Women's Law Journal* 17 (1994): 5–16; Rhonda Copelon, 'Surfacing Gender: Re-Engraving Crimes against Women in Humanitarian Law', *Hastings Women's Law Journal* 5 (1994): 243–266, at 264.

8 Dubravka Žarkov, 'Ontologies of International Humanitarian and Criminal Law: "Locals" and "Internationals" in Discourses and Practices of Justice', in Marlies Glasius and Dubravka Žarkov (eds), *Narratives of Justice in and out of the Courtroom: Former Yugoslavia and Beyond* (Cham, Switzerland: Springer, 2006), 3–21, at 6.

9 See, for example, Susan Brownmiller, *Against our Will: Men, Women and Rape* (New York: Fawcett Columbine, 1975), 15; Lisa S. Price, 'Finding the Man in the Soldier-Rapist: Some Reflections on Comprehension and Accountability', *Women's Studies International Forum* 24 (2001): 211–227, at 214.

10 Žarkov, *supra* note 8, at 6.

11 Olivera Simić, 'Challenging Bosnian Women's Identity as Rape Victims, as Unending Victims: The Other "Sex" in Times of War', *Journal of International Women's Studies* 13 (2012): 129–142, at 137.

12 Author interview, 4 March 2015. According to a recent study by *Medica Zenica* and *Medica Modiale* involving 51 female survivors of rape and sexual violence in BiH, 'Most of them do not like hearing themselves described as victims, and preferred to see themselves in positive ways such as being strong, active, fighters, sensible, caring, fair, correct and persistent'.

suffered rape and sexual violence during the war are survivors because many of them, despite their war trauma, continue to fight – for their children, for their families, for a better life. Nevertheless, this does not mean that we should minimize or overlook the diverse ways in which they continue to struggle as a result of what they endured during the war. Engle questions whether 'rape is really a fate worse than death', insisting that 'Many women, including rape victims, in Bosnia and Herzegovina arguably saw a worse fate – death – befall their family members'.[13] The reality, however, is that for some individuals, rape *is* a fate worse than death. It is unhelpful, therefore, to make sweeping generalizations about this crime and how it is experienced. To do so is itself a form of disempowerment that disallows individualized responses and reactions.

It is also imperative to stress that vulnerability and agency are not mutually exclusive. One does not negate or cancel out the other.[14] Illustrative of this is Fineman's concept of the 'vulnerable legal subject'. While vulnerability is part of the human condition, it is not a constant. Rather, 'We will be dependent, weak, in need, as well as empowered and strong at different developmental stages in our lives… We are situated beings who live with the ever-present possibility of changing needs and circumstances in our individual and collective lives'.[15] Hence, the fact that an individual is rendered vulnerable in a particular situation at a particular time does not mean that this vulnerability is permanent or that it precludes the expression of agency and agentic behaviour. For Fineman, thus, 'the counterpoint to vulnerability is *not* invulnerability, for that is impossible to achieve, but rather the *resilience* that comes from having some means with which to address and confront misfortune'.[16]

Resilience is a concept that has 'recently experienced surging popularity',[17] and the growing volume of academic research on the topic clearly reflects this. Extant scholarship on resilience, which can be defined as 'a dynamic process encompassing positive adaptation within the context of significant adversity',[18] focuses

Medica Zenica and Medica Mondiale, *"We are still Alive", "We have been Harmed but We are Brave and Strong": Research on the Long-Term Consequences of War Rape and Coping Strategies of Survivors in Bosnia and Herzegovina* (Zenica, BiH: *Medica*, 2014), 124.

13 Engle, *supra* note 4, at 813.

14 Carine M. Mardorossian, 'Toward a New Feminist Theory of Rape', *Signs* 27 (2002): 743–775, at 771; Nicola Henry, 'The Fixation on Wartime Rape: Feminist Critique and International Criminal Law', *Social and Legal Studies* 23 (2014): 93–111, at 103.

15 Martha Albertson Fineman, 'Feminism, Masculinities and Multiple Identities', *Nevada Law Journal* 13 (2013): 619–639, at 637.

16 Martha Albertson Fineman, 'The Vulnerable Subject and the Responsive State', *Emory Law Journal* 60 (2010): 251–275, at 269.

17 Katarina Kolar, 'Resilience: Revisiting the Concept and its Utility for Social Research', *International Journal of Mental Health Addiction* 9 (2011): 421–433, at 421.

18 Suniya S. Luthar, Dante Cicchetti and Bronwyn Becker, 'Research on Resilience: Response to Commentaries', *Child Development* 71 (2000): 543–562, at 543.

heavily on children and adolescents[19] and on adults who experienced childhood sexual abuse.[20] In contradistinction, there has been surprisingly little research on resilience in survivors of rape and sexual violence – and in particular survivors of war rape and sexual violence. While this book is not specifically about resilience,[21] it is important to emphasize that resilience cannot easily flourish if the long-term effects of rape and sexual violence – and the needs to which they give rise – are neglected and overlooked.

According to some feminist scholars, the international attention that is now being given to rape and sexual violence in conflict unduly detracts from other forms of gender-based violence in warfare.[22] Related to this is the more specific concern that a focus on 'exceptional' wartime violence necessarily marginalizes the 'ordinary' everyday violence that women suffer. For Bueno-Hansen, thus, 'The idea of "exceptional violence" is particularly problematic when investigating how conflict impacts women'.[23] The boundaries between 'exceptional' and 'ordinary' violence, however, are fluid and porous rather than fixed and clearly defined. Some female interviewees, for example, disclosed that they had experienced or were experiencing domestic violence (verbal and/or physical); others were worried that their own trauma was having a negative effect on their children. Three of them revealed that their sons had been violent towards them and/or their own wives. In other words, violence can 'travel' between war and post-war contexts, and 'everyday' peacetime violence can hence become part of the long-term legacy of 'exceptional' war violence.

When feminists write about rape and sexual violence, they are primarily concerned with male-on-female violence. Such violence, in turn, is commonly framed as reflecting and manifesting wider forms of structural violence against women.[24]

19 See, for example, Steven J. Condly, 'Resilience in Children: A Review of Literature with Implications for Education', *Urban Education* 41 (2006): 211–236; Peggy C. Giordano, *Legacies of Crime: A Follow-Up of the Children of Delinquent Girls and Boys* (Cambridge: Cambridge University Press, 2010).

20 See, for example, Margaret O'Dougherty Wright, Joan Fopma-Loy and Stephanie Fischer, 'Multidimensional Assessment of Resilience in Mothers who are Child Sex Abuse Survivors', *Child Abuse and Neglect* 29 (2005): 1173–1193; Christine B. Bogar and Diana Hulse-Killacky, 'Resiliency Determinants among Female Adult Survivors of Childhood Sexual Abuse', *Journal of Counselling and Development* 84 (2006): 318–327.

21 The author has recently been awarded a European Research Council Consolidator Grant to undertake a five-year comparative study of resilience in survivors of war rape and sexual violence in BiH, Colombia and Uganda.

22 Susan Harris-Rimmer, 'Sexing the Subject of Transitional Justice', *Australian Law Journal* 32 (2010): 123–147, at 132; Fionnuala Ní Aoláin, Dina F. Haynes and Naomi Cahn, 'Criminal Justice for Gendered Violence and Beyond', *International Criminal Law Review* 7 (2011): 425–443, at 426–427.

23 Pascha Bueno-Hansen, 'Engendering Transitional Justice: Reflections on the Case of Peru', *Journal of Peacebuilding and Development* 5 (2010): 61–74, at 64.

24 See, for example, Brownmiller, *supra* note 9; MacKinnon, *supra* note 7; Jacqui True, *The Political Economy of Violence against Women* (Oxford: Oxford University Press, 2012); Sara E. Davies and Jacqui True, 'The Pandemic of Conflict-Related Sexual Violence and the

As Alison argues, however, 'explanations for the widespread, often systematic and orchestrated occurrences of wartime rape need to be more complicated'.[25] Fundamentally, rape and sexual violence are highly useful weapons of war.[26] This utility, in turn, leaves both men and women exposed to the risk of these crimes. It is essential, therefore, that more attention is given to male survivors and their needs.[27] It is also essential that men's experiences of rape and sexual violence are studied in their own right and not 'squeezed' into a particular gender narrative, whereby they are 'reduced to exceptions to the (implied) real victims of sexual violence: women and girls'.[28]

This book is about the long-term effects of rape and sexual violence for male and female survivors in BiH. Its first key objective is to provide a rich qualitative analysis of some of the problems and challenges that these individuals face today, as they themselves described them, and to examine the wider impact of their war trauma on their families. Pupavac has consistently criticized what she terms 'international therapeutic governance', a model which 'pathologizes war-affected populations as psychologically dysfunctional'.[29] While it is impossible to analyse the long-term effects of rape and sexual violence without a trauma referent, it is not the aim of this research to portray survivors as 'psychologically dysfunctional'. What it seeks to emphasize is the fact that more than 20 years after the Bosnian war ended, survivors of war rape and sexual violence are still affected by and living with the consequences of what they went through during the conflict.

These long-term consequences have wider implications for transitional justice, which the UN has defined as the 'full range of processes and mechanisms associated with a society's attempt to come to terms with a legacy of large-scale past

Political Economy of Gender Inequality', in Anastasia Powell, Nicola Henry and Asher Flynn (eds), *Rape Justice: Beyond the Criminal Law* (London: Palgrave MacMillan, 2015), 160–181.

25 Miranda Alison, 'Wartime Sexual Violence: Women's Rights and Questions of War', *Review of International Studies* 33 (2007): 75–90, at 78.

26 See, for example, Patricia A. Weitsman 'The Politics of Identity and Sexual Violence: A Review of Bosnia and Rwanda', *Human Rights Quarterly* 30 (2008): 561–578. Crawford maintains that the effectiveness of rape as a weapon of war stems from 'gender norms and the power relationships inextricably tied to them'. Kerry F. Crawford, 'From Spoils to Weapons: Framing Wartime Sexual Violence', *Gender and Development* 21 (2013): 505–517, at 510. This, however, is a reductionist approach to the utility of rape in war. See, for example, Dara J. Cohen, 'Explaining Rape during Civil War: Cross-National Evidence (1980–2009)', *American Political Science Review* 107 (2013): 461–477.

27 Some feminist scholars have themselves acknowledged this. See, for example, Olivera Simić, 'Engendering Transitional Justice: Silence, Absence and Repair', *Human Rights Review* 17 (2016): 1–8, at 3.

28 Maria Eriksson Baaz and Maria Stern, *Sexual Violence as a Weapon of War? Perceptions, Prescriptions, Problems in the Congo and Beyond* (London: Zed Books, 2013), 36.

29 Vanessa Pupavac, 'International Therapeutic Peace and Justice in Bosnia', *Social and Legal Studies* 13 (2004): 377–401, at 378.

abuses'.[30] All human rights abuses leave a grassroots legacy and a deep imprint on individual lives. Yet, transitional justice typically assumes an ad hoc and temporally bounded form characterized by one-off events and processes – the formation of a court; the creation of a truth and reconciliation commission (TRC); the issuing of an apology; the introduction of a vetting system. Operating 'across a temporal shift',[31] transitional justice is quintessentially about addressing the past in order to create a better present and future. The boundaries between these temporal periods, however, are innately fluid; and if little attention is given to the long-term consequences of human rights violations, 'legacy' issues are necessarily dealt with in only a partial and compromised way. The second key aim of this book, thus, is to develop a new holistic approach to transitional justice that comprehensively addresses the legacy of rape and sexual violence.

## Transitional justice and legacy issues

Transitional justice is a burgeoning field, and this is reflected in a rich and growing body of literature. Diverse viewpoints exist, however, on what exactly transitional justice is and what it encompasses.[32] For some scholars, transitional justice is primarily about legal accountability. Teitel, for example, defines it as 'the conception of justice associated with periods of political change, characterized by legal responses to confront the wrongdoings of repressive predecessor regimes'.[33] In a similar vein, Bell, Campbell and Ní Aoláin note that, 'As generally understood, "transitional justice" encompasses the legal, moral and political dilemmas that arise in holding human rights abusers accountable at the end of conflict'.[34] Beyond these 'violation-centric' definitions,[35] transitional justice has also been defined and conceptualized in much wider terms. According to Pham, Vinck and Weinstein, transitional justice 'lies at the nexus of public health, conflict and social reconstruction';[36] for David and Choi, it consists of 'policy interventions

30 UN, *Guidance Note of the Secretary-General: United Nations Approach to Transitional Justice* (March 2010), 2, available at: www.un.org/ruleoflaw/files/TJ_Guidance_Note_March_2010FINAL.pdf (accessed 8 September 2016).

31 Alex Jeffrey, 'The Political Geographies of Transitional Justice', *Transactions of the Institute of British Geographers* 36 (2011): 344–359, at 347.

32 Catherine O'Rourke, *Gender Politics in Transitional Justice* (Abingdon: Routledge, 2013), 10.

33 Ruti G. Teitel, 'Transitional Justice Genealogy', *Harvard Human Rights Journal* 16 (2003): 69–94, at 69.

34 Christine Bell, Colm Campbell and Fionnuala Ní Aoláin, 'Justice Discourses in Transition', *Social and Legal Studies* 13 (2004): 305–328, at 305.

35 Brandon Hamber, 'There is a Crack in Everything: Problematising Masculinities, Peacebuilding and Transitional Justice', *Human Rights Review* 17 (2016): 9–34, at 17.

36 Phuong N. Pham, Patrick Vinck and Harvey M. Weinstein, 'Human Rights, Transitional Justice, Public Health and Social Reconstruction', *Social Science and Medicine* 70 (2008): 98–105, at 98.

designed to bring justice, disclose truth, and promote reconciliation in order to foster peace and establish democracy in the aftermath of political conflicts and authoritarian regimes';[37] and Kent maintains that 'At its core, transitional justice works discursively to establish a break between the violent past and a peaceful, democratic future, and is based upon compelling frameworks of resolution, rupture and transition'.[38]

Alongside definitional debates, questions have increasingly been asked about the inclusivity of transitional justice. Concerns that it often operates in ways that are disconnected from on-the-ground realities and priorities have led to growing calls for more bottom-up and participatory ways of dealing with the past that give local communities an opportunity to be 'listened to and heeded'.[39] Greater grassroots involvement and participation are seen as crucial for enabling more victim-centred forms of transitional justice.[40] This strand of scholarship reflects a normative view of transitional justice as a quintessentially dialectic process. If it operates simply as a 'global project',[41] formulated and developed from the top down, this will circumscribe its grassroots impact. This book builds on and adds to these inclusivity critiques. Fundamentally, the long-term effects of rape and

37 Roman David and Susanne Y.P. Choi, 'Getting Even or Getting Equal? Retributive Desires and Transitional Justice', *Political Psychology* 30 (2009): 161–192, at 162.

38 Lia Kent, 'Transitional Justice in Law, History and Anthropology', *Australian Feminist Law Journal* 42 (2016): 1–11, at 1.

39 Patricia Lundy and Mark McGovern, 'Whose Justice? Rethinking Transitional Justice from the Bottom Up', *Journal of Law and Society* 35 (2008): 265–292, at 284. See also Kieran McEvoy and Lorna McGregor, *Transitional Justice from Below: Grassroots Activism and the Struggle for Change* (Portland, OR: Hart Publishing, 2008); Wendy Lambourne, 'Transitional Justice and Peacebuilding after Mass Violence', *International Journal of Transitional Justice* 3 (2009) 28–48; Rosalind Shaw and Lars Waldorf, with Pierre Hazan (eds), *Localizing Transitional Justice: Interventions and Priorities after Mass Violence* (Stanford, CA: Stanford University Press, 2010); Paul Gready and Simon Robins, 'From Transitional to Transformative Justice: A New Agenda for Practice', *International Journal of Transitional Justice* 8 (2014) 339–361; Annika Björkdahl and Johanna Mannergren Selimovic, 'Gendering Agency in Transitional Justice', *Security Dialogue* 46 (2015): 165–182; Simon Robins and Erik Wilson, 'Participatory Methodologies with Victims: An Emancipatory Approach to Transitional Justice Research', *Canadian Journal of Law and Society* 30 (2015): 219–236; Nina Schneider and Marcia Ezparza (eds), *Legacies of State Violence and Transitional Justice in Latin America: A Janus-Faced Paradigm?* (Lanham, MD: Lexington Books, 2015).

40 Jonathan Doak, 'The Therapeutic Dimension of Transitional Justice: Emotional Repair and Victim Satisfaction in International Trials and Truth Commissions', *International Criminal Law Review* 11 (2011): 263–298; Simon Robins, 'Towards Victim-Centred Transitional Justice: Understanding the Needs of Families of the Disappeared in Post-Conflict Nepal', *International Journal of Transitional Justice* 5 (2011): 75–98; *idem*, 'Challenging the Therapeutic Effect: A Victim-Centred Evaluation of Transitional Justice Process in Timor-Leste', *International Journal of Transitional Justice* 6 (2012): 83–105.

41 Rosemary Nagy, 'Transitional Justice as Global Project: Critical Reflections', *Third World Quarterly* 29 (2008): 275–289, at 276.

sexual violence underscore the need for a more inclusive approach to the concept of 'legacy'.

### *Holistic transitional justice*

Olsen, Payne and Reiter distinguish between four main existing approaches to transitional justice, namely 'maximalist, minimalist, moderate, and holistic'.[42] Holistic approaches can be defined as compound approaches that seek to address and overcome the limitations of individual transitional justice mechanisms. According to Boraine, for example, a holistic approach to transitional justice consists of five 'key pillars' – namely accountability, truth recovery, reconciliation, institutional reform and reparations – and thus combines retributive, restorative and reparative justice.[43] In a similar vein, Duthie maintains that 'it is precisely the individual weakness of each measure taken on its own that strengthens the argument for a holistic approach to transitional justice, in which the different measures are employed in an integrated manner'.[44]

In BiH, there has been a strong emphasis on criminal prosecutions. Trials at the International Criminal Tribunal for the former Yugoslavia (ICTY)[45] – established by the UN Security Council in 1993 – have focused heavily on atrocities committed during the Bosnian war; and as part of its completion strategy, the Tribunal has transferred cases, expertise and materials to courts in BiH. These national and local institutions are now prosecuting their own war crimes cases.[46] However, transitional justice in BiH has also taken non-judicial forms, including several short-lived truth commissions,[47] memorials,[48] a Women's Court[49] and an ongoing campaign (which is not confined to BiH) to establish a regional

42 Tricia D. Olsen, Leigh A. Payne and Andrew G. Reiter, 'The Justice Balance: When Transitional Justice Improves Human Rights and Democracy', *Human Rights Quarterly* 32 (2010): 980–1007, at 982.

43 Alexander L. Boraine, 'Transitional Justice: A Holistic Interpretation', *Journal of International Affairs* 60 (2006): 17–28, at 19.

44 Roger Duthie, 'Afterword: The Consequences of Transitional Justice in Particular Contexts', in Alexander L. Hinton (ed.), *Transitional Justice: Global Mechanisms and Local Realities after Genocide and Mass Violence* (New Brunswick: Rutgers University Press, 2011), 249–256, at 255.

45 See www.icty.org/

46 See, for example, www.sudbih.gov.ba/

47 See Jelena Subotić, *Hikacked Justice: Dealing with the Past in the Balkans* (Ithaca: Cornell University Press, 2009), 146–153.

48 See, for example, Sebina Sivac-Bryant, 'The Omarska Memorial Project as an Example of How Transitional Justice Interventions Can Produce Hidden Harms', *International Journal of Transitional Justice* 9 (2015): 170–180; Janine N. Clark, 'Are there "Greener" Ways of Doing Transitional Justice? Some Reflections on Srebrenica, Nature and Memorialisation', *International Journal of Human Rights* 8 (2016): 1199–1218.

49 Janine N. Clark, 'Transitional Justice as Recognition: An Analysis of the Women's Court in Sarajevo', *International Journal of Transitional Justice* 10 (2016): 67–87.

fact-finding commission (RECOM).[50] In other words, even if they have not been 'employed in an integrated manner', different types of transitional justice have nevertheless been used in BiH.

This book, however, ultimately conceptualizes holistic transitional justice as something more than just a fusion of retributive, restorative and reparative justice. Rather than addressing the individual components of transitional justice and how they fit together ('bricolage'), it is mainly concerned with the broader operationalization of transitional justice as a process. Its central argument is that transitional justice must be more holistic in how it *deals* with the legacy of human rights abuses – and specifically rape and sexual violence. In developing a holistic approach to transitional justice, moreover, it foregrounds three core dimensions of holism focused around time, socio-economic factors and gender respectively.

### *A temporal dimension of holism*

The concept of time is inherently embedded in transitional justice. Underpinning all transitional justice processes is the notion of moving on from the past. As Nagy remarks, transitional justice 'implies a fixed interregnum period with a distinct end… Notions of "breaking with the past" and "never again", which align with the dominant transitional mechanisms, mould a definitive sense of "now" and "then"'.[51] In order for societies to move on from and break with the past, it is essential that the past is dealt with. Unaddressed injustices fester, becoming a 'spectral presence'[52] that overshadows the present. The process of dealing with past injustices, in turn, often necessitates a temporal 'shrinkage' or compression, particularly when these injustices span an extended period of time. As Hinton argues, 'Long, complicated histories are reduced to an immediate past of conflict; future horizons are delimited by the promised end of the transition, an idyllic state of civilized democracy'.[53] What this book is calling for, however, is a temporal broadening.

The temporally bounded way in which transitional justice typically operates, through the creation of ad hoc mechanisms and processes focused on precisely demarcated time periods, is intrinsically discordant with the temporal expansiveness of rape and sexual violence.[54] As an Amnesty International report underlines,

50 See www.recom.link/
51 Nagy, *supra* note 41, at 280.
52 Christiane Wilke, 'Enter Ghost: Haunting Courts and Haunting Judgments in Transitional Justice', *Law and Critique* 21 (2010): 73–92, at 74.
53 Alexander L. Hinton, 'Introduction: Toward an Anthropology of Transitional Justice', in Alexander L. Hinton (ed.), *Transitional Justice: Global Mechanisms and Local Realities after Genocide and Mass Violence* (New Brunswick: Rutgers University Press, 2011), 1–22, at 7.
54 Michelle S. Kelsall and Shanee Stepakoff, '"When We Wanted to Talk about Rape": Silencing Sexual Violence at the Special Court for Sierra Leone', *International Journal of Transitional Justice* 1 (2007): 355–374; Doak, *supra* note 40; Gearoid Millar, 'Local Evaluations of

'For many survivors of rape and other forms of sexual violence, the story does not necessarily end in a courtroom. Many still struggle in their daily lives with the physical, emotional and social consequences of the crimes committed against them'.[55] Transitional justice therefore needs to operate in a more longitudinal way and to acknowledge the relevance of what Neimanis and Walker have termed 'thick time'. This refers to 'a transcorporeal stretching between present, future, and past, that foregrounds a nonchronological durationality'.[56] Crimes of rape and sexual violence epitomize this 'stretching' across different time periods, and the final chapter explores possible ways of operationalizing a temporal broadening of transitional justice that respects thick time.

## *A socio-economic dimension of holism*

One of the growing debates within existing scholarship is whether transitional justice should deal with violations of economic and social rights.[57] For those who maintain that it should, 'holistic' transitional justice necessarily includes social justice. In a speech delivered in October 2006, for example, Louise Arbour, a former chief prosecutor at the ICTY, emphasized that 'By reaching beyond its criminal law-rooted mechanisms to achieve social justice, transitional justice could contribute to expand our traditional and reductive understanding of "justice" by rendering it its full meaning'.[58] For some, the development of a more expansive conception of

Justice through Truth Telling in Sierra Leone: Postwar Needs and Transitional Justice', *Human Rights Review* 12 (2011): 515–535.

55 Amnesty International, *When Everyone is Silent: Reparation for Survivors of Wartime Rape in Republika Srpska in Bosnia and Herzegovina* (1 October 2012), 4, available at: www.amnesty.org/en/documents/EUR63/012/2012/en/ (accessed 5 May 2016).

56 Astrida Neimanis and Rachel L. Walker, '*Weathering*: Climate Change and the "Thick Time" of Transcorporeality', *Hypatia: A Journal of Feminist Philosophy* 29 (2014): 558–575, at 561.

57 Louise Arbour, 'Economic and Social Justice for Societies in Transition', *New York University Journal of International Law and Politics* 40 (2007): 1–28; Tafadzwa Pasipanodya, 'A Deeper Justice: Economic and Social Justice as Transitional Justice in Nepal', *International Journal of Transitional Justice* 2 (2008): 378–397; Ismael Muvingi, 'Sitting on Powder Kegs: Socioeconomic Rights in Transitional Societies', *International Journal of Transitional Justice* 3 (2009): 163–182; Eibe Riedel, Gilles Giacca and Christophe Golay (eds), *Economic, Social, and Cultural Rights in International Law: Contemporary Issues and Challenges* (Oxford: Oxford University Press, 2014); Evelyn Schmid and Aoife Nolan, '"Do No Harm": Exploring the Scope of Economic and Social Rights in Transitional Justice', *International Journal of Transitional Justice* 8 (2014): 362–382; Madeleine Rees and Christine Chinkin, 'Exposing the Gendered Myth of Post Conflict Transition: The Transformative Power of Economic and Social Rights', *International Law and Politics* 48 (2016): 1211–1226.

58 Louise Arbour, 'Economic and Social Justice for Societies in Transition', Second Annual Transitional Justice Lecture hosted by the Center for Human Rights and Global Justice at New York University School of Law and by the International Center for Transitional Justice (25 October 2006), 14, available at: http://graduateinstitute.ch/files/live/sites/iheid/files/shared/executive_education/IMAS/IMAS_2011_2012/Modules%202010-2011_S3/Droits/FR_LArbour_25102006_ENG.pdf (accessed 8 June 2016). See also Amanda

justice is also critically linked to the realization of core transitional justice aims. If, for example, violations of economic and social rights are excluded from the remit of transitional justice, 'we are left with only uncertain guarantees of nonrepetition';[59] which by extension impacts on the goal of prevention. Some scholars, however, have voiced concerns about expanding transitional justice in a socio-economic direction.[60] According to Waldorf, the strongest argument for broadening transitional justice to include socio-economic wrongs is that victims and survivors themselves may prioritize them.[61] Yet, he also questions whether transitional justice mechanisms are 'practically suited' to addressing these wrongs.[62] This would require a long-term commitment that is temporally incongruous with the fact that transitional justice, according to Waldorf, is 'inherently short-term, legalistic and corrective'.[63]

This book does not specifically engage in the debate on whether transitional justice should deal with economic and social rights. It does, however, respond to a particular concern that Schmid and Nolan have articulated. According to them, 'arguments for and against more attention being paid to economic and social issues in transitional justice cannot be properly addressed until we know what exactly an author is arguing that transitional justice mechanisms should, or should not, be taking on'.[64] This book contends that transitional justice, theorized holistically, needs to address the long-term legacy of human rights abuses – specifically rape and sexual violence – and that this legacy has a socio-economic dimension. Economically, survivors must have 'their basic needs met before they can begin the process of healing and speaking out'.[65] Socially, rape and sexual violence affect not only individuals, but also families and communities. They can trigger the breakdown of relationships; they can create fear; they can weaken community bonds. The final chapter of the book explores how a holistic approach to transitional justice might address these socio-economic legacy strands.

Cahill-Ripley, 'Foregrounding Socio-Economic Rights in Transitional Justice: Realising Justice for Violations of Economic and Social Rights', *Netherlands Quarterly of Human Rights* 32 (2014): 183–213, at 185; Rees and Chinkin, *supra* note 57, at 1219.

59 Lisa J. Laplante, 'Transitional Justice and Peace Building: Diagnosing and Addressing the Socioeconomic Roots of Violence through a Human Rights Framework', *International Journal of Transitional Justice* 2 (2008): 331–355, at 333.

60 See, for example, Rama Mani, 'Dilemmas of Expanding Transitional Justice, or Forging the Nexus between Transitional Justice and Development', *International Journal of Transitional Justice* 2 (2008): 253–265, at 255.

61 See, for example, Robins, *supra* note 40, at 86.

62 Lars Waldorf, 'Anticipating the Past: Transitional Justice and Socio-Economic Wrongs', *Social and Legal Studies* 21 (2012): 171–186, at 175.

63 Ibid., at 179.

64 Schmid and Nolan, *supra* note 57, at 378.

65 Anne-Marie de Brouwer and Sandra Ka Hon Chu, *The Men Who Killed Me: Rwandan Survivors of Sexual Violence* (Vancouver: Douglas & McIntyre, 2009), 158. More broadly, Millar pertinently asks: 'What would be the point in knowing who had chopped off your child's hands, when you can't afford to feed her breakfast, cure her boils, or send her to school?' Millar, *supra* note 54, at 530.

### *A gender dimension of holism*

Within existing scholarship on gender and transitional justice, the absence/exclusion of women constitutes a central theme. Transitional justice is depicted as a primarily 'masculine' field that neglects women and the harms that women suffer, from gender-based violence in the private realm to everyday forms of structural violence.[66] Bell and O'Rourke remark that 'Efforts to "add gender" to transitional justice have been most prominent with respect to the legal treatment of sexual violence in conflict'.[67] Yet, for some feminists, as previously noted, the prosecution of rape and sexual violence does not represent an unequivocal step forward. Not only does it risk essentializing women as victims,[68] but it further contributes to marginalizing the 'wider harm spectrum' that women experience.[69] However, such arguments do not take sufficient account of the fact that the long-term consequences of rape and sexual violence can include 'everyday' and structural forms of violence, from domestic abuse[70] to poverty fuelled by unaddressed health needs.[71] Greater attention to the wider legacy of these sexual crimes would therefore help to bring other examples of gender-based violence more squarely within the purview of transitional justice processes. This 'gender broadening' must also include gender-based violence against men.

More attention is now being given to the use of rape and sexual violence against men in conflict.[72] Nevertheless, it still remains a comparatively under-researched

66 Nagy, *supra* note 41, at 285; Kent, *supra* note 38, at 3.

67 Christine Bell and Catherine O'Rourke, 'Does Feminism Need a Theory of Transitional Justice? An Introductory Essay', *International Journal of Transitional Justice* 1 (2007): 22–44, at 26.

68 Susanne Buckley-Zistel, 'Redressing Sexual Violence in Transitional Justice and the Labelling Women as "Victims"', in Thorsten Bonacker and Christoph Safferling (eds), *Victims in Transitional Justice* (The Hague: T.C.M. Asser Press, 2013), 91–100, at 96; Bueno-Hansen, *supra* note 23, at 320.

69 Ní Aoláin, Haynes and Cahn, *supra* note 22, at 429.

70 In 2014, for example, Human Rights Watch interviewed 163 women and nine men who experienced and/or witnessed rape and sexual violence committed during the post-election violence in Kenya that occurred between December 2007 and February 2008. Eighty-one survivors admitted that they had subsequently experienced physical and verbal domestic abuse. According to the report, 'Some of the women Human Rights Watch interviewed said their husbands blamed them for being "unfaithful" and for infecting them with diseases if they contracted HIV and other sexually transmitted infections. Others said their husbands constantly accused them of having affairs with their rapists'. Human Rights Watch, *I Just Sit and Wait to Die: Reparations for Survivors of Kenya's 2007–2008 Post-Election Sexual Violence* (15 February 2016), 53, available at: www.hrw.org/sites/default/files/report_pdf/kenya0216_web.pdf (accessed 9 December 2016).

71 See Helen Liebling-Kalifani, Angela Marshall, Ruth Ojiambo-Ochieng and Nassozi Margaret Kakembo, 'Experiences of Women War-Torture Survivors in Uganda: Implications for Health and Human Rights', *Journal of International Women's Studies* 8 (2007), 1–17, at 8.

72 See, for example, Sandesh Sivakumaran, 'Sexual Violence against Men in Armed Conflict', *European Journal of International Law* 18 (2007): 253–276; Chris Dolan, 'Has Patriarchy

issue and feminist concerns with the totality of 'women's experiences'[73] have contributed to the marginalization of men's experiences. Both women and men are subjected to rape and sexual violence in conflict, and both women and men can suffer profound long-term consequences. Gender is thus an important dimension of holistic transitional justice, and the long-term legacy of rape and sexual violence necessarily includes the legacy for male and female survivors.

It is important to note that there is a growing body of literature on masculinity and transitional justice.[74] As will be discussed in the final chapter, however, this literature has mainly looked at men as perpetrators, through an emphasis on violent masculinity and what Theidon has termed 'militarized masculinity'.[75] What is needed is a stronger focus on male survivors and their experiences of rape and sexual violence. Within existing scholarship, the concept of impugned masculinity is often foregrounded.[76] According to Sivakumaran, 'Today, there is in society the idea that male victims of sexual violence are not "real men" for "real men" would not have let this happen to them'.[77] Not only should this relationship between rape, sexual violence and masculinity be empirically explored rather than simply assumed a priori, but as this book argues attention must also be given to how the long-term consequences of rape and sexual violence themselves shape and impact on male survivors' individual sense of masculine self.

## Methodology and fieldwork

### *Ethical issues*

According to Rosenbaum and Langhinrichsen-Rohling, 'Too often, researchers and reviewers focus on the results of a study and whether they were significant

been Stealing the Feminists' Clothes? Conflict-Related Sexual Violence and UN Security Council Resolutions', *IDS Bulletin* 45 (2014): 80–84; Heleen Touquet and Ellen Gorris, 'Out of the Shadows? The Inclusion of Men and Boys in Conceptualisations of Wartime Sexual Violence', *Reproductive Health Matters* 24 (2016): 36–46; Amrita Kapur and Kelli Muddell, *When No One Calls it Rape: Addressing Sexual Violence against Men and Boys in Transitional Contexts*, International Center for Transitional Justice (ICTJ) (December 2016), available at: www.ictj.org/sites/default/files/ICTJ_Report_SexualViolenceMen_2016.pdf (accessed 9 January 2017).

73 Fionnuala Ní Aoláin, 'Advancing Feminist Positioning in the Field of Transitional Justice', *International Journal of Transitional Justice* 6 (2012): 205–228, at 225.

74 See, for example, Brandon Hamber, 'Masculinity and Transitional Justice: An Exploratory Essay', *International Journal of Transitional Justice* 1 (2007): 375–390; *idem*, *supra* note 35; Naomi Cahn and Fionnuala Ní Aolaín, 'Hirsch Lecture: Gender, Masculinities and Transition in Conflicted Societies', *New England Law Review* 44 (2009): 1–24; Erin Baines, 'Gender, Responsibility and the Grey Zone: Considerations for Transitional Justice', *Journal of Human Rights* 10 (2011): 477–493.

75 Kimberly Theidon, 'Transitional Subjects: The Disarmament, Demobilization and Reintegration of Former Combatants in Colombia', *International Journal of Transitional Justice* 1 (2007): 66–90, at 76.

76 See, for example, Alison, *supra* note 25, at 81.

77 Sivakumaran, *supra* note 72, at 270.

and meaningful. It is possible for the findings to become separated from the people and processes that generated the particular results'.[78] At the heart of this book are 79 men and women who suffered rape and sexual violence during the Bosnian war. Interviewing survivors, however, necessarily raises complex ethical issues, and foremost among these is the potential for re-traumatization.[79] Three particular steps were taken throughout the research process to minimize this risk.

Firstly, none of the survivors who participated in this research were asked direct, probing or intrusive questions about their trauma. Rather, one of the opening prompts used was: 'Could you tell me something about your war story?' Some interviewees gave only a brief response and moved on to talk about their current problems. Others, however, spoke in far more detail. Interviewees who were raped in camps, for example, frequently described the general living conditions, and in particular the lack of sufficient food and sanitation. When they reached the point in their stories where they were sexually violated, some interviewees never used the word 'rape' and simply said something like: 'Then he did with me whatever he wanted'. Some used the term rape, but metaphorically closed the door on that part of their war experience. What occurred behind that door was something that they did not want to speak about, or perhaps could not speak about. Others, in contrast, shared certain details – the number of times that they were raped and by how many soldiers, how they were raped, what their rapists said to them. However, there is nothing 'voyeuristic' about the data.[80] Survivors were given the space to say as much or as little as they wanted, and they used this space in diverse ways. In all cases, their stories are presented with sensitivity and care.

Secondly, the interviews were grounded in an empowerment approach. Ullman and Townsend point out that 'Because the act of rape constitutes having someone take away control from the victim, it is crucial that survivors regain control in any and all ways possible to facilitate their empowerment'.[81] In this research, therefore, a key priority was to give survivors a sense of control over the interview process. Although the interviews were semi-structured, they often assumed the

78 Alan Rosenbaum and Jennifer Langhinrichsen-Rohling, 'Meta Research on Violence and Victims: The Impact of Data Collection Methods on Findings and Participants', *Violence and Victims* 21 (2006): 404–409, at 408.

79 Lisa Aronson Fontes, 'Ethics in Violence against Women Research: The Sensitive, the Dangerous and the Overlooked', *Ethics and Behaviour* 14 (2004): 141–174, at 165.

80 Stiglmayer's book on the use of rape in the Bosnian war contains some extremely graphic content. One survivor revealed, for example, that: 'They pushed bottle necks into our sex, they even stuck shattered, broken bottles into some women ... Guns too'. Alexandra Stiglmayer, 'The Rapes in Bosnia-Herzegovina', in Alexandra Stiglmayer (ed.), *Mass Rape: The War against Women in Bosnia-Herzegovina* (Lincoln, NE: University of Nebraska Press, 1994), 82–169, at 118. While these descriptions are very explicit, they capture the full brutality of rape and this reality cannot be – and should not be – glossed over or diluted.

81 Sarah E. Ullman and Stephanie M. Townsend, 'What is an Empowerment Approach to Working with Sexual Assault Survivors?' *Journal of Community Psychology* 36 (2008): 299–312, at 305.

form of free-flowing conversations based around several core themes.[82] Survivors set the pace of the interviews and they could pause or stop them at any time. Some of them did become upset, although not necessarily when speaking about their war trauma per se. One interviewee cried, for example, when she talked about her son who had died as a result of a brain tumour. Another interviewee became distressed when describing the challenges that she had faced in trying to achieve status as a civilian victim of war.[83] None of them, however, chose to stop the interviews. By telling their stories, they took control of them and told them in the way that they wanted to tell them. Some interviews lasted for an hour. Some lasted for four hours.

Thirdly, Ullman and Townsend further note that implicit in an empowerment approach is the idea that 'no one can really make things better for the survivor or fix the problem, which is likely a common well-intentioned, yet ultimately negative reaction of those around the survivor'.[84] It was always made clear to interviewees that the purpose of this research was to explore and understand the long-term impact of their war trauma and not to 'fix' their current problems. It is regrettable that some researchers and journalists have interviewed survivors in BiH and made various pledges of assistance and financial support which, in most cases, ultimately came to nothing. In north-west BiH, for example, an interviewee who was living in extremely poor conditions described how she had previously told her story to a young woman who claimed to work for an overseas aid organization. It turned out that this self-declared humanitarian was in fact a student writing her Master's dissertation. The food parcels that she had promised her interviewees never materialized. It is unsurprising, therefore, that many survivors – as well as NGO staff – have become jaded. In short, there exists a deep research fatigue in BiH. This made the process of doing fieldwork extremely challenging. In some cases, moreover, NGO leaders (although by no means all) were openly hostile, insisting that they needed to protect 'their women' from further trauma.[85] Some of them also assumed that this research was financially motivated.

All of this raises a second important ethical issue relating to the impact of research. Fundamentally, how can we ensure that the work we do has some positive benefits on the ground? While this research was never about 'fixing' people's

82 Although an interview guide was used, this was not rigidly adhered to. The questions in the interview guide were divided into five sections addressing the following key topics: the Bosnian war, the long-term effects of rape and sexual violence (psychological and physical), the wider ricochet effects, everyday life and transitional justice.

83 The process of obtaining this status is complex. Those survivors in BiH who have civilian victim of war status receive a monthly social payment. This will be discussed in Chapter 6.

84 Ullman and Townsend, *supra* note 81, at 305.

85 Janine N. Clark, 'Working with Survivors of War Rape and Sexual Violence: Fieldwork Reflections from Bosnia-Hercegovina', *Qualitative Research* (published online 17 October 2016), available at: http://journals.sagepub.com/doi/abs/10.1177/1468794116671987.

problems, efforts were made to 'give something back' wherever possible. As one illustration, some interviewees were either unaware that they could apply for civilian victim of war status or knew nothing about the process of applying. In these situations, I always offered information and provided the contact details of a relevant NGO. In some cases, and with the interviewees' consent, I also passed on certain information to *Snaga Žene*, the Tuzla-based NGO with which I closely collaborated during my time in the field. As a result of this information-sharing, *Snaga Žene* is now working with some of the survivors who participated in this research, including several male survivors whom I interviewed in August and October 2014 and a group of female survivors whom I first met in November 2014. These men and women are currently receiving occupational therapy as well as regular visits from the NGO.

### *The interviewees*

During a month-long scoping visit to BiH in August 2014 and a subsequent year-long field visit from October 2014 to October 2015, I interviewed 79 survivors.[86] Key information regarding these men and women is summarized in Table 0.1. I conducted the interviews in Bosnian/Croatian/Serbian and no translators were used.

Sixty-six of the interviewees were women and 13 were men. The interview sample would ideally have been more gender-balanced. However, while there are a number of NGOs in BiH that offer support to female survivors, male survivors have been decidedly neglected. Finding and gaining access to these men was therefore immensely challenging. In this regard, several organizations of former camp detainees – including in Sarajevo and Velika Kladuša – played a critical facilitating role. If the number of men who participated in this research was small, the interviews with male survivors also tended to generate rather 'thin' data. As previously noted, some of the female interviewees spoke directly about being raped. In contrast, the male interviewees did not, although some of them described sexual abuses inflicted on other men that they had witnessed. One interviewee showed me a statement that he had previously given to the Bosnian police, disclosing that he had been forced to perform oral sex on a fellow camp detainee. He stressed that he could not talk about this. As Scarce has argued, 'Perhaps the most powerful effect of male rape is the stigma, shame, and embarrassment that follows as survivors begin to cope with what has happened to them'.[87]

86 In addition, 16 key informant interviews were conducted to further enrich the data. These interviewees included NGO leaders, a lawyer and four psychologists.

87 Michael Scarce, *Male on Male Rape: The Hidden Toll of Stigma and Shame* (Cambridge, MA: Perseus Publishing, 1997), 19. According to the Institute for International Criminal Investigations, 'male victims of SGBV [sexual and gender-based violence]

*Table 0.1* The interviewees

| *Gender* | *Age* | *Ethnicity* | *Birthplace* | *Current residence situation* | *Place of trauma* |
|---|---|---|---|---|---|
| Female: 66 | Under 40: 11 | Bosniak: 57 | Sarajevo: 4 | Living in same pre-war location: 47 | Camp: 46 |
| Male: 13 | 40s: 18 | Serb: 15 | Central BiH: 16 | Internally displaced (own entity): 23 | Other place of detention: 10 |
| | 50s: 34 | Croat: 6 | North-east BiH: 15 | Internally displaced (different entity): 6 | Own home: 10 |
| | Over 60: 16 | Other: 1 | Brčko District: 8 | Living in another country: 3 | Other: 13 |
| | | | Posavina: 5 | | |
| | | | Eastern BiH: 6 | | |
| | | | North-west BiH: 12 | | |
| | | | Herzegovina: 12 | | |
| | | | Other: 1 | | |

Furthermore, none of the male interviewees directly expressed how they felt or spoke about their emotions. They overwhelmingly focused on their current problems. In doing so, they did offer important glimpses into how the trauma of their war experiences continues to affect their lives today. Overall, however, if it is 'the interviewer's task to help in unpacking an experience and gaining access to deeper levels and more nuanced descriptions of the experience',[88] there were clear

generally are especially loath to talk about the violations they have been subjected to'. Institute for International Criminal Investigations, *Guidelines for Investigating Conflict-Related Sexual and Gender-Based Violence against Men and Boys* (29 February 2016), 12, available at: www.iici.info/uploads/docs/160229_IICI_InvestigationGuidelines_ConflictRelatedSGBVagainstMenBoys.pdf (accessed 6 May 2016).

88 Donald E. Polkinghorne, 'Language and Meaning: Data Collection in Qualitative Research', *Journal of Counselling Psychology* 52 (2005): 137–145, at 143.

differences between male and female interviewees in how much of their experiences they were willing to share. One possible explanation is that the men had previously had few opportunities to tell their stories and thus to gain control over them.

In addition to including men, the interview sample also needed to be ethnically inclusive. Although the largest number of rapes committed during the Bosnian war involved Serb/Bosnian Serb forces and Bosniak women[89] – and the interview data reflects this – it must be acknowledged that crimes of rape and sexual violence occurred on all sides. Of the total 79 interviewees, 57 were Bosnian Muslims (Bosniaks), 15 were Bosnian Serbs, six were Bosnian Croats and one was Macedonian (she had moved to BiH during the 1970s). The process of creating an ethnically mixed sample, however, was extremely difficult. The main survivor-focused associations and NGOs in BiH are based in Bosniak-majority areas in the Federation and they work primarily (although not exclusively) with Bosniak women. To the extent that these organizations were willing to endorse this research, and not all of them were, they mainly facilitated contact with Bosniak survivors. NGOs working with Bosnian Serb and Bosnian Croat survivors are considerably fewer, less organized and generally less visible, and regrettably neither of the main organizations supported this research.

If, as Goodman notes, 'Hard-to-reach populations are hard to reach',[90] survivors of rape and sexual violence are an epitomizing example of this. *Snaga Žene*, a highly respected NGO that works with survivors from all ethnic groups across large areas of BiH, played a crucial enabling role in this research. The head of the NGO provided me with invaluable opportunities to meet survivors, to get to know them as individuals and ultimately to interview some of them. Several other organizations also facilitated access to survivors. Additionally, snowball sampling was used; interviewees were asked if they knew other survivors who might be willing to participate in the research. This proved to be an effective way of meeting new survivors. Purposive sampling, moreover, was employed to ensure that male survivors and survivors from all ethnic groups were included in the interview sample. Although I was based in Tuzla, I travelled extensively across BiH and conducted interviews in almost 30 different places across the Federation, Republika Srpska (RS) and Brčko District. One interview (and one key informant interview) took place in Croatia. Interviewees came from four main areas, namely central BiH (16), north-east BiH (15), north-west BiH (12) and Herzegovina (12). Within the total sample, however, 29 interviewees were internally displaced. Of these, 23 were still living in the same entity (i.e. the Federation or RS) and six were not. An interviewee from Vlasenica in RS, for example, was now living in Tuzla (in the Federation); and an interviewee who was born in Sarajevo (part of the Federation) was now living near Bijeljina (RS). Interviewees were mainly

89 UN, *Security Council Resolution 780*, S/RES/780 (6 October 1992), §251.

90 Leo A. Goodman, 'Comment: On Respondent-Driven Sampling and Snowball Sampling in Hard-to-Reach Populations and Snowball Sampling not in Hard-to-Reach Populations', *Sociological Methodology* 41 (2011): 347–353, at 350.

raped in formal camps, including Sušica in Vlasenica, Viktor Bubanj in Sarajevo and Luka in Brčko District.

The men and women who participated in this research are not statistics or percentages. They are individuals with individual stories. This book cannot tell 'their' stories.[91] Only they themselves can do that. As Hill Bailey and Tilley have argued, however, 'The goal of qualitative researchers is to provide ways of understanding experience from the perspective of those who live it'.[92] By presenting the data in the form of vignettes, this book demonstrates the diverse ways in which the rapes and sexual violence committed during the Bosnian war continue to impact on survivors' individual lives today – and the lives of their families[93] – and why transitional justice needs to address the long-term legacy of these crimes. Due to the sensitive nature of the research, no names or other identifying information will be used.

## Structure of the book

This book consists of seven chapters. Chapter 1 is a crucial background chapter. Emphasizing the intrinsic and multi-dimensional usefulness of rape and sexual violence in situations of war and armed conflict, it also underlines that this usefulness now comes at a potential price. Today, rape and sexual violence are widely recognized as constituting heinous weapons of war that inflict incalculable suffering. Normatively and juridically, the international landscape has changed and 'no impunity' has become the dominant discourse. The news of mass rapes occurring in the Bosnian war fundamentally contributed to these macro developments. The remainder of the chapter provides key background information about the war and the ways in which rape and sexual violence were used. It draws attention to the fact that these crimes were committed by all sides, although not to the same extent; it underscores that both women and men were targeted; and it highlights the neglected issue of intra-ethnic rapes.

Chapter 2 examines existing scholarship on the long-term effects of rape and sexual violence in conflict. Few major studies exist and long-term effects are often analysed quantitatively. This has the effect of depersonalizing survivors and their experiences. Qualitative studies have primarily focused on Africa. While significant research has been conducted on the use of rape and sexual violence during the Bosnian war, little attention has been given to the long-term legacy of

91 Tshepo Madlingozi, 'On Justice Entrepreneurs and the Production of Victims', *International Journal of Transitional Justice* 2 (2010): 208–228.

92 Patricia Hill Bailey and Stephen Tilly, 'Storytelling and the Interpretation of Meaning in Qualitative Research', *JAN: Informing Practice and Policy Worldwide through Research and Scholarship* 38 (2002): 574–583, at 575.

93 Interviews were also conducted with a young man and woman who were both born as a result of rape. One of them had spoken publicly on a number of occasions. The other was the daughter of one of the female survivors whom I interviewed.

these crimes. To date, only one major study exists. Conducted by the Bosnian NGO *Medica Zenica* and its partner organization *Medica Mondiale*, the study was published as a report in 2014.[94] Although it constitutes extremely important and valuable research, it is limited in several ways. Most significantly, all of the 51 research participants were women, and, overwhelmingly, Bosnian Muslim women. This book is based on a larger and more diverse sample. What further distinguishes it, both from the *Medica* study and from broader existing scholarship on the long-term consequences of rape and sexual violence, is that it goes beyond simply documenting these consequences. It also reflects on and analyses their implications for transitional justice.

Chapter 3 is the book's first empirical chapter. It explores some of the long-term psychological effects of the rapes and sexual violence committed during the Bosnian war. However, it also demonstrates that other factors and intervening variables may have contributed to or exacerbated survivors' ongoing problems and difficulties. In other words, the trauma of rape and sexual violence needs to be situated within a broader matrix of contextual stressors. The chapter discusses three in particular. Firstly, it introduces the notion of 'entangled traumas', to emphasize that many of the survivors who participated in this research had endured multiple traumas during the Bosnian war. Secondly, it examines some of the possible linkages between interviewees' health conditions – including diabetes and heart arrhythmias – and unhealed trauma. Thirdly, it considers how socio-economic conditions in BiH, including high levels of unemployment, are negatively fuelling the long-term effects of rape and sexual violence.

Chapter 4 looks at some of the wider long-term effects of these crimes on families and family relationships. One of the central themes that emerged from the interview data was the 'unsupportive husband'; the majority of female interviewees spoke about marital problems directly or indirectly related to their war trauma. Many of them felt that they had not received the understanding and support that they needed from their husbands, and some of them had experienced/were experiencing domestic abuse. Male interviewees, in contrast, often had more positive marital relations. Relationships with children emerged from the interview data as a second major theme. While female survivors frequently stressed that their children must never know that they were raped, some male and female interviewees also expressed concerns that their own trauma was affecting their children. The topic of transgenerational transmission of trauma is therefore discussed. The chapter additionally addresses the neglected issue of children born as a result of rape, presenting the stories of three particular interviewees.

Chapter 5 and the remaining chapters shift the focus to transitional justice. Criminal trials, both at the ICTY and in national/local courts, have been the primary transitional justice response to the rapes and sexual violence committed during the Bosnian war. This emphasis on criminal prosecutions exemplifies

94 Medica Zenica and Medica Mondiale, *supra* note 12.

what Sikkink has termed a 'justice cascade'.[95] The first part of the chapter takes a top-down perspective. It examines some of the major developments over the last two decades in the international prosecution of rape and sexual violence. The second part looks at the criminal trial process from the 'bottom up', by asking how survivors *experience* the process of testifying in a court of law. As just under half of the interviewees had testified in court, the chapter examines their personal experiences. By using this top-down/bottom-up structural juxtaposition, it seeks to demonstrate that while criminal trials are important, they leave the long-term legacy of rape and sexual violence critically unaddressed.

Chapter 6 is about reparations, the most 'victim-centred' type of transitional justice. At the international level, victims' right to a remedy has long been recognized. The chapter briefly considers three key international documents, namely: the UN Basic Principles and Guidelines on the Right to a Remedy and Reparation for Victims of Gross Violations of International Human Rights Law and Serious Violations of International Humanitarian Law; the Nairobi Declaration on Women and Girls' Right to a Remedy and Reparation; and the UN Secretary-General's Guidance Note on Reparations for Conflict-Related Sexual Violence. The chapter moves on to examine whether and to what extent survivors in BiH have received reparative justice. There is a Strategy for Transitional Justice in BiH that makes important provision for reparations to all war victims. However, it has not been adopted and it is flawed on a number of levels. The remainder of the chapter explores two particular routes to reparations in BiH – a legal route and an administrative route. The former has been little utilized. The latter is more common, but the payments that survivors receive as civilian victims of war are primarily social payments rather than reparations per se. Furthermore, the lack of a state law on civilian victims of war means that survivors have different rights depending on where in BiH they live.

Chapter 7 offers a new way forward. In BiH, neither criminal trials nor the limited use of reparations have sufficiently addressed the long-term consequences of rape and sexual violence. The chapter therefore develops a new holistic approach to transitional justice, but it goes beyond simply stating that retributive, restorative and reparative forms of justice should be combined. Rather, it posits that transitional justice needs to be more holistic in how it deals with the legacy of rape and sexual violence. Building on the three dimensions of holistic transitional justice outlined in this introduction – namely a temporal dimension, a socio-economic dimension and a gender dimension – the chapter seeks to operationalize these dimensions by examining what they might look like in practice.

The conclusion reflects on some of the broader implications of this research. It links holistic transitional justice with the just war notion of *jus post bellum* or justice after war. It also shows that notwithstanding the book's specific focus,

95 Kathryn Sikkink, *The Justice Cascade: How Human Rights Prosecutions are Changing World Politics* (New York: W.W. Norton & Company, 2011).

the conceptualization and development of a more legacy-inclusive approach to transitional justice has a wider application and relevance both beyond BiH and beyond crimes of rape and sexual violence. Vigorously eschewing template or 'cookie cutter' methods of doing transitional justice, it frames the approach as a meta model which must be adapted to country-specific and local needs.

Chapter 1

# Rape and sexual violence in conflict

## A historical overview

'I told him not to touch me and begged him to let me go… I told him to take me to my mother. I was a young girl, and I asked him, "What do you want from me?" He spent three days having sex with me'.[1] These are the words of a 12-year-old Yazidi girl in northern Iraq. Islamic State fighters have heavily targeted women and girls from the Yazidi religious minority, subjecting them to brutal crimes – including rape[2] – and often forcing them to become sex slaves.[3] As these crimes continue to occur, reports have emerged of the widespread use of rape against women in the escalating conflict in South Sudan;[4] of sexual abuses committed by members of the Burmese military;[5] and of conflict-related sexual violence in Ukraine, primarily in places of detention.[6]

1 Cited in Human Rights Watch, 'Iraq: ISIS Escapees Describe Systematic Rape' (15 April 2015), available at: www.hrw.org/news/2015/04/14/iraq-isis-escapees-describe-systematic-rape (accessed 2 March 2016).
2 Michael Georgy, 'Captive Islamic State Militant Says Mass Rapes were "Normal"' (17 February 2017), available at: www.reuters.com/article/us-mideast-crisis-mosul-prisoners-idUSKBN15W1N0 (accessed 19 February 2017).
3 See Human Rights Watch, 'Iraq: Forced Marriage, Conversion for Yezidis – Victims, Witnesses Describe Islamic State's Brutality to Captives' (11 October 2014), available at: www.hrw.org/news/2014/10/11/iraq-forced-marriage-conversion-yezidis (accessed 3 March 2016).
4 Ben Quinn, 'Makeshift Justice the Only Recourse for Ill-Protected Women at South Sudan Camp' (16 January 2017), available at: www.theguardian.com/global-development/2017/jan/16/makeshift-justice-ill-protected-women-south-sudan-un-camp-malakal-protection-of-civilians-sexual-violence (accessed 18 January 2017).
5 David Scott Mathieson, 'Dispatches: Impunity for Sexual Violence in Burma's Kachin Conflict' (21 January 2016), available at: www.hrw.org/news/2016/01/21/dispatches-impunity-sexual-violence-burmas-kachin-conflict (accessed 25 March 2016); Human Rights Watch, 'Burma: Security Forces Raped Rohingya Women, Girls' (6 February 2017), available at: www.hrw.org/news/2017/02/06/burma-security-forces-raped-rohingya-women-girls (11 February 2017).
6 Magdalena Mis, 'Rape, Sexual Assault in Ukraine Conflict May Amount to War Crimes – U.N.' (16 February 2017), available at: http://news.trust.org/item/20170216165120-xlxq8 (accessed 19 February 2017).

These examples attest to the sobering fact that rape and sexual violence remain persistent scourges of war and armed conflict. Yet, there have also been many positive developments and steps forward. In March 2015, for example, military commanders from the Armed Forces of the Democratic Republic of Congo (DRC) signed a declaration to combat sexual violence in war. They pledged, inter alia, to take action against any soldiers under their command who commit acts of rape and sexual violence, to ensure that their soldiers understand the zero tolerance policy and to co-operate with military prosecutors in bringing perpetrators to justice.[7] In May 2015, the Croatian parliament (Sabor) adopted a new law which provides survivors of rape and sexual violence committed during the war in Croatia (1991–1995) with a comprehensive range of rights, from compensation and health insurance to psycho-social assistance and legal support.[8] In February 2016, in the Sepur Zarco trial, a court in Guatemala found two former military officers guilty of crimes against humanity – including sexual violence and sexual slavery – against 11 women from the indigenous Maya Q'eqchi' community. A month later, the court issued a landmark decision in which it ordered both the payment of compensation to the women and the adoption of wider community-focused measures to address the legacy of sexual violence suffered by the Q'eqchi' during the 1980s.[9] In June 2016, the International Criminal Court (ICC) sentenced the former Congolese vice-president, Jean-Pierre Bemba Gombo, to 18 years' imprisonment. He is the first person convicted at the ICC of rape.[10]

The issue of conflict-related rape and sexual violence illuminates a fundamental interplay of continuity and progress. The ongoing use of rape and sexual violence in conflict attests to the usefulness of these crimes in warfare. What has changed, however, is that they are no longer seen internationally as mere by-products or legitimate 'spoils' of war. In June 2014, the organization of the first Global Summit to End Sexual Violence in Conflict – held in London – reflected a widespread normative consensus that rape and sexual violence constitute dangerous and destructive weapons of war, the deployment of which must be punished and outlawed.[11] This chapter moves from the general to the particular. The first sections focus on the international

7 Zainab Hawa Bangura, 'DRC: Military Pledge Marks Milestone on Road to Ending Conflict-Related Sexual Violence' (31 March 2015), available at: www.un.org/sexualviolenceinconflict/press-release/drc-military-pledge-marks-milestone-on-road-to-ending-conflict-related-sexual-violence/ (accessed 5 April 2015).

8 Janine N. Clark, 'In from the Margins: Survivors of Wartime Sexual Violence in Croatia and an Early Analysis of the New Law', *Journal of Human Rights Practice* 8 (2016): 128–147.

9 UN Women, 'Landmark Ruling in Guatemala a Victory against Sexual Violence in Armed Conflict' (3 March 2016), available at: www.unwomen.org/en/news/stories/2016/3/guatemala-victory-against-sexual-violence-in-armed-conflict (accessed 11 March 2016).

10 *Prosecutor v. Jean-Pierre Bemba Gombo*, ICC-01/05-01/08, ICC Decision on Sentence pursuant to Article 76 of the Rome Statute (21 June 2016).

11 Foreign and Commonwealth Office, *Summit Report: The Global Summit to End Sexual Violence in Conflict, London 2014* (2014), available at: www.gov.uk/government/publications/summit-report-the-global-summit-to-end-sexual-violence-in-conflict-june-2014 (accessed 7 June 2016).

level, while the remaining sections are specifically about the widespread use of rape and sexual violence in BiH during the 1990s. The scale of these crimes had 'an electrifying effect…';[12] the international community could not simply turn a blind eye and do nothing. Thematically, therefore, the Bosnian war can itself be associated with both continuity and progress. The crimes committed were not new, but they contributed to new developments – normative and legal – internationally.

## Continuities of violence

Just as human suffering and loss have always accompanied warfare, so too have rape and sexual violence. To cite Mitchell, 'Rape, torture, and sexual violence have been endemic during armed conflict for centuries'.[13] It was during the twentieth century, however, that some of the most well-known and documented cases occurred. The mass rapes committed by Red Army soldiers in Germany at the end of World War II;[14] the Japanese imperial army's 'Rape of Nanking' in 1931[15] and its use of 'comfort women' during the 1930s;[16] the rapes of an estimated 200,000 Bengali women during the Bangladesh Liberation War in 1971;[17] the use of rape and sexual torture by US soldiers during the Vietnam war;[18] the 'widespread and systematic sexual violence' carried out by rebel forces during the 1991–2002 civil war in Sierra Leone;[19] the high levels of rape and sexual violence that occurred during the 1992–1995 Bosnian war;[20]

12 Rhonda Copelon, 'Surfacing Gender: Re-Engraving Crimes against Women in Humanitarian Law', *Hastings Women's Law Journal* 5 (1994): 243–266, at 248.

13 David S. Mitchell, 'The Prohibition of Rape in International Humanitarian Law as a Norm of *Jus Cogens*: Clarifying the Doctrine', *Duke Journal of Comparative and International Law* 15 (2005): 219–257, at 219–220.

14 Thomas Goodrich, *Rape Hate: Sex and Violence in War and Peace* (Manasota Key, FL: Pineapple Press, 2015).

15 Iris Chang, *The Rape of Nanking: The Forgotten Holocaust of World War II* (New York: Basic Books, 1997).

16 Caroline Norma, *The Japanese Comfort Women and Sexual Slavery during the China and Pacific Wars* (London: Bloomsbury Academic, 2016).

17 Nayanika Mookherjee, '"Remembering to Forget": Public Secrecy and Memory of Sexual Violence in the Bangladesh War of 1971', *Journal of the Royal Anthropological Institute* 12 (2006): 433–450.

18 Highlighting the fact that it is not only women and girls who are vulnerable to rape and sexual violence in conflict, Bourke notes that in Vietnam, 'male prisoners of war found themselves vulnerable to rape and other forms of sexual abuse during questioning and as part of interrogation techniques'. Joanna Bourke, *Rape: A History from 1860 to the Present* (London: Virago Press, 2007), 362.

19 Human Rights Watch, *"We'll Kill You if You Cry": Sexual Violence in the Sierra Leone Conflict* (January 2003), available at: www.hrw.org/reports/2003/sierraleone/sierleon0103.pdf (accessed 8 November 2015).

20 M. Cherif Bassiouni and Marcia McCormick, 'Sexual Violence: An Invisible Weapon of War in the former Yugoslavia', *Occasional Paper No. 1* (Chicago, IL: DePaul University College of Law, 1996), 15.

the systematic rape of between 100,000 and 250,000 people (mainly ethnic Tutsis) during the 1994 Rwandan genocide;[21] the ongoing rape of women and men in the DRC, earning the country the infamous title of 'rape capital of the world'.[22] These are just some examples of the crimes committed in a century that Hobsbawn has termed 'the most murderous in recorded history'.[23]

The recurrent use of rape and sexual violence in war has inevitably given rise to a wealth of different causal theories, from biological[24] and social constructivist accounts[25] to purposive/strategic[26] and feminist explanations.[27] However, no single theory is sufficient to explain the pervasiveness of war rape and sexual violence across time and space. They are crimes that occur within the unique context and dynamics of individual conflicts and their use may further specific conflict-related goals. Such goals can include genocide (as in Rwanda in 1994);[28] troop motivation (South Sudan offers a recent example);[29] group bonding (illustrated by the use of gang rape in Sierra

21 UN, 'Background Information on Sexual Violence Used as a Tool of War' (n.d.), available at: www.un.org/en/preventgenocide/rwanda/about/bgsexualviolence.shtml (accessed 5 February 2016).

22 It was Margot Wallström, the UN's Special Representative on Sexual Violence in Conflict, who first described the DRC as the 'rape capital of the world'. BBC, 'UN Official Calls DR Congo "Rape Capital of the World"' (28 April 2010), available at: http://news.bbc.co.uk/1/hi/world/africa/8650112.stm (accessed 8 October 2015).

23 Eric Hobsbawn, 'War and Peace' (23 February 2002), available at: www.theguardian.com/education/2002/feb/23/artsandhumanities.highereducation (accessed 5 March 2016).

24 Michael P. Ghiglieri, *The Dark Side of Man: Tracing the Origins of Male Violence* (Cambridge, MA: Perseus Books, 2000); Randy Thornhill and Craig Palmer, *A Natural History of Rape* (Cambridge, MA: MIT Press, 2000).

25 Janie L. Leatherman, *Sexual Violence and Armed Conflict* (Cambridge: Polity Press, 2011); Inger Skjelsbaek, *The Political Psychology of War Rape: Studies from Bosnia and Herzegovina* (Abingdon: Routledge, 2012).

26 Paul Kirby, 'How is Rape a Weapon of War? Feminist International Relations, Modes of Critical Explanation and the Study of Wartime Sexual Violence', *European Journal of International Relations* 19 (2013): 797–821; Zoe Marks, 'Sexual Violence in Sierra Leone's Civil War: "Virgination", Rape and Marriage', *African Affairs* 113 (2014): 67–87.

27 Susan Brownmiller, *Against Our Will: Men, Women and Rape* (New York: Fawcett Columbine, 1975); Catharine A. MacKinnon, 'War, Genocide and Women's Human Rights', *Harvard Women's Law Journal* 17 (1994): 5–16; Meredith Turshen, 'The Political Economy of Violence against Women during Armed Conflict in Uganda', *Social Research* 67 (2000), 803–824.

28 In the Trial of Jean-Paul Akayesu at the International Criminal Tribunal for Rwanda (ICTR), the Trial Chamber found that 'These rapes resulted in physical and psychological destruction of Tutsi women, their families and their communities. Sexual violence was an integral part of the process of destruction, specifically targeting Tutsi women and specifically contributing to their destruction and to the destruction of the Tutsi group as a whole'. *Prosecutor v. Jean-Paul Akayesu*, ICTR-96-4-T, ICTR Trial Chamber Judgement (2 September 1998), §731.

29 BBC, 'South Sudan: Women Raped as "Reward for Fighters"' (11 March 2016), available at: www.bbc.co.uk/news/world-africa-35780777 (accessed 1 May 2016).

Leone's civil war);[30] and the defeat of an armed insurgency (highlighted by the Sri Lankan military's use of sexual violence against members of the Tamil Tigers).[31]

In other words, significant micro variation exists alongside the macro narrative of continuity.[32] As Bourke underlines, rape 'varies between countries; it changes over time. There is nothing timeless or random about it'.[33] These variations across different conflicts and contexts point to the multi-dimensional and polyvalent utility of rape and sexual violence in warfare. This utility, in turn, helps to explain both the persistent use of these crimes in war and the related fact that, historically, they were often viewed as 'mere inevitable consequences or side effects of armed conflict'.[34]

## Impunity and the changing international landscape

The use of rape and sexual violence in conflict highlights a fundamental disconnect between formal rules of war and the informal codes of conduct that develop and solidify on the battlefield. As Aydelott argues, 'The treatment of civilian women during war is an issue in which the law often clashes with the expectations of the soldier... In this conflict between law and man, the women are the losers'.[35] While this is largely true, it is not the case that rape in war has always gone unpunished historically. For example, some soldiers were 'subjected to capital punishment under national military codes, such as those of Richard

30 Dara K. Cohen, 'Female Combatants and the Perpetration of Violence: Wartime Rape in the Sierra Leone Civil War', *World Politics* 65 (2013): 383–415.

31 Dean Nelson, 'Sri Lankan Military "Raping Tamil Tigers"' (26 February 2013), available at: www.telegraph.co.uk/news/worldnews/asia/srilanka/9894458/Sri-Lankan-military-raping-Tamil-Tigers.html (accessed 8 October 2015).

32 Elisabeth J. Wood, 'Variation in Sexual Violence during War', *Politics and Society* 34 (2006): 307–341; Michele Leiby, 'Wartime Sexual Violence in Guatemala and Peru', *International Studies Quarterly* 53 (2009): 445–468; Dara K. Cohen, Amelia Hoover Green and Elisabeth J. Wood, *Wartime Sexual Violence: Misconceptions, Implications and Ways Forward*, United States Institute of Peace Special Report 323 (February 2013), available at: www.usip.org/sites/default/files/resources/SR323.pdf (accessed 10 November 2015); Janine N. Clark, 'Untangling Rape Causation and the Importance of the Micro Level: Elucidating the Use of Mass Rape during the Bosnian War', *Ethnopolitics* (published online 14 April 2016), available at: www.tandfonline.com/doi/abs/10.1080/17449057.2016.1165919.

33 Bourke, *supra* note 18, at 6. A further dimension of variation derives from the particular meanings that different individuals and communities attach to rape. See, for example, Jelke Boesten, 'Analyzing Rape Regimes at the Interface of War and Peace in Peru', *International Journal of Transitional Justice* 4 (2010): 110–129, at 115.

34 Kelly D. Askin, 'Prosecuting Wartime Rape and other Gender-Related Crimes under International Law: Extraordinary Advances, Enduring Obstacles', *Berkeley Journal of International Law* 21 (2003): 288–349, at 296.

35 Denise Aydelott, 'Mass Rape during War: Prosecuting Bosnian Rapists under International Law', *Emory International Law Review* 7 (1993): 585–631, at 587.

II (1385) and Henry V (1419)';[36] and in 1474, an international tribunal of the Holy Roman Empire sentenced a military commander, Peter von Hagenbach, to death for crimes committed by his troops – including rape – in Breisach in the Rhine Valley. Nevertheless, these were isolated ad hoc developments, and several centuries were to pass before any serious and sustained efforts were made to outlaw the use of rape and sexual violence in war.

In 1863, the United States adopted the Lieber Code, Article 44 of which stated that: 'all rape, wounding, maiming, or killing of such inhabitants are prohibited under the penalty of death, or such other severe punishment as may seem adequate for the gravity of the offense'.[37] This collocation of rape with offences such as killing and maiming was in itself highly significant. Rape was thus repositioned as a violent crime instead of simply 'an affront to a man's pride as guardian of his women'.[38] Although the Lieber Code was not an international document, it helped to pave the way for the Hague Conventions, which 'are generally considered by international law scholars to be the crowning achievement of the effort to humanize war through law'.[39]

Article 1 of the 1899 Hague Convention (II) entreated armies, militias and volunteers to 'conduct their operations in accordance with the laws and customs of war';[40] and similarly Article 1 of the 1907 Hague Convention (IV) stipulated that 'The Contracting Powers shall issue instructions to their armed land forces which shall be in conformity with the Regulations respecting the laws and customs of war on land'.[41] More importantly, Article 46 of the 1907 Convention implicitly proscribed the use of sexual violence in war by declaring that: 'Family honour and rights, the lives of persons, and private property, as well as religious convictions and practice, must be respected'.[42] This implicit conceptualization of sexual violence as a crime of honour, even if it reflected social attitudes at the time,[43] was nevertheless a step backwards from the Lieber Code. In the 1907

36 Theodor Meron, 'Rape as a Crime under International Humanitarian Law', *American Journal of International Law* 89 (1993): 424–428, at 425.

37 The Lieber Code (24 April 1863), Article 44, available at: http://avalon.law.yale.edu/19th_century/lieber.asp#art44 (accessed 28 November 2015).

38 Suzanne Gibson, 'The Discourse of Sex/War: Thoughts on Catharine MacKinnon's 1993 Oxford Amnesty Lecture', *Feminist Legal Studies* 1 (1993): 179–188, at 179.

39 Chris af Jochnick and Roger Normand, 'The Legitimation of Violence: A Critical History of the Laws of War', *Harvard International Law Journal* 35 (1994): 49–95, at 68.

40 Hague Convention (II), *Laws and Customs of War on Land* (29 July 1899), Article 1, available at: http://avalon.law.yale.edu/19th_century/hague02.asp#art1 (accessed 4 March 2016).

41 Hague Convention (IV), *Laws and Customs of War on Land* (18 October 1907), Article 1, available at: http://avalon.law.yale.edu/20th_century/hague04.asp#art1 (accessed 4 March 2016).

42 Ibid., Article 46.

43 Askin points out that 'At the turn of the twentieth century, a violation of family "honor" was commonly understood as encompassing sexual assault'. Askin, *supra* note 34, at 300.

Hague Convention, 'the Lieber Code's alternative characterization of rape as a violent crime was abandoned'.[44]

If the Hague Conventions omitted any explicit reference to rape and sexual violence, the statutes of the post-World War II Nuremberg and Tokyo military tribunals did not mention them at all – one of the most glaring examples of the historical 'silence' surrounding these crimes.[45] Apropos of Nuremberg and the trial of 22 leading Nazi war criminals, Askin notes that although the voluminous trial transcripts contained extensive evidence of sexual violence, this was not reflected in the 732-page index that accompanied them: 'Neither "rape" nor "women" is included in any heading or subheading in this index'.[46] The word rape was similarly absent from the Tribunal's judgement,[47] although evidence of mass rapes introduced by French and Soviet prosecutors helped to secure convictions for crimes against humanity.[48]

These omissions at Nuremberg, while regrettable, are important because they draw attention to some of the myriad factors which, collectively, have contributed to the marginalization of rape and sexual violence throughout history. At the Tribunal, for example, the French prosecutor largely glossed over these crimes, claiming: 'The Tribunal will forgive me if I avoid citing the atrocious details'.[49] Yet, it is precisely these 'atrocious details' that bring home the true gravity and brutality of rape and sexual violence. Pushing such details to one side effectively dilutes these crimes, rendering them anodyne, and perpetuates the dangerous and fallacious idea that they are somehow 'incidental to "real" crimes like the killing of unarmed civilians and other types of mistreatment of prisoners of war'.[50] In other words, rape and sexual violence got 'lost' at Nuremberg, just as they did in the 1907 Hague Convention *qua* euphemistic references to 'family honour'.

Events at Nuremberg also powerfully illustrated that justice can clash with *Realpolitik*; and when the latter dominates, the outcome is a deeply compromised 'justice' that reflects political trade-offs and self-interest. Hence, a key reason why rape received so little attention at Nuremberg, according to Chinkin, is 'not because the Germans were not guilty of rape, but because the allied forces,

44 Catherine N. Niarchos, 'Women, War and Rape: Challenges Facing the International Tribunal for the former Yugoslavia', *Human Rights Quarterly* 17 (1995): 649–690, at 672–673.

45 UN Women refers to crimes of rape and sexual violence as constituting one of 'history's greatest silences'. UN Women, 'Addressing Conflict-Related Sexual Violence: An Analytical Inventory of Peacekeeping Practice' (October 2012), available at: www.unwomen.org/~/media/Headquarters/Media/Publications/en/04DAnAnalyticalinventoryofPeacekeepingPracti.pdf (accessed 7 March 2016), at 9.

46 Askin, *supra* note 34, at 295.

47 Richard J. Goldstone, 'Prosecuting Rape as a War Crime', *Case Western Reserve Journal of International Law* 34 (2002): 277–285, at 279.

48 Aydelott, *supra* note 35, at 592.

49 Cited in Bassiouni and McCormick, *supra* note 20, at 4.

50 Ibid.

especially the Russians and the Moroccan forces under French control, were also guilty of many rapes'.[51] That Allied Powers themselves engaged in rape and sexual violence underscores the discomforting reality that crimes committed in the context of war and armed conflict rarely evince a straightforward Manichean character. Despite this, the 'banality of evil in militarized patriarchal culture'[52] is too often portrayed as a one-sided banality precisely because the preservation of a war's meta narrative necessitates this. The result is that certain crimes and victims are always neglected and overlooked, and Nuremberg is a powerful example of top-down political agendas submerging on-the-ground suffering, including rape and sexual violence.

The International Military Tribunal for the Far East (the Tokyo Tribunal) did not receive the same level of attention as the Nuremberg Tribunal and it is often regarded as less important.[53] Vis-à-vis rape and sexual violence, however, the Tokyo Tribunal made considerably more progress than its counterpart in Germany. For example, 'the Tokyo Indictment did include allegations of gender-related crimes'.[54] Furthermore, although the Tribunal did not give any rape survivors the opportunity to testify, its judgement recorded the mass rapes of approximately 20,000 Chinese women in Nanking in 1937.[55] Nevertheless, it critically ignored the existence of the thousands of 'Comfort Women' (an estimated 200,000) who were forced into sexual slavery to serve the needs of the Japanese imperial army.[56] In Copelon's words, 'Calling the "comfort stations" brothels, not rape camps, and referring to the women as prostitutes and not sexual slaves, obfuscated the horrors of the system through a suggestion of immorality and voluntariness'.[57] Highlighting, once again, that political interests can crucially shape the 'justice agenda', Copelon further suggested that the existence of the 'comfort stations' may have been too close to the bone for some of the Allied nations – and

51 Christine Chinkin, 'Rape and Sexual Abuse of Women in International Law', *European Journal of International Law* 5 (1994): 326–341, at 334.

52 Rhonda Copelon, 'Gender Crimes as War Crimes: Integrating Crimes against Women into International Criminal Law', *McGill Law Journal* 46 (2000): 218–240, at 222.

53 According to Meron, 'The Tokyo Tribunal's more cavalier attitude toward the law and the defendants largely explains its relative marginality during the past sixty years, and its near-total lack of influence on international law'. Theodor Meron, 'Reflections on the Prosecution of War Crimes by International Tribunals', *American Journal of International Law* 100 (2006): 551–579, at 571.

54 Askin, *supra* note 34, at 302.

55 Goldstone, *supra* note 47, at 279.

56 Meade notes that: 'It was a common belief that soldiers should not die as virgins, and many thought that sex before battle protected soldiers against death. Additionally, the leadership hoped that by providing a system of closely regulated brothels it could present the soldiers with a sexual outlet while simultaneously lowering the incidence of venereal disease and the opportunity for espionage that existed with private brothels'. Christopher P. Meade, 'From Shanghai to Globocourt: An Analysis of the "Comfort Women's" Defeat in Hwang v. Japan', *Vanderbilt Journal of Transnational Law* 35 (2002): 211–289, at 220.

57 Copelon, *supra* note 52, at 223.

specifically the United States, whose military had itself 'organized and directed men to STD [sexually transmitted disease]-safe brothels'.[58] Large numbers of American occupation soldiers had also used Japan's 'comfort stations'.[59]

If the Nuremberg and Tokyo Tribunals were an elemental part of World War II's multi-dimensional legacy, so too were the four Geneva Conventions, adopted in 1949. Effectively a codified version of *jus in bello* or justice in war, the Conventions regulate the conduct of war and seek to minimize its nefarious effects. They protect those who are no longer able to fight, namely sick and wounded soldiers (the First and Second Geneva Conventions) and prisoners of war (the Third Geneva Convention), as well as civilians (the Fourth Geneva Convention). As regards offering protection from rape and sexual violence, however, the Geneva Conventions are limited. Only one article in the Fourth Geneva Convention, for example, refers to rape. Article 27 states:

> Protected persons are entitled, in all circumstances, to respect for their persons, their honour, their family rights, their religious convictions and practices, and their manners and customs. They shall at all times be humanely treated, and shall be protected especially against all acts of violence or threats thereof and against insults and public curiosity.
>
> Women shall be especially protected against any attack on their honour, in particular against rape, enforced prostitution, or any form of indecent assault.[60]

It is unfortunate that the protection of women is thus subsumed within a paragraph on the protection of civilians in general, which has the effect of tempering the specificity of rape and sexual violence. It is also regrettable that, like the 1907 Hague Convention, the Fourth Geneva Convention adopts a highly reductionist approach to these crimes by framing them as attacks on a woman's honour. 'Women's honour', however, is not a stand-alone concept, but rather a socially constructed idea that is intricately intertwined with patriarchy and its structures.[61] That it is ultimately men who define the normative standard of the 'honourable woman' means that when rape and sexual violence are essentially theorized as honour crimes, a victimological displacement occurs. The multiple harms done to the individual woman become secondary to the harms brought about by the impugning of her honour; and hence victimhood is effectively transferred from

58 Ibid.

59 Goodrich, *supra* note 14, at 86.

60 Fourth Geneva Convention Relative to the Protection of Civilian Persons in Time of War (12 August 1949), Article 27, available at: www.icrc.org/applic/ihl/ihl.nsf/Article.xsp?action=openDocument&documentId=FFCB180D4E99CB26C12563CD0051BBD9 (accessed 3 March 2016).

61 Laura Sjoberg, *Women Wartime Rapists: Beyond Sensation and Stereotyping* (New York: New York University Press, 2016), 56.

the direct victim to her husband, father and family (or even her community).[62] The fact that Article 27 of the Fourth Geneva Convention links 'honour' with 'family rights' further illustrates this point.[63] As Pinker aptly underlines, 'one has to look long and hard through history and across cultures to find an acknowledgement of the harm of rape *from the viewpoint of the victim*'.[64]

Changes in the nature of warfare, and in particular the increase in the number of non-international armed conflicts – including some of the many proxy wars fought during the Cold War – led in 1977 to the adoption of the two Additional Protocols to the Geneva Conventions. As Askin points out, however, 'only one sentence in each explicitly prohibits sexual violence'.[65] Article 76 (explicitly entitled 'Protection of Women') of Additional Protocol I declares in its first paragraph that: 'Women shall be the object of special respect and shall be protected in particular against rape, forced prostitution and any other form of indecent assault'.[66] In contrast to Article 27 of the Fourth Geneva Convention, Article 76 does not expressly link these crimes with the concept of honour. The accompanying commentary, however, makes it clear that Article 76 is simply building on, rather than departing from, Article 27. In particular, the commentary states that 'The rule [in paragraph 1 of Article 76] relates to respect for the person and honour, as laid down in paragraph 1 of Article 75'.[67] Article 75, which addresses 'Fundamental Guarantees', underscores in paragraph 1 that 'Each Party shall respect the person, honour, convictions and religious practices of all such persons [covered by the Geneva Conventions]'. Paragraph 2 goes on to list those acts which 'are and shall remain prohibited at any time and in any place whatsoever, whether committed by civilian or by military agents'.[68] It does not specifically mention rape and instead refers more generally to 'outrages upon personal

62 Coulter observes that 'When shifting the perspective from the woman who is raped to that of her husband, family, community, ethnic group or nation, many seem to forget who the actual victim of a violent crime is'. Chris Coulter, *Bush Wives and Girl Soldiers: Women's Lives through War and Peace in Sierra Leone* (Ithaca: Cornell University Press, 2009), 133.

63 The commentary to Article 27 explicitly states that 'Respect for family life is also covered by the clause prohibiting rape and other attacks on women's honour'. International Committee of the Red Cross (ICRC), 'Commentary of 1958 – Article 27' (1958), available at: https://ihl-databases.icrc.org/applic/ihl/ihl.nsf/Treaty.xsp?documentId=AE2D398352C5B028C12563CD002D6B5C&action=openDocument (accessed 3 March 2016).

64 Steven Pinker, *The Better Angels of Our Nature: A History of Violence and Humanity* (London: Penguin, 2011), 476.

65 Askin, *supra* note 34, at 295.

66 Protocol Additional I Relating to the Protection of Victims of International Armed Conflicts (8 June 1977), Article 76, available at: www.icrc.org/eng/assets/files/other/icrc_002_0321.pdf (accessed 3 January 2016).

67 ICRC, 'Commentary of 1987 – Protection of Women' (1987), available at: https://ihl-databases.icrc.org/ihl/COM/470-750098?OpenDocument (accessed 3 January 2016).

68 Protocol Additional I Relating to the Protection of Victims of International Armed Conflicts (8 June 1977), Article 75, available at: www.icrc.org/eng/assets/files/other/icrc_002_0321.pdf (accessed 3 January 2016).

dignity, in particular humiliating and degrading treatment, enforced prostitution and any form of indecent assault'.[69] This emphasis on dignity is closely related to honour, and once again it deflects from the 'embodied violation of another person' that is intrinsic to rape and sexual violence.[70]

Unlike Additional Protocol I, Additional Protocol II – which covers the protection of civilians in non-international armed conflicts – does not have an article which specifically addresses the protection of women. Rather, Article 4(2)(e) provides a list of acts against the person which 'are and shall remain prohibited at any time and in any place whatsoever', including 'outrages upon personal dignity, in particular humiliating and degrading treatment, rape, enforced prostitution and any form of indecent assault'.[71] According to the commentary to Article 4(2)(e), the ICRC's draft included a separate paragraph focused on the protection of women. As the discussions progressed, it became clear that 'children and adolescents who may also be the victims of rape, enforced prostitution or indecent assault' themselves needed greater protection; and hence 'a reference to such acts was added to sub-paragraph (e)'.[72] This recognition that children and adolescents are also vulnerable to rape in war partly diluted the association of the crime with honour. Overall, however, the Geneva Conventions and their Additional Protocols construed the crime of rape very narrowly and thus 'reinforced the secondary importance as well as the shame and stigma of the victimized women'.[73]

Even if the rules of war now outlawed rape and sexual violence, moreover, they continued to be flouted with impunity because the machinery of international law had not yet caught up. Over the last 20 years it has steadily done so, and rape and sexual violence are now recognized as constituting war crimes, crimes against humanity and even genocide. It is prudent not to over-emphasize the importance of criminal trials. Like all transitional justice mechanisms, they have limitations. The important point, however, is that the international landscape has changed, and the Bosnian war was a significant contributing factor. The scale of the abuses committed in BiH during the 1990s, the locus of these crimes in the heart of Europe and the 'copious media coverage' of the hostilities[74] made the international community sit up and take notice.[75] Fundamentally, the Bosnian

69 Ibid.

70 Bourke, *supra* note 18, at 6. See also Ann J. Cahill, *Rethinking Rape* (Ithaca: Cornell University Press, 2001).

71 Protocol Additional II Relating to the Protection of Victims of International Armed Conflicts (8 June 1977), Article 4(2)(e), available at: www.icrc.org/eng/assets/files/other/icrc_002_0321.pdf (accessed 3 January 2016).

72 ICRC, 'Commentary of 1987 – Fundamental Guarantees' (1987), available at: https://ihl-databases.icrc.org/ihl/COM/475-760008?OpenDocument (accessed 9 February 2016).

73 Copelon, *supra* note 52, at 221.

74 Kate Fitzgerald, 'Problems of Prosecution and Adjudication of Rape and Other Sexual Assaults under International Law', *European Journal of International Law* 8 (1997): 638–663, at 638.

75 Jelena Batinic, 'Feminism, Nationalism and War: The "Yugoslav Case" in Feminist Texts', *Journal of International Women's Studies* 3 (2001): 1–23, at 1. See also Inger Skjelsbaek,

war contributed to fostering a new international consensus around rape and sexual violence. According to a lawyer from the ICTY:

> When the OTP [Office of the Prosecutor] was created in 1993, the international community expressed its determination that sexual violence crimes would be prosecuted along with all of the other crimes committed during the conflicts. For the first time in history, the rhetoric of accountability for sexual violence flowed readily around the globe.[76]

## Background to the Bosnian war

> BOREDOM!!! SHOOTING!!! SHELLING!!! PEOPLE BEING KILLED!!! DESPAIR!!! HUNGER!!! MISERY!!! FEAR!!!
>
> That's my life! The life of an innocent eleven-year-old schoolgirl!! A schoolgirl without a school, without the fun and excitement of school. A child without games, without friends, without the sun, without nature, without fruit, without chocolate or sweets, with just a little powdered milk. In short, a child without a childhood. A wartime child.[77]

These are the powerful words of Zlata Filipović, a Bosnian Muslim girl from Sarajevo who wrote a diary about the siege of her beloved city during the Bosnian war. Like so many people, both inside and outside of BiH, she struggled to make any sense of what was happening or why.

BiH was one of six republics[78] that constituted the Socialist Federal Republic of Yugoslavia (SFRY). Today, there is deep and widespread nostalgia for Yugoslavia[79] – for a period when everyone had jobs, money, existential security. However, the Yugoslavia that many people fondly remember – particularly the older generation – was partly a myth. In a quest to achieve unity and harmony, President Josip Broz Tito chose to focus on the present and the future rather than on the past. Hence, the legacy of the internecine civil war that had ripped

'Victim and Survivor: Narrated Social Identities of Women who Experienced Rape during the War in Bosnia-Herzegovina', *Feminism and Psychology* 16 (2006): 373–403, at 373.

76 Michelle Jarvis, 'Overview: The Challenge of Accountability for Conflict-Related Sexual Violence Crimes', in Serge Brammertz and Michelle Jarvis (eds), *Prosecuting Conflict-Related Sexual Violence at the ICTY* (Oxford: Oxford University Press, 2016), 1–18, at 1–2.

77 Zlata Filipović, *Zlata's Diary: A Child's Life in Sarajevo* (London: Puffin Books, 1995), 60.

78 The other republics were Croatia, Macedonia, Montenegro, Serbia (which had two autonomous provinces, Kosovo and Vojvodina) and Slovenia.

79 Marija Ristić, 'Yugo-Nostalgia Thrives at Tito Memorials' (25 June 2013), available at: www.balkaninsight.com/en/article/yugo-nostalgia-thrives-at-tito-memorials (accessed 20 February 2017); Pål Kolstø, 'Identifying with the Old or the New State: Nation-Building vs. Yugonostalgia in the Yugoslav Successor States', *Nations and Nationalism* 20 (2014): 760–781.

Yugoslavia apart during World War II was simply buried and never dealt with. While Tito successfully rallied people under the banner of 'brotherhood and unity', there were always centripetal forces and rumblings of discontent. A nationalist revival in Croatia during the late 1960s, known as the Croatian Spring, was just one example.[80] The more intrinsic problem, according to Lendvai and Parcell, was that:

> Yugoslavia is a country without Yugoslavs. That is, it lacks people prepared to declare themselves as belonging to a Yugoslav entity as opposed to a specific nationality. According to the last census in 1981, only 1.2 million people out of a total population of 22.4 million declared themselves as Yugoslavs.[81]

In other words, not everyone was committed to Tito's Yugoslav ideal, and it was always a highly fragile construction. Nevertheless, the fact that people enjoyed a good standard of living allowed Tito to keep nationalism in check. As Tanner notes, 'The late 1970s was a time of *la dolce vita* for most Yugoslavs'.[82] Inevitably, this 'good life' came at a cost. The SFRY was mired in national debt, and 'in the last five years of Tito's life it ballooned to just under $20bn'.[83] Tito was the glue that held the troubled Yugoslavia together. Following his death on 4 May 1980, the forces which had always posed a threat to Yugoslavia's existence – nationalism, the unresolved past, political ambitions – gradually came to the fore. Politicians such as Serbia's Slobodan Milošević and Croatia's Franjo Tuđman, who deliberately exploited and instrumentalized nationalist sentiments and long-suppressed grievances, rose to fill the void that Tito's passing had created.

The League of Communists of Yugoslavia met for the last time in January 1990. This was the beginning of the end. In June 1991, both Slovenia and Croatia declared independence. Slovenia was largely ethnically homogenous, with Slovenes constituting 90 per cent of the population. This made its secession from Yugoslavia relatively straightforward. However, as the president of the largest Yugoslav republic, and as someone who publicly presented himself as a leader committed to defending the SFRY, Milošević 'could not be seen to sit back contentedly and watch Yugoslavia's richest republic stroll off into the European dawn'.[84] The Serbian leader thus sent the Yugoslav National Army (JNA) into

80 As Dragojević notes, this 'culminated in the 1974 initiative calling for the change of the language name in the Constitution from "Serbo-Croatian" to "Croatian or Serbian"'. Mila Dragojević, 'Competing Institutions in National Identity Construction: The Croatian Case', *Nationalism and Ethnic Politics* 11 (2005): 61–87, at 68.

81 Paul Lendvai and Lis Parcell, 'Yugoslavia without Yugoslavs: The Roots of the Crisis', *International Affairs* 67 (1991): 251–261, at 253.

82 Marcus Tanner, *Croatia: A Nation Forged in War*, 3rd edn (New Haven, CT: Yale University Press 2010), 206.

83 Ibid., at 207.

84 Adam LeBor, *Milošević: A Biography* (London: Bloomsbury Publishing, 2002), 137.

Slovenia, triggering a ten-day war. Croatia's decision to leave Yugoslavia led to far greater bloodshed. Croatia had a significant Serb minority that accounted for approximately 12 per cent of the population; and these Serbs had no desire to live in an independent Croatia. During World War II, thousands of Serbs perished in the Independent State of Croatia (NDH), a Nazi puppet state[85] headed by Ante Pavelić, the leader of the far-right *Ustaše*. According to Goldstein, 'The actions of the Ustasha[86] became infamous, even outdoing the Nazis' brutality'.[87]

If this violent past made Serbs deeply fearful of living in another independent Croatia, decisions taken by the new Croatian leadership and President Tuđman further exacerbated their insecurities. On 22 December 1990, for example, parliament adopted a new constitution that relegated Serbs from a constituent nation within Croatia to a minority.[88] In May 1991, the Serb leadership in Croatia organized a referendum and local Serbs were asked whether they wanted to remain in Yugoslavia. A huge 99.8 per cent answered in the affirmative.[89] Just a week later, the Croatian leadership organized its own referendum, in which 94.1 per cent of the population voted for Croatia's independence from Yugoslavia. Even before Croatia declared independence on 25 June 1991, armed conflict had broken out in several areas. Milošević sent in the JNA to aid local Serbs, and by the end of 1991 Croatia had lost approximately one third of its territory to Serb forces.[90] A UN-sponsored ceasefire was agreed in January 1992. The final stage of the conflict occurred in August 1995, when Croat forces launched Operation 'Storm' and expelled thousands of Serbs from their ancestral homes in Croatia.[91]

Developments in Slovenia and Croatia had major domino effects. During the Cold War, 'The domino theory was originally an expression of a U.S. foreign policy directed towards the maintenance of an anti-communist and committed pro-Western position among the states of Southeast Asia'.[92] In the former Yugoslavia, once Slovenia and Croatia seceded from the SFRY, it was only a matter of time before the BiH 'domino' would fall. BiH was the most ethnically diverse of all the Yugoslav republics. Bosnian Muslims

85 According to Tanner, 'The first acts of the NDH made it clear that the new state was to be a carbon copy of Nazi Germany'. Tanner, *supra* note 82, at 144.

86 Here, Goldstein is using the English spelling rather than the Croatian spelling (*Ustaše*).

87 Ivo Goldstein, 'Ante Pavelić, Charisma and National Mission in Wartime Croatia', *Politics, Religion and Ideology* 7 (2006): 225–234, at 233.

88 *Prosecutor v. Milan Martić*, IT-95-11-T, ICTY Trial Chamber Judgement (12 June 2007), §130.

89 Ibid., at §134.

90 *Prosecutor v. Ante Gotovina, Ivan Čermak and Mladen Markač*, IT-06-90-T, ICTY Trial Chamber Judgement, Vol. I (15 April 2011), §2.

91 Marija Ristić, Ivana Nikolić and Sven Milekić, 'Operation Storm: Croatia's Triumph, Serbia's Grief' (3 August 2015), available at: www.balkaninsight.com/en/article/operation-storm-croatia-s-triumph-serbia-s-grief-07-31-2015 (accessed 7 December 2016).

92 Jerry Mark Silverman, 'The Domino Theory: Alternatives to a Self-Fulfilling Prophecy', *Asian Survey* 15 (1975): 915–939, at 916.

(Bosniaks) constituted 44 per cent of the population, Serbs made up 33 per cent and Croats formed 17 per cent (with the remainder declaring themselves as Yugoslavs).[93] The challenges involved in reaching any sort of agreement on BiH's future were thus enormous, particularly in a context of growing nationalism which fostered political divides and polarization. Slovenia and Croatia's secession from Yugoslavia created a crucial dilemma for BiH. As Tabeau and Bijak explain:

> If Bosnian Muslims remained in the post-1991 Bosnia that would belong to the rump Yugoslavia, their educational or job opportunities would be severely limited by the dominance of Serbs. Their fate in the already independent Croatia would not be much different. But breaking away from Yugoslavia put Bosnian Muslims in a particularly difficult position, as they were left with no support other than the one expected from the international community.[94]

A referendum took place on 1 March 1992, which Bosnian Serbs boycotted. A massive 98 per cent of the votes cast favoured independence. President Alija Izetbegović declared BiH's independence on 3 March 1992 and this was recognized by the European Community on 6 April 1992. Serbs in BiH, however, like their ethnic kin in Croatia, wished to remain part of Yugoslavia. The Bosnian Serb leader, Radovan Karadžić, who had warned that an independent Bosnian state would be 'still-born',[95] declared the existence of an independent Serbian Republic of BiH (which was later renamed Republika Srpska) on 27 March 1992. The war thus began. It lasted for three long years, created 1.2 million refugees[96] and resulted in the deaths of more than 100,000 people.[97] A particular dimension of the conflict that attracted widespread international attention was the use of rape and sexual violence. To cite Neill, 'The backdrop of the Balkans provides one of the most contemporary and publicized examples of the mass perpetration of rape'.[98]

93 LeBor, *supra* note 84, at 171.

94 Ewa Tabeau and Jakub Bijak, 'War-Related Deaths in the 1992–1995 Armed Conflicts in Bosnia-Herzegovina: A Critique of Previous Estimates and Recent Results', *European Journal of Population* 21 (2005): 187–215, at 189.

95 Nick Hawton, *Europe's Most Wanted Man: The Quest for Radovan Karadžić* (London: Arrow Books, 2009), 104.

96 International Crisis Group, *Going Nowhere Fast: Refugees and Internally Displaced Persons in Bosnia and Herzegovina*, Europe Report No. 23 (1 May 1997), 5, available at: http://repository.forcedmigration.org/show_metadata.jsp?pid=fmo:1740 (accessed 8 January 2017).

97 Denis Džidić, '"Bosnian Book of the Dead" Published' (22 January 2013), available at: www.balkaninsight.com/en/article/bosnian-ngo-presents-written-memorial-to-victims (accessed 8 September 2015).

98 Kevin Gerard Neill, 'Duty, Honour, Rape: Sexual Assault against Women during War', *Journal of International Women's Studies* 2 (2000), 43–51, at 48.

## Rape and sexual violence in the Bosnian war

On 6 October 1992, the UN Security Council adopted Resolution 780, in which it expressed its 'grave alarm at continuing reports of widespread violations of international humanitarian law occurring within the territory of the former Yugoslavia and especially in Bosnia-Herzegovina'.[99] It accordingly requested the UN Secretary-General to 'establish, as a matter of urgency, an impartial Commission of Experts' to investigate these violations.[100] The Commission commenced its work in November 1992, and after 18 months of investigations it issued its final report in May 1994. In the 'Notes' section at the end of the report, the Commission found that:

> The rape and sexual assault study and investigation discussed in paragraphs 232–253 suggests a very high number of rapes and sexual assaults in custodial and non-custodial settings. Thus, the earlier projection of 20,000 rapes made by other sources[101] is not unreasonable considering the number of actual reported cases.[102]

In a separate paper, the Commission's Rapporteur on the Gathering and Analysis of Facts, M. Cherif Bassiouni, and the Assistant Attorney General in the State of Illinois, Marcia McCormick, wrote that 'In the former Yugoslavia, as many as 20,000 women may have been raped'.[103] It is important to stress that these numbers must be treated with caution. Some men and women were killed after being raped and sexually abused;[104] some survivors moved overseas; some may never disclose what happened to them, due to fear or shame.[105] Hence, it will never be

99 UN Security Council Resolution 780, S/RES/780 (6 October 1992), Preamble.

100 Ibid., at §2.

101 Skjelsbaek notes that: 'At the end of 1992, the Bosnian government released a figure stating that the number of women who had been raped was about 14,000... Later the same year (in December), the European Community set the number of women of Muslim ethnicity who had been raped by Bosnian Serb soldiers at around 20,000. The Bosnian Ministry of the Interior set the number at around 50,000'. Skjelsbaek, *supra* note 75, at 398 n 1.

102 M. Cherif Bassiouni, *Final Report of the Commission of Experts Established Pursuant to Security Council Resolution 780*, S/1994/674 (27 May 1994), §87, available at: www.icty.org/x/file/About/OTP/un_commission_of_experts_report1994_en.pdf (accessed 5 January 2016).

103 Bassiouni and McCormick, *supra* note 20, at 6.

104 M. Cherif Bassiouni, *Final Report of the United Nations Commission of Experts Established Pursuant to Security Council Resolution 780 (1992), Annex VIII – Prison Camps*, S/1994/674/Add.2, Vol. IV (27 May 1994), §42, available at: http://mcherifbassiouni.com/wp-content/uploads/2015/08/Yugoslavia-Report-Vol-4-Annex-VIII.pdf (accessed 5 January 2016).

105 Denis Džidić, 'Bosnian War Victims Urged to Speak Out' (9 April 2015), available at: www.balkaninsight.com/en/article/bosnian-rape-victims-called-to-speak-up (accessed 7 July 2015).

known exactly how individuals were subjected to rape and sexual violence during the Bosnian war; and as the leader of one NGO emphasized, it is essential that the figures do not become a cynical numbers game.[106]

More than the scope and scale of the rapes and sexual violence in BiH, it was a third 'S' that made these crimes appear particularly shocking, namely the seemingly systematic way in which they were being committed. In a 1993 report, for example, Amnesty International found that:

> the rape and sexual abuse of women, the great majority of them Muslims, by Serbian forces has occurred in many places in Bosnia-Herzegovina and in some cases has been carried out in an organized or systematic way, with the deliberate detention of women for the purpose of rape and sexual abuse.[107]

The aforementioned UN Commission of Experts itself concluded that these crimes 'have been carried out by some of the parties so systematically that they strongly appear to be the product of a policy'.[108] The fact that soldiers were raping with impunity further reinforced this notion.[109] Whether or not military and political leaders – and specifically the Bosnian Serb military and political leadership – expressly consented to the commission of these crimes, as Bassiouni and McCormick surmised,[110] or whether they simply turned a blind eye to them, what is clear is that there were some recurrent patterns of perpetration, and during my fieldwork in BiH some common themes began to emerge. For example, people of all ages were raped and sexually abused during the Bosnian war, but younger women were particularly vulnerable.[111] Of the 66 female interviewees, 53 had been in their teens, twenties or thirties when they were violated, while only 13

106 Author interview, Sarajevo, 13 August 2014.

107 Amnesty International, *Bosnia Herzegovina: Rape and Sexual Abuse by Armed Forces* (21 January 1993), 7, available at: www.amnesty.org/en/documents/eur63/001/1993/en/ (accessed 8 May 2016).

108 Bassiouni, *supra* note 102, at §313.

109 Ibid. Helsinki Watch noted, for example, that 'soldiers often rape without regard for witnesses, and, on occasion, identify themselves to their victims. These are not the actions of men who fear retribution'. Helsinki Watch, *War Crimes in Bosnia-Hercegovina – Volume II* (New York: Human Rights Watch, 1996), 22.

110 They acknowledged, however, that 'this remains to be definitively proven'. Bassiouni and McCormick, *supra* note 20, at 21. For MacKinnon, in contrast, sufficient proof of what was happening already existed. According to her, 'It is specifically rape under orders. This is not rape out of control. It is rape under control'. MacKinnon, *supra* note 27, at 11.

111 Discussing the rapes committed in the Trnopolje camp in Prijedor municipality between May and October 1992, for example, the ICTY found that 'Not all of the perpetrators were camp personnel. Some were allowed to visit the camp from the outside. Soldiers took out girls aged 16 or 17 from the camp and raped them on the way to Kozarac [in close vicinity to the Trnopolje camp] on a truck. In one case, a 13-year-old Bosnian Muslim girl was raped'. *Prosecutor v. Radoslav Brđanin*, IT- 99-36-T, ICTY Trial Chamber Judgement (1 September 2004), §514.

had been in their forties or fifties. Indeed, younger women were often separated from older women to be raped. At Caparde, for example, in the municipality of Kalesija in eastern BiH, 'The younger women were held for several nights in a furniture warehouse in the town. Serbian soldiers selected and raped 40 of the women between the ages of 15 and 30 years'.[112] Six of the interviewees were themselves raped at Caparde and all of them were in their late teens or early twenties at the time.

Several other commonalities developed from the research data. All of the 66 female interviewees were raped and one of the male interviewees showed me documentation which stated that he was raped. Of these 67 interviewees, just over one third were raped by a single perpetrator (with other soldiers typically close by), one third of them were raped by two or more perpetrators (either in quick secession or on separate occasions) and slightly under one third did not disclose this information. Many interviewees were forced to hand over money and valuables;[113] and just under half of the total 79 men and women were raped and/or sexually abused in camps such as Omarska and Trnopolje (Prijedor municipality), Čelebići (Konjic municipality), Dretelj (Čapljina municipality), Luka (Brčko District), Čelopek (Zvornik municipality), Sušica (Vlasenica municipality) and Viktor Bubanj (Sarajevo). Indeed, Engle notes that 80 per cent of the rapes committed during the Bosnian war reportedly occurred in camps.[114] More informal places of detention were also used, including hotels[115] and apartments. In the ICTY's leading case on rape and sexual violence, which centred on war events in the eastern Bosnian town of Foča:

> [Witness] FWS-87 testified that she stayed at the apartment of Radomir Kovač [a sub-commander of the military police of the Bosnian Serb army] in the Lepa Brena block for about four months, and had almost daily contact with him. She was raped by him vaginally and orally almost every night, and sometimes also by Jagos Kostić who lived in the apartment together with the accused Kovač. [Witness] FWS-75 was also raped by Radomir Kovač, and [Witness] A.S. would generally be raped by Jagos Kostić. During her time in the apartment, the girls were frequently threatened with murder; they were locked up and had no contact whatsoever with the outside world.

112 Amnesty International, *supra* note 107, at 14.

113 In its final report, the UN Commission of Experts identified five patterns of rape in BiH, the first of which involved 'individuals or small groups committing sexual assault in conjunction with looting and intimidation of the target ethnic group'. Bassiouni, *supra* note 102, at §245.

114 Karen Engle, 'Feminism and its (Dis)contents: Criminalizing Wartime Rape in Bosnia and Herzegovina', *American Journal of International Law* 39 (2005): 778–816, at 785.

115 Some women, for example, were detained 'in hotels or similar facilities for the sole purpose of sexually entertaining soldiers', after which these women were reportedly often killed. Bassiouni, *supra* note 102, at §249.

> While in the apartment, the girls were obliged to cook, clean and wash clothes.[116]

Interviewees who were interned in camps, homes and other buildings during the Bosnian war described how the soldiers came and went as they pleased and did 'whatever they wanted'. In the camps, rapes and sexual violence typically happened at night. A soldier would point at an individual woman, signalling to her that she had been 'chosen' and should go outside. She would return, sometimes several hours later, rarely speaking about what had happened to her. It was not safe to do so. But everyone knew. It was an open secret. Some rapes were also committed in public. The UN Commission of Experts, for example, found that 'Mothers of young children are often raped in front of their children and are threatened with the death of their children if they do not submit to being raped'.[117] Some of the women who took part in this research disclosed that their children were held in camps or private dwellings alongside them, but none of them claimed to have been raped in front of their offspring. Without exception, the male interviewees provided few details of their experiences. Several of them who were together in the same camp, however, recalled that crimes and abuses were committed in the presence of other camp inmates.

If the rapes and sexual violence committed during the Bosnian war attracted huge international attention from policymakers, scholars and the media, a number of important sub-themes have been consistently neglected or downplayed. Three in particular can be highlighted, which individually and in combination reveal a more nuanced picture than the dominant narrative of Serb military formations raping Bosnian Muslim women.[118]

## The use of rape and sexual violence by non-Serb forces

The UN Commission of Experts found that of the 677 alleged camps in BiH, 381 were corroborated (i.e. reported by a neutral source or multiple neutral

116 *Prosecutor v. Dragoljub Kunarac, Radomir Kovač and Zoran Vuković*, IT-96-23-T& IT-96-23/1-T, ICTY Trial Chamber Judgement (22 February 2001), §68.

117 Bassiouni, *supra* note 102, at §230.

118 See, for example, Beverley Allen, *Rape Warfare: The Hidden Genocide in Bosnia and Herzegovina* (Minneapolis, MN: University of Minnesota Press, 1996); Thomas Salzman, 'Rape Camps as a Means of Ethnic Cleansing: Religious, Cultural and Ethical Responses to Rape Victims in the former Yugoslavia, *Human Rights Quarterly* 20 (1998): 348–378; Leah Hansen, 'Gender, Nation, Rape: Bosnia and the Construction of Security', *International Feminist Journal of Politics* 3 (2001): 55–75; Lynda E. Boose, 'National Countermemories: Crossing the River Drina: Bosnian Rape Camps, Turkish Impalement and Serb Cultural Memory', *Signs: Journal of Women in Culture and Society* 28 (2002): 71–96.

sources) and 296 were uncorroborated.[119] Serb-run camps were the most numerous and were particularly concentrated in areas such as Prijedor (28 camps)[120] and Brčko (24 camps).[121] However, it was not only the Bosnian Serb army (VRS) that used camps. There were six corroborated Bosnian Muslim camps and four corroborated Bosnian Muslim/Bosnian Croat camps in Konjic, for example;[122] 11 corroborated Bosnian Muslim camps in Sarajevo;[123] and five corroborated Bosnian Croat camps in Mostar.[124]

Relatedly, it is important to acknowledge that all sides in the Bosnian war committed rape and sexual violence, albeit not to the same extent.[125] The UN Commission of Experts referred to, inter alia, a Bosniak-run detention facility in Breza, near Vareš in central BiH, where Serb women 'were reportedly raped by as many as 20 men at a time, one after another'.[126] Indeed, the first rape trial at the ICTY focused on the crimes committed by a Bosnian Muslim soldier in the Čelebići camp, while the second trial centred on the rape of a Bosnian Muslim woman detained by Bosnian Croat soldiers.[127] To cite Engle, 'It was not until Kunarac [in 2001], the case involving Foča, that Serbian men were convicted for raping Bosnian Muslim women'.[128] Some of the reported abuses that occurred in Bosnian Croat-run camps included indiscriminate beatings, public humiliation and rape; and '[e]lectric shock and forced same-sex sexual acts were also alleged as common methods of torture and abuse'.[129] In a 1993 report, Amnesty International described how seven soldiers from the *Vatreni konji* (Fire Horses), a military brigade of the Croatian Defence Council (HVO), raped a group of Serb women in a house in Novi Grad, in the municipality of Odžak in northern BiH.[130] More recently, in the trial of *Prlić et al.*,

119 Bassiouni, *supra* note 104, at §74.
120 Ibid., at §134.
121 Ibid., at §85.
122 Ibid., at §114.
123 Ibid., at §140.
124 Ibid., at §127.
125 Bassiouni, *supra* note 102, at §251.
126 Ibid., at §871.
127 *Prosecutor v. Zejnil Delalić, Zdravko Mucić, Hazim Delić and Esad Landžo*, IT-96-21-T, ICTY Trial Chamber Judgement (16 November 1998); *Prosecutor v. Anto Furundžija*, IT-95-17/1-T, ICTY Trial Chamber Judgement (10 December 1998).
128 Engle, *supra* note 114, at 798.
129 Bassiouni, *supra* note 104, at §172.
130 Amnesty International, *supra* note 107, at 14. In October 2014, four former members of the *Vatreni Konji* went on trial at the State Court of BiH (*Prosecutor v. Marijan Brnjić, Martin Barukčić, Pavo Glavaš and Ilija Glavaš*). A year later, only one of them – Marijan Brnjić – was found guilty of rape and sentenced to six years' imprisonment. This was upheld on appeal in May 2016. The other defendants in the case were acquitted on the grounds of lack of evidence. See www.sudbih.gov.ba/predmet/3287/show. In a subsequent separate trial, which commenced on 20 January 2016, Brnjić was again convicted of raping a Serb woman. See www.sudbih.gov.ba/predmet/3491/show.

the ICTY similarly documented sexual abuses committed by HVO soldiers. It found, for example, that 'in August 1993 members of the HVO raped several Muslim women and girls held in the Podgrađe neighbourhood [in Prozor municipality in northern Herzegovina] while under the guard of the Military Police'.[131] It further established that during the same period, 'several women being held in houses in the village of Duge [close to the town of Prozor] were forced to have sexual relations with HVO soldiers and members of the HVO Military Police'.[132]

To reiterate, Bosniak and Croat forces did not commit rape and sexual violence on the same scale as Serb forces, and the UN Commission underlined that it could not 'detect any particular pattern or policy' operating in Bosniak- and Croat-run camps.[133] However, this does not mean that certain groups of survivors should be overlooked or ignored, or that variation across the three 'S's' of scope, scale and systematization justifies the creation of victimological echelons.[134] Fundamentally, the motives imputed to perpetrators should not determine or affect how survivors themselves are perceived, or how their trauma is understood. Moreover, the maintenance of 'binary and hierarchical representations of wartime sexual violence that further polarised and fastened on divisive nationalist discourse'[135] is inimical to the realization of key transitional justice goals, including justice and reconciliation.

If little attention has been given to the use of rape and sexual violence by Bosnian Croat and Bosniak forces, the occurrence of intra-ethnic rape has been even more neglected. One Bosnian Croat interviewee described how she was raped by members of the aforementioned *Vatreni konji*; this was her 'punishment' for marrying a Bosnian Serb.[136] Intra-ethnic rapes, however, primarily occurred in the context of an 'ultimately unsuccessful [Muslim] rebellion against the Sarajevo government'.[137]

131 *Prosecutor v. Jadranko Prlić, Bruno Stojić, Slobodan Praljak, Milivoj Petković, Valentin Ćorić and Berislav Pušić*, IT-04-74-T, ICTY Trial Chamber Judgement, Vol. III (29 May 2013), §757. This case is currently on appeal.
132 Ibid., at §759.
133 Bassiouni, *supra* note 102, at §227–228.
134 See Olivera Simić, *Silenced Victims of Wartime Sexual Violence* (Abingdon: Routledge, forthcoming September 2017).
135 Olivera Simić, 'Rape, Silence and Denial', in Martina Fischer and Olivera Simić (eds), *Transitional Justice and Reconciliation: Lessons from the Balkans* (Abingdon: Routledge, 2016), 102–120, at 104.
136 Author interview, 24 June 2015.
137 Sarah Kenyon Lischer, 'Militarized Refugee Populations: Humanitarian Challenges in the Former Yugoslavia', *The Rosemary Rogers Working Paper Series, Working Paper #5* (August 1999), available at: http://web.mit.edu/CIS/www/migration/pubs/rrwp/5_militarized.pdf (accessed 8 February 2016).

## Intra-ethnic rapes

In September 1993, Fikret Abdić – a Bosniak politician and the owner of the *Agrokomerc* conglomerate in Velika Kladuša, in the Bosnian Krajina area of north-west BiH – declared the establishment of the Autonomous Province of Western Bosnia (APWB) in opposition to the official Bosnian government in Sarajevo. Abdić formed his own army, the National Defence of the APWB, which fought against the Fifth Corps of the Bosnian army (ABiH) in Velika Kladuša (and collaborated with Serb rebels from Croatia and Serbia). Viewing anyone who remained loyal to the Bosnian state as an enemy and a traitor, soldiers from Abdić's army – known as *Autonomaši* – arrested large numbers of Bosniaks and sent them to camps.[138] Between 1993 and 1995, there were eight camps in the municipality of Velika Kladuša, of which the two largest were Nepek (where 2,383 civilians were held) and Drmeljevo (where 1,500 civilians and captured soldiers were detained).[139] Prisoners were subjected to inhumane treatment, and some acts of rape and sexual violence occurred. On 21 January 2016, for example, the County Court in Rijeka in Croatia sentenced Ćazim Behrić – the commander of the Drmeljevo camp – to four years' imprisonment for, inter alia, raping a Bosniak woman in the camp.[140]

Allegations of rape and sexual abuses committed by members of the Fifth Corps of the ABiH also began to emerge. In 1995, for example, the UN noted that:

> In one reported case, the wife of a senior Abdić army official was interrogated several times in her home by members of the Fifth Corps. Finally, on 10 August, she was abducted from her home, beaten and raped. In another case investigated by international monitors, a 67-year-old woman, who had been forced to stay behind in Velika Kladuša to look after her paralysed husband, was raped in her home at night by an armed man in uniform. In another case, a woman and her two daughters were repeatedly beaten and harassed by soldiers from the Fifth Corps on several occasions, and interrogated about the military activities of male relatives.[141]

138 Kemal Mujagić, *Istina o "Autonomnoj Pokrajini Zapadna Bosna" 1993–1995* (Cazin, BiH: Grafis, 2013), 216.

139 Ibid., at 310.

140 Tamara Opačak Klobučar, 'Ćazim Behrić osuđen na četiri godine zatvora zbog ratnog zločina protiv civila' (21 January 2016), available at: www.vecernji.hr/hrvatska/rijeka-cazim-behric-osuden-na-cetiri-godine-zatvora-zbog-ratnog-zlocina-protiv-civila-1053898 (accessed 9 March 2016). In total, eight female Bosniak interviewees maintained that they were raped by *Autonomaši* (and, in one case, by Serb soldiers too). Two male interviewees also identified their perpetrators as *Autonomaši*.

141 UN General Assembly, *Human Rights Questions: Human Rights Situations and Reports of Special Rapporteurs and Representatives – Situation of Human Rights in the former Yugoslavia – Note by the Secretary-General*, A/50/727, S/1995/933 (7 November 1995), §76, available at: www.refworld.org/pdfid/3ae6af351b.pdf (accessed 9 December 2015).

In 2012, the Cantonal Court in Bihać sentenced Safet Delić to three-and-a-half years' imprisonment for raping a Bosniak woman in Velika Kladuša in August 1995. Delić was fighting in the ABiH and his victim's brother was part of Abdić's army.[142] Several former members of the 505th Bužim Brigade of the Fifth Corps of the ABiH are currently on trial at the State Court of BiH. They are charged with war crimes against civilians and war crimes against prisoners of war, including acts of rape and sexual violence, committed in an improvised prison in the Radoč Hotel in Bužim, close to Velika Kladuša.[143] According to a journalist following the case, 'Detainees were allegedly forced to commit sexual and physical violence upon each other'.[144]

There is a critical lack of data regarding the sexual crimes committed in the Bosnian Krajina. Moreover, this intra-ethnic aspect of the Bosnian war is rarely spoken about,[145] particularly in Velika Kladuša which remains deeply divided.[146] In its judgement against Suljo Karajić, who fought in the Fifth Corps of the ABiH, the State Court of BiH emphasized that 'This was an extremely painful conflict. It was Muslim against Muslim. It was clear for some of the witnesses that many young people were caught up in this conflict without any clear sense of why this conflict was occurring'.[147] One interviewee explained that he no longer has any communication with his brother. The two men were always close, but the war destroyed their relationship. The interviewee insisted that his brother, who joined the *Autonomaši*, could have intervened when he was sent to a camp and saved him from the 'hell' that he endured.[148] The interviewee's story, in turn, highlights a third important dimension of the rapes and sexual violence committed during the Bosnian war that has been heavily neglected.

142 Balkan Transitional Justice, 'Bosniak Sentenced for Velika Kladuša War Rape' (7 December 2012), available at: www.balkaninsight.com/en/article/bosniak-sentenced-to-three-and-a-half-years-for-wartime-rape (accessed 17 March 2016).

143 *Prosecutor v. Zijad Nanić et al.*, S1 1 K 016629 15 Krl, see www.sudbih.gov.ba/predmet/3492/show; *Prosecutor v. Mehmed Alšević*, S1 1 K 016629 15 Krl, see www.sudbih.gov.ba/predmet/3555/show.

144 Emina Diždarević, 'Trial for Bužim Crimes has Begun' (15 March 2016), available at: www.justice-report.com/en/articles/po%C4%8Delo-su%C4%91enje-za-zlo%C4%8Dine-u-bu%C5%BEimu-1 (accessed 4 February 2017).

145 According to Mujagić, it is especially difficult for survivors to come to terms with the fact that their rapists were fellow Bosniaks. Mujagić, *supra* note 138, at 420.

146 Abdić himself was sentenced by a Croatian court in 2002 to 20 years' imprisonment – later reduced to 15 years – for war crimes. He was released from prison in 2012 and still enjoys significant popular support. His nickname, '*Babo*', is scrawled in graffiti around the town of Velika Kladuša, which highlights the persistence of intra-Bosniak cleavages.

147 *Prosecutor v. Suljo Karajić*, X-KR-07/336, State Court of BiH First Instance Verdict (13 April 2010), §325.

148 Author interview, 29 November 2014.

## The rape and sexual abuse of men

At an international level, as previously noted, greater attention is gradually being given to male survivors of rape and sexual violence. The Summit Report that followed the 2014 Global Summit to End Sexual Violence in Conflict, for example, emphasizes, inter alia, that 'Sexual violence is indiscriminate, affecting men and boys as well as women and girls'.[149] A year earlier, the UN Security Council acknowledged for the first time that men and boys can suffer sexual violence in conflict. The Preamble to UN Security Council Resolution 2106 notes 'with concern that sexual violence in armed conflict and post-conflict situations disproportionately affects women and girls, as well as groups that are particularly vulnerable or may be specifically targeted, while also affecting men and boys'.[150] Although this acknowledgement 'is rather tentative', it nevertheless marks an important departure from 'the complete silence of the preceding 13 years of such resolutions'.[151] UN Security Council Resolution 1325, for example, calls on all parties involved in armed conflict 'to take special measures to protect women and girls from gender-based violence, particularly rape and other forms of sexual abuse'.[152] In a similar vein, UN Security Council Resolution 1820 demands that 'all parties to armed conflict immediately take appropriate measures to protect civilians, including women and girls, from all forms of sexual violence'.[153] There is no recognition that men and boys also need protection. As Scully argues apropos of Resolution 1820, 'the phrase "women and girls" is used thirteen times in the document, while no explicit mention is made of how men and boys are also victims'.[154]

During the Bosnian war, there was some acknowledgement that men were being subjected to acts of rape and sexual violence. In a 1993 report, Amnesty International noted that it had 'received allegations of instances of male prisoners in detention under the control of both Serbian and Bosnian Government forces being made to perform sexual acts with each other'.[155] In a similar vein, the UN Commission of Experts found that men were being 'forced to rape women and to perform sex acts on guards or each other';[156] and some had also been 'subjected to castration, circumcision or other sexual mutilation'.[157] Additionally, the

149 Foreign and Commonwealth Office, *supra* note 11, at 8.
150 UN Security Council Resolution 2106, SRES/2106 (24 June 2013), Preamble.
151 Chris Dolan, 'Has Patriarchy been Stealing the Feminists' Clothes? Conflict-Related Sexual Violence and UN Security Council Resolutions', *IDS Bulletin* 45 (2014): 80–84, at 80.
152 UN Security Council Resolution 1325, S/RES/1325 (31 October 2000), §10.
153 UN Security Council Resolution 1820, S/RES/1820 (19 June 2008), §3.
154 Pamela Scully, 'Vulnerable Women: A Critical Reflection on Human Rights Discourse and Sexual Violence', *Emory International Law Review* 24 (2009): 113–123, at 118.
155 Amnesty International, *supra* note 107, at 9.
156 Bassiouni, *supra* note 102, at §235.
157 Ibid.

ICTY became the first international tribunal to prosecute sexual violence against men. The trial of Duško Tadić, the president of the local board of the Serb Democratic Party in Kozarac in north-western BiH, partly focused on the castration and sexual mutilation of Fikret Harambašić, a Bosnian Muslim detained in the infamous Omarska camp in Prijedor municipality (further discussed in Chapter 5).[158] Looking at the overall picture, however, it is unquestionably the case that male survivors in BiH have been significantly overlooked, and few scholars have endeavoured to correct this.[159]

In her work on male rape in prison contexts, Stemple discusses the positioning of male survivors within a 'sexual violence hierarchy'. According to her:

> Chastity is not a virtue to which men are generally taught to aspire and is not an attribute associated with proper manhood. That men are often raped in unappealing contexts such as prisons – one cannot imagine a setting in which 'innocence' is less prevalent – helps propel male victims to the bottom of a hierarchy of victim sympathy.[160]

Male survivors in BiH are similarly at the bottom of a hierarchy, not because there is little sympathy for them but simply because they have never received the level of attention that female survivors have. One explanation, which is not specific to BiH, is that men are not 'supposed' to be vulnerable. In war situations, moreover, they are expected to defend not only their own boundaries, but also the boundaries of their communities. The reality of their own vulnerability is thus deeply problematic and indeed unsettling; it challenges the heteronormative order and thereby reveals a deeper vulnerability that potentially has far-reaching security implications. As Bourke argues apropos of the sexual abuse of Iraqi prisoners at Abu Ghraib, 'The photographs were a stark reminder of an uncomfortable observation: not only the female body, but the male body as well, is violable, penetrable'.[161] We therefore focus on

158 *Prosecutor v. Duško Tadić*, IT-94-1-T, ICTY Trial Chamber Opinion and Judgement (7 May 1997), §20.

159 There are some exceptions. See, for example, R. Charli Carpenter, 'Recognizing Gender-Based Violence against Civilian Men and Boys in Conflict Situations', *Security Dialogue* 37 (2006): 83–103; Sandesh Sivakumaran, 'Sexual Violence against Men in Armed Conflict', *European Journal of International Law* 18 (2007): 253–276; Sarah Solangon and Preeti Patel, 'Sexual Violence against Men in Countries Affected by Armed Conflict', *Conflict, Security and Development* 2 (2012): 417–442. However, these articles address the general issue of conflict-related rape and sexual violence against men and do not specifically focus on BiH.

160 Lara Stemple, 'Male Rape and Human Rights', *Hastings Law Journal* 60 (2009): 605–646, at 630.

161 Bourke, *supra* note 18, at 211–212.

the penetrated female body, pushing male survivors into the background. It is easier to do this than to 'acknowledge the vulnerability of masculinity and manhood'.[162]

Relatedly, male survivors may be unwilling or reluctant to tell their stories. They might struggle to acknowledge that they have suffered sexual violence;[163] they might be apprehensive of other people's reactions;[164] they might be afraid of being viewed as a 'failed man';[165] they might worry that people will question their sexuality.[166] Indeed, men who have a physical response (erection, ejaculation) while being raped/sexually abused may themselves become deeply confused about their sexual identity; '"My mind was saying no, but my body seemed to say yes. Why did my body betray me in this way?"'[167] Although I was able to interview 13 Bosnian men (12 Bosnian Muslims and one Bosnian Serb), which was fewer than I had hoped, the extent to which they really spoke about their experiences was extremely limited. With only one exception, the interviews with these men felt 'threadbare'. There were many holes and many fibres that were broken off. Story-telling, of course, is a process and it takes time. Most of these men were only at the start of that process.

*****

The Bosnian war fundamentally contributed to putting the issue of conflict-related rape and sexual violence firmly on the international agenda. This was one of the war's long-term legacies. Yet, what this chapter has also sought to show is that the situation on the ground was more complex and nuanced than the dominant narrative of Bosnian Serb soldiers raping Bosnian Muslim women suggested. A key aim of the following chapters is precisely to add shades of grey by presenting stories from all sides, and from both male and female survivors. The next three chapters are about the long-term effects of rape and sexual violence.

162 Michael Scarce, *Male on Male Rape: The Hidden Toll of Stigma and Shame* (Cambridge, MA: Perseus Publishing, 1997), 9.
163 Kay L. Levine, 'No Penis, No Problem', *Fordham Urban Law Journal* 33 (2005): 100–147, at 128.
164 As Rentoul and Appleboom point out, 'The experiences of male victims of sexual assault may be antithetical to cultural notions of what it means to be a man (strong, sexually active and able to defend himself)'. Lynett Rentoul and Nicola Appleboom, 'Understanding the Psychological Impact of Rape and Serious Sexual Assault of Men: A Literature Review', *Journal of Psychiatric and Mental Health Nursing* 4 (1997): 267–274, at 268.
165 Aliraza Javaid, 'Feminism, Masculinity and Male Rape: Bringing Male Rape "Out of the Closet"', *Journal of Gender Studies* 25 (2014): 283–293, at 291.
166 Sandesh Sivakumaran, 'Male/Male Rape and the "Taint" of Homosexuality', *Human Rights Quarterly* 27 (2005): 1274–1306.
167 Scarce, *supra* note 162, at 60.

These long-term effects are a critically neglected dimension of the Bosnian war, and indeed of many other conflicts. As Chapter 2 will explore, existing studies – although important – are limited in number, are mainly focused on Africa and have tended to explore 'long-term' effects within a relatively compressed time period.

Chapter 2

# The long-term effects of rape and sexual violence

## A legacy gap

Kira Salak is an American travel writer. Her powerful book, *Four Corners*, describes her journey through Papua New Guinea. However, the book begins four year earlier, in Africa. Salak was in Malawi and trying to get to Zimbabwe, via Mozambique. It was 1992 and the civil war in Mozambique was still raging. Taken by a group of soldiers to a building near the border with Zimbabwe, Salak came close to being gang raped. She escaped, yet the memory of that night remained with her. 'I think about the trip I took four years earlier, to Mozambique', she writes. 'I never put that place behind me – I don't know how to get over it. If there's some magic elixir that allows one to forget, I haven't been given it. Mozambique stays'.[1]

Traumatic experiences leave a deep imprint, and this is particularly true of rape and sexual violence.[2] These are crimes that have a myriad of long-term effects, including physical, psychological, socio-economic and familial. Often, however, this longevity of impact is neglected.[3] As Amone-P'Olak et al. accentuate, 'Although incidents of sexual violence have been reported in many theatres of war by international bodies such as the United Nations... research on its long-term

1 Kira Salak, *Four Corners: A Journey into the Heart of Papua New Guinea* (Washington, D.C: National Geographic, 2001), 50.

2 See, for example, Ann W. Burgess and Lynda L. Holmstrom, 'Rape Trauma Syndrome', *American Journal of Psychiatry* 131 (1974): 981–986; Ann W. Burgess, 'Rape Trauma Syndrome', *Behavioral Sciences and the Law* 1 (1983): 97–113.

3 In contrast, there are many studies on the long-term effects of childhood sex abuse. See, for example, John N. Briere and Diana M. Elliott, 'Immediate and Long-Term Impacts of Child Sexual Abuse', *The Future of Children* 4 (1994): 54–69; Shanta R. Dube, Robert F. Anda, Charles L. Whitfield, David W. Brown, Vincent J. Felitti, Maxia Dong and Wayne H. Giles, 'Long-Term Consequences of Childhood Sexual Abuse by Gender of Victim', *American Journal of Preventive Medicine* 28 (2005): 430–438; David M. Fergusson, Geraldine F.H. McLeod and L. John Horwood, 'Childhood Sexual Abuse and Adult Developmental Outcomes: Findings from a 30-year Longitudinal Study in New Zealand', *Child Abuse and Neglect* 37 (2013): 664–674; Joanna C. Young and Cathy S. Widom, 'Long-Term Effects of Child Abuse and Neglect on Emotion Processing in Adulthood', *Child Abuse and Neglect* 38 (2014): 1369–1381.

adverse physical, mental, and social consequences has lagged behind'.[4] One explanation is that rape and sexual violence typically galvanize the most interest – especially at the policy level – in live conflict situations, which in turn leads to a strong emphasis on immediate/short-term trauma. Consequently, there are still few detailed empirical studies – and, in particular, qualitative studies – addressing the long-term consequences of conflict-related rape and sexual violence.

The first half of this chapter examines some of the extant scholarship on long-term consequences, in order to lay the foundations for the forthcoming empirical chapters. Although limited, this scholarship does at least provide some important insights into the multi-dimensional and multi-layered long-term effects of rape and sexual violence. In relation to the rapes and sexual violence committed during the Bosnian war, however, very significant gaps exist. Where are the survivors today? To what extent does their war trauma continue to affect their lives? Have they been able to move on? The second half of the chapter, which shifts the focus back to BiH, shows that these questions remain largely unanswered – and explores some of the possible reasons for this.

## Life after rape and sexual violence

On 4 May 1992, the first shells – 'apparently fired by the JNA and other Serb forces'[5] – fell on Konjic, a town and municipality in Herzegovina. Life became increasingly difficult for the local inhabitants,[6] and armed Serb forces blocked the two routes in and out of Konjic, namely the M17 road to Sarajevo and the highway to Mostar. For the HVO and Konjic Territorial Defence (TO) units in the area, unblocking these roads was a major priority. In the second half of 1992, after negotiations with Serb forces failed, they launched a series of attacks on Serb villages around Konjic. As the ICTY has noted, 'These military operations resulted in the arrest of many members of the Serb population and it was

4 Kennedy Amone-P'Olak, Tlholego Molemane Lekhutlile, Emilio Ovuga, Rosemary Ann Abbott, Richard Meiser-Stedman, David Gage Stewart and Peter Brian Jones, 'Sexual Violence and General Functioning among Formerly Abducted Girls in Northern Uganda: The Mediating Roles of Stigma and Community Relations – The WAYS Study', *BMC Public Health* 16 (2016): 1–10, at 2. See also Corey Barr, 'Making Connections: Bridging Transitional Justice and Security Sector Reform to Confront Conflict-Related Sexual and Gender-Based Violence', *Praxis: The Fletcher Journal of Human Security* 26 (2011): 5–23, at 12; Nicola Jones, Janice Cooper, Elizabeth Presler-Marshall and David Walker, *The Fallout of Rape as a Weapon of War: The Life-Long and Intergenerational Impacts of Sexual Violence in Conflict* (June 2014), 2, available at www.odi.org/sites/odi.org.uk/files/odi-assets/publications-opinion-files/8990.pdf (accessed 9 June 2016).

5 *Prosecutor v. Zejnil Delalić, Zdravko Mucić, Hazim Delić and Esad Landžo*, IT-96-21-T, ICTY Trial Chamber Judgement (16 November 1998), §134.

6 'The population of the municipality, according to the 1991 census, was 43,878, of which 54.3 per cent were designated Muslims, 26.2 per cent Croats, 15 per cent Serbs, 3 per cent Yugoslavs and 1.3 per cent others'. Ibid., at §121.

thus necessary to create a facility where they could be housed'.[7] The chosen facility was a compound consisting of barracks and warehouses in the village of Čelebići, also in the municipality of Konjic. Four men subsequently went on trial at the ICTY for crimes committed against these Serb prisoners. During the trial, a Serb woman described how she felt as a result of being raped by the camp's deputy commander, Hazim Delić. According to the Trial Chamber judgement, 'The effect of this rape by Hazim Delić was expressed by Ms. Ćećez when she stated: "he trampled on my pride and I will never be able to be the woman that I was." '[8]

On 26 April 2012, the Special Court for Sierra Leone (SCSL) convicted its most high-profile defendant, Charles Taylor. The former president of Liberia was found guilty of 11 counts of, inter alia, planning, aiding and abetting crimes committed by rebel forces – the Revolutionary United Front (RUF) and the Armed Forces Revolutionary Council (AFRC) – during the 11-year civil war in Sierra Leone (1991–2002). These crimes included rape.[9] Commenting on the verdict, Prosecutor Brenda Hollis declared: 'Victims were savagely and repeatedly raped, and were then used as sex slaves, handed from owner to owner. The emotional and physical trauma suffered by these victims will continue for a lifetime'.[10]

More recently, on 21 March 2016, Trial Chamber III of the ICC delivered its judgement against Jean-Pierre Bemba Gombo, a former deputy president of the DRC and leader of the *Mouvement de libération du Congo* (MLC).[11] The Trial Chamber held Bemba responsible, under Article 28 of the Rome Statute,[12] for crimes committed by MLC soldiers in the Central African Republic, including rape. The judgement discusses some of the ways in which the rapes committed by MLC soldiers had a long-term impact on the lives of the victims. For example, 12 soldiers raped Witness V1 orally, vaginally and anally. As well as subsequently experiencing pain in her vagina and lungs, and having psychological problems,

7 Ibid., at §141.

8 Ibid., at §938.

9 The judgement documents, for example, that 'From February 1998 to December 1998, human rights abuses intensified, leaving thousands of civilians killed or mutilated by RUF and AFRC fighters. Hundreds of civilians were abducted, raped and the burning of houses and looting continued to occur'. *Prosecutor v. Charles Taylor*, SCSL-01-03-T, SCSL Trial Chamber Judgement (26 April 2012), §555. Taylor's conviction and 50-year sentence were upheld on appeal a year later.

10 Special Court for Sierra Leone, 'Brenda Hollis Hails the Historic Conviction of Charles Taylor' (26 April 2012), available at: www.rscsl.org/Documents/Press/OTP/prosecutor-042612.pdf (accessed 5 April 2016).

11 See Janine N. Clark, 'The First Conviction at the ICC: An Analysis of the Bemba Judgment', *Journal of International Criminal Justice* 14 (2016): 667–687.

12 Article 28 defines liability based on command responsibility. See ICC, *Rome Statute of the International Criminal Court* (17 July 1998), available at: www.icc-cpi.int/nr/rdonlyres/ea9aeff7-5752-4f84-be94-0a655eb30e16/0/rome_statute_english.pdf (accessed 8 July 2016).

'She felt like she was no longer treated as a human being and was called the "Banyamulengué wife"'.[13] She became a social outcast within her own community, lost her job and could no longer provide for her children.[14] After Witness P23 was raped, he no longer felt respected within his community and saw himself as a 'dead man'.[15]

It is widely noted within extant scholarship that war rape and sexual violence can have major long-term effects. Chinkin, for example, underlines that 'The consequences of rape continue beyond the actual attack or attacks, often lasting for the rest of the women's lives. As well as the degradation, pain and terror caused at the time, the fear engendered remains long after'.[16] Looking beyond the men and women who directly experience these crimes, Jones et al. draw particular attention to some of the wider effects of war rape and sexual violence, including effects on family members who are forced to watch their loved-ones suffer.[17] Rarely, however, are these long-term consequences explored empirically within the framework of specific case studies. Most frequently, they are simply listed in a decontextualized way without any concrete connection to individual lives and realities. Illustrative of this is Wing and Merchán's observation that 'Long-term consequences for women may include mistrust, negative attitudes toward men, chronic depression, and fear of being left alone'.[18]

Some survivors, of course, may react to and deal with their experiences in broadly similar ways. Based on a study of 146 women and children who entered the emergency ward of the Boston City Hospital between July 1972 and July 1973, the therapists Burgess and Holmstrom introduced the term 'rape trauma syndrome' to encapsulate a composite of behavioural, somatic and psychological stress reactions. As they define it, this syndrome is 'the acute phase and long-term reorganization process that occurs as a result of forcible rape or attempted forcible rape'.[19] Potentially common stress reactions, however, are only one part

13 *Prosecutor v. Jean-Pierre Bemba Gombo*, ICC-01/05-01/08, ICC Trial Judgement pursuant to Article 74 of the Rome Statute (21 March 2016), §551. The Trial Chamber remarked that 'Many CAR (Central African Republic) civilians used the term "Banyamulengué" (or phonetically similar terms) to refer to the MLC troops' (§563).

14 Ibid., at §551.

15 Ibid., at §494.

16 Christine Chinkin, 'Rape and Sexual Abuse of Women in International Law', *European Journal of International Law* 5 (1994): 326–341, at 329.

17 Jones et al., *supra* note 4, at 2–3.

18 Adrien K. Wing and Sylke Merchán, 'Rape, Ethnicity and Culture: Spirit Injury from Bosnia to Black America', *Columbia Human Rights Law Review* 25 (1993): 1–48, at 4. See also Cassandra Clifford, 'Rape as a Weapon of War and Its Long-Term Effects on Victims and Society', 7th Global Conference on Violence and the Contexts of Hostility, Budapest (May 2008), available at: www.inter-disciplinary.net/ptb/hhv/vcce/vch7/Clifford%20paper.pdf (accessed 8 June 2016); Evelyne Josse, '"They Came with Two Guns": The Consequences of Sexual Violence for the Mental Health of Women in Armed Conflicts', *International Review of the Red Cross* 92 (2010): 177–195.

19 Burgess and Holmstrom, *supra* note 2, at 982.

of a more complex picture, and sweeping claims about the long-term effects of rape and sexual violence critically mask and distort the reality of more variegated individualized responses to trauma.[20]

A strong emphasis on psychological consequences has further contributed to the de-individualization of survivors. Because psychological consequences are typically assessed quantitatively, this often leads to survivors being represented simply as percentages. Kuwert et al., for example, carried out a study comparing the long-term effects of conflict-related sexual trauma and non-sexual trauma experienced at the end of World War II. The aim was to investigate the lasting impact of conflict-related sexual violence on mental health and sexual functioning, and a total of 27 elderly war rape survivors participated in the study. The authors found, inter alia, that women who had been exposed to conflict-related sexual violence during the war 'reported greater severity of PTSD [post-traumatic stress disorder]-related avoidance and hyperarousal symptoms, as well as anxiety, compared to female long-term survivors of non-sexual WWII trauma'.[21] Furthermore, 80.9 per cent of the women who had suffered wartime sexual trauma reported subsequently experiencing severe sexual problems throughout their life. This was compared to only 19.0 per cent of the women who had faced non-sexual war trauma.[22] These findings, although important, are not groundbreaking; and while they powerfully highlight the longevity of sexual violence impact, they offer limited insights into the everyday and individualized dimensions of this impact.

In a similar vein, Lueger-Schuster et al. examined the long-term mental health impact of sexual violence committed on a group of Austrian survivors during World War II. As part of a larger epidemiological study on war traumatization, the authors interviewed 298 elderly Austrians, 12 of whom reported direct experience of sexual violence. A further 33 had witnessed acts of sexual violence. Like Kuwert et al.'s study, the research draws valuable attention to the enduring effects of sexual violence seven decades on. The authors found, for example, that the female interviewees who had experienced or witnessed such violence were more likely to display symptoms of PTSD; and that 'Victims were more likely to show clinically relevant levels of depression and phobic fear and also reported higher levels of distress than non-victims, although not in a clinically relevant

20 Robert J. Ursano, Carol S. Fullerton and Brian G. McCaughey, 'Trauma and Disaster', in Robert J. Ursano, Brian G. McCaughey and Carol S. Fullerton (eds), *Individual and Community Responses to Trauma and Disaster: The Structure of Human Chaos* (Cambridge: Cambridge University Press, 1994), 1–27, at 5.

21 Philipp Kuwert, Heide Glaesmer, Svenja Eichhorn, Elena Grundke, Robert H. Pietrzak, Harald J. Freyberger and Thomas Klauer, 'Long-Term Effects of Conflict-Related Sexual Violence Compared with Non-Sexual War Trauma in Female World War II Survivors: A Matched Pairs Study', *Archives of Sexual Behavior* 43 (2014): 1059–1064, at 1062.

22 Ibid.

range'.[23] Again, however, these findings are somewhat abstract and disconnected from individual lives.

It is important to acknowledge that quantitative research is primarily about breadth rather than depth, and it is not aimed at capturing individuality and individual experiences. Yet, this is precisely why purely quantitative approaches to exploring the long-term effects of rape and sexual violence can only take us so far. These crimes profoundly affect human lives, and a comprehensive analysis of long-term effects requires attention to these lives – and specifically to the personal stories of survivors. In short, this is a field of research where qualitative studies, focused on 'the depths of the human experience',[24] are especially valuable. Relatedly, it must be emphasized that the long-term effects of rape and sexual violence extend far beyond psychological trauma and its diverse expressions. These are ricochet crimes that affect not only individuals but also entire families and communities. Hence, their diverse long-term effects are both multi-dimensional (affecting different aspects of a person's life) and multi-layered (affecting not only the direct victim). What follows is a review of some of the existing qualitative studies investigating these long-term effects.

## The multi-dimensional effects of rape and sexual violence

In April 1994, as the Bosnian war continued unabated, Hutu extremists in Rwanda began a genocidal campaign of mass slaughter aimed at exterminating the ethnic Tutsi. In the 100 days of ensuing bloodshed, an estimated 800,000 Tutsi and moderate Hutu were killed.[25] Furthermore, in his report to the UN Economic and Social Council in May 1994, René Degni-Ségui, the Special Rapporteur of the UN Commission on Human Rights, stressed that 'According to consistent and reliable testimony, a great many women were raped; rape was the rule and its absence the exception'.[26] Employing a phenomenological approach, Mukamana

23 Brigitte Lueger-Schuster, Tobias M. Glück, Ulrich S. Tran and Elisabeth L. Zeilinger, 'Sexual Violence by Occupational Forces during and after World War II: Influence of Experiencing and Witnessing of Sexual Violence on Current Mental Health in a Sample of Elderly Austrians', *International Psychogeriatrics* 24 (2012): 1354–1358, at 1356.

24 Jill E. Trenholm, Pia Olsson and Beth M. Ahlberg, 'Battles on Women's Bodies: War, Rape and Traumatisation in Eastern Democratic Republic of Congo', *Global Public Health: An International Journal for Research, Policy and Practice* 6 (2011): 139–152, at 147.

25 Lt. Gen. Roméo Dallaire, *Shake Hands with the Devil: The Failure of Humanity in Rwanda* (London: Arrow Books, 2004), xv.

26 René Degni-Ségui, *Report on the Situation of Human Rights in Rwanda* (25 May 1994), §15, available at: http://repository.un.org/bitstream/handle/11176/213419/E_CN.4_1996_68-EN.pdf?sequence=3&isAllowed=y (accessed 27 February 2017). Bijleveld, Morssinkhof and Smeulers estimate that 354,440 women were raped during the Rwandan genocide. According to them, 'Based on an estimated population of approximately 7.7 million… of whom just less than 4 million were female, more than 350,000 women were raped. This translates to approximately 8,972 rapes per 100,000 women'. Catrien Bijleveld, Aafke

and Brysiewicz's study explores the lived experiences of seven women who were raped during the 1994 Rwandan genocide. The aim was expressly to allow these individuals to focus on those aspects of their experiences that were most important to them and to speak about their current problems. The research variously addresses their sense of humiliation, loss of identity (linked to the loss of virginity) and social isolation. Unfortunately, each of these issues is examined only briefly, and indeed the entire article is just six pages in length. The data is thus presented in a somewhat superficial way. What the research clearly demonstrates, however, is that the long-term effects of rape are defined and shaped by diverse and assorted factors. For example, some of the research participants had been infected with the HIV virus. For these women, living with the virus and with their husbands' changed behaviours towards them were enduring consequences of rape. One participant, Furaha, 'described her husband's refusal to have sex with her because he did not want to use condoms'.[27]

The study also underlines that negative community attitudes can hugely affect survivors' ability to cope,[28] thereby exacerbating the long-term effects of rape. This, by extension, spotlights the critical importance of support networks. Two of the participants in the study, for example, were involved in a basket-making project. This provided them with opportunities not only to earn money, but also to share their stories with other women.[29] It cannot be assumed that story-telling is always, or necessarily, therapeutic.[30] However, while it is usually discussed in the context of formal transitional justice processes, such as criminal trials and TRCs, intra-survivor forms of story-telling are far less explored. By talking to each other and sharing their stories, survivors can regain a sense of meaning,[31] and this is crucial for enabling them to process and integrate their trauma.[32] The creation of support networks for survivors is thus an essential part of addressing the long-term consequences of rape and sexual violence.

The genocide in Rwanda significantly contributed to destabilizing its western neighbour, the DRC, as large numbers of Hutus crossed the border to avoid

Morssinkhof and Alette Smeulers, 'Counting the Countless: Rape Victimization during the Rwandan Genocide', *International Criminal Justice Review* 19 (2009): 208–224, at 219.

27 Donatilla Mukamana and Petra Brysiewicz, 'The Lived Experience of Genocide Rape Survivors in Rwanda', *Journal of Nursing Scholarship* 40 (2008): 379–384, at 380.

28 Ibid., at 383.

29 Ibid., at 382.

30 Claire Hackett and Bill Rolston, 'The Burden of Memory: Victims, Storytelling and Resistance in Northern Ireland', *Memory Studies* 2 (2009): 355–376, at 360.

31 Mukamana and Brysiewicz, *supra* note 27, at 383.

32 As Trenholm et al. underline, 'To share one's traumatic experience with another human being can be markedly painful and potentially retraumatising to the victim, but it can also serve as a powerful affirmation on the journey toward healing, sense-making and integrating the experience'. Jill Trenholm, Pia Olsson, Martha Blomqvist and Beth M. Alhberg, 'The Global, the Ethnic and the Gendered War: Women and Rape in Eastern Democratic Republic of Congo', *Gender, Place and Culture* 23 (2016): 484–501, at 495–496.

revenge attacks by the Rwandan Patriotic Front (RPF) in July 1994.[33] Over the last two decades, thousands of men, women and children have been subjected to rape and sexual violence in the DRC, particularly in the east of the country.[34] In 2007–2008, Kelly et al. surveyed 255 women in the DRC, 75.7 per cent of whom had experienced rape. The authors additionally conducted focus groups with a further 48 survivors of gender-based violence, in order to explore the multiple effects of war and violence on individuals and communities. Consistent with Mukamana and Brysiewicz's findings in Rwanda, the study powerfully demonstrates how the long-term effects of rape stem not only from the physical act itself, but also from the reactions that it provokes in others – and from the social context that feeds and sustains those reactions. The issue of stigma, for example, emerged as a dominant theme during the focus group discussions;[35] and common expressions of stigma – such as gossip and finger-pointing – were fuelling survivors' sense of humiliation and shame. Beyond noting the effects of rape stigma, however, the research also discusses some of the social factors and customs underpinning it, as identified by the women themselves. For example, 'customs that had previously been directed towards female adulterers were now applied to victims of rape'; and women who had been 'unfaithful' – regardless of the circumstances – 'were perceived to bring misfortune to the household'.[36] The

33 These Hutus took refuge in various camps in the DRC. According to Prunier, five camps alone (Katale, Kahindo, Mugunga, Lac Vert and Sake) together 'held no fewer than 850,000 people, including the 30,000 to 40,000 men of the ex-FAR [Forces Armées Rwandaises], the army of the genocide, complete with its heavy and light weapons, its officer corps, and its transport echelon'. Gérard Prunier, *From Genocide to Continental War: The "Congolese" Conflict and the Crisis of Contemporary Africa* (London: Hurst & Co., 2009), 25.

34 Amber Peterman, Tia Palermo and Caryn Bredenkamp, 'Estimates and Determinants of Sexual Violence against Women in the Democratic Republic of Congo', *American Journal of Public Health* 101 (2011): 1060–1067; Trenholm et al., *supra* note 32, at 484. According to a report by the UN Secretary General, 'From January to September 2014, the United Nations Population Fund (UNFPA) recorded 11,769 cases of sexual and gender-based violence in the provinces of North Kivu, South Kivu, Orientale, Katanga and Maniema; 39 per cent of these cases were considered to be directly related to the dynamics of conflict, perpetrated by armed individuals'. UN Security Council, *Conflict-Related Sexual Violence: Report of the Secretary General* (23 March 2015), 7, available at: www.securitycouncilreport.org/atf/cf/%7B65BFCF9B-6D27-4E9C-8CD3-CF6E4FF96FF9%7D/s_2015_203.pdf (accessed 8 May 2016). As several experts have pointed out, however, it is unhelpful to reductively focus only on the use of rape and sexual violence in the DRC. These crimes are part of a more complex web of violence. See, for example, Séverine Autesserre, 'Dangerous Tales: Dominant Narratives on the Congo and their Unintended Consequences', *African Affairs* 111 (2012): 202–222, at 216; Maria Eriksson Baaz and Maria Stern, *Sexual Violence as a Weapon of War? Perceptions, Prescriptions, Problems in the Congo and Beyond* (London: Zed Books, 2013), 32.

35 Jocelyn T. Kelly, Theresa S. Betancourt, Denis Mukwege, Robert Lipton and Michael J. VanRooyen, 'Experiences of Female Survivors of Sexual Violence in Eastern Democratic Republic of the Congo: A Mixed Methods Study', *Conflict and Health* 5 (2011): 1–8, at 5.

36 Ibid.

study thereby offers valuable emic insights into the problem of rape stigma in the women's communities. Unusually, it also allows the women to express their own opinions on how to tackle the problem.[37]

Challenging the more common idea that husbands can exacerbate their wives' trauma,[38] the research participants in Kelly et al.'s study suggested an alternative narrative that associated men with the alleviation of suffering. Support from husbands, the women argued, 'can act as a powerful resource to help the survivor resist community stigmatization'.[39] Those who have been infected with the HIV virus are often at a higher risk of being rejected by their husbands.[40] While this is a major issue in its own right that reinforces the critical need for more education and sensitization vis-à-vis HIV/AIDS, even the suspicion that a woman may be infected with the HIV virus can lead to her becoming a social outcast.[41] To address this problem, the research participants in Kelly et al.'s study suggested that women who have not been infected with HIV – or with any other sexually transmitted infections (STIs) – should be given the opportunity to prove this to their husbands and families. In short, 'STI testing was described as an extremely important intervention that may act as a first step towards reintegration'.[42] Such testing could help survivors to regain control of their lives and thereby reduce some of the long-term effects of rape.

Trenholm et al. have undertaken a more detailed study of the effects of war rape in the DRC. They note that although there are numerous testimonies of survivors, 'a deeper analysis into the intricacies of the aftermath of war rape from the perspectives of the affected women is lacking'.[43] The research employs an

37 Researchers typically voice their own views on this. See, for example, Susan Bartels, Jennifer Scott, Jennifer Leaning, Denis Mukwege and Robert Lipton, 'Surviving Sexual Violence in Eastern Democratic Republic of Congo', *Journal of International Women's Studies* 11 (2010): 37–49, at 44.

38 During their ethnographic research in the DRC, for example, Trenholm et al. found that 'For married women, rejection by husbands and the loss of their mutual children was expressed as a major cause of suffering'. Trenholm et al., *supra* note 32, at 493.

39 Kelly et al., *supra* note 35, at 5.

40 Amnesty International, *Rwanda: "Marked for Death", Rape Survivors Living with HIV/AIDS in Rwanda* (5 April 2004), available at: www.amnesty.org/en/documents/afr47/007/2004/en/ (accessed 9 January 2016).

41 According to Trenholm et al.'s research in the DRC, 'Those showing signs of weight loss, despite food insecurity and a negative HIV test, remained suspect'. Trenholm et al. *supra* note 32, at 497. In an earlier study, Trenholm, Olsson and Ahlberg spoke to ten local leaders in South Kivu about war rape and its effects. The interviews revealed that 'Most rape survivors are assumed to be infected by HIV so rather than receiving an empathetic healing reception, according to the leaders, they are promptly ostracised from their communities. In the case where a man has accepted his wife back, sexual relations were said to be curtailed. Contracting AIDS was also expressed as men's greatest fear concerning acceptance of their violated wives. Society was seen as implicit in the rejection'. Trenholm, Olsson and Ahlberg, *supra* note 24, at 143.

42 Kelly et al., *supra* note 35, at 5.

43 Trenholm et al., *supra* note 32, at 485.

ethnographic approach; Trenholm spent seven months working with 15 women over a six-year period. Written narratives and in-depth interviews were also part of the research methodology. The research discusses how the trauma and experience of being raped had affected multiple dimensions of the women's lives, from their physical health[44] and social identities[45] to their livelihoods[46] and mothering abilities.[47]

Trenholm et al. explicitly seek to counter the 'collectivization' of rape trauma,[48] by reasserting the individuality of survivors and their experiences. Indeed, they maintain that 'one of the reasons why rape has such profound effects on women's lives is precisely because people respond to them in a way that effectively strips them of their individuality'.[49] This further draws attention to the vital importance of social context in framing and shaping the long-term effects of rape and sexual violence. The authors, however, look beyond simply the local/community context. Rather, using an intersectional approach, they position the suffering of survivors within a broader macro framework of structural violence and gender inequalities. Viewed in this way, local responses to rape survivors simply reflect a wider set of dynamics – political, economic, global – that subordinate women. In the authors' words, 'Being a raped woman and barred from community underscores an already subservient gendered position'.[50] By situating rape and sexual violence within a wider narrative, this intersectional approach usefully provides a more holistic and layered understanding of the long-term effects of rape and sexual violence.

Trenholm et al. accordingly advocate a composite and multi-dimensional approach to aiding survivors, in recognition of complex and inter-related needs. While it is essential, for example, that survivors have access to adequate health

44 Ibid., at 492.
45 Ibid., at 494.
46 Ibid., at 491.
47 Ibid., at 493.
48 Kinyanda et al., for example, carried out a study in northern Uganda in 2005 involving structured interviews with 810 respondents. Within the total sample, 28.7 per cent of the women and 6.7 per cent of the men had reported experiencing at least one form of war-related sexual violence. The study provides useful data on some of the problems that these survivors now face. For example, 'About three quarters (72.4 per cent) of the respondents had "at least one gynaecological complaint" with the most commonly reported complaints being chronic lower abdominal pain (52.2 per cent), abnormal vaginal bleeding (27.4 per cent), infertility (26.6 per cent), genital sores (25.3 per cent), and swellings in the abdomen (22.5 per cent)'. Eugene Kinyanda, Seggane Musisi, Christine Biryabarema, Isaac Ezati, Henry Oboke, Ruth Ojiambo-Ochieng, Juliet Were-Oguttu, Jonathan Levin, Heiner Grosskurth and James Walugembe, 'War Related Sexual Violence and Its Medical and Psychological Consequences as Seen in Kitgum, Northern Uganda: A Cross-Sectional Study', *BMC International Health and Human Rights* 10 (2010): 1–8, at 4. The study's 'collective' approach to the effects of rape and sexual violence, however, homogenizes survivors and their experiences.
49 Trenholm et al., *supra* note 32, at 494.
50 Ibid.

care and appropriate drugs,[51] their health issues may be exacerbated if more existential needs remain unmet. Hence, any health interventions – and in particular mental health interventions – 'require that at a minimum livelihoods are restored and basic needs met'.[52] If this does not happen, women may be unable to perform their expected social roles,[53] making it more difficult for them to regain a crucial sense of purpose. This potentially makes them more vulnerable to social stigma, which can further impact upon their health. In their longitudinal study of formerly abducted girls in northern Uganda, for example, 65 per cent of whom claimed to have experienced sexual violence while in captivity, Amone-P'Olak et al. found that stigma and poor community relations increased the young women's susceptibility to mental health problems. These factors also complicated the women's access to mental and other health services.[54]

## The multi-layered effects of rape and sexual violence

Just as bullets can bounce or ricochet off an object,[55] the long-term effects of rape and sexual violence can be far-reaching and ricochet beyond those directly affected. As one illustration, Porter interviewed 187 women drawn from a random sample of two villages in northern Uganda. Seventy-six of these women had been raped, some by combatants from the Lord's Resistance Army (LRA) and some by civilians. The research revealed that these crimes had profoundly affected the community, particularly in cases where the women had been forced to marry LRA rebels. Quintessentially, 'the rape that happened as part of forced marriage was experienced as a crime against the individual, her family, and her clan, as well as the general mores of Acholi society'.[56] The crimes had also, in some cases, impacted on the women's children. One of the research participants, for example, explained that while she herself had intense dreams and nightmares, so too did her children (both those fathered by her 'bush' husband and by her current husband).[57] From a Western perspective, the children's nightmares might be interpreted through the lens of transgenerational transmission of trauma.[58]

51 Ibid., at 498.

52 Ibid., at 496.

53 The authors underline, for example, that 'The demands inherent in child-rearing and role-modeling, when one's own rudimentary needs are unfulfilled, is hardly sustainable'. Ibid., at 498.

54 Amone-P'Olak et al., *supra* note 4, at 6.

55 Robert C. Shaler, *Crime Scene Forensics: A Scientific Method Approach* (Boca Raton, FL: CRC Press, 2012), 527.

56 Holly E. Porter, 'Justice and Rape on the Periphery: The Supremacy of Social Harmony in the Space between Local Solutions and Formal Judicial Systems in Northern Uganda', *Journal of Eastern African Studies* 6 (2012): 81–97, at 86.

57 Ibid., at 87.

58 Ibid. According to Suarez, 'The intergenerational transmission of violent trauma is indeed an important yet under examined public health problem, and given the extensiveness of

Porter's research, however, offers a more emic explanation; both the woman and her husband attributed these bad dreams to the fact that they had not yet performed any rituals to deal with the 'cosmological consequences of sex in the bush'.[59]

As part of their ricochet effects, rape and sexual violence can also impact on survivors' husbands and have a vicarious traumatizing effect. Trenholm, Olsson and Ahlberg conducted a study in South Kivu in eastern Congo, in which they interviewed ten local leaders about the use of rape in war and what it does to individuals and communities. One of these leaders spoke about a man in the community who had witnessed his wife being raped. The man's sense of powerlessness at being unable to protect or defend her had not only traumatized him, but had completely altered his relationship with his wife. He no longer had any desire to make love to her, not because he had stopped loving her but because the sight of her naked body was a constant reminder of what the rapists had done to her.[60] Although this was only one case in the context of a very small study, the issue of how rape and sexual violence impact upon husbands merits further research, not least because it suggests the need for a more inclusive approach to dealing with rape trauma that encompasses both survivors and those within their immediate environments.

If existing scholarship has largely overlooked the effects of war rape and sexual violence on husbands, it has similarly neglected how these crimes affect male survivors. Christian et al.'s research in South Kivu is one of the rare studies. In 2010, the authors conducted 27 interviews and three focus groups with men who had faced war-related sexual violence between 2002 and 2007. Interestingly, the research participants often positioned their own experiences within a comparative framework, emphasizing that the long-term effects of rape for men and women differ. Most obviously, women may fall pregnant after being raped, which potentially exposes them to additional risks of social ostracism and stigmatization.[61]

The men's stories also exposed more complex linkages between gender and the impact of rape. For example, 'The majority of survivors reported shame and

populations affected by armed conflicts, it is important that intensified efforts be directed at understanding and reducing the effects that extreme violence can have on victims and their children'. Eliana Barrios Suarez, 'Two Decades Later: The Resilience and Post-Traumatic Responses of Indigenous Quechua Girls and Adolescents in the Aftermath of the Peruvian Armed Conflict', *Child Abuse and Neglect* 37 (2013): 200–210, at 208.

59 Porter explains that in Acholi culture, 'there are strong beliefs that sex "in the bush" is inappropriate and carries negative cosmological consequences. It violates norms that define the purposes of sex around the creation of and cementation of "a home"'. Porter, *supra* note 56, at 87.

60 Trenholm, Olsson and Ahlberg, *supra* note 24, at 144.

61 Mervyn Christian, Octave Safari, Paul Ramazani, Gilbert Burnham and Nancy Glass, 'Sexual and Gender Based Violence against Men in the Democratic Republic of Congo: Effects on Survivors, their Family and the Community', *Medicine, Conflict and Survival* 27 (2011): 227–246, at 234.

stigma for self and family, resulting in isolation. Shame and stigma was related to no longer being considered a man, the rape "transforming" him into a woman in the view of self, family and village'.[62] Believing that it was unacceptable for two women to live together as intimate partners, many of these men felt that they needed to leave their families and villages as a way of dealing with stigma and discrimination.[63] By doing so, however, they can create additional problems for their families, exposing their wives and children to stigmatization and leaving them economically vulnerable.[64] These are some of the further ripple effects of rape.

All of the qualitative studies that have been discussed in this chapter are extremely valuable and add vital texture and richness to quantitative studies. Many of them, however, were conducted only several years after the crimes in question took place. Hence, although they provide insights into some of the longer-term consequences of rape and sexual violence, studies of long-term effects over a more extended time period remain noticeably lacking. In this regard, BiH offers a crucial case study; 22 years have passed since the Bosnian war ended and many of the rapes were committed during the first year of the conflict (1992–1993). Despite the volume of scholarship on the use of rape and sexual violence during the Bosnian war, there is a pronounced dearth of research on the lasting effects of these crimes.

## Explaining rape and sexual violence in the Bosnian war

A significant proportion of existing scholarship on the rapes and sexual violence committed during the Bosnian war was written during the 1990s and, in many cases, during the conflict itself.[65] This early literature placed a strong emphasis on the importance of criminal prosecutions.[66] Additionally, it heavily focused on

62 Ibid., at 238.
63 Ibid., at 237–238.
64 Ibid.
65 See, for example, Cheryl Benard, 'Rape as Terror: The Case of Bosnia', *Terrorism and Political Violence* 6 (1994): 29–43; Dorean M. Koenig, 'Women and Rape in Ethnic Conflict and War', *Hastings Women's Law Journal* 5 (1994): 129–141; Elizabeth A. Kohn, 'Rape as a Weapon of War: Women's Human Rights during the Dissolution of Yugoslavia', *Golden Gate University Law Review* 24 (1994): 199–221; Hastings Law School Symposium, 'Rape as a Weapon of War in the Former Yugoslavia', *Hastings Women's Law Journal* 5 (1994): 69–88; Alexandra Stiglmayer (ed.), *Mass Rape: The War against Women in Bosnia-Herzegovina* (Lincoln, NE: University of Nebraska Press, 1994); Beverly Allen, *Rape Warfare: Hidden Genocide in Bosnia-Herzegovina and Croatia* (Minneapolis, MN: University of Minnesota Press, 1996); Maria B. Olujic, 'Embodiment of Terror: Gendered Violence in Peacetime and Wartime in Croatia and Bosnia-Herzegovina', *Medical Anthropology Quarterly: International Journal for the Analysis of Health* 12 (1998): 31–50; Todd A. Salzman, 'Rape Camps as Means of Ethnic Cleansing: Religious, Cultural, and Ethical Responses to Rape Victims in the Former Yugoslavia', *Human Rights Quarterly* 20 (1998): 348–378.
66 Denise Aydelott, 'Mass Rape during War: Prosecuting Bosnian Rapists under International Law', *Emory International Law Review* 7 (1993): 585–632; Kathleen M. Pratt and Laurel E. Fletcher, 'Time for Justice: The Case for International Prosecutions of Rape

the issue of classification. What was happening in BiH? Was the use of mass rape a form of genocide? Were the rapes purely ethnically motivated? Copelon was insistent that women were being raped not simply because of their ethnicity and religion, but also because of their gender.[67] The very characteristics that made them women, including their sexual and reproductive power, she argued, left them vulnerable in war and critically defined their enemy status.[68] For Copelon, therefore, it was this gender dimension of rape in conflict that needed to be foregrounded. This was essential 'not only to surfacing women as full subjects of sexual violence in war, but also to recognizing the atrocity of rape in the time called peace'.[69] Although she neglected the issue of male rape, Copelon's emphasis on 'surfacing gender', through an exploration of the intersections of gender and ethnicity, did at least allow for a more individualist and experiential approach to rape than one narrowly centred solely on ethnicity. The victims and survivors of rape are ultimately people and not simply ethnic groups or cultures.

Many scholars, however, did focus heavily on ethnicity, and indeed on the idea that Serb forces in BiH were committing ethnically driven genocidal rape. According to MacKinnon, for example, 'this is rape as ethnic expansion through forced reproduction... Croatian and Muslim women are being raped, and then denied abortions, to help make a Serbian state by making Serbian babies'.[70] Allen similarly embraced this genocidal rape thesis. Admitting that she had 'definitely taken sides',[71] she insisted that official Serb policy not only condoned but actively ordered the commission of atrocities, including genocidal rape, in order to further the creation of a Greater Serbia.[72] It is interesting how many scholars, often with little or no prior knowledge or experience of the former Yugoslavia, became overnight 'experts' on Serb military and political strategy.[73]

and Gender-Based Violence in the Former Yugoslavia', *Berkeley Women's Law Journal* 9 (1994): 77–102; Tamara L. Tompkins, 'Prosecuting Rape as a War Crime: Speaking the Unspeakable', *Notre Dame Law Review* 70 (1994): 845–890; Sharon A. Healey, 'Prosecuting Rape under the Statute of the War Crimes Tribunal for the Former Yugoslavia', *Brook Journal of International Law* 2 (1995): 327–383; Catherine N. Niarchos, 'Women, War and Rape: Challenges Facing the International Tribunal for the Former Yugoslavia', *Human Rights Quarterly* 17 (1995): 649–690; Kelly D. Askin, *War Crimes against Women: Prosecution in International War Crimes Tribunals* (The Hague: Kluwer Law International, 1997); Anne M. Hoefgen, ' "There will be no Justice unless Women are part of that Justice": Rape in Bosnia, the ICTY and "Gender Sensitive" Prosecution', *Wisconsin Women's Law Journal* 14 (1999): 155–179.

67 Rhonda Copelon, 'Surfacing Gender: Re-Engraving Crimes against Women in Humanitarian Law', *Hastings Women's Law Journal* 5 (1994): 243–266, at 260.

68 Ibid., at 262.

69 Ibid., at 264.

70 Catharine A. MacKinnon, 'Rape, Genocide and Women's Human Rights', *Harvard Women's Law Journal* 17 (1994): 5–16, at 13.

71 Allen, *supra* note 65, at 42.

72 Ibid., at 43.

73 Some commentators also made hugely sweeping claims. The journalist Stephen Schwartz, for example, postulated that 'The Serbian intention has been to rape whole cultures, to rape

This genocidal rape discourse strongly detracted from the suffering of individual survivors. Their unique stories became subsumed with a broader macro rape narrative centred on the destruction of a group – the essence of genocide[74] – rather than the destruction of individual lives. The emphasis placed on Serb military and political objectives similarly deflected from individual suffering. Illustrative of this is Hansen's claim that 'The large-scale raping of Bosnian women – commonly suggested to be as many as 20,000 – and the perceived inability of the Bosnian men to provide protection were part of Serbian attempts to constitute the entire Bosnian nation as humiliated, inferior, weak and feminine'.[75] In short, the effects of rape and sexual violence on individual survivors often appeared secondary to their purported national effects, with survivors themselves becoming mere statistics. Based on 7,000 testimonies, for example, the feminist human rights organization BISER claimed that 65,000 Bosniak women had been raped during the war.[76]

women and men, to rape social relationships going back five hundred years, to rape religion and art'. He made the further bizarre assertion that 'One of the under-reported parts of this tragedy is that the sexual terror has been directed against men as well as women. Serbian racism has always evoked hatred of the Balkan Muslims for their acceptance of gayness'. Hastings Law School Symposium, *supra* note 65, at 70. As anyone with sufficient knowledge of the former Yugoslavia will know, there are high levels of prejudice against the LGBTI (lesbian, gay, bisexual, transsexual, intersex) community, including in BiH. According to a 2014 progress report on BiH by the European Commission, 'Discrimination against LGBTI people remains widespread. Hate speech, hate crimes and violent attacks against LGBTI people and human rights defenders have increased along with the higher visibility of the LGBTI community... Awareness on LGBTI rights remains very low among the judiciary, law enforcement agencies and the general public'. European Commission, *Bosnia and Herzegovina Progress Report* (October 2014), 20, available at: https://ec.europa.eu/neighbourhood-enlargement/sites/near/files/pdf/key_documents/2014/20141008-bosnia-and-herzegovina-progress-report_en.pdf (accessed 9 October 2016).

74 According to the legal definition of genocide, as contained in the 1948 Convention on the Prevention and Punishment of the Crime of Genocide, 'genocide means any of the following acts committed with intent to destroy, in whole or in part, a national, ethnical, racial or religious group, as such:

(a) Killing members of the group;
(b) Causing serious bodily or mental harm to members of the group;
(c) Deliberately inflicting on the group conditions of life calculated to bring about its physical destruction in whole or in part;
(d) Imposing measures intended to prevent births within the group;
(e) Forcibly transferring children of the group to another group'.

Convention on the Prevention and Punishment of the Crime of Genocide (9 December 1948), Article II, available at: https://treaties.un.org/doc/publication/unts/volume%2078/volume-78-i-1021-english.pdf (accessed 8 May 2016).

75 Lene Hansen, 'Gender, Nation, Rape: Bosnia and the Construction of Security', *International Feminist Journal of Politics* 3 (2000): 55–75, at 56.

76 Diana Kapidzic and Aida Daidzic, 'BISER: A Conversation with Bosnian Women Living in Exile', *Hastings Women's Law Journal* 5 (1994): 55–68, at 60.

The overwhelming focus on Bosnian Muslim women meant that the effects of rape and sexual violence were typically situated and discussed within a specific cultural and religious framework. The significance of Muslim honour, in particular, was frequently underlined. Wing and Merchán, for example, insisted that the rape of a Muslim woman 'is a complete affront to her honor, and it is nearly impossible for Muslim culture to reconcile the rape with the concept of honor'.[77] One of the consequences of the mass rapes, thus, would be the 'ostracism of entire groups of Muslim women and/or their mixed children', whom society regarded as 'impure'.[78] In a similar vein, Bresnick maintained that 'Muslims view rape victims as particularly shameful... If the victim is raped in her home or village, she may refuse to return home'.[79] Such arguments simplistically homogenize 'Muslim' culture and treat it as determinative of particular outcomes. By extension, they foster a highly reductive approach to the effects of rape, thereby further detracting from the individuality of survivors. Perhaps most problematically, they suggest that there is something specific to Muslim culture that renders rape and sexual violence uniquely harmful and damaging to Bosniak women.

Some survivors have themselves fostered this idea. As one illustration, Bakira Hasečić, the head of the Sarajevo-based NGO *Žena Žrtva Rata* (ŽŽR), was extremely vocal in her opposition to Angelina Jolie's 2011 film, *In the Land of Blood and Honey*.[80] The film centres on a Bosnian Muslim woman who is taken to a camp where her pre-war Serb boyfriend is one of the commanders. While it is a love story, it is not a story about a survivor falling in love with her rapist as Hasečić claimed. Prior to the film's release in 2011, she wrote an open letter to Jolie, insisting that:

> All those who know the psychology of a victim who is a woman and upon whom a horrendous war crime of rape was committed know that it is not possible that a woman thus raped, unless she is a pathological case, fall in love

77 Wing and Merchán, *supra* note 18, at 24.

78 Ibid., at 25.

79 Rebecca O. Bresnick, 'Reproductive Ability as a Sixth Ground of Persecution under the Domestic and International Definitions of Refugee', *Syracuse Journal of International Law and Commerce* 21 (1995): 121–153, at 126. See also Adriana Kovalovska, 'Rape of Muslim Women in Wartime Bosnia', *ILSA Journal of International and Comparative Law* 3 (1997): 931–945, at 935; Janie L. Leatherman, *Sexual Violence and Armed Conflict* (Cambridge: Polity Press, 2011), 48.

80 Among survivors, reactions to the film were mixed. Even those who praised it found the film difficult to watch. Elissa Helms, *Innocence and Victimhood: Gender, Nation and Women's Activism in Postwar Bosnia-Herzegovina* (Madison, WI: University of Wisconsin Press, 2013), 217. For an analysis of the film's impact, see Zala Volčič and Karmen Erjavec, 'Transnational Celebrity Activism in Bosnia and Herzegovina: Local Responses to Angelina Jolie's Film *In the Land of Blood and Honey*', *European Journal of Cultural Studies* 18 (2015): 356–375.

> with her rapist. That is well known to those who know and understand the culture and tradition of Muslim women, Bosniak women.[81]

According to Helms, this reference to 'culture and tradition' conveys the idea that Bosnian Muslim women 'were more seriously injured by rape' and particularly suffered due to fear of their families and communities rejecting them.[82] During her extensive research in BiH, however, she found 'no indication that Bosniac women experienced rape any differently from women of other ethnic or religious backgrounds'.[83] Skjelsbaek's research, which will be discussed in more detail below, further supports this. In autumn 2001 and early spring 2002, she interviewed five women who were raped during the Bosnian war. Although all of them were Bosnian Muslims, this did not mean – contrary to the 'ostracism narrative' – that their husbands and families rejected them. Indeed, the stories of two of the women, Danira and Azra, particularly 'contradict prevalent assumptions about the status of raped women'.[84] In both cases, the women's husbands – far from rejecting them – strongly supported them.

During my own fieldwork in BiH, similarly, I found little evidence of ethnicity and culture distinctively shaping the effects of rape and sexual violence. Although many of the female interviewees spoke about marital problems – from indifferent to abusive husbands – this was a theme that transcended ethnic belonging. Only one interviewee had been abandoned by her husband; she was a Bosniak and he was a Bosnian Croat. Moreover, the four interviewees who spoke about the enormous support that they had received from their husbands were all Bosniaks; one of them was married to a Bosnian Croat and the other three were married to fellow Bosnian Muslims. A small number of female interviewees had experienced problems with neighbours, but again there was no discernible ethnic pattern. Indeed, gender appeared to be a more significant factor. As will be discussed in Chapter 7, often it was fellow women within the community who exhibited a lack of empathy. Regardless of their ethnicity, moreover, interviewees frequently described what had happened to them during the war as 'shameful'.

To summarize, notwithstanding the volume of existing scholarship on the use of rape and sexual violence during the Bosnian war, significant gaps remain as

81 Cited in Elissa Helms, 'Rejecting Angelina: Bosnian War Rape Survivors and the Ambiguities of Sex in War', *Slavic Review* 73 (2014): 612–634, at 624.

82 Ibid.

83 Helms, *supra* note 80, at 67. She underlines that 'This does not mean there was no stigma against raped women or the children born from the rapes… It also does not mean that women themselves, including women rape survivors, did not reproduce these Orientialized tropes'. Helms, *supra* note 80, at 67.

84 Inger Skjelsbaek, 'Victim and Survivor: Narrated Social Identities of Women who Experienced Rape during the War in Bosnia-Herzegovina', *Feminism and Psychology* 16 (2006): 373–403, at 386. The third interviewee had not told her husband that she was raped, the fourth was a widow and the fifth was not married.

regards the legacy of those crimes. As the final section of this chapter will now explore, there are a small number of empirical studies focused on the effects of the rapes and sexual violence committed during the Bosnian war. However, as these studies were mainly undertaken during the 1990s, they do not deal with long-term effects.

## Studying the effects of rape and sexual violence in BiH

Beginning in February 1993, Kozarić-Kovačić et al. worked with 25 Bosnian Muslim and Croat women who had been admitted to the Zagreb Obstetrics and Gynaecological Clinic or its associated regional centres. All of the women had been raped and had suffered multiple traumas, and 14 of them had become pregnant as a result of rape. The authors greatly enrich the data by presenting – in the form of short vignettes – the stories of three of the women. Like the 79 survivors who participated in this research, these women had suffered compound traumas. 'Mrs B', for example, was raped in front of her mother-in-law and 17-year-old daughter. Her daughter was then raped by two of the soldiers and subsequently killed a month later. 'Ms C' was detained in a camp and both she and her mother were raped. Her brother was killed in battle. She gave birth to a child born of rape and left the hospital without the baby. While the article is brief and does not address long-term effects, it is important for several reasons.

Firstly, it makes clear that in cases of composite traumas, 'it is difficult to disentangle the factors that contribute to the subsequent constellation of symptoms'.[85] In other words, when speaking about the 'effects' of rape and sexual violence, it is essential to keep in mind that these effects may form part of and reflect more complex webs of trauma. This is further discussed in Chapter 3.

Secondly, although the research offers a partly cultural explanation for the women's sense of shame in speaking about their trauma, it does not fixate on Muslim culture or suggest that Bosnian Muslim women experienced particularly high levels of shame. Rather, the authors make the broader argument that 'rape carries stigma, leading the victimized women to hide the occurrence from their physicians and families, much as did raped women in the Khmer conflict [in Cambodia]'.[86]

Thirdly, Kozarić-Kovačić et al.'s study provides important insights into the emotional states of those women who became pregnant after being raped, an

85 Dragica Kozarić-Kovačić, Vera Folnegović Šmalc, Jarmila Škrinjarić, Nathan Szajnberg and Ana Marušić, 'Rape, Torture and Traumatization of Bosnian and Croatian Women: Psychological Sequelae', *American Journal of Orthopsychiatry* 65 (1995): 428–433, at 431.

86 Ibid. Further highlighting this point, Van Boeschoten emphasizes that 'The silence of raped women is of course a general phenomenon'. Riki Van Boeschoten, 'The Trauma of War Rape: A Comparative View on the Bosnian Conflict and the Greek Civil War', *History and Anthropology* 14 (2003): 41–54, at 46.

issue around which there is little research. None of the women who carried their pregnancies to term wanted to keep their babies; 'They wished that they had a tumor instead of a baby, because a tumor could be removed easily'.[87] Once they had given birth, the women were keen to leave the hospital and none of them showed any interest in their child's future. According to the authors, this is a powerful illustration of the impact of violence on human reactions.[88]

Fourthly, the research cautions against premature psychological interventions aimed at reducing the effects of trauma. For the women in the study, dealing with their trauma was simply not a priority and all of them had rejected psychotherapy. Survival was their main focus and, for the time being at least, it took precedence over 'the discussion of traumatic experiences that psychotherapy would involve'.[89]

Similarly focusing on women from BiH and Croatia, Lončar et al. conducted a study of 68 rape survivors.[90] Although the research, undertaken between April 1992 and December 1995, was specifically looking at both the short-term and long-term effects of rape, in most cases the study participants had been raped – on average – just several months earlier. Methodologically, the authors combined a testimony method with the use of a multi-choice questionnaire and structured clinical interviews. They found that 'At the time of the study, i.e., approximately a year after the trauma, most victims suffered from depression and social phobia, whereas PTSD and sexual dysfunctions were present in fewer women'.[91] Many of the participants, moreover, had comorbid or co-occurring conditions.[92] Logistic regression analysis revealed that the women's age, nationality, marital status, education, and duration of captivity did not constitute predictive variables with regards to their psychological disorders.[93] The study did, however, find different distributions in the prevalence rates of psychological disorders. For example, 'Impaired relationship with a partner was more pronounced among women who were in a relationship but not married'.[94] The authors deduced from this that marriage itself offers some level of support and protection,[95] although my own research generally suggested the opposite to be true. They further found that

87 Kozarić-Kovačić et al., *supra* note 85, at 431–432.
88 Ibid., at 432.
89 Ibid. Lončar et al., however, argue that 'Providing counseling and psychiatric care immediately after the rape might be crucial in promoting recovery and preventing later problems'. Mladen Lončar, Vesna Medved, Nikolina Jovanović and Ljubomir Hotujac, 'Psychological Consequences of Rape on Women in 1991–1995 War in Croatia and Bosnia-Herzegovina', *Croatian Medical Journal* 47 (2006): 67–75, at 68.
90 The authors note that 'Initially, there were 100 raped women recruited for the study, but 32 emigrated from Croatia and Bosnia and Herzegovina during the course of the study, which reduced the size of the study sample'. Lončar et al., ibid., at 69.
91 Ibid., at 72.
92 Ibid.
93 Ibid.
94 Ibid.
95 Ibid., at 73.

more Bosnian Muslim than Croat women felt that their trauma had negatively impacted on their relationships with partners. It is unfortunate that the authors simply offer the 'more traditional culture' of Bosniak women as a possible explanation,[96] without elaborating on this and without discussing the women's views on their relationships.

To reiterate, while the study is important, it does not deal with the long-term effects of rape and sexual violence because of when it was conducted.[97] It is also interesting to note that like Kozarić-Kovačić et al., the authors underline the difficulties of establishing clear causal relations between rape per se and psychological consequences, due to the fact that rape in conflict situations rarely occurs as an isolated trauma.[98] They suggest, therefore, that 'Future studies are needed to establish to what extent the psychological consequences depend on a multi-dimensional nature of trauma in situations of war'.[99] It is not the purpose of this book to specifically investigate and elucidate that relationship. However, by qualitatively exploring the individual stories of survivors, it contextualizes the effects of rape and sexual violence within broader frameworks of trauma.

While male survivors are often overlooked, Lončar, Henigsberg and Hrabac conducted interviews in 1992 with 60 men who experienced sexual violence during the wars in BiH and Croatia, most frequently while detained in camps. Of these, 68.3 per cent had suffered severe beatings of the testes or genitals; 25 per cent had endured objects being forcefully inserted into their rectum; 21.6 per cent had been made to perform fellatio on other prisoners; and 3.3 per cent had been raped.[100] Focusing on the psychological consequences of rape and sexual violence, the authors found that:

96 Ibid.

97 Klarić et al. sought to explore the psychological consequences of war trauma over the longer term. Their study involved a cluster sample of 367 adult women. Divided into two groups, the 187 women in the first group were from the west side of Mostar (now an overwhelmingly Bosnian Croat area) and had experienced high levels of trauma during the Bosnian war. The second group consisted of 180 women from urban areas in western Herzegovina who had experienced the war indirectly. The authors found that 'women in Bosnia and Herzegovina who were directly exposed to long-term and extreme war trauma had serious posttraumatic and general psychological symptoms even 10 years after the war'. Miro Klarić, Branka Klarić, Aleksandra Stevanović, Jasna Grković and Suzana Jonovska, 'Psychological Consequences of War Trauma and Postwar Social Stressors in Bosnia and Herzegovina', *Croatian Medical Journal* 48 (2007): 167–176, at 173. While the study thus highlights the longevity of trauma and its effects, it is about war trauma in general. None of the research participants are referred to as rape survivors.

98 Lončar et al., *supra* note 89, at 75.

99 Ibid.

100 Mladen Lončar, Neven Henigsberg and Pero Hrabac, 'Mental Health Consequences in Men Exposed to Sexual Abuse during the War in Croatia and Bosnia', *Journal of Interpersonal Violence* 25 (2010): 191–203, at 196.

> In all, 46 patients had difficulties concentrating on any specific job, 57 suffered from nightmares and flashbacks, and 47 were experiencing feelings of hopelessness. As many as 40 of the interviewed persons admitted putting an active effort in[to] avoiding any situation that could remind them of the traumatic experience, and 47 patients complained of constant headaches. Close to half of the patients (29) exhibited symptoms of sexual dysfunction, ranging from erectile dysfunction (26 patients) and orgasmic dysfunction (13 patients) to coital pains (31 patients).[101]

While this is important data, the psychological consequences of rape and sexual violence that the men were experiencing are not explored in any depth (structured interviews were used) and are often discussed in a highly generalized way. One illustration is the claim, which is not elaborated on, that 'Most of them [the men] exhibited castration anxiety as well as homophobia and symptoms of identity crisis'.[102] Furthermore, the reflections on why rape and sexual violence are used in war[103] detract from the men themselves; and the use of the term 'homosexual rape'[104] is problematic as it suggests that it is gay men who rape and sexually abuse other men in war and conflict situations. This is erroneous, and by implying that there is a sexual motive involved in male-on-male rape it dilutes the complexities of causation.[105] At the end of the article, the authors explain that 'To our regret, after the present study was completed, no new study was authorized by the Croatian Ministry of Health'.[106] This is indeed regrettable. A newer study would have been extremely valuable, not only for analysing the long-term effects of rape and sexual violence on male survivors but also for enabling future gender-based comparative research.

More recently, in 2001–2002, Skjelsbaek interviewed five Bosniak women who were raped during the Bosnian war. Using narrative analysis, her two-fold aim was to explore how the women constructed their identities through the narratives that they told, and to examine how the trauma of being raped had influenced this identity construction process. Two of the women placed a strong emphasis on ethnicity and their identity as Bosnian Muslims. This is consistent with much of the existing scholarship on the Bosnian war, and in particular the aforementioned genocidal rape discourse and focus on Serb objectives. Contrary, however, to the commonly made claim that Bosnian Muslim women particularly suffered as a

101 Ibid.
102 Ibid., at 200.
103 Ibid., at 199–201.
104 Ibid., at 192.
105 Amrita Kapur and Kelli Muddel, *When No One Calls It Rape: Addressing Sexual Violence against Men and Boys in Transitional Contexts*, ICTJ (December 2016), 6–9, available at: www.ictj.org/sites/default/files/ICTJ_Report_SexualViolenceMen_2016.pdf (accessed 9 January 2017).
106 Lončar et al., *supra* note 100, at 201.

result of being raped, due to cultural reasons, Skjelsbaek's research reveals a more complex and less deterministic picture. '[W]hen the victim positions herself as an ethnic subject', she argues, 'this also creates a possibility for a new-found solidarity between men and women of the same ethnic belonging, a solidarity that supersedes traditional patriarchal relationships within the family'.[107]

Furthermore, while ethnically driven rape is so often associated with destruction, as seen in the previous section, Skjelsbaek shows that the two women who foregrounded ethnic dimensions of their stories partly viewed themselves as survivors. Because they were specifically targeted as Bosnian Muslims, their female identities as wives and mothers remained intact.[108] However, victim and survivor identities can closely overlap and coalesce, and both of these women also spoke of their continuing suffering. They therefore situated themselves 'as victims of war in their accounts'.[109] What is interesting is that the women's current circumstances and ongoing problems were strongly fuelling their perceptions of themselves as victims, which reinforces the argument that survivors' long-term needs must be addressed.

For the remaining three women in Skjelsbaek's study who accentuated the gender aspects of rape, the impact of their trauma similarly assumed a more gendered form. Focusing on their bodies, they narrated the rapes 'as having destroyed the core of their female identities: their sexual and procreative abilities'.[110] As they saw it, thus, their experiences had left an indelible imprint on their family relationships, in addition to affecting their relations with men in general. Their 'trauma triggers', which themselves were clearly gendered, included sexual contact, the sight of men in uniform and the birth of a son.[111] For these three women, therefore, rape was a more 'embodied experience'.[112] Their bodies were damaged and they viewed themselves as 'damaged goods'. One of the women, for example, feared that she would never marry because 'everybody knows'.[113]

While Skjelsbaek's study is small, it nevertheless offers a deep analysis of individual experiences. It also powerfully shows that even within a very limited sample, there can be considerable variations in rape impact. Furthermore, these variations derive, in part, from survivors' own agency. How they perceive themselves and how they make sense of their experiences can intimately shape the long-term impact of rape and sexual violence. Hence, Skjelsbaek's work highlights the critical need for more empirical – and specifically qualitative – research on the long-term effects of these crimes in BiH. Indeed, 'No systematic study on the *specific*

107 Inger Skjelsbaek, *The Political Psychology of War Rape: Studies from Bosnia and Herzegovina* (Abingdon: Routledge, 2012), 34.
108 Ibid., at 35.
109 Ibid.
110 Ibid., at 40.
111 Ibid., at 41.
112 Ann J. Cahill, *Rethinking Rape* (Ithaca: Cornell University Press, 2001).
113 Skjelsbaek, *supra* note 107, at 44.

consequences of war rape has been undertaken in Bosnia-Herzegovina' since the aforementioned studies by Kozarić-Kovačić et al. and Lončar et al.[114]

The Bosnian NGO *Medica Zenica* and its partner organization, *Medica Mondiale*, sought to address this by conducting the only major study – up until now – of the long-term effects of war rape in BiH. Published in 2014 and centred on 51 women who were raped early in the Bosnian war, the research examines four particular issues: the impact of rape on the women's lives, health and families; levels of social support; coping strategies and sources of resilience; and *Medica Zenica*'s impact on the women's lives. Methodologically rich, the research uses several different questionnaires, including one that was specially designed for the study and consisted of both closed and open-ended questions.[115] In addition, qualitative interviews were conducted with seven of the study participants.

The research provides valuable data on the multiple and long-term consequences of rape for the 51 women, including the consequences for their psychological health and relationships. For example, 57 per cent of the women were found to have symptoms of PTSD; and '76 per cent of the participants said that the rape affects their current relationship with their husband and/or men in general either completely or to some extent, most often in relation to sexual problems'.[116] The research also looks at how contextual factors, such as social attitudes and support, have affected the women and their coping abilities. Rape stigma clearly emerges as a theme.[117] However, whereas many of the African studies referred to in this chapter primarily discussed rape stigma as a community problem, the Bosnian study exposes an additional institutional dimension of rape stigma. Specifically, some of the research participants had experienced a lack of understanding and insensitivity from staff working in state institutions.[118] One of the study's conclusions, thus, is that 'Representatives of the relevant institutions, neighbours, and society in general stigmatise the survivors of war rape and sexual violence'.[119]

In relation to coping, the researchers found that the women used a variety of coping strategies to come to terms with what had happened to them during the Bosnian war, from seeking advice and help from others to engaging in prayer and proactively endeavouring to solve their problems.[120] Understanding from family and friends, and the knowledge that other women had also suffered rape and sexual violence during the war, emerged as key sources of resilience.[121] The

114 Medica Zenica and Medica Mondiale, *"We are still Alive", "We have been Harmed but We are Brave and Strong": Research on the Long-Term Consequences of War Rape and Coping Strategies of Survivors in Bosnia and Herzegovina* (Zenica, BiH: *Medica*, 2014), 26.
115 Ibid., at 56–58.
116 Ibid., at 91.
117 Ibid., at 105.
118 Ibid., at 106–107.
119 Ibid., at 110.
120 Ibid., at 115.
121 Ibid., at 124.

fact, however, that all of the 51 participants had received help and support from *Medica Zenica*, which does exceptional work with survivors, potentially creates a 'resilience bias' within the sample. Certain parts of BiH, and particularly more rural areas, are off the 'radar' of major NGOs. The reality, hence, is that many survivors do not have support, including from their own families, and must deal with their trauma alone. In post-conflict societies that have experienced large-scale rape and sexual violence, every effort should therefore be made to establish not just lasting support networks for survivors, but also – as much as possible – an even geographical spread of such networks.

*****

More of the findings from the *Medica Zenica* and *Medica Mondiale* study will be discussed in the forthcoming chapters. While this monograph builds on that research, it also seeks to address some of its weaknesses. In particular, *Medica Zenica* and *Medica Mondiale* focused only on women who were raped during the war; all except four of the 51 research participants were Bosnian Muslims; qualitative interviews were conducted with only seven of the women; and the study appears geographically limited. *Medica Zenica* is based in central BiH and because all of the study participants had used the NGO's services, it is reasonable to assume that they were mainly women from Central Bosnia Canton and Zenica-Doboj Canton (although this is not explicitly stated). What primarily distinguishes this book from the research by *Medica Zenica* and *Medica Mondiale*, however, is that it is not simply, or even primarily, a psychological study. Rather, it is an interdisciplinary work that innovatively explores the long-term effects of rape and sexual violence within a transitional justice framework. The next two chapters, which constitute the book's empirical building blocks, present and analyse the data from my own fieldwork in BiH.

Chapter 3

# Survivors of war rape and sexual violence in Bosnia-Herzegovina

## Long-term psychological effects and contributory contextual stressors

Although more than 20 years have passed since the Bosnian war ended, many survivors continue to struggle and to suffer. They still live with the consequences of what happened to them during the war and some of them have little or no help and support. According to Tomkins, 'Rape, like genocide, will not be deterred unless and until the stories are heard. People must hear the horrifying, think the unthinkable and speak the unspeakable'.[1] Whether and to what extent rape and sexual violence can be deterred is a separate issue that is not the focus of this research. It is crucial, however, that the stories of survivors – and not only their war stories but also the stories of their lives today – are heard and taken seriously. Both the present chapter and the following chapter are constructed from the stories of the 79 men and women who participated in this research. The aim is not to tell their stories for them, but rather to use the stories as a way to present and analyse some of the complex and multiple-stranded long-term consequences of rape and sexual violence committed during the Bosnian war.

This chapter begins by exploring some of the long-term psychological effects. Due to the amount of time that has passed since the Bosnian war ended, however, these psychological effects cannot be viewed in isolation. In other words, a more sophisticated and contextualized approach to causation is required. Significantly, a number of coterminous and intervening variables, or aggravating factors, emerged from the research data which themselves have potential causal relevance. In short, these additional factors, which are discussed in the chapter's final three sections, were almost certainly contributing – directly or indirectly – to some of the ongoing psychological issues that so many of the interviewees talked about. Firstly, the majority of them had endured multiple traumas during the war, including forced displacement and the loss of loved-ones. It is helpful, therefore, to situate the long-term psychological consequences of rape and sexual violence in BiH within this broader context of 'entangled traumas'. Secondly, all of the interviewees had at least one physical health issue, ranging from general

1 Tamara L. Tomkins, 'Prosecuting Rape as a War Crime: Speaking the Unspeakable', *Notre Dame Law Review* 70 (1995): 845–890, at 852.

aches and pains to more serious conditions such as diabetes and heart problems. In some cases, these health issues were potentially linked, at least indirectly, to war trauma. Furthermore, interviewees repeatedly articulated concerns about the cost of medicine in BiH, which for many was an additional source of stress and anxiety. Thirdly, and relatedly, the majority of interviewees were unemployed and struggling to make ends meet. Although economic-related worries are common in BiH,[2] the frequency with which interviewees expressed them is noteworthy. Fundamentally, it points to the fact that the long-term psychological effects of rape and sexual violence exist within a wider socio-economic milieu.

The previous chapter was critical of quantitative studies that present survivors simply as percentages. A key concern of this research is precisely to individualize survivors by examining the problems that they face today against the background of their own particular stories. To this end, it employs a narrative approach, with the empirical data primarily presented in the form of interwoven vignettes. As Sinclair Bell underlines, 'Narratives allow researchers to present experience holistically in all its complexity and richness'.[3] By extension, a narrative approach is especially suited for capturing and conveying the multiple and intersectional needs of survivors. One of the key limitations of such an approach, however, is that it cannot tell us anything about the relationship between an individual's experiences, problems, etc., and the data as a whole. In other words, it does not lend itself to more generalizable conclusions. To address this, some statistical analysis of the data is provided as a complement to the rich qualitative analysis. No interviewees are identified. They are referred to using a random letter from their names combined with their individual interviewee number. To further protect their identities, no specific place names (towns, villages) are used.

## Long-term psychological trauma

M72 lived in Herzegovina-Neretva Canton before the war. In 1993, Bosniaks from her village began sleeping in the forest at night and only came back to their homes during the day to get food and other essentials. This became a common practice during the Bosnian war. Forests offered protection and a chance to survive.[4] One day in May 1993, she returned to her family home. While she was

2 See, for example, Janine N. Clark, *International Trials and Reconciliation: Assessing the Impact of the International Criminal Tribunal for the former Yugoslavia* (Abingdon: Routledge, 2014), 111–112.

3 Jill Sinclair Bell, 'Narrative Inquiry: More than Just Telling Stories', *TESOL Quarterly* 36 (2002): 207–211, at 213.

4 When the Bosniak town of Srebrenica fell to Bosnian Serb forces on 11 July 1995, for example, large numbers of men fled through the forest in the hope of reaching ABiH-controlled territory. Some of them made it to safety. Balkan Transitional Justice, 'Escaping Death on the Flight from Srebrenica' (11 July 2013), available at: www.balkaninsight.com/en/article/escaping-death-on-the-flight-from-srebrenica (accessed 3 June 2016).

there, a group of six HVO soldiers entered the village. When they found her, they raped her. Afterwards, she re-joined her family in the forest. She was 17 years old. Her father asked her 'Are you alive?' She did not disclose to anyone that she had been raped. Today, she is married and has two children. When she told her husband what had happened to her in the war, he did not say anything and has never mentioned it since. She has not told her children and never will. She fears that they would be disappointed in her if they knew the truth. Unlike many survivors, M72 has a job. Several years ago, there was an explosion at her workplace and at that point something 'cracked' in her. The explosion acted as a trigger and re-awakened her war trauma and memories. Up until that point, she had kept everything suppressed inside her, but after the explosion she decided that she needed to speak to someone. She began seeing a psychologist and was diagnosed as having PTSD, anxiety and depression. She has regular flashbacks. Sometimes she finds her job too much – the noise bothers her – and she dislikes being in a confined space. She feels most at peace when she is working in her garden, but she has little time for herself. Her father was killed during the war. Whenever she thinks about him, she recalls his words 'Are you alive?' They remind her of what the HVO soldiers did to her. She has never told her mother that she was raped; there is no reason to. M72 sees herself as a person in two halves: the woman who was raped, and the wife and mother.[5]

L15 looked nervous and clutched the box of sedatives that she had purchased that morning. She also lived in Herzegovina-Neretva Canton prior to the war. In June 1992, five armed men from the Croatian Defence Forces (HOS)[6] came to her apartment. They questioned her and her family and took them to a nearby military building. L15 and her mother were locked in a room with two other Serb women. One of the HOS soldiers subsequently took her into a separate room. She remembers that he looked as though he had not shaved for four or five

5 Author interview, 25 April 2015. M72's way of seeing is consistent with the fact that individuals who have suffered trauma may 'live in two different worlds: the realm of trauma and the realm of their current ordinary life'. Bessel A. van der Kolk and Onno van der Hart, 'The Intrusive Past: The Flexibility of Memory and the Engraving of Trauma', in Cathy Caruth (ed.), *Trauma: Explorations in Memory* (Baltimore: John Hopkins University Press, 1995), 158–182, at 176. The realm of trauma, however, inevitably encroaches upon and intrudes into the realm of daily life.

6 The HOS, established in 1991, were the paramilitary wing of the ultra-nationalist Croatian Party of Rights. As Irvine notes, HOS troops 'quickly gained a reputation as ruthless and effective fighters'. Jill A. Irvine, 'Ultranationalist Ideology and State-Building in Croatia, 1990–1996', *Problems of Post-Communism* 44 (1997): 30–43, at 36. HOS units competed with the HVO for power and influence during the early part of the Bosnian war. On 7 August 1992, HVO forces assassinated Blaž Kraljević – the HOS commander in BiH – and eight of his staff members. This led to the dismantling of the HOS. On 23 August 1992, former HOS soldiers reached an agreement with the HVO and joined the latter's ranks. *Prosecutor v. Jadranko Prlić, Bruno Stojić, Slobodan Praljak, Milivoj Petković, Valentin Ćorić and Berislav Pušić*, IT-04-74-T, ICTY Trial Chamber Judgement, Vol. III (29 May 2013), §778.

days. She was made to perform oral sex on him, which made her retch. He then ordered her to strip and vaginally raped her. She wondered whether she was alive or dead. He took her back to the room where her mother and the other women were being held. Due to a sense of shame, she did not tell any of them what had happened to her. Later that night, another soldier entered the room. He was bald and wearing a black uniform.[7] He too raped her. She was 27 years old. The next morning, she and her mother were taken to the Dretelj camp in the municipality of Čapljina. Conditions were 'catastrophic' and there were no hygiene facilities.[8] HOS soldiers used to fire bullets to frighten the prisoners, and she never knew whether her loved-ones had been shot. After her parents were released as part of a prisoner exchange, L15 was taken to several other camps in Herzegovina – where she cooked and cleaned for HVO soldiers. She was exchanged as a prisoner of war in October 1992. Today, both of her parents are dead and she feels alone. She repeated several times that the two men who raped her destroyed both her life and the life of her family. She still sees the soldiers' faces; sometimes they fade but then they reappear. She does not know who they were or whether they have been prosecuted. Several years after the war ended, she began a relationship and became pregnant, but later suffered a miscarriage. Her partner left her because she could not give him children. Every day, she experiences the pain and consequences of what happened to her in 1992. Sometimes she does not know where she is, and she cannot function without sedatives and tablets to help her sleep. She has not received any counselling or therapy. Her pain is with her every day and it does not go away.[9]

7 Black was the official colour of the HOS. This was a way of paying homage to the *Ustaše*, a right-wing fascistic militia established in 1941.

8 In 2015, the State Court of BiH in Sarajevo convicted four former members of the HOS for crimes committed against Serbs in Dretelj. They received prison terms of between five and seven years. Balkan Transitional Justice, 'Bosnia Convicts Four of Dretelj Jail Camp Abuses' (14 April 2015), available at: www.balkaninsight.com/en/article/bosnia-sentences-four-for-dretelj-camp-crimes (accessed 9 June 2016). In 2013, a Trial Chamber of the ICTY sentenced six high-ranking Bosnian Croats – including the president of the HVO, Jadranko Prlić – to prison terms of between ten and 25 years for crimes against humanity, graves breaches of the Geneva Conventions and violations of the laws or customs or war committed, inter alia, against Bosnian Muslims in Dretelj. See *Prlić et al., supra* note 6 (the case is currently on appeal). These crimes took place in 1993, after the military alliance between the HVO and the ABiH broke down amid growing tensions between the two armies. According to Nizich, 'Bosnian Croats grew increasingly resentful of Muslims, claiming that the Muslims were avoiding battle, leaving the Croats to fight for them. At the same time, Muslims grew angry at the Bosnian Croats, claiming that the Bosnian Croats were disregarding the authority of the Sarajevo-based Bosnian government in areas where Croats were in the majority or where the HVO maintained a strong military presence'. Ivana Nizich, 'Violations of the Rules of War by Bosnian Croat and Muslim Forces in Bosnia-Herzegovina', *Hastings Women's Law Journal* 5 (1994) 25–52, at 27. The crimes against Serbs in Dretelj occurred in 1992 and have not been prosecuted at the ICTY.

9 Author interview, 8 October 2014.

N34, aged 56, looked thin and gaunt, and she said that her stomach was hurting. She was raped by two Serb soldiers in Brčko District in 1992. She was menstruating at the time and recalled how the soldiers had her blood on their penises. One of them has since died and the other was killed during the war. She said that she does not have the strength to live with what happened to her. She takes antidepressants and sleeping tablets, she is anxious and her stomach is always painful. She struggles to eat, she cannot stay in one room for any length of time and she no longer has a sex life with her husband. Having sex is too painful for her.[10] She rarely goes out and has no desire to. She used to sew, but now it hurts her eyes too much and she cannot afford to see an optician. She needs 50 Bosnian Marks (KM) each month (£21) just for medicine, and her husband's pension is only 300 KM per month (£131). He knows that she was raped, but he does not understand. She spoke out for the first time only in 2012. If she was not married, she probably would have done so much earlier. She and her husband had problems when they returned to their village after the war ended. On one occasion, somebody wrote 'Death to *Balijas*'[11] on their wall. She has vivid dreams that soldiers are shooting all around her and that she is unable to escape. She regularly goes to see a neuro-psychiatrist, but her appointments last less than 15 minutes. She is just given more pills to take. She knows that these tablets are not the solution, yet she cannot eat or function without them. She feels that nobody has any time for women like her and she has lost interest in everything.[12]

U36 was in several camps in north-west BiH between 1994 and 1995 and he weighed just 60 kilograms when he was released. He said little about what happened to him in these camps but took out a report from his psychologist; this stated that he was raped and has PTSD. It also noted that his daughter was killed during the war. U36 has a number of health issues, including diabetes, chronic asthma, a heart arrhythmia and high blood pressure. He cannot afford to buy all of the medicines that he needs and he has not had any health insurance for ten years. One of his inhalers alone costs 20 KM (£8) and he tries to make it last for two months instead of one. He used to feel like a 'gentleman', but a

10 *Medica Zenica* and *Medica Mondiale's* aforementioned study in BiH identified a high prevalence (44 per cent) of gynaecological conditions among the 51 research participants. These included vaginismus, which refers to the involuntary contraction and tightening of the vaginal muscles when sexual penetration is attempted. Medica Zenica and Medica Mondiale, *"We are still Alive", "We have been Harmed but We are Brave and Strong": Research on the Long-Term Consequences of War Rape and Coping Strategies of Survivors in Bosnia and Herzegovina* (Zenica, BiH: *Medica*, 2014), 78. During my own interviews, only three female survivors talked about sexual intercourse being too painful for them. It is perhaps the case that interviewees simply did not feel comfortable speaking about intimate gynaecological problems with someone whom they had just met. In contrast, *Medica Zenica* already had a long-standing relationship with the women who participated in its study with *Medica Mondiale.*

11 This is a derogatory and insulting word used to describe Bosnian Muslims.

12 Author interview, 20 November 2014.

gentleman is someone who has enough money to look after his family and to eat properly. U36 wears second-hand clothes and he and his wife largely subsist on the food that they grow themselves. He finds it difficult to sleep and images from the past regularly intrude into his life, particularly when he is alone. He testified against one of his perpetrators; this man received a seven-year sentence.[13]

What these vignettes powerfully convey is that every survivor is an individual with his or her own unique war story. It was especially frustrating, therefore, when some local NGOs insisted that 'their women'[14] did not want to speak and tell their stories, as if these women are a homogenous and undifferentiated group.[15] Notwithstanding the intrinsic individuality of survivors, a number of common themes did nevertheless emerge from the interview data. For example, interviewees frequently spoke about experiencing sleep problems, disliking enclosed spaces[16] and fearing large crowds.[17] Furthermore, while many of them acknowledged that they themselves were not to blame for what happened to them – their rapists were often armed and 'did what they wanted' – almost half of them maintained that they had experienced something that was deeply shameful.[18] By extension, some of them expressed feeling alone, unsure of whom they could confide in. As Hind asserts, 'Rape silences the victim because it creates the potential for censure from others beyond the perpetrator – the shame of exposure acts as a powerful social sanction against self-expression'.[19]

13 Author interview, 29 November 2014.

14 While there are numerous women's NGOs in BiH, there are no equivalent men's NGOs. In May 2015, I visited the NGO *Budućnost*, located in Modriča in northern BiH, which established a Men's Centre in 2010. This Men's Centre, however, does not aid male survivors of wartime sexual violence. Rather, it mainly works with men who have committed/are committing domestic violence, a significant problem in post-war BiH. See, for example, Lisa R. Muftić and Jennifer R. Cruze, 'The Laws Have Changed but What About the Police? Policing Domestic Violence in Bosnia-Herzegovina', *Violence against Women* 20 (2014): 695–715.

15 See Janine N. Clark, 'Working with Survivors of War Rape and Sexual Violence: Fieldwork Reflections from Bosnia-Hercegovina', *Qualitative Research* (published online 17 October 2016), available at: http://journals.sagepub.com/doi/abs/10.1177/1468794116671987

16 This can be partly attributed to the fact that more than half of them were raped in camps or other places of detention, as shown in Table 0.1 in the introduction.

17 Based on their research with 146 rape survivors in the US in the 1970s, Burgess and Holmstrom found that 'Many victims were quite apprehensive when they had to be in crowds or ride on public transport'. Ann W. Burgess and Lynda L. Holmstrom, 'Rape Trauma Syndrome', *American Journal of Psychiatry* 131 (1974): 981–986, at 984. Crowds may be experienced as intimidating and threatening.

18 In this regard, the interview data appears to problematize Phasha's claim that 'an individual who does not blame himself or herself for the occurrence of the abuse or fate is capable of recovering quickly because he or she can claim back his or her personal power to function better than those who are overwhelmed with self-blaming attitudes'. Tlakale Nareadi Phasha, 'Educational Resilience among African Survivors of Child Sexual Abuse in South Africa', *Journal of Black Studies* 40 (2010): 1234–1253, at 1247.

19 Heather Hind, 'Women and Shame', *Women: A Cultural Review* 26 (2015) 178–181, at 179.

Almost 18 per cent of interviewees explicitly stated that they were not the same person that they were before the war and that their trauma had irrevocably changed them; they laughed less now, were easily irritated and had mood swings. Somewhat consistent with Mertus' claim that 'The most devastating psychological trauma of rape is that it takes away a person's sense that life has meaning',[20] a small number of interviewees no longer saw any meaning or purpose in life and 10 per cent admitted that they had struggled with suicidal thoughts. Approximately a quarter of the interviewees had been diagnosed as having PTSD,[21] and a similar proportion of them were experiencing flashbacks and intrusive memories from the past – the 'hallmark PTSD symptom'.[22] Some interviewees, moreover, still looked visibly traumatized. One spoke in a flat and monotonous way and appeared wooden; five of them appeared to be talking though gritted teeth (this was especially pronounced among male interviewees); and some of them had a noticeably far-away look in their eyes, characteristic of dissociation. According to Josse, 'People are considered to suffer from "dissociation" when they are disconnected from part of reality. They give the impression of "not being there" or of "being elsewhere" '.[23] Linked to this, several of the female survivors explained that when they were raped, it was as if they were watching a film about someone else.[24] Dissociation is also linked to PTSD.

In total, 62 per cent of interviewees had received some form of psychotherapy/counselling (often from NGOs) and/or had access to a psychologist/neuropsychiatrist. Nevertheless, a very high percentage of them (73.4 per cent) were using anti-depressants, sleeping tablets and other benzodiazepines. They insisted that they needed these tablets in order to get through each day. In the 2014 study conducted by *Medica Zenica* and *Medica Mondiale*, similarly, 65.3 per cent of respondents said that they were taking medicines on a regular basis. Of these,

20 Julie Merus, 'Shouting from the Bottom of the Well: The Impact of International Trials for Wartime Rape on Women's Agency', *International Feminist Journal of Politics* 6 (2004): 110–128, at 119.

21 Paulson and Krippner note that 'The "stress" of PTSD describes the residual strain on the mind/body system caused by the initial catastrophic "stressor". Unlike psychic or physical wounds that are resolved, eased, or healed but may be stored as vivid memories, traumas responsible for PTSD remain a source of distress'. Daryl S. Pauldon and Stanley Krippner, *Haunted by Combat: Understanding PTSD in War Veterans* (Lanham, MD: Rowman & Littlefield, 2010), 3.

22 Corin Bourne, Clare E. McKay and Emily A. Holmes, 'The Neural Basis of Flashback Formation: The Impact of Viewing Trauma', *Psychological Medicine* 43 (2013): 1521–1532, at 1521.

23 Evelyne Josse, '"They Came with Two Guns": The Consequences of Sexual Violence for the Mental Health of Women in Armed Conflicts', *International Review of the Red Cross* 92 (2010): 177–195, at 190.

24 As Mason and Lodrick explain, 'dissociation (a sense of being cut off from the actual situation) can result from extreme fear'. Fiona Mason and Zoe Lodrick, 'Psychological Consequences of Sexual Assault', *Best Practice and Research: Clinical Obstetrics and Gynaecology* 27 (2013): 27–37, at 29.

90.0 per cent disclosed that they were using psycho-pharmacological drugs.[25] 'Recovery' from rape and sexual violence is not an end state but rather a 'life-long healing process'.[26] In BiH, sophomoric drugs and sedatives have seemingly become crucial parts of this healing process, due to their easy accessibility and the frequency with which they are prescribed in lieu of long-term psycho-social care.

Although a number of common patterns thus emerged from the interview data, it is arguably too simplistic merely to posit a clear-cut causal relationship between rape and sexual violence, on one hand, and long-term psychological effects on the other. The remaining sections of the chapter therefore seek to complexify this relationship through an analysis of possible 'aggravating' factors. These factors, in turn, provide an important contextual framework. The first factor in this framework relates to the interconnections between rape trauma and other types of trauma. In short, many of the interviewees told stories in which these different traumas were deeply entangled.

## Entangled traumas

At the end of May 1992, D64 was taken from her home in eastern BiH and imprisoned in a building in a nearby town. After a prisoner exchange took place, she was left in the building with eight other women and girls. Serb soldiers raped all of them, and D64 was sexually violated multiple times. She was 15 years old. After almost a month, she and the other prisoners were taken to a collective centre. She spent one and a half months there, and during this time she met a fellow Bosnian Muslim whom she subsequently married. Separated from her parents, she viewed this man as representing safety. After leaving the collective centre, the two of them briefly went to Hungary and he soon became violent towards her. In his eyes, it was her fault that she was raped, and he became intensely jealous whenever she spoke to other men. She distinctly remembers the first time that he hit her. She had gone to buy bread and he wanted to know why she had started a conversation with the male shop assistant. The two of them returned to BiH (the Federation) in 1993. The domestic abuse continued; he accused her of being a whore and of sleeping with male neighbours. She gave birth to her first child and struggled to put food on the table. Her neighbours called her a 'refugee' and told her to go back to where she had come from. She will never go back there.[27] Now divorced, D64 is considering leaving BiH, but she does not want to do so until she has received 'justice'. None of her rapists have been prosecuted and two of them have public profiles on Facebook.

25 Medica Zenica and Medica Mondiale, *supra* note 10, at 77.

26 Colleen Galambos, 'Community Healing Rituals for Survivors of Rape', *Smith College Studies in Social Work* 71 (2001): 441–457, at 445.

27 Author interview, 30 March 2015.

A76 was three years old when her father murdered her mother. She and her siblings witnessed it. When the war began, she was living in the north of BiH. She was taken to a building opposite the local school. She was with her baby son, her sister and two other women. The five of them were subsequently taken to a private house and imprisoned for three months. HVO soldiers came to the house every night and raped the women. She remembers the first time that she was raped. There were four soldiers and all of them had nicknames. 'You had to give them what they wanted', she stressed. 'You had no choice'. She begged them to kill her, but they refused. If she was dead, they would not be able to have any fun with her. She told them that she was a Bosnian Croat, in the hope that this would save her, but it made no difference. They were angry that she had married a '*četnik*' (Serb). She weighed just 42 kilograms when she was released from the house. Her husband and her son both drink heavily and have PTSD. Her son has been violent towards her. One of A76's brothers was killed in an accident after the war. Now in her early 40s, she stroked her granddaughter's pink teddy bear as she told her story.[28]

J70 lived in south-west BiH before the war. In April 1992, a group of HVO soldiers – his neighbours – came for him and took him to a town close to the Bosnian-Croatian border. From there, he was taken to the Lora camp near Split in Croatia. 'There is nothing that they didn't do to us', he recalled. One day, the commander of the camp, Tomislav Duić, ordered J70 and his fellow prisoners to leave the room where they were being held. J70 saw three soldiers wearing JNA uniforms. The men were Montenegrins and they were covered in blood. Duić told J70 and his fellow prisoners that soon they too would look like the JNA soldiers. On another occasion, Duić introduced J70 to a blonde woman and left him alone with her. She took out her breasts and asked him if he liked them. She suddenly began to scream and Duić and his friend came to her 'rescue'. They severely beat J70, including on his testicles.[29] The woman was Duić's wife.[30] Physical and sexual violence were regular occurrences in Lora, particularly

28 Author interview, 24 June 2015. Interviewees who were raped at a young age often seemed childlike in certain ways. They stressed that their war experiences had destroyed their childhood/youth, and it was as if some of them wanted to claw back those lost years. An interviewee in Brčko District, for example, was raped when she was 19. Not long after we had first met, she suddenly hugged me, called me '*pahuljica*' (snowflake) and sat down on the floor next to me with her legs crossed.

29 One explanation for the persistent neglect of male survivors – both in BiH and more generally – is that sexual violence against men is not always recognized for what it actually is. Regarding blunt trauma to the male genitals, for example, Carlson points out that: 'being hit in the testicles during peacetime activities is generally considered a "normal occurrence" … [M]en's testicles are hit in soccer, American football and in many other contact sports, where the players are expected to "take it like a man"'. Eric S. Carlson, 'The Hidden Prevalence of Male Sexual Assault during War: Observations on Blunt Trauma to the Male Genitals', *British Journal of Criminology* 46 (2006): 16–25, at 20.

30 Women participated in some of the crimes committed in Lora. According to Dobrivoje Bojović, who has spoken publicly about his time in the camp, 'the worst was when they

when the HVO soldiers were drunk. One of their favourite games was 'Tuta'. The prisoners had to wear military boots and then jump and kick each other in the back. If they failed to kick hard enough, Duić and his colleagues would show the prisoners how it 'should be done'. J70 regularly had to clean blood from the walls, and he stressed that he will never forget Duić's face.[31] However, there were two HVO soldiers in Lora who did not hurt him, and he would like to be able to see them again in order to thank them. From Lora, he was taken to the military investigation prison in Ljubuški in BiH where he suffered further abuses,[32] and he was finally part of a prisoner exchange in August 1992. Due to the injuries that he sustained in Lora, J70 has a disability and problems with his back. He has not been able to return to his pre-war home; he said that he would not feel safe there. He is retired and drinks to numb his pain.[33]

The stories of D64, A76 and J70 are powerful illustrations of multi-stranded trauma. They also underscore the critical point that any discussion of the long-term psychological effects of rape and sexual violence should take account of related and interwoven traumas. In situations of war and armed conflict, trauma rarely occurs as a singular event. As Cloitre et al. emphasize, 'The importance

[HVO soldiers] brought [in] some females in the evening and gave them sticks. They were beating us all night. Not only were they beating us, but you had to tell them "Thank you lady, and come again"'. Marija Taušan and Erna Mačkić, 'Crime across the Border' (28 October 2014), available at: www.justice-report.com/en/articles/crime-across-the-border (accessed 11 May 2016).

31 In 2006, in the so-called 'Lora 1' case, the District Court in Split in Croatia convicted Tomislav Duić – who was tried in absentia – of war crimes committed in Lora and sentenced him to eight years' imprisonment (this was upheld on appeal one year later). Duić was on the run for 11 years but was finally arrested (bizarrely in Split) in February 2016. He is currently on trial in the 'Lora 2' case, together with four co-defendants. Sven Milekić, 'Croatian War Criminal Caught after 11 Years' (19 February 2016), available at: www.balkaninsight.com/en/article/croatian-war-criminal-caught-after-11-years-02-19-2016 (accessed 3 March 2016). Thirty-seven prisoners of war were tortured in the Lora camp, three of whom died from their injuries. Documenta, 'Crime in Lora 2' (Tomislav Duić et al.) (n.d.), available at: www.documenta.hr/en/crime-in-lora-2-tomislav-dui%C4%87-et-all.html (accessed 9 May 2016). Interestingly, the Republic of Croatia recently erected a monument in front of the former Lora camp, in honour of 12 HVO soldiers who were killed during the war in Croatia. Sven Milekić, 'Croatia Unveils Military Monument at Prison Camp Site' (13 December 2016), available at: www.balkaninsight.com/en/article/croatia-s-battalion-gets-monument-on-prison-camp-site-12-13-2016 (accessed 27 February 2017).

32 Seven former HVO soldiers are currently on trial at the State Court of BiH for crimes committed in the military investigation prison. Three of them – Ivan Kraljević, Mate Jelčić and Slakvo Skender – are former wardens of the prison. Denis Džidić, 'Bosnian Croats' Trial for Ljubuški Prison Abuse Opens' (27 October 2015), available at: www.balkaninsight.com/en/article/trial-for-ljubuski-crimes-opens-10-27-2015/1458/5 (accessed 25 May 2016). The trial began in October 2015 and the defendants are charged with crimes against humanity and the criminal offence of war crimes against prisoners of war. See www.sudbih.gov.ba/predmet/3463/show

33 Author interview, 23 April 2015.

of evaluating the effects of multiple traumas in their cumulative form is critical as this circumstance characterizes the experience of the majority of trauma survivors'.[34] The phenomenon of entangled trauma, moreover, operates across different levels, and interviewees' own multiple traumas were frequently further entangled with the trauma that their own loved-ones had gone through during the war.

B10 is from eastern BiH. Early in the war, she and her youngest son were taken to the local *Dom kulture* (House of Culture). They spent 24 hours there. During the night, a Serb soldier called her outside. He grabbed her breasts and she pushed him away. He then raped her at knifepoint. Would he have left her alone, she still asks herself, if she had not cried. She was menstruating at the time and the soldier vaginally and anally raped her. She said that he 'enjoyed himself'. He was in his twenties and he told her that she should be happy that other soldiers had not joined them. Her husband was killed early in the war and her eldest son and daughter fled to Srebrenica, thinking that they would be safe there.[35] When Srebrenica fell to the VRS in July 1995, B10's daughter was one of the thousands of women who were put on buses and taken to ABiH-controlled territory. B10's son did not survive the slaughter. The last thing he had said to her was that he would see her soon. When the war ended, B10 had an opportunity to move abroad, but she did not want to leave BiH. She was waiting for her son to return home. She has only been able to bury five of his bones[36] and she sobbed every time that she spoke about him. She partly blames herself for his death; she should have protected him and her daughter from harm.[37]

In 1993, R38 was imprisoned in three separate camps. Beatings and sexual violence were daily occurrences and she was raped. During this period, she did not know whether her children were safe or where they were, and she cried every day. When she was released from the third camp, she found out that her children had been taken to an abandoned house and held there for a month and a half. Soldiers came and went as they pleased, and her two eldest daughters were raped. R38 struggles with intense feelings of guilt and believes that she failed her

34 Marylene Cloitre, Bradley C. Stolbach, Judith L. Herman, Bessel van der Kolk, Robert Pynoos, Jing Wang and Eva Petkova, 'A Developmental Approach to Complex PTSD: Childhood and Adult Cumulative Trauma as Predictors of Symptom Complexity', *Journal of Traumatic Stress* 22 (2009): 399–408, at 400.

35 On 16 April 1993, the UN Security Council adopted Resolution 819 which demanded that 'all parties and others concerned treat Srebrenica and its surroundings as a safe area which should be free from any armed act or any other hostile act'. UN Security Council Resolution 819, S/RES/819 (16 April 1993). Many Bosniaks therefore flocked to Srebrenica, believing that the town would offer them safety and security.

36 Locating and exhuming mass graves, and identifying victims' remains, are tasks that present enormous challenges. See Erin D. Williams and John D. Crews, 'From Dust to Dust: Ethical and Practical Issues Involved in the Location, Exhumation and Identification of Bodies from Mass Graves', *Croatian Medical Journal* 44 (2003): 251–258, at 255.

37 Author interview, 27 August 2014.

children. She carries their trauma together with her own trauma. Her brothers could have saved her and her children, but they joined Fikret Abdić's *Autonomaši* (discussed in Chapter 1) and turned their backs on the family. She no longer has any relationship with her siblings.[38]

Interviewees' entangled traumas, however, were not always related exclusively to the war. Highlighting temporal dimensions of entanglement, some interviewees had also suffered more recent traumas involving their loved-ones. One of the most difficult interviews was with Š24, a survivor from eastern BiH. When the war began, she was 28 years old and was taken to the Sušica camp in Vlasenica. She spent a week there[39] and described one particular night in the camp. A group of soldiers pointed at her, and one of them grabbed her hands and took her to a place behind the camp.[40] He punched her in the face, tore off her clothes and raped her. He warned her that if she ever told anyone, he would kill her. She was too afraid even to tell her mother and sister, who were also in the camp. For a long time afterwards, she feared men, but several years later she began a relationship and became pregnant. The relationship ended when she discovered that the father of her unborn child was married. After giving birth, Š24 largely raised her son alone, but when he was 13 years old he developed a brain tumour. He died less than a year later. Through her tears, Š24 stressed how much his death continues to hurt her and how much she misses him.[41]

P17, a Serb, was raped during the war by both HVO and ABiH soldiers. Several years after the war ended, her daughter was killed in a road traffic accident. She seemed convinced that someone had deliberately killed her, although there was no evidence of this. Her daughter, who was in her early twenties when she died, had wanted her mother to talk to her about the war and to speak about what she had gone through, but P17 always refused to do so. She was determined to protect her daughter from the truth.[42] She needed to protect her. Today, it hurts her

38 Author interview, 30 November 2014.

39 According to the ICTY's Sentencing Judgement against Dragan Nikolić, the former commander of the Sušica camp, 'Men, women and children were detained in Sušica camp, some being detained as entire families. Women and children were usually only detained for short periods of time and then forcibly transferred to nearby Muslim areas. Before being forcibly transferred, non-Serbs usually had to sign a document stating that they were leaving the area voluntarily and giving up their property'. *Prosecutor v. Dragan Nikolić*, IT-94-2-S, ICTY Sentencing Judgement (18 December 2003), §59. After initially pleading not guilty, Nikolić subsequently pleaded guilty to crimes against humanity. He was sentenced to 23 years' imprisonment in 2003 (reduced to 20 years on appeal in 2005), and in August 2013 he was granted early release.

40 The ICTY has noted that in Sušica, 'Many of the detained women were subjected to sexual assaults, including rape. Camp guards or other men who were allowed to enter the camp frequently took women out of the hangar at night. When the women returned, they were often in a traumatised state and distraught'. Ibid., at §61.

41 Author interview, 29 October 2014.

42 As will be discussed in the next chapter, interviewees frequently insisted that they would never tell their children what they had endured during the war. Some worried that their children would view them differently or be disappointed in them. Almost all of the male

deeply that she never had that conversation with her daughter and never shared her story with her.[43]

E30 spent three years in a camp in north-west BiH and suffered multiple rapes and abuses. During this time she was separated from her mother, who did not know whether her teenage daughter was dead or alive. Throughout the war years, E30's mother used to paint at night when she could not sleep.[44] Her paintings were visual representations of her innermost fears – a picture of a naked young woman on all fours; the same naked woman with her legs drawn up to her chest and her face pressed against her knees (see figure 3.1); four faces without any distinguishing features, their eyes devoid of any detail and their mouths wide open in fear.[45] Reunited after the war ended, E30 was still coming to terms with the fact that her mother – her biggest support – had recently died from illness.[46]

In addition to the complex traumas that they had suffered during the war and, in some cases, post war, almost all of the interviewees were also facing a variety of everyday challenges and difficulties. Indeed, some of them barely spoke about their war trauma and focused on their current problems. Several of them described their lives as a constant fight or struggle, and few of them had time to deal with and work through their own trauma. It was simply not a priority. Bread and butter issues were more important. This highlights a critical broader point. As a leading psychologist-psychotherapist in Zagreb underlined, 'You need to holistically repair and improve all the pieces of a woman's life. It is not enough to focus only on her psychological state'.[47] In other words, if crucial pieces remain damaged or broken, this will almost certainly have a psychological impact. For many of the

interviewees, however, said that their children knew what had happened to them in the war. One explanation may be that these men were living in small communities where it was difficult to have 'secrets' (and indeed two of them had spoken publicly). Yet, it was also striking that they did not express the same fears and concerns about their children that many female interviewees expressed.

43 Author interview, 13 October 2014.

44 Art therapy 'enables the processing of traumatic experiences by accessing and integrating traumatic memories, by communicating and documenting images of traumatic memories and through rituals'. Karin Alice Schouten, Gerrit J. de Niet, Jeroen W. Knipscheer, Rolf J. Kleber and Giel J.M. Hutschemaekers, 'The Effectiveness of Art Therapy in the Treatment of Traumatized Adults: A Systematic Review on Art Therapy and Trauma', *Trauma, Violence and Abuse* 16 (2015): 220–228, at 221. Through her trauma, one interviewee had discovered that she is an extremely gifted painter. She eloquently described the sense of liberation that she feels each time that she allows her paintbrush to freely glide across a canvas. Author interview, 16 April 2015.

45 During my first meeting with E30, I spent two days with her and her family. Shortly before I was due to leave, she began showing me her mother's paintings. She did do entirely spontaneously and revealed afterwards that it felt 'right' at that particular point to share them with me.

46 Author interview, 12 November 2014.

47 Author interview, 29 August 2015.

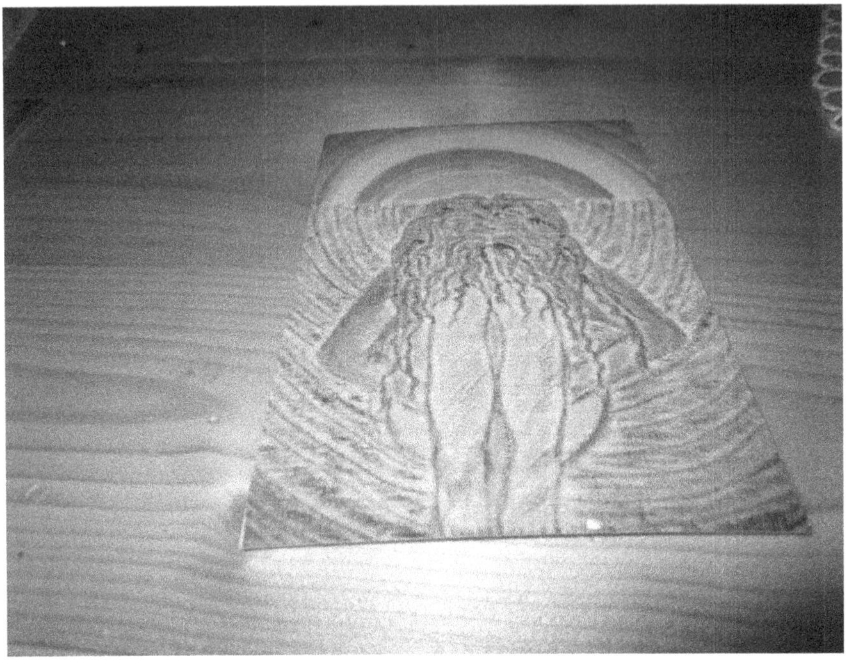

*Figure 3.1* A mother's fears

survivors who participated in this research, one of the defective pieces of their lives was their physical health.

## Physical health issues

The long-term physical health effects of war rape and sexual violence, direct and indirect, remain under-investigated. Significant research exists on the health effects of intimate partner violence,[48] and this form of violence has been linked to multiple chronic health effects. These include '[h]eadaches, back pain, fainting, seizures or related central nervous system complaints, chronic pain, irritable bowel syndrome, pelvic inflammatory disease, persistent skin disorders, and

48 See, for example, Ann L. Coker, Paige H. Smith, Lesa Bethea, Melissa R. King and Robert E. McKeown, 'Physical Health Consequences of Physical and Psychological Intimate Partner Violence', *Archives of Family Medicine* 9 (2000): 451–457; Jacquelyn Campbell, Alison S. Jones, Jacqueline Dienemann, Joan Kub, Janet Schollenberger and Patricia O'Campo, 'Intimate Partner Violence and Physical Health Consequences', *Archives of Internal Medicine* 162 (2002): 1157–1163; Therese Zink, C. Jeffrey Jacobson, Saundra Regan and Stephanie Pabst, 'Hidden Victims: The Healthcare Needs and Experiences of Older Women in Abusive Relationships', *Journal of Women's Health* 13 (2004): 898–908.

adverse pregnancy outcomes'.[49] In the context of war rape and sexual violence, scholarship has predominantly focused on the psychological legacies of these crimes.[50] When the purview is broadened to include physical sequelae, the emphasis is most commonly placed on traumatic fistula[51] and gynaecological issues.[52] Liebling-Kalifani et al.'s research with female survivors of rape and sexual violence in northern Uganda illustrates this point. Among the health complications that the authors discuss are 'painful intercourse, unwanted pregnancies, prolapses, genital sores, swelling in the abdomen, chronic pelvic pain, fistula causing leaking of urine and faeces, and vaginal tears'.[53]

Researching the physical and psycho-social consequences of rape in the eastern DRC, Bartels et al. reviewed 1,021 patient medical records at the Panzi Hospital in Bukavu. These records revealed a broader range of physical consequences following rape and sexual violence, including 'pelvic pain (22 per cent of women), lumbar pain (11 per cent), abdominal pain (7 per cent)'.[54] These consequences, however, are simply stated rather than explored. The identification of these consequences, moreover, necessarily raises a number of important causation questions that are similarly left unaddressed. Was lumbar pain, for example, a direct result of rape? Was pelvic pain linked to a contracted STI? Critically, claims that rape and sexual violence

49 Susan C. Modesitt, Alisa C. Gambrell, Hope M. Cottrill, Lon R. Hayes, Robert Walker, Brent J. Shelton, Carol E. Jordan and James E. Ferguson, 'Adverse Impact of History of Violence for Women with Breast, Cervical, Endometrial or Ovarian Cancer', *Obstetrics and Gynaecology* 107 (2006): 1330–1336, at 1330.

50 Sadler et al. underline that 'Clinical research has focused on the psychologic effects of sexual victimization with limited recognition of the health-related consequences'. Anne G. Sadler, Brenda M. Booth, Deanna Nielson and Bradley N. Doebbeling, 'Health-Related Consequences of Physical and Sexual Violence: Women in the Military', *Obstetrics and Gynaecology* 96 (2000): 473–480, at 473.

51 Research on traumatic fistula overwhelmingly focuses on the DRC. See, for example, Haleigh Hanlon, 'Implications for Health Care Practice and Improved Policies for Victims of Sexual Violence in the Democratic Republic of Congo', *Journal of International Women's Studies* 10 (2008): 64–72; Ahuka O. Longombe, Kasereka M. Claude and Joseph Ruminjo, 'Fistula and Traumatic Genital Injury from Sexual Violence in a Conflict Setting in Eastern Congo: Case Studies', *Reproductive Health Matters* 16 (2008): 132–141; Mathias Onsrud, Solbjørg Sjøveian, Roger Luhiriri and Denis Mukwege, 'Sexual Violence-Related Fistulas in the Democratic Republic of Congo', *International Journal of Gynaecology and Obstetrics* 103 (2008): 265–269.

52 See, for example, Ruxana Jina and Leena S. Thomas, 'Health Consequences of Sexual Violence against Women', *Clinical Obstetrics and Gynaecology* 27 (2013): 15–26, at 18.

53 Helen Liebling-Kalifani, Ruth Ojiiambo-Ochieng, Angela Marshall, Juliet Were-Oguttu, Seggane Musisi and Eugene Kinyanda, 'Violence against Women in Northern Uganda: The Neglected Health Consequences of War', *Journal of International Women's Studies* 9 (2008): 174–192, at 180.

54 Susan Bartels, Jennifer Scott, Jennifer Leaning, Denis Mukwege, Robert Lipton and Michael VanRooyen, 'Surviving Sexual Violence in Eastern Democratic Republic of Congo', *Journal of International Women's Studies* 11 (2010): 37–49, at 38.

'can have serious physical, social, and psychological consequences'[55] are often left insufficiently undeveloped, and this is especially true vis-à-vis arguments about physical consequences.

According to *Medica Zenica* and *Medica Mondiale*'s research with 51 survivors in BiH, 57.1 per cent of them described their health as bad;[56] 85.4 per cent said that they visit the doctor on a regular basis;[57] 51.5 per cent were using cardiovascular medications;[58] and 10.6 per cent had been diagnosed with cancer in the last ten years.[59] Consistent with these findings, almost all of the survivors whom I interviewed were suffering from at least one health issue (and often multiple health issues). These ranged from general aches and pains to chronic conditions including diabetes, high blood pressure, heart problems and cancer; and one interviewee had suffered a stroke eight years earlier when she was in her 40s. Some of these health issues may be indirectly linked to rape and sexual violence. Although it is impossible to indubitably establish this, a number of possible correlations might be made based on existing medical research and knowledge. One such potential correlation relates to cancer.[60]

A year earlier, an interviewee in her 40s had undergone an operation to have a brain tumour removed. Her face was partially paralysed as a result of the operation and she had lost all her hair. She spoke out for the first time about being raped only in 2013. For 20 years, she remained silent about what had happened to her, to protect her family and children. Eventually, however, she reached the point where she needed to tell her story. Shortly after she spoke about her trauma for the first time, she discovered that she had a brain tumour. A second interviewee, in her 60s, had also been diagnosed with (and overcome) a brain tumour several years earlier, which she partly attributed to the beatings that she sustained during her detention in a camp. An interviewee in her early 70s had early stage ovarian cancer, and a younger interviewee in her 50s had previously had one of her ovaries removed due to a tumour. Another interviewee had needed to have

55 Kirsten Johnson, Jennifer Scott, Bigy Rughita, Michael Kisielewski, Jane Asher, Ricardo Ong and Lynn Lawry, 'Associations of Sexual Violence and Human Rights Violations with Physical and Mental Health in Territories of the Eastern Democratic Republic of Congo', *Journal of the American Medical Association* 304 (2010): 553–562, at 561.

56 Medica Zenica and Medica Mondiale, *supra* note 10, at 76.

57 Ibid., at 77.

58 Ibid.

59 Ibid., at 78. The authors further note that '7 rape survivors who we tried to contact to participate in [the] research had died from cancer'. Ibid., at 78.

60 It is important, however, to look at the broader picture. According to the World Bank Group, for example, 'The disease burden in BiH has shifted to a majority of chronic and noncommunicable conditions. Cardiovascular diseases, for example, are the leading cause of death, and cancer is the second most frequent cause'. World Bank Group, 'World Bank Group – Bosnia and Herzegovina Partnership: Country Program Snapshot' (October 2015), available at: http://pubdocs.worldbank.org/pubdocs/publicdoc/2015/10/779381443795253068/BiH-Snapshot.pdf (accessed 9 July 2017).

her uterus and ovaries removed three years earlier – at the age of 45 – due to a large uterine tumour; and an interviewee in her late 30s was awaiting a hysterectomy because of tumours on her uterus. None of the male interviewees, in contrast, had suffered from cancer.

Every cancer is unique and there are no single causes. Age, lifestyle, genetics, hormones and diet are just some of the myriad contributing factors. Research has indicated, however, that stress may also play a part. Cohen, Janicki-Deverts and Miller, for example, note that 'Experimental research in animals has found that stress contributes to the initiation, growth, and metastasis of select tumors'.[61] They further point out that although the evidence linking stress and cancer in humans is far more mixed, stress effects are likely to be most pronounced in certain types of cancers, 'especially those facilitated by impairments in antiviral immunity and sustained activation of hormonal response', including cervical cancer.[62] Similarly relevant, Modesitt et al.'s research points to possible links between violence and cancer. Between 2004 and 2005, they interviewed 101 women with breast, cervical, endometrial (uterine) or ovarian cancer. It emerged that half of these women were victims of childhood or adult violence, and that they were often at a more advanced stage of cancer when diagnosed with the disease.[63] Although the reasons for this were unclear, the authors suggest that 'Possible explanations... could include decreased access to health care providers, decreased adherence to recommended cancer screening, or potentially, increased stress and compromised immune function'.[64]

Shifting to a war context, Ghobarah, Huth and Russett have explored the long-term public health effects of civil wars using World Health Organization (WHO) data on disability-adjusted life years. While they found that civil wars appear to increase rates of cervical cancer, they offer no real causal explanation for this. One of their arguments is simply that civil wars lead to a breakdown in social norms, including norms against forced sexual relations.[65] This is not, however, especially telling. More significant in this regard is the fact that the human papilloma virus (HPV), which has been strongly linked to cervical cancer,[66] is sexually

61 Sheldon Cohen, Denise Janicki-Deverts and Gregory E. Miller, 'Psychological Stress and Disease', *Journal of the American Medical Association* 298 (2007): 1685–1687, at 1686.

62 Ibid., at 1687.

63 Modesitt et al., *supra* note 49, at 1333.

64 Ibid., at 1334.

65 Hazem A. Ghobarah, Paul Huth and Bruce Russett, 'Civil Wars Kill and Main People – Long after the Shooting Stops', *American Political Science Review* 97 (2003): 189–202, at 199.

66 According to Bosch et al., 'By the year 2000, the epidemiological evidence included a large and consistent body of studies indicating, beyond any reasonable doubt, strong and specific associations relating HPV infections to cervical cancer. The observations have been reported from all countries where investigations have taken place'. F. Xavier Bosch, Attila Lorincz, Nubia Muñoz, Chris J.L.M. Meijer and Keerti V. Shah, 'The Causal Relation between Human Papillomavirus and Cervical Cancer', *Journal of Clinical Pathology* 55 (2002): 244–265, at 244.

transmitted.[67] Potentially, thus, rape in war – and not just civil wars – exposes women to a greater risk of contracting HPV, and thus of developing cervical cancer. None of the survivors who took part in this research had specifically suffered from cervical cancer, which begins in the neck of the uterus as opposed to in the uterus itself. However, the relationship between rape, trauma and cancer, and in particular gynaecological cancers, merits further investigation and research.

If six interviewees (7.6 per cent) had battled with cancer, 12 interviewees (15.2 per cent) disclosed that they had heart arrhythmias (abnormal heart rhythm). Three of these were male interviewees. Here again, a possible link with rape and sexual violence might be made. Many of the interviewees had multiple stressors in their lives that were inter-connected with these traumas (and with broader entangled traumas), including family problems (discussed in Chapter 4) and difficulties obtaining their rights as civilian victims of war (discussed in Chapter 6). In short, they were dealing with cumulative stress, and 'Episodes of acute emotional stress can have significant adverse effects on the heart', including 'disturbances of cardiac rhythm'.[68] It is also important to note that linkages have been made between heart irregularities and PTSD. According to Lee and Theus, for example, 'Women are almost 3 times more likely to develop PTSD and have greater reactivity to stress at the sinus and atrioventricular node than men'.[69] It is precisely the sinus and atrioventricular nodes, in turn, that are crucial for regulating heartbeat.[70] Of the 12 interviewees who revealed that they had a heart arrhythmia, nine of them had also been diagnosed with PTSD.

Some research has additionally pointed to a correlation between PTSD and diabetes.[71] Trief et al., for example, note that 'From a biomedical perspective, chronic

67 Cancer Research UK, 'HPV and Cancer' (2 September 2016), available at: www.cancerresearchuk.org/about-cancer/cancers-in-general/cancer-questions/what-is-the-hpv-virus (accessed 9 October 2016).

68 Roy C. Ziegelstein, 'Acute Emotional Stress and Cardiac Arrhythmias', *Journal of the American Medical Association* 298 (2007): 324–329 at 329.

69 Elizabeth A.D. Lee and Sue A. Theus, 'Lower Heart Rate Variability Associated with Military Sexual Trauma Rape and Posttraumatic Stress Disorder', *Biological Research for Nursing* 41 (2012): 412–418, at 412.

70 According to the University Hospital Southampton in the UK, 'The sinus node is responsible for setting the rate and rhythm of the heart and is therefore referred to as the heart's pacemaker'; and the atrioventricular node 'acts as a gateway, slowing and regulating the impulses travelling between the atria [upper chambers of the heart] and the ventricles [lower chambers]'. University Hospital Southampton, 'Patient Information Factsheet: Atrioventricular (AV) Node Ablation' (April 2015), available at: www.uhs.nhs.uk/Media/Controlleddocuments/Patientinformation/Heartandlungs/Atrioventricularnodeablation-patientinformation.pdf (accessed 30 June 2016).

71 These studies include Renee D. Goodwin and Jonathan D. Davidson, 'Self-Reported Diabetes and Posttraumatic Stress Disorder among Adults in the Community', *Preventive Medicine* 40 (2005): 570–574; Charles Agyemang, Simone Goosen, Kenneth Anujuo and Gbenga Ogedegbe, 'Relationship between Posttraumatic Stress Disorder and Diabetes among Asylum Seekers in the Netherlands', *European Journal of Public Health* 22 (2012): 658–662; Karoline Lukaschek, Jens Baumert, Johannes Kruse, Rebecca Thwing Emeny,

stress has been linked to endocrinological abnormalities' – including changes in thyroid function and hormonal changes – 'which may also relate to diabetes and insulin resistance'.[72] Miller-Archie et al. conducted a study of 36,899 people who were affected by the terrorist attacks on the World Trade Centre (WTC) on 11 September 2001. They observed 'a significant association between 9/11-related PTSD at Registry enrollment and new-onset diabetes reported at follow-up'.[73] Specifically, of the total number of study participants, 2,143 (or 5.8 per cent) had been diagnosed with diabetes between 2003/2004, when they registered at the WTC Health Registry, and March 2012.[74] According to the authors, 'Established diabetes risk factors, including non-white race/ethnicity, older age, lower educational attainment, and overweight/obesity, were highly associated with diabetes in this study, as were hypertension and high cholesterol'.[75] These established risk factors were present in my own research; interviewees with diabetes (16.5 per cent) tended to be over 55 and, in some cases, slightly overweight. Significantly, however, all of them stressed that they were fit and healthy before the war. Their diabetes had only developed post trauma, and in four out of 13 cases within the first five years of the war ending.

In considering the relationship between trauma and health, it is important to take account of country-specific factors. For example, BiH 'has one of the highest rates of smoking prevalence in the world'; and the 'screening and clinical management of chronic diseases remains inadequate'.[76] Nevertheless, the fact that 91.2 per cent of interviewees had one or more health issues seems more than simply coincidental. According to Zinzow et al., 'rape victims are at particular risk for comorbid diagnoses'.[77] It is also noteworthy that 21.6 per cent of interviewees

Maria Elena Lacruz, Cornelia Huff, Barbara Thorand, Rolf Holle, Wolfgang Rathmann, Christa Meisinger and Karl-Heinz Ladwig, 'Relationship between Posttraumatic Stress Disorder and Type 2 Diabetes in a Population-Based Cross-Sectional Study with 2970 Participants', *Journal of Psychosomatic Research* 74 (2013): 340–345.

72 Paula M. Trief, Paige Ouimette, Michael Wade, Paul Shanahan and Ruth S. Weinstock, 'Post-Traumatic Stress Disorder and Diabetes: Co-Morbidity and Outcomes in a Male Veterans Sample', *Journal of Behavioral Medicine* 29 (2006): 411–418, at 412.

73 Sara A. Miller-Archie, Hannah T. Jordan, Ryan R. Ruff, Shadi Chamany, James E. Cone, Robert M. Brackbill, Joanna, Felix Ortega and Steven D. Stellman, 'Posttraumatic Stress Disorder and New-Onset Diabetes among Adult Survivors of the World Trade Center Disaster', *Preventive Medicine* 66 (2014): 34–38, at 37.

74 Ibid., at 35.

75 Ibid., at 37.

76 World Bank, 'Project Information Document (PID) Concept Stage' (November 2015), available at: www-wds.worldbank.org/external/default/WDSContentServer/WDSP/ECA/2015/11/19/090224b0831ed6cf/1_0/Rendered/PDF/Project0Inform0or0Project000P149920.pdf (accessed 18 May 2016).

77 Heidi M. Zinzow, Heidi S. Resnick, Jenna L. McCauley, Ananda B. Amstadter, Kenneth J. Ruggiero and Dean G. Kilpatrick, 'Prevalence and Risk of Psychiatric Disorders as a Function of Variant Rape Histories: Results from a National Survey of Women', *Social Psychiatry and Psychiatric Epidemiology* 47 (2012): 893–902, at 901.

primarily complained of common bodily pains – in particular headaches, back pain and joint pain. This further offers potential insights into how rape and sexual violence – individually or as part of combined traumas – indirectly impact on the body's functioning over the long term. It is has been long established that chronic stress can have adverse health effects.[78] However, it can also induce and be a significant source of pain. Particularly when caused by traumatic events, it 'may lead to imbalance in the body's adaptive stress response and dysregulation of both cortisol levels and proinflammatory cytokines[79] that may lead to an increase in the autoimmune/inflammatory response and, subsequently, chronic pain'.[80]

In addition to these linkages between trauma and ill-health, interviewees' health issues were themselves a frequent cause of stress. In BiH, only medication that is on the so-called 'essential list' is free of charge. All other medicines are to be paid for (or paid for in part); and BiH is the only country in the Balkans that does not have any law limiting the prices that pharmaceutical companies can charge.[81] The cost of medication in BiH was a recurring theme during my fieldwork and 83.6 per cent of interviewees explicitly raised it as an issue. For many of them, finding the money to pay for the medication that they needed was a daily source of worry and a serious financial burden. An interviewee in north-east BiH, for example, became very upset when speaking about her health problems. She opened a cupboard in her lounge and pulled out a carrier bag full of small boxes and blister packs, many of which were empty. She explained that apart from her insulin, she must pay for all of her medication. Effectively, therefore, she had to choose which of her tablets she needed the most.[82] An interviewee in central BiH complained that she has constant pain in her kidneys, which she believed was linked to the regular beatings that she suffered for many months during the war while held in a camp. Insisting that she could not afford to see a doctor, she was attempting to treat the problem herself by drinking herbal teas, using herbs from her own garden. She would only go to the doctor, she maintained, if one

78 Dhabhar, for example, notes that 'chronic stress induced acceleration of immune cell aging can have significant deleterious effects on immune function because it is likely to result in suppression of immunoprotection and exacerbation of immune dysregulation and immunopathology [how the immune system deals with disease]'. Firdaus S. Dhabar, 'Effects of Stress on Immune Function: The Good, the Bad and the Beautiful', *Immunologic Research* 58 (2014): 193–210, at 200.

79 Cytokines are small proteins produced in the immune system which impact on other cells.

80 Judith Wuest, Marilyn Merritt-Gray, Marilyn Ford-Gilboe, Barbara Lent, Colleen Varcoe and Jacquelyn C. Campbell, 'Chronic Pain in Women Survivors of Intimate Partner Violence', *Journal of Pain* 9 (2004): 1049–1057, at 1054.

81 Rodolfo Toe, 'Bosnia Urged to Limit Price of Medicines' (31 May 2016), available at: www.balkaninsight.com/en/article/bosnia-urged-to-adopt-drug-price-regulation-05-30-2016 (accessed 9 July 2016).

82 Author interview, 5 November 2014.

of her children became ill.[83] These examples, in turn, draw attention to another factor that is potentially aggravating or fuelling the long-term psychological consequences of rape and sexual violence in BiH, namely economic hardship.

## Existential insecurities and the struggle to make ends meet

C77 has a small room in an old building. Five other internally displaced women also live there. There is a sink in one corner of her room and a refrigerator in another corner, but it does not work. She stores her food in a carrier bag which she attaches to the door handle. She does not have a cooker, and has to rely on a one-ring hob that wobbles unsteadily whenever she places something on it. Her diet consists mainly of cheap, starchy foods such as bread, pasta and potatoes. Her only means of warming the room is a small fan heater, and she has to use this sparingly in order not to run up a large electricity bill. Until recently, she slept on the floor, but a couple of months earlier a local NGO had bought her a sofa which doubles as a bed. Because she lives in RS, she cannot claim civilian victim of war status[84] and she has no option of moving to the Federation. After the war ended, she worked for 16 years, but her bosses constantly harassed her and made her life a misery. After she fell one day at work and broke her hand, they used this as an excuse to sack her. She has no pension and no income. She does occasional cleaning work to earn money, and one of her neighbours sometimes gives her 10 KM (£4) from her own pension when she can spare it. C77 revealed that her nephew would shortly be getting married, but she could not afford the cost of a bus ticket to Serbia to attend the wedding. She started to cry.[85] Of all the interviewees, her situation seemed particularly desperate (see figure 3.2).

E30 lives in a ramshackle house with her husband and three children. Every time it rains, the roof leaks. She worries about how the dampness is affecting her children's health. Rental options in the town are limited and the family cannot afford to pay much. Neither E30 nor her husband has a job, and the family relies on the money that she receives as a civilian victim of war. This should be 586 KM (£262) a month. However, because the canton in which she lives is several

83 Author interview, 12 November 2014. This interviewee did not have health insurance, and several others were similarly without it. A male interviewee living in RS, for example, explained that in order for him to qualify for medical insurance, he would need to register with the local employment bureau, and he could only do so by first applying for a personal identity (ID) card from the local municipality. His ID card, however, had been issued by a municipality in the Federation. If he were now to register in RS, he would lose his right to civilian victim of war status, which he had obtained by registering in the Federation. Author interview, 23 August 2014.

84 While this will be explained further in Chapter 6, the crucial point is that survivors in RS only had until 31 December 2007 to seek civilian victim of war status. In the Federation, in contrast, there are no such deadlines and survivors can apply at any time.

85 Author interview, 26 June 2015.

*Figure 3.2* An interviewee's tiny one-room living accommodation

months in arrears,[86] she usually only receives 440 KM (£194) a month – and this often arrives late. Money is always tight. The family's food budget for the month is around 160 KM (£71) and they grow what they can. E30 stressed that she would love to have a five-year period in her life where she could live normally, be happy and take her children to the sea. Describing her life as one of 'constant suffering', she revealed that she often feels demoralized and exhausted.[87]

S43 is an ex-combatant and she fought in the ABiH during the Bosnian war. Because of this, she has been unable to claim civilian victim of war status,[88] despite her efforts to do so. She remained silent about what had happened to her

86 The BiH Federation is divided into ten cantons. The social payments that civilian victims of war receive each month partly come from the State and partly from the particular canton in which the individual survivor lives. Some cantons have considerably more money than others. See, for example, Elvira M. Jukić, 'Bosnia Cantons say Sarajevo gets too much Cash' (10 March 2015), available at: www.balkaninsight.com/en/article/bosnia-cantons-demand-new-distribution-of-tax-revenues (accessed 9 June 2016).

87 Author interview, 12 November 2014.

88 Similarly, one of the male interviewees was unable to apply for civilian victim of war status because he had been a combatant and not a civilian when he suffered sexual violence. He had a disability pension of 140 KM (£61) a month.

for 18 years, due to fear and shame. When she finally told her husband that she had been raped, she hoped that he would understand. She just wanted him to hold her. Instead, he became abusive towards her and the marriage ended. S43 was left homeless. The municipality (essentially a local council) provided her with temporary accommodation – a small apartment – and she has been living there ever since. She does not know when she will be asked to vacate the property and constantly worries that she could become homeless again. It was December and the apartment felt cold. She was struggling to pay the bills and had previously gone to see the local mayor to ask for help. He told her that she could not build her life on the municipality. She questions why she fought in the war. She still has to fight.[89]

The concept of human security 'broadens the scope of security analysis and policy from territorial security to the security of people',[90] and it necessarily has an economic dimension. Interviewees repeatedly stressed that in order to rebuild their lives and move forward, they needed to be able to 'live normally'. Yet, as long as their circumstances required them to worry about putting food on the table, paying their bills, keeping warm in the winter, 'normality' was impossible. The crimes that they had experienced during the war often made them feel physically powerless and vulnerable. These sentiments had now taken on a new economic form.

All interviewees – even the 21.5 per cent who were in their 60s and 70s – underlined the critical importance of employment. Only eight of them (10.1 per cent) currently had a job,[91] and a handful of them did casual (mainly cleaning) work. Some of the younger interviewees – and specifically those who were raped in their teens – had never had a job. With no qualifications or work experience, they maintained that the war had put an end to both their education and their dreams. One interviewee had planned to become a doctor. Another had wanted to work with children. Although this was still possible, this young woman seemed completely demotivated and spent most of the day sleeping, unable to do so at night. Seventy per cent of interviewees emphasized that they wanted to work. When they were busy, they had less time to think about the past. In BiH, however,

89 Author interview, 2 December 2014.

90 Oscar A. Gómez and Des Gasper, *Human Security: A Thematic Guidance Note for Regional and National Human Development Report Teams* (2013), 2, available at: http://hdr.undp.org/sites/default/files/human_security_guidance_note_r-nhdrs.pdf (accessed 19 July 2016). The concept of people-centred human security was first introduced in the 1994 Human Development Report. This Report concomitantly emphasized the need for sustainable human development which, inter alia, 'empowers people rather than marginalizing them'. United Nations Development Programme, *Human Development Report 1994* (New York: Oxford University Press, 1994), iii, available at: http://hdr.undp.org/sites/default/files/reports/255/hdr_1994_en_complete_nostats.pdf (accessed 8 August 2016).

91 These eight interviewees had a range of different jobs, from company director and doctor to accounts clerk and warehouse assistant.

the job market remains stagnant,[92] and the European Parliament recently stressed that the country needs to 'address the persistently high long-term unemployment rate (27.6 per cent), including very high youth unemployment (62.7 per cent)'.[93]

Prior to the 1990s, BiH had numerous factories which provided thousands of people with jobs. Today, however, many of these hulking edifices have become rusty and derelict shells, poignant reminders of a bygone socialist era – and powerful symbols of failed privatization in BiH (see figure 3.3).[94] To cite Judah, 'Privatisations were often corrupt, with well-connected people buying companies to strip them of their assets to make a quick profit – before declaring them bankrupt'.[95] The 'Bosnian Spring' in 2014 – when mass protests swept through major cities such as Sarajevo, Tuzla and Zenica – was a delayed response to years of economic mismanagement and hardship.[96] The protests ultimately lost momentum, however, and people returned to their homes. Nothing changed, and the unrest further confirmed that any foreign investment in BiH necessarily carries risks.[97]

During my fieldwork in BiH, I worked closely with *Snaga Žene*. In November 2014, the NGO took approximately 45 Bosniak women from Srebrenica and

92 See, for example, International Monetary Fund, 'Bosnia and Herzegovina: Concluding Statement of the 2015 Article IV Mission' (12 May 2015), available at: www.imf.org/external/np/ms/2015/051215.htm (accessed 7 July 2016).

93 European Parliament, *Motion for a Resolution to Wind Up the Debate on the Statements by the Council and the Commission Pursuant to Rule 123(2) of the Rules of Procedure on the 2015 Report on Bosnia and Herzegovina (2015/2897(RSP))* (5 April 2016), available at: www.europarl.europa.eu/sides/getDoc.do?pubRef=-//EP//NONSGML+MOTION+B8-2016-0441+0+DOC+PDF+V0//EN (accessed 15 June 2016). According to the European Commission, youth unemployment among enlargement states is highest in Kosovo (61.1 per cent) and in BiH (62.7 per cent). European Commission, 'Enlargement Countries – Labour Market Statistics' (September 2015), available at: http://ec.europa.eu/eurostat/statistics-explained/index.php/Enlargement_countries_-_labour_market_statistics#Unemployment_rates (accessed 15 June 2016)). The lack of job opportunities for young people in BiH was a significant cause of concern among interviewees who had children.

94 Timothy Donnais, 'The Politics of Privatization in Post-Dayton Bosnia', *Southeast European Politics* 3 (2002): 3–19.

95 Tim Judah, 'Bosnian Protests: A Balkan Spring?' (7 February 2014), available at: www.bbc.co.uk/news/world-europe-26093160 (accessed 9 June 2016).

96 Denis Džidić, 'Bosnia-Herzegovina Hit by Wave of Violent Protests' (7 February 2014), available at: www.theguardian.com/world/2014/feb/07/bosnia-herzegovina-wave-violent-protests (accessed 9 June 2016).

97 The UK Foreign and Commonwealth Office has observed that, 'Although investors are guaranteed free transfer of capital as well as repatriation of profit, foreign direct investment remains modest and is hindered by excessive layers of bureaucracy and corruption. According to Central Bank data, most investments between 1994 and 2014 came from Austria, Serbia and Croatia'. Foreign and Commonwealth Office, 'Overseas Business Risk – Bosnia-Herzegovina' (18 May 2016), available at: www.gov.uk/government/publications/overseas-business-risk-bosnia-and-herzegovina/overseas-business-risk-bosnia-and-herzegovina (accessed 19 July 2016).

*Figure 3.3* A former factory in central BiH

Potočari – those who had lost loved-ones in the genocide in July 1995 – to Mostar to meet a group of Bosnian Croat women who had also suffered during the Bosnian war. In October 2015, another trip was organized to enable women from Srebrenica and Potočari to meet women in Croatia who had lost husbands and sons in the siege of Vukovar in 1991.[98] As there was only one coach on both occasions, places were necessarily limited, and the women from eastern BiH who did not secure a seat were deeply disappointed. These trips offered a rare opportunity to do something different, to see something new – and all of them wanted to go. Similarly, interviewees frequently stressed how much they would like to go to the sea, to visit a spa or to go on an excursion, in order to 're-charge their batteries' and break the routine of their daily lives. However, they needed their money for food, medicines and other essentials. There was nothing left for extras. Few of them felt optimistic about the future, and their grinding economic worries were an integral part of their daily lives. They had little time to focus on themselves.

*****

98 See Janine N. Clark, 'The ICTY and Reconciliation in Vukovar', *Journal of International Criminal Justice* 10 (2012): 397–422.

The rapes and sexual violence committed during the Bosnian war have left a long-term legacy, and this legacy has a significant psychological dimension. While emphasizing the individuality of survivors, this chapter has also shown that some common psychological themes developed from the interview data. Rather than simply focusing on psychological issues, however, the chapter has also sought to do something different, by demonstrating that some of the psychological problems that interviewees spoke about – such as anxiety, depression and insomnia – should be seen in a broader context. This is not to detract from the fact that rape and sexual violence clearly have deep long-term psychological effects – as the interviewees' stories show – but rather to stress that additional factors may be adding to or fuelling these effects. By exploring interviewees' entangled traumas, physical health issues and socio-economic challenges, moreover, this chapter has sought to provide deeper insights into their current lives than would be possible from a purely psychological analysis. The next chapter also does something different. Broadening the purview beyond the interviewees themselves, it moves up a level and focuses on their families. Rape and sexual violence can provoke strong reactions in family members, particularly husbands, and can heavily impact on family relationships and dynamics.

Chapter 4

# The wider impact of war rape and sexual violence in Bosnia-Herzegovina

## Survivors and their families

According to Harvey, 'A host of person, event and environmental factors may influence individual posttraumatic response and recovery'.[1] Families are an important environmental factor that can contribute to shaping the long-term effects of rape and sexual violence. Equally, the long-term effects of these crimes can extend to families themselves. The various studies discussed in Chapter 2 were highly illustrative in this regard. Those studies, however, primarily focused on African countries, and especially the DRC. In the context of BiH, existing research on rape and sexual violence has given little attention to the families of survivors. This chapter addresses that gap. If, as Erikson maintains, rape can be described as a 'blow to the basic tissues of social life that damages the bonds attaching people together and impairing the prevailing sense of community',[2] the central aim of this chapter is to examine the multiple effects of rape and sexual violence on the 'basic tissues' of family life. One of the central themes within the interview data was the 'unsupportive husband'; female interviewees often spoke about marital problems directly or indirectly related to their war trauma. The first half of this chapter accordingly explores some of the long-term 'ripple effects' of rape and sexual violence on marital relations – and on the dynamics within those relations. The second half of the chapter shifts the focus to survivors' children. More specifically, it addresses the dual themes of transgenerational transmission of trauma and children born of rape.

### Family and marital relations

Danieli maintains that 'you need to heal the sociopolitical context for the full healing of the individuals and their families, as you need to heal the individuals to

1 Mary R. Harvey, 'An Ecological View of Psychological Trauma and Trauma Recovery', *Journal of Traumatic Stress* 9 (1996): 3–23, at 7.
2 Kai Erikson, *A New Species of Trouble: The Human Experience of Modern Disasters* (New York, NY: Norton, 1994), 233.

heal the sociopolitical context'.[3] From a social-ecological perspective, however, it is not only the macro socio-political context that is significant. So too is the meso context, and families are a critical meso environmental variable that can profoundly affect survivors' 'recovery environment'[4] and how they cope with their trauma. As Campbell et al. underscore, 'The ways in which families... respond to survivors may have a profound effect on victims' well-being'.[5] While these responses and their effects can be extremely positive, in BiH the majority of interviewees – and specifically female interviewees – gave primarily negative examples.

Z40 explained that she only spoke out for the first time in 2010. For many years, she had wanted to break her silence, to talk to other survivors and to seek help, yet she had felt unable to do so because of her brother-in-law. During the war, he held an important position in the Fifth Corps of the ABiH, and he insisted that she should not speak about her experiences. He did not want people to know that a member of his family had been raped. He felt humiliated. She respected his wishes, but recalled that there were times when she felt as though she might 'explode'. Only after her brother-in-law died did she speak out for the first time and make contact with other survivors in the area.[6] More commonly, however, interviewees who had kept their war trauma a secret for many years had done so, in large part, because of their husbands. They feared how their spouses might react.[7]

### *What husbands 'know'*

Of the 66 female interviewees who took part in this research, 56 per cent were married, 29 per cent were not married (some had never been married and some were divorced) and 15 per were widows. Five of the 37 interviewees who were married were still concealing the truth from their husbands. In one case, a Serb

3 Yael Danieli, 'Massive Trauma and the Healing Role of Reparative Justice', in Carla Ferstman, Mariana Goetz and Alan Stephens (eds), *Reparations for Victims of Genocide, War Crimes and Crimes against Humanity: Systems in Place and Systems in the Making* (Leiden: Brill, 2009), 41–78, at 56.

4 Harvey, *supra* note 1, at 8.

5 Rebecca Campbell, Courtney E. Ahrens, Tracy Sefl, Sharon M. Wasco and Holly E. Barnes, 'Social Reactions to Rape Victims: Healing and Hurtful Effects on Psychological and Physical Health Outcomes', *Violence and Victims* 16 (2001): 287–302, at 288.

6 Author interview, 1 December 2014.

7 Speaking in 2013, the then UN Special Rapporteur on Violence against Women, Rashida Manjoo, observed that 'Many women [in BiH] have only recently started speaking out and service providers continue to meet victims who have remained silent for 18 or 20 years... Women keep silent out of fear of their perpetrators, fear of disclosing their experiences to their husbands, their children and other family, and fear of social stigmatization'. Rashida Manjoo, *Report of the Special Rapporteur on Violence against Women, its Causes and Consequences, on her Mission to Bosnia and Herzegovina (28 October – 6 November 2012)*, A/HRC/23/49/Add.3 (4 June 2013), §25, available at: www.ohchr.org/Documents/HRBodies/HRCouncil/RegularSession/Session23/A-HRC-23-49-Add3_en.pdf (accessed 10 April 2016).

interviewee, V28, initially refused to take part in this research because of her husband. She subsequently agreed to talk when he had gone out, but she was clearly on edge and stressed several times that her husband must never know her story. For her, the fact that she was raped during the war – in the Viktor Bubanj camp in Sarajevo[8] – was a huge 'disgrace'. She further explained that after her daughter was killed by a sniper in 1993, her husband started drinking heavily. She found him difficult to deal with when he was drunk, and this had further strengthened her resolve never to tell him that she was raped. 'It would only create more problems', she stressed.[9] M1, a Bosniak who was raped in a camp in Goražde in eastern BiH when she was 18 years old, disclosed that she has never told her husband because she sees no reason for doing so. She maintained that 'Even if husbands know, they don't ask any questions and just sweep it under the carpet'.[10]

When asked directly whether their husbands knew that they had been raped during the war, female interviewees frequently answered: 'He knows, but he doesn't know'. This essentially meant that although they had spoken to their husbands, albeit not in detail, rape was nevertheless a 'taboo topic' within their marriages and was never discussed.[11] P17, a Bosnian Croat, recalled the night, several years after the war ended, that she had told her husband she was raped. When she had finished her story, he silently left the house, returning a couple of hours later. To this day, he has never spoken about that evening or initiated any discussion. It is as if the conversation never happened.[12] Simply asking interviewees whether their husbands 'knew', thus, was in many ways too simplistic to capture the intricacies of undesirable knowledge. The word 'undesirable' is pivotal. In this context, the issue is not only what individuals ***know***, but also what they *want* to know.[13]

8 On 26 February 2016, the State Court of BiH in Sarajevo convicted Ramiz Avdović, the former commander of the Viktor Bubanj camp guards, and Iuliana-Nicola Vintila, a cook and guard in the camp, of war crimes against civilians (in violation of article 142 of the Criminal Code of the SFRY). They were sentenced to prison terms of three years and two years respectively. The third defendant in the case, Besim Muderizović, who was the military prison commander, died in 2012. See www.sudbih.gov.ba/predmet/2881/show

9 Author interview, 5 November 2014.

10 Author interview, 7 August 2014.

11 Such avoidance, however, is not specific to BiH. In one of the rare studies of how married couples deal with rape, Burgess and Holmstrom spoke to 146 survivors and focused on a sub-sample of 16 survivors (aged between 17 and 40) who were either married or living with partners. They discovered that 'The couples found the rape very difficult to discuss openly with each other. In most of the couples, it was not discussed openly; they had only minimal discussion or no discussion. They talked neither about their feelings nor the details of what occurred. Avoidance of the topic was the pattern in 12 of 15 couples for whom we have data'. Lynda L. Holmstrom and Ann W. Burgess, 'Rape: The Husband's and Boyfriend's Initial Reactions', *The Family Coordinator* 28 (1979): 321–330, at 325.

12 Author interview, 13 October 2014.

13 Judith L. Alpert, 'Enduring Mothers, Enduring Knowledge: On Rape and History', *Contemporary Psychoanalysis* 51 (2015): 296–311, at 297.

A further layer of complexity arises from the degree of information that is imparted and shared. Some interviewees, for example, disclosed that they had not told their husbands the entire truth. L40 explained that her husband had been badly beaten by five *Autonomaši* and had his own trauma. When asked whether he knew what had happened to her, she was somewhat vague and simply said that he knew 'one part' but not 'the other part'. She did not elaborate further and changed the subject, but she admitted that she was raped twice. It is therefore probable that she had only told her husband about one of the rapes.[14] This is consistent with the fact that several other interviewees who were raped more than once had similarly only revealed to their husbands that they were raped on one occasion. N21 was raped in her apartment in Zvornik. She spoke in some detail about this and described how the Serb soldiers came and went as they pleased, 'did what they wanted' with her, verbally abused her and extinguished their cigarette butts on her skin. A Serb neighbour found her and helped her, putting her on a bus from Zvornik to ABiH-controlled territory via Bijeljina. On Majevica Mountain, four soldiers boarded the bus and asked to see everyone's ID cards. She was instructed to get off the bus and the soldiers took her into a nearby building. She stopped at this point and said simply: 'And that's when it happened again'.[15] It was as though she herself had not yet come to terms with this second rape and she continued to keep it a secret from her husband.

Among the 37 female interviewees who were married, 85.5 per cent claimed that their husbands knew at least part of their 'rape story'. Significantly, however, 62.5 per cent of these women claimed that they had marital problems. Of the 51 survivors in *Medica Zenica* and *Medica Mondiale's* study in BiH, 45.7 per cent maintained that their rape trauma continues to completely influence their relationships with their husbands or with men in general. A further 30.4 per cent opined that it did so to a certain extent, and 23.9 per cent felt that it did not do so at all.[16] From my own research, it emerged that rape had affected interviewees' marital relations in two main ways, namely via the conduits of blame and sex.

## Wife blaming

Some interviewees revealed how their husbands, instead of offering support and understanding, actually blamed them for being raped. Interviewee N34, for example, who was introduced in the previous chapter, recalled that her husband – a fellow Bosnian Muslim – was aggressive when she told him her story. Angrily, he asked her why she did not 'say no' to the two Serb soldiers who raped her.

14 Author interview, 30 November 2014.

15 Author interview, 26 October 2014.

16 Medica Zenica and Medica Mondiale, *"We are still Alive", "We have been Harmed but We are Brave and Strong": Research on the Long-Term Consequences of War Rape and Coping Strategies of Survivors in Bosnia and Herzegovina* (Zenica, BiH: Medica, 2014), 81.

She responded by asking him why he himself did not 'say no' when a group of Serb soldiers came to take him to the Batković camp,[17] near Bijeljina, in 1992.[18] Part of A76's story was also discussed in the previous chapter. Towards the end of 1993, this Bosnian Croat woman mustered the courage to tell her Serb husband that she had endured – just a year earlier – multiple rapes by a group of HVO soldiers over a three-month period. Her husband did not react in the way that she had hoped and accused her of having willingly 'slept' with the soldiers.[19] Examples of husbands blaming their wives – which frequently emerged from the interview data and were not confined to Bosnian Muslim interviewees – attest to the influence of pernicious rape myths. According to Moor, 'Rape myths… proclaim that women can prevent rape if they truly want to, and that no woman can be forced to have sex against her will. Hence if a woman is raped, she obviously did not mind it or worse yet, secretly desired it'.[20] From the stories they told, some interviewees were married to men who appeared to strongly believe that rape is a crime in which, oxymoronically, women have a choice.

The former UN Special Rapporteur on Violence against Women, Rashida Manjoo, has observed that 'In the cultural context of Bosnia and Herzegovina, women are generally portrayed vis-à-vis their relations to men, that is, as mothers, wives, sisters or intimate partners, but rarely as businesswomen, intellectuals or leaders'.[21] In other words, broader cultural ideas about women,[22] and about their place in Bosnian society, can foster 'wife blaming'. These ideas can also encourage victimological displacement. If, historically, rape was construed as a property crime that devalued a man's 'estate',[23] vestiges of this idea persist in the allocation and apportioning of rape harm. Fundamentally, in some cases, interviewees'

17 The Batković camp was established on the outskirts of Bijeljina, in north-east BiH, in June 1992. According to the ICTY, 'Between 2,000 and 3,000 non-Serbs went through the camp after its establishment with new groups arriving when other groups left. The exchange of detainees in groups of 50 to 100 began in August 1992'. *Prosecutor v. Radovan Karadžić*, IT-95-5/18-T, ICTY Trial Chamber Judgement (24 March 2016), §648. Detainees were periodically beaten, and those who became ill were refused medical treatment (§654). More than half of the male interviewees had spent time in Batković during the Bosnian war.

18 Author interview, 20 November 2014.

19 Author interview, 24 June 2015.

20 Avigail Moor, 'When Recounting the Traumatic Memories is Not Enough: Treating Persistent Self-Devaluation Associated with Rape and Victim-Blaming Rape Myths', *Women and Therapy* 30 (2007): 19–33, at 22. See also A. Nicholas Groth, *Men Who Rape: The Psychology of the Offender* (Cambridge, MA: Basic Books, 1979), 7

21 Manjoo, *supra* note 7, at §12.

22 Victoria L. Banyard, Elizabethe G. Plante and Mary M. Moynihan, 'Bystander Education: Bringing a Broader Community Perspective to Sexual Violence Prevention', *Journal of Community Psychology* 32 (2004): 61–79, at 63.

23 Brownmiller notes that 'The historic price of woman's protection by man against man was the imposition of chastity and monogamy. A crime committed against her body became a crime against the male estate'. Susan Brownmiller, *Against Our Will: Men, Women and Rape* (New York: Fawcett Columbine, 1975), 17.

husbands seemingly perceived themselves as the injured party rather than their wives. R50's story was one of the most extreme examples.

The day after Srebrenica fell, on 11 July 1995, three masked men took R50 away for 'questioning'. They repeatedly asked her about her eldest brother, who had fought alongside Naser Orić, the ABiH commander in eastern BiH. Unsatisfied with her answers, they proceeded to rape her. In her words, 'They were drunk and like animals'. When the VRS overran Srebrenica, R50's husband fled through the forest to reach ABiH-held territory. He survived but his father was killed. As soon as R50 was reunited with her husband, she told him that she had been raped. He said little and asked nothing. However, after he watched the infamous 'Scorpions' video, which showed the killing of six Bosniak men following the fall of Srebrenica,[24] something 'changed in him' and he began to drink heavily. He became aggressive towards his wife and partly blamed her for the fact that she was raped. Speaking softly, and looking embarrassed, she revealed that he no longer wants to have sex with her 'in the normal way' – the rapists had encroached upon his sexual 'territory' – and that he only desires (anal) sex when he is drunk. She added that when they have sex, she feels as though she is not there.[25] There is no connection between them, and there is no love or tenderness. She always bleeds afterwards. She started to cry and divulged that her husband had recently forced himself on her. He had also reminded her that she did not say no to 'them'. Was she afraid of her husband? 'Always'. Nevertheless, she did not wish to go to the police and insisted that she still loves him.[26]

In addition to containing elements of wife blaming, R50's story also points to a second important way in which rape can put a strain on marital relations. In her case, rape had primarily affected her husband's sexual behaviour and preferences.

24 The Scorpions (*Škorpioni*) were a paramilitary unit attached to the Serbian Ministry of Internal Affairs. A video showing members of the Scorpions killing six Bosnian Muslim civilians in Srebrenica in July 1995 was made public during the Milošević trial at the ICTY. According to Zveržhanovski, 'On 1 June 2005, while cross-examining a defense witness, police General Obrad Stevanović, the Prosecutor introduced a videotape showing the murder of six young Bosnian Muslim men at the hands of what it claimed were special forces of the Serbian Ministry of Internal Affairs, the MUP. The idea was to re-enforce the Prosecutor's case that Serbia was an active participant in the war in Bosnia, rather than just a supporter of the Bosnian Serbs, thus challenging the witness's statement that no Serbian MUP units and no members of the State Security… were present in the vicinity of Srebrenica during the massacre'. Ivan Zveržhanovski, 'Watching War Crimes: The Srebrenica Video and Serbian Attitudes to the Srebrenica Massacre', *Southeast European and Black Sea Studies* 7 (2007): 417–430, at 424.

25 According to Burgess and Holmstrom's aforementioned research with 16 couples, 'The typical sexual response for the men was to want to have sex with the raped partner quite soon after the rape… In some cases, the man seemed to focus exclusively on his own sexual needs. He wanted to have sex quickly either (a) to test himself to see if he would be able to do it, or (b) to prove to himself that things will remain as they had always been, that the rape would not interfere'. Burgess and Holmstrom, *supra* note 11, at 328.

26 Author interview, 20 January 2015.

More commonly, however, it can alter survivors' own feelings about sex and their physiological responses. According to Moor, 'The penetration into the uniquely private space ordinarily associated with meaningful connections frequently contaminates the sphere of sexuality, obstructs intimacy, and further augments many survivors' sense of unworthiness and dishonor'.[27]

## Sexual relations

In *Medica Zenica* and *Medica Mondiale*'s study in BiH, 28.9 per cent of respondents said that they either avoided having, or were reluctant to have, sexual intercourse.[28] One of them revealed that 'In intimate relations with my husband, some movements remind me of the rape'.[29] In my research, none of the interviewees were asked questions about their sexual relations. However, five of them openly admitted that their rape trauma had affected their sex lives – and thus their marital relations. Z31, a Bosniak woman in her 50s, was raped by a HVO soldier in 1993 while her mother and sister were in the room next door. She explained that she has not been able to have sex with her husband for 18 years and that this has created 'many problems' in her marriage.[30] M62, also a Bosnian Muslim and aged 60, related how she developed a 'phobia' of men after she was raped. She could not bear her husband touching her, and seeing him physically aroused frightened her.[31] They are now separated and she lives alone.[32] A further three female interviewees simply mentioned that sex had become too painful for them.

Interviewees who spoke about physical intimacy stressed that their husbands could have helped them by being more understanding and supportive. One survivor's story was particularly moving in this regard. E30, who was in her late 30s when I interviewed her, had an extremely positive relationship with her husband. I was able to stay with them on three separate occasions and to thereby observe at first hand the strong bond and solid partnership between them. E30 was in a camp for three years during the Bosnian war and suffered multiple rapes. Although I became close to her during my fieldwork in BiH (and we have remained in contact), she was less forthcoming than many of the other interviewees and spoke

27 Moor, *supra* note 20, at 21. See also Helen A. Neville and Mary J. Heppner, 'Contextualizing Sequelae and Proposing a Culturally Inclusive Ecological Model of Sexual Assault Recovery', *Applied and Preventive Psychology* 8 (1999): 41–62, at 44.

28 Medica Zenica and Medica Mondiale, *supra* note 16, at 81.

29 Ibid., at 82.

30 Author interview, 13 November 2014.

31 According to Yehuda, Lehrner and Rosenbaum, 'The pairing of physiological arousal with fear or horror may override healthy sexual functioning, so that arousal signals impending threat rather than pleasure'. Rachel Yehuda, Amy Lehrner and Talli Y. Rosenbaum, 'PTSD and Sexual Dysfunction in Men and Women', *The Journal of Sexual Medicine* 12 (2015): 1107–1119, at 1108.

32 Author interview, 19 March 2015.

very little about the past. During my second visit to her home, however, she suddenly disclosed that after everything that she went through during the war, she doubted that she would ever be able to love a man or have a relationship with one. Everything changed when she met her husband. In her words, 'He awakened something in me that I had thought was dead. I can't believe that after everything that has happened to me, I have the feelings and desires of a real woman'.[33] If, as Yehuda, Lehrner and Rosenbaum argue, trauma can 'profoundly rupture' an individual's sense of safety and ability to trust others,[34] E30's husband had helped to repair this damage.

The discussion thus far has focused on female interviewees. Rape and sexual violence, however, can also significantly affect sex drive and sexual functioning in male survivors. Scarce, who was raped as a university student in Ohio, notes that 'Some survivors may have less sex after their rape, whereas others may have more sex in an attempt to reestablish a normalcy of sexual experience'.[35] In a recently published book about his own experience of being raped at the age of 18, Douglas writes that he did not date until he was 36; and after he got married:

> Most nights there were two people in our bedroom, but sometimes there were three. The fact that the interloper was occupying head-space in my brain, rather than bed-space in the physical realm, did not make his presence any less real or disquieting. Trying to contrive matters so that nothing in our lovemaking should even by implication resemble what transpired in another bedroom, years earlier, while not shutting out my wife… did not conduce to the light-hearted, playful attitude toward marital intimacy that I had always hoped to cultivate.[36]

Not only are male survivors frequently overlooked – although this is starting to change[37] – but we also rarely hear from these men directly. Books such as those

33 Author interview, 12 November 2014.

34 Yehuda, Lehrner and Rosenbaum, *supra* note 31, at 117.

35 Michael L. Scarce, *Male on Male Rape: The Hidden Toll of Stigma and Shame* (Cambridge, MA: Perseus Publishing, 1997), 73–74.

36 Raymond M. Douglas, *On Being Raped* (Boson, MA: Beacon Press, 2016), 68–69.

37 See, for example, R. Charli Carpenter, 'Recognizing Gender-Based Violence against Civilian Men and Boys in Conflict Situations', *Security Dialogue* 37 (2006): 83–103; Sandesh Sivakumaran, 'Sexual Violence against Men in Armed Conflict', *European Journal of International Law* 18 (2007): 253–276; *idem*, 'Lost in Translation: UN Responses to Sexual Violence against Men and Boys in Situations of Armed Conflict', *International Review of the Red Cross* 92 (2010): 259–277; Dustin A. Lewis, 'Unrecognized Victims: Sexual Violence against Men in Conflict Settings under International Law', *Wisconsin International Law Journal* 27 (2009): 1–49; Chris A. Dolan, 'Into the Mainstream: Addressing Sexual Violence against Men and Boys in Conflict', a briefing paper prepared for the workshop held at the Overseas Development Institute, London (14 May 2014), available at: www.refugeelawproject.org/files/briefing_papers/Into_The_Mainstream-Addressing_Sexual_Violence_against_Men_and_Boys_in_Conflict.pdf (accessed 7 May 2016); Jerker Edström,

written by Scarce and Douglas, and the work of men's groups such as the Men of Hope in Uganda,[38] are thus extremely valuable and offer important insights into some of the ways that rape and sexual violence affect men as individuals. As previously noted in the introduction and in Chapter 1, the male survivors who participated in this research avoided (with only one exception) speaking about what they themselves had endured during the war, although they talked about some of the crimes that they had witnessed against others. Similarly, they did not discuss their feelings and emotions, and overwhelmingly gave the impression of simply wanting to carry on 'as usual'. They gave no indication of whether their war experiences had affected their sexual relations with their wives, which was not surprising; and indeed I had expected male interviewees to be more guarded than female interviewees.[39]

Interestingly, however, none of the male interviewees had hidden their war stories from their wives, and none of them spoke about marital tensions or problems. I had the opportunity to meet four of the men's wives, and these women were clearly a strong source of support for their husbands. As one illustration, I spoke to J70 in his lounge while his wife was cooking in the adjoining kitchen. Towards the end of the interview, she came and sat next to her husband on the sofa. J70 was explaining that his entire body hurt, in particular his head, and at this point his wife suddenly began to laugh. For a second, it seemed highly incongruous and inappropriate, but then she joked that every part of her husband's body hurts except his tongue – and so he has no problems talking. He found this amusing and laughed with her. Her presence lifted the mood in the

Chris Dolan and Thea Shahrokh, with Onen David, *Therapeutic Activism: Men of Hope Refugee Association Uganda Breaking the Silence over Male Rape in Conflict-Related Sexual Violence*, IDS Development Report 182 (March 2016), available at: www.refugeelawproject.org/files/others/Therapeutic_Activism_MOH.pdf (accessed 9 April 2016).

38 The Men of Hope Refugee Association in Uganda was formed by male survivors of rape and sexual violence from the DRC and neighbouring countries, in collaboration with the Refugee Law Project in Kampala. One of the major aims of the Men of Hope is to raise awareness of the particular challenges that male survivors face. According to the former president of the association, Alain Kabenga, '[i]t has affected so much my personality… also my gender. I was born a man, [but] when these things happened to me, it affected how I felt I was a man. I had so many questions'. Cited in Edström et al., ibid., at 26. As part of their efforts to foster awareness, male survivors from Men of Hope have made a powerful film entitled *Men can be Raped too* (2015). See www.youtube.com/watch?v=iktuUoZGq48

39 It was always much easier to 'connect' with female interviewees. Frequently, for example, they would ask me questions about my age, marital status, family and so on. As Brown points out, 'The separation of the public and the private is a fiction that is hard to maintain in most research sites'. Stephen Brown, 'Dilemmas of Self-Representation and Conduct in the Field', in Chandra L. Sriram, John C. King, Julie A. Mertus, Olga Martin-Ortega and Johanna Herman (eds), *Surviving Fieldwork: Working in Violent and Difficult Situations* (Abingdon: Routledge, 2009), 213–226, at 215. When interviewees posed their own questions, this helped to close the gap between researcher and 'researched'. It was striking that none of the male interviewees asked me any personal questions.

room. It was also striking that J70 only talked – and very briefly – about the sexual violence that he had endured during the war when his wife went outside to get something from the garden. He revealed that he and another man had been forced to perform fellatio on each other in the Lora camp in Split in Croatia. He said this in a hushed voice and gestured with his hands what he had been made to do. He evidently did not wish for his wife to overhear.[40]

Although all of the male interviewees were married, they tended primarily to mention their wives in passing. These women were in the background of their stories. Pointedly, none of them spoke about their wives' own war experiences. As all of these men had been held in camps, they had been separated from their wives for a period during the war and thus unable to protect them. The fact, therefore, that they did not share any details of their wives' own stories was perhaps their way of now protecting and shielding these women – and hence of reasserting their masculinity. The men's stories, in short, contained narrative 'enclaves',[41] and both their own experiences and their wives' war experiences were positioned safely within these enclaves. In contrast, approximately a quarter of the female interviewees talked about their husbands' own war trauma, thereby highlighting the important issue of combined or dual marital traumas.

## Combined marital traumas

Č18 was raped during the war close to her home. She did not tell her husband for seven years because she felt deeply ashamed. However, the stress and worry of keeping everything hidden from him affected her health, and, with strong encouragement from her doctor, she finally confided in her husband that she was raped. He asked her why she had waited so long to tell him. They have never spoken about it since.[42] Two weeks after I interviewed Č18 in October 2014, she and her husband invited me to spend a night with them in their home. They were concerned that I would feel lonely staying in one of the local hotels. As the evening went on, they seemed increasingly disconnected from each other. According to Backer, 'Trauma implies a complete psychological breakdown of an individual'.[43] The fact that Č18 and her husband had their own individual war traumas had seemingly contributed to a breakdown in their relationship with each other. Throughout the evening, she smoked cigarette after cigarette and chatted constantly. She laughed a great deal, but it did not always seem natural and her smile

40 Author interview, 23 April 2015.

41 According to Young, 'stories can be seen as an enclave within conversation, framed off from it as a different order of discourse'. Katharine Young, 'Ontological Puzzles about Narrative', *Poetics* 13 (1984): 239–259, at 239.

42 Author interview, 16 October 2014.

43 David Backer, 'A Contextual Approach to Fear, Trauma and Loss: Growing with *Vive Žene*', in Mima Dahić and Jasna Zečević (eds), *A Contextual Approach to Fear, Trauma and Loss* (Tuzla: *Vive Žene*, 2008), 9–29, at 13.

never reached her eyes. Her husband sat at the table making his own cigarettes and drinking Rakija, a strong brandy. At around 11pm, he announced that he was going to bed, but he did not wish his wife good night. He always slept in a room next to the bathroom and she slept in the lounge.

On a previous occasion, I had spoken one-to-one with this man. He revealed that during the war, he had spent two months in the Luka camp in Brčko, before being transferred to Batković. He was badly beaten in Luka and no longer has any sight in his right eye.[44] He explained that he has taken Seroxat, an anti-depressant, for the last 17 years. The fact that I was able to talk to both Č18 and her husband was unusual, and it was striking that she herself said nothing about his war experiences, except to briefly mention that he was sent to the Luka camp. When I informally spoke to her a month later, it emerged that she was in fact harbouring considerable resentment towards her husband. She complained that he is only good to other people but not to her, and claimed that he expects her to pay for everything in their marriage.

More commonly, female interviewees readily disclosed that their husbands had their own war trauma, and they offered this as a major reason why they could not rely upon these men for support and understanding. They did not want to 'burden' them with their own trauma. The following two examples are particularly illustrative. G29 lives in RS, but prior to the war she resided in what is now the Federation. In 1992, she was raped by two Bosniak soldiers in her bathroom. Her two young children (aged eight and 10) were downstairs. Today, she has various health problems, including diabetes and high blood pressure, and has not received any help for her trauma. She lives with her husband, grown-up son, daughter-in-law and granddaughter. Nobody in the family has a job, and she feels that she needs to be strong and to 'hold everything together'. During the war, her husband spent 22 months in the Music School and KP Dom (Penal and Correctional Facility) in Zenica,[45] in central BiH, and suffered severe beatings.

44 Heinous crimes were committed in Luka and serious beatings were a daily occurrence. For example, in its sentencing judgement against Goran Jelišić, who held a position of authority in the camp, the ICTY described the suffering experienced by a prisoner called Muhamad Bukvić. According to the judgement, 'this man was very severely beaten by Goran Jelišić during an interrogation which he underwent in the administrative offices in Luka camp. The victim, already covered in bruises from the beating he received the previous day from another guard at the camp named Kosta, was beaten all over his body by Goran Jelišić with a truncheon. The accused, using his fingers to squeeze the victim's cheeks up towards his eyes, hit him with his truncheon at eye level'. *Prosecutor v. Goran Jelišić*, IT-95-10-T, ICTY Sentencing Judgement (14 December 1999), §43. Jelišić pleaded guilty to 16 counts of violations of the laws or customs of war and 15 counts of crimes against humanity. He was sentenced to 40 years' imprisonment, which was upheld on appeal in 2001. See also *Prosecutor v. Ranko Češić*, IT-95-10/1-S, ICTY Sentencing Judgement (11 March 2004), §§11–17.

45 Bosnian Croats and Bosnian Serbs detained in the Music School and KP Dom in 1993 were subjected to crimes committed by members of the Third Corps (and within this the Seventh Mountain Brigade) of the ABiH. In the trial of Enver Hadžihasanović (the commander of the Third Corps) and Amir Kubura (the commander-in-chief of the Seventh

He knew nothing about his family for most of this period. When I interviewed G29 in her home, her husband briefly entered the room and sat next to her. With one of his hands withered as a result of the injuries that he sustained in the camp, he looked disorientated and appeared not to register anything that was going on. After a couple of minutes, he left the room without saying anything. By way of explanation, his wife said that he refuses to take any medication and finds refuge in alcohol. This was evident in his red 'drinker's nose'.[46] She further insisted that her husband is in a worse psychological state than she is and that he is unable to deal with her trauma as well as his own. Consequently, she cannot speak about the past in front of him and even has to hide all of her war-related documentation – including information regarding her rapists' trial.[47]

I52, also a Serb, was raped in 1992. She had been to visit the local doctor and as she was returning home, she was stopped by three ABiH soldiers. They took her away for 'questioning' and subsequently raped her. Her husband, a Bosnian Croat, was in the HVO. When the war ended, they moved to the United States and she started to feel happy again. She worked in a restaurant as a waitress and her husband was employed in the kitchen. However, he started to become violent towards her and could not deal with her speaking to other men – an example of what Zimmer-Tamakoshi terms 'troubled masculinity'.[48] He knew that his wife was raped during the war, but he never showed any understanding and wanted her to remain at home. As his jealousy grew, she made the decision that they should move back to BiH. She hoped that he would be more relaxed in his own surroundings and that his physical and verbal abuse of her would stop, but it only got worse.[49] He frequently called her a whore and demanded to know

Mountain Brigade), the ICTY Trial Chamber noted that 'All the Prosecution witnesses are consistent in stating that, throughout their detention in the Music School, they repeatedly underwent cruel treatment and lived in a permanent state of anxiety. Thus, upon their arrival at the School, the detainees were almost systematically kicked and beaten with rubber cable and wooden shovel handles by the soldiers and guards of the School'. *Prosecutor v. Enver Hadžihasanović and Amir Kubura*, IT-01-47/T, ICTY Trial Judgement (15 March 2006), §1180. The Trial Chamber also described the 'atmosphere of terror that prevailed at the KP Dom in Zenica' (§184). Hadžihasanović and Kubura were found guilty, on the basis of command responsibility, of violations of the laws or customs of war and sentenced to prison terms of five years and two-and-a-half years respectively. These sentences were subsequently reduced on appeal to three-and-a-half years and two years.

46 Karlheinz Woeber, 'The Skin in Diagnosis of Alcoholism', *Annals of the New York Academy of Sciences* 252 (1975): 292–295, at 292.

47 Author interview, 5 November 2014. The interviewee's rapists were tried in 1998 and received sentences of less than eight years each.

48 Laura Zimmer-Tamakoshi, 'Troubled Masculinities and Gender Violence in Melanesia', in Margaret Jolly, Christine Stewart and Carolyn Brewer (eds), *Engendering Violence in Papua New Guinea* (Canberra: Australian National University Press, 2010), 73–105, at 74.

49 Post-conflict domestic violence may be interpreted, in part, as an attempt by men to assert and regain lost power and authority. See, for example, Angela Radan, 'Exposure to Violence and Expressions of Resilience in Central American Women Survivors of War', *Journal of Aggression, Maltreatment and Trauma* 14 (2007): 147–164, at 151. In total, 6.6 per cent

why she did not resist the three ABiH soldiers in 1992. The domestic abuse lasted for six years. She explained that her husband is much calmer now because he takes medication. However, there is little communication between them and they largely live separate lives. Describing her husband as a heavy smoker, she stressed that he only cares about his cigarettes. He rarely leaves the house and she has to do everything for him. Why had she resigned herself to this situation? When I asked her this, she simply smiled and sighed. Her husband had sustained shrapnel injuries during the war, and according to her his trauma is far worse than her own.[50]

McEvoy and McConnachie argue that within transitional justice, there are 'hierarchies of victimhood'. Some individuals are seen as more deserving of the 'victim' label than others, and 'the "innocent" victim is placed at the apex of a hierarchy of victimhood'.[51] Most commonly, these hierarchies operate inter-ethnically, with the ethnic 'in-group' seeking to demonstrate that it suffered more than the aggressor 'out-group'.[52] What emerged from the data in BiH, however, is that some female interviewees had constructed their own hierarchies of victimhood, through their insistence that their husbands had gone through far more than they themselves had. The creation of these family-based hierarchies of victimhood, and the implicit notion that male suffering is more important, reflect broader gender dynamics in a country that remains heavily patriarchal.[53]

From the above examples and vignettes, it is clear that the mass rapes and sexual violence committed during the Bosnian war have left a legacy that is multi-layered and extends beyond survivors themselves. This legacy includes altered family dynamics and marital problems which, in turn, can prolong and exacerbate survivors' individual traumas. Although the thematic of marital relations emerged very prominently from the research data, interviewees' stories also revealed a second important familial dimension of legacy, highlighting that the long-term

of female interviewees who participated in my research admitted that they had suffered domestic abuse since the Bosnian war ended, and two of these ten women were still enduring such abuse. According to Björkdahl and Selimovic, 'A legacy of the [Bosnian] war is that violence experienced during the conflict now seems to manifest itself in increased and more severe cases of domestic violence'. Annika Björkdahl and Johanna M. Selimovic, 'Gendering Agency in Transitional Justice', *Security Dialogue* 48 (2015): 165–182, at 175.

50 Author interview, 3 February 2015.

51 Kieran McEvoy and Kirsten McConnachie, 'Victimology in Transitional Justice: Victimhood, Innocence and Hierarchy', *European Journal of Criminology* 9 (2012): 527–538, at 532.

52 Andrighetto et al. note that in conflict situations, 'people often interpret the impact of the conflict subjectively, viewing their own group as the only legitimate victim and the rivals as the illegitimate perpetrators of unjust and immoral misdeeds'. Luca Andrighetto, Silvia Mari, Chiara Volpato and Burim Buhluli, 'Reducing Competitive Victimhood in Kosovo: The Role of Extended Contact and Common Ingroup Identity', *Political Psychology* 33 (2012): 513–529, at 513.

53 Danijela Majstorović, 'Femininity, Patriarchy and Resistance in the Postwar Bosnia and Herzegovina', *International Review of Sociology* 21 (2011): 277–299, at 278.

effects of rape and sexual violence have impacted on children and, in some cases, on survivors' relationships with their children.

## Family relations and children

In the study conducted by *Medica Zenica* and *Medica Mondiale*, the 51 female research participants were asked about the impact of their rape trauma on their children. In total, 25.6 per cent of the women opined that the trauma they went through during the Bosnian war completely affects their children today, 32.5 per cent adjudged that it affects them to some extent and 41.9 per cent felt that it does not affect their children at all.[54] During my interviews in BiH, children became an important theme in two key ways. Firstly, some female interviewees emphatically stressed that their children must be protected from the truth and must never know that their mothers were raped. Secondly, some male and female interviewees expressed concerns that their own trauma was impacting on their children, thereby implicitly raising the issue of transgenerational transmission of trauma.

### *Protecting children from the truth*

For many interviewees (and specifically female interviewees), a key priority was to protect their children from ever finding out the truth. Some insisted that they would never tell their children that they were raped; a common concern was that their sons and daughters might start to view them differently and be ashamed of them. One interviewee was extremely worried about her 15-year-old daughter. A couple of days earlier, the teenager had discovered her mother's paperwork from ŽŽR, an NGO which helps rape survivors to obtain civilian victim of war status. The interviewee explained that since finding the paperwork, her daughter had shut herself in her bedroom and was refusing to go to school.[55]

Other interviewees were simply unsure how to tell their children that they were raped. What should they say to them? K61 was one of the few Bosnian Croat women whom I was able to interview. She had suffered from a serious stroke several years earlier and was now unable to walk. Her 21-year-old daughter, AJ, was her full-time carer. When I visited the interviewee in her home, her daughter sat next to her, holding her hand. She was there not only for support, but because she desperately wanted to know what had happened to her mother during the war. AJ recalled that when she was around 16 years old, two police officers from the State Investigation and Protection Agency (SIPA) had visited the family home and spoken to her mother. She had overheard parts of the conversation and strongly suspected that her mother was raped during the war.

54 Medica Zenica and Medica Mondiale, *supra* note 16, at 82.
55 Author interview, 3 December 2014.

Born in 1994, AJ was concerned that she herself may have been conceived as a result of rape. Was the man she called her father actually her biological father? She needed to know the truth, but her mother struggled to tell her story. K61 recounted how, during one summer's day in 1993, a group of ABiH soldiers approached her house. She was outside with her two young children. One of the soldiers insisted that she must enter the house with him while he looked for weapons. He scoured the entire house, without finding anything, and finally he searched in the basement. It was here that he asked K61 how she would feel if he were to kill her husband. AJ interjected and asked her mother what happened next. She was unsatisfied with the response. What did her mother mean when she said 'I surrendered myself'? At this point, it felt as though AJ was conducting the interview. She was taking control, asking the questions that she needed answers to, and I became merely an observer to a powerful exchange between a mother and a daughter. Although both of them wanted me to stay, it felt somewhat awkward. Engaging in what Primeau terms '*reflexivity* in action',[56] I started to question whether it was appropriate for me to be there. It was a private, family matter.

AJ wanted to know what happened next. Her mother explained that in order to save her husband, she told the ABiH soldier to 'do what he wanted' with her. He told her to lie down and he lay on top of her, kissing her and touching her breasts. He tried to have sex with her, but she closed her legs and held her skirt down. AJ started to become frustrated with her mother, sensing that she was holding back and not telling her the entire truth. Her mother mentioned several times that she had 'done her job' to save her husband's life, but each time her daughter asked her if the soldier had raped her, she insisted that he had not. She described how the soldier, after kissing and touching her, turned her onto her stomach and masturbated on her skirt. Regarding her husband – whom she stressed was indeed her daughter's biological father – she recalled that she had been afraid to tell him what had happened in the basement, anxious that he might reject her. Her daughter asked her once again if she was raped. The answer was still no.[57] Four days later, AJ called me. She had been trying to find out from her mother what had happened in the basement that day in 1993, but she still had so many unanswered questions. AJ hoped that her mother, who kept repeating that what had happened to her was a 'disgrace', would eventually feel comfortable enough to tell her everything.

56 According to Primeau, reflexivity requires that 'we', as researchers, are 'aware of our presence in the research… Such awareness comes through our internal dialogues with ourselves and continuous, intensive scrutiny of "what we know" and "how we know it" as we participate in the research process'. Loree A. Primeau, 'Reflection on Self in Qualitative Research: Stories of Family', *American Journal of Occupational Therapy* 57 (2003): 9–16, at 10.

57 Author interview, 19 March 2015.

### *Transgenerational transmission of trauma*

According to a psychologist in Tuzla who has worked for many years with survivors of rape and sexual violence, 'It is important for survivors to understand their behaviour and to understand how it affects those around them, and in particular their children'. She also noted that 'Sometimes they cannot talk to their children and push them away'.[58] A59's story powerfully illustrates this last point. A Bosniak woman in her early 40s, A59 said very little about the war and what she had personally gone through. She stressed that every time she speaks about the past, she re-lives her trauma. She thus focused almost exclusively on her current problems, and in particular she talked about her relationship with her 15-year-old son. She described how, for the last six years, she has been unable to show him any love or affection. When he tries to hug her, she turns away.[59] She was deeply concerned about how this situation might be affecting him. If she could not emotionally connect with her son, would he turn to other people – 'bad people, drug dealers' – to get what he could not get from her? This was her greatest fear. Her anxieties, in turn, were manifesting themselves in her dreams. 'I often have dreams where my son is missing and I can't find him', she explained. Her brother was taken away in 1992 and she never saw him again. He was found in a mass grave in 2006. She has not told her son that she was raped. She does not know how to tell him or when would be the right time to do so. She feels an overwhelming sense of guilt that she is emotionally distant towards him and cannot reciprocate his affections.[60]

A59's concerns regarding her son raise the important issue of trans-generational transmission of trauma, whereby trauma is transferred from one generation to the next. According to Kellermann, just as 'heat, light, sound, and electricity can be invisibly carried from a transmitter to a receiver', it is similarly possible that parents can transmit unconscious experiences to their children 'through some complex process of extrasensory communication'.[61] Research on transgenerational transmission of trauma has predominantly focused on children of Holocaust survivors[62] and, to a lesser extent, on children of

58 Author interview, Tuzla, 21 August 2014.

59 In *Medica Zenica* and *Medica Mondiale*'s study, similarly, one of the respondents said of her children: 'I cannot show love or emotions towards them. Everything died in me'. Medica Zenica and Medica Mondiale, *supra* note 16, at 83.

60 Author interview, 14 February 2015.

61 Natan P.F. Kellermann, 'Transmission of Holocaust Trauma: An Integrative View', *Psychiatry* 64 (2001): 256–267, at 260.

62 See, for example, Kellermann, ibid.; Abraham Sagi-Schwartz, Marinus H. van Ijzendoorn, Klaus E. Grossman, Tirtsa Joels, Karin Grossman, Miri Scharf, Nina Koren-Karie and Sarit Alkalay, 'Attachment and Traumatic Stress in Female Holocaust Children Survivors and their Daughters', *American Journal of Psychiatry* 160 (2003): 1086–1092; Pierre Fossion, Christophe Leys, Caroline Vandeleur, Chantal Kempanaers, Stéphanie Braun, Paul Verbanck and Paul Linkowski, 'Transgenerational Transmission of Trauma in Families of Holocaust

ex-combatants.[63] In contrast, there is a major gap vis-à-vis transgenerational transmission of trauma from survivors of rape and sexual violence to their children.

Like A59, several of the interviewees expressed concerns that their war trauma might be negatively affecting their children. D51 spent two-and-a-half months in the Batković camp during the Bosnian war. His hand and nose were broken as a result of the beatings that he received, and he also suffered injuries to his back. He was just 20 years old at the time and the Serb soldier who sexually abused him was approximately the same age. While not disclosing anything about this abuse, he maintained that it was 'deeply shameful and humiliating'. He does not like speaking about the past because he worries that people will laugh at him and mock him. They might ask him why he did not resist or fight back.[64] When he was released from Batković, he became heavily dependent on alcohol. It was the only way that he could cope. He was 'completely broken' when he came out of the camp, and his experiences there will always follow him. He no longer drinks, but he struggles to concentrate and has withdrawn into himself, to ensure that his wife and, in particular, his daughter do not feel his pain. Despite endeavouring to protect his five-year-old daughter,[65] he expressed concerns about her: 'She doesn't eat much and only wants orange juice'. He admitted that he rarely plays with her because he does not feel in the right frame of mind.[66]

Survivors: The Consequences of Extreme Family Functioning on Resilience, Sense of Coherence, Anxiety and Coherence', *Journal of Affective Disorders* 171 (2015): 48–53.

63 See, for example, Ann C. Davidson and David J. Mellor, 'The Adjustment of Children of Australian Vietnam Veterans: Is there Evidence for the Transgenerational Transmission of the Effects of War-Related Trauma?' *Australian and New Zealand Journal of Psychiatry* 35 (2001): 345–351; Rachel Dekel and Hadass Goldblatt, 'Is there Intergenerational Transmission of Trauma? The Case of Combat Veterans' Children', *American Journal of Orthopsychiatry* 78 (2008): 281–289; Miro Klarić, Tanja Frančišković, Branka Klarić, Ante Kvesić, Ana Kaštelan, Mirjana Graovac, Ines Diminić Lisica, 'Psychological Problems in Children of War Veterans with Posttraumatic Stress Disorder in Bosnia and Herzegovina: Cross-Sectional Study', *Croatian Medical Journal* 49 (2008): 491–498.

64 There is often an expectation that men should be able to fight back and defend themselves. To cite Weiss, 'With "real" men expected to avoid behaviors associated with femininity, men who are overpowered by others may be judged to have failed in their masculine duty to stick up for themselves'. Karen G. Weiss, 'Male Sexual Victimization: Examining Men's Experiences of Rape and Rape Assault', *Men and Masculinities* 12 (2010): 275–298, at 277. A male survivor's own belief that he has failed as a man may compound and aggravate his trauma. Jayne Walker, John Archer and Michelle Davies, 'Effects of Rape on Men: A Descriptive Problem', *Archives of Sexual Behavior* 35 (2005): 69–80, at 78.

65 According to Daud, Skoglund and Rydelius, 'Undergoing a psychic trauma affects the parent's ability to function as a protective shield for their children'. Atia Daud, Erling Skoglund and Per-Anders Rydelius, 'Children in Families of Torture Victims: Transgenerational Transmission of Parents' Traumatic Experiences to their Children', *International Journal of Social Welfare* 14 (2005): 23–32, at 23.

66 Author interview, 30 January 2015.

Alpert herself was five years old when she 'caught' her mother's trauma.[67] She only found out many years later that her mother had been raped,[68] but somehow she had always known this. When she started seeing a child therapist, she habitually played with the same two toys. One was a doll's house. She used to place the mother doll in the safest position within the house and moved the furniture around to further achieve maximum security. The other toy was a wooden block with holes in it. She reflects:

> I hammered fat wooden round pegs into a piece of wood with round holes. Over and over again I did this. What was my play about? Was I announcing that I knew some secret about forbidden entry of some fat round thing being hammered into a hole? Did I repeat the hammering in an effort to have control of this forbidden entry, this violation that never should have happened? I wonder now.[69]

Parents can 'pass on' their trauma to their children in a variety of different ways, including through their fears, anxieties and emotional state.[70] In 1993, J56 – then aged 26 – was raped by one of her neighbours who had joined the HVO. She explained that she frequently cries, only leaves the house when she has to and constantly feels dirty and sullied. When she eventually told her two adult children what had happened to her, they already knew. During the interview, she expressed concerns about her 34-year-old son, who was still living with her. She worried that he was becoming overweight and depressed. She also talked about his anxiety. For years, he has been checking on her while she is asleep, to make sure that she is breathing.[71]

In some cases, moreover, survivors' children had experienced their own war trauma, which added a further layer of complexity. R38 was introduced in the previous chapter. She was held in a camp for three months during the Bosnian war and her children were effectively imprisoned in an abandoned house. A group of *Autonomaši* came and went as they pleased, and R38's two eldest daughters were raped. Her son was 10 years old at the time and he is now a drug addict. He briefly emerged from upstairs and appeared 'high'. He spoke as if through gritted teeth and explained that he needed some time to 'get myself together'. I saw him the next day, standing on the street with a group of men. When I greeted him, he seemed not to recognize me and just stared blankly. His mother admitted that

67 Alpert, *supra* note 13, at 298.

68 Alpert's mother had also been affected by her own mother's trauma of living through three pogroms directed at Russian Jews from 1881 to 1921.

69 Alpert, *supra* note 13, at 298.

70 Kami L. Schwerdtfeger and Briana S. Nelson Goff, 'Intergenerational Transmission of Trauma: Exploring Mother-Infant Pre-Natal Attachment', *Journal of Traumatic Stress* 20 (2007): 39–51, at 40.

71 Author interview, 5 February 2015.

she is afraid of him. The previous night, he had pulled a knife on her husband. The situation was so bad that she could not leave them alone for long as she never knew what might happen. The war had destroyed her son's childhood, she emphasized, and all of her children's childhoods. All of them now had psychological problems.[72]

According to Khamis, 'The parent-child relationship involves a dynamic interplay between dyadic emotions and behaviors'.[73] What some of the interviewees' stories also demonstrated, however, is that this relationship can additionally involve a dynamic interplay of different individual traumas. Fundamentally, the trauma of rape survivors may co-exist and co-mingle with their children's own trauma. This further evinces the concept of entangled traumas, which was discussed and explored in Chapter 3. A particularly important example of entangled parent–child traumas pertains to children who were conceived through rape. These children are a critical part of the long-term legacy of rape in BiH, yet, as Helms points out, 'There is still much that is unknown about the very complex social and psychological dynamics affecting rape survivors and the lives of children they bore in relation to questions of stigma, ethnic identities, and gender'.[74]

## Children born of rape

Notwithstanding the volume of academic scholarship on rape in conflict, the issue of children born as a consequence of rape remains surprisingly under-researched. According to Denov, 'The overall silence, invisibility and inattention that this population has faced, at the level of policy, practice, and research, can be seen to parallel other populations who have experienced war-related trauma and abuse'.[75] It is certainly the case that children born as a result of war rape in BiH have been heavily neglected.[76] Carpenter is one of the few scholars to have extensively studied this topic. She recalls that:

> Rape-related pregnancies were a staple trope in media accounts of the [Bosnian] war. I was told in interviews with women's organizations in

72 Author interview, 30 November 2014.

73 Vivian Khamis, 'Does Parent's Psychological Stress Mediate the Relationship between War Trauma and Psychological Adjustment in Children?' *Journal of Health Psychology* 21 (2016): 1361–1370, at 1367.

74 Elissa Helms, *Innocence and Victimhood: Gender, Nation and Women's Activism in Postwar Bosnia-Herzegovina* (Madison, WI: University of Wisconsin Press, 2013), 69.

75 Myriam Denov, 'Children Born of Wartime Rape: The Intergenerational Realities of Sexual Violence and Abuse', *Ethics, Medicine and Public Health* 1 (2015): 61–68, at 66.

76 In one of the few studies, Erjavec and Volčič interviewed 11 teenage girls – aged between 14 and 16 – born of rape in BiH. Karmen Erjavec and Zala Volčič, 'Living with the Sins of Their Fathers: An Analysis of Self-Representation of Adolescents Born of War Rape', *Journal of Adolescent Research* 25 (2010): 359–386.

> Bosnia-Herzegovina that the ideal rape survivor sought by journalists during the war was "preferably someone who had had a baby born of war" during this period.[77]

While they once attracted considerable media interest, little is known about these children born of rape, including their numbers.[78] One of the reasons for this is that complete records were not always kept. An employee working at an orphanage in Tuzla, for example, told Bećirbašić and Sačić that: 'In 1993 alone, we admitted 700 children and the capacity of the orphanage was only 110. It is possible that many of those were the babies of raped women, but there was chaos at the time and we had more important tasks than keeping detailed records'.[79] Of the 66 women whom I interviewed in BiH, two of them – a Bosnian Muslim and a Bosnian Serb – admitted that they had become pregnant and obtained an abortion. A further three interviewees, all of them Bosnian Muslims, revealed that they had carried their pregnancies to term.[80] Manifesting the multiple and diverse ways in which rape can affect families over the long term, these three women – despite their common ethnicity and religion – had very different stories.

In 1992, H58 spent ten days in the Sušica camp in Vlasenica with her son and two daughters. After they were released from the camp, they travelled to the small town of Cerska – which was under the control of the ABiH – and spent a year living in a collective centre. In March 1993, however, Serb forces overran Cerska[81] and it was in the ensuing chaos that H58 was raped. Together with all

77 R. Charli Carpenter, *Forgetting Children Born of War: Setting the Human Rights Agenda in Bosnia and Herzegovina* (New York: Columbia University Press, 2010), 59.

78 According to Daniel-Wrabetz, 'the exact number of children born as a result of the mass rapes and forced impregnation is not known, but anecdotal evidence suggests that many of the war-rape pregnancies were carried to term during the war. Although many of these children left Bosnia with their mothers, some are likely to have been raised within Bosnia after the war'. Joana Daniel-Wrabetz, 'Children Born of War Rape in Bosnia-Herzegovina and the Convention on the Rights of the Child', in R. Charli Carpenter (ed.), *Born of War: Protecting Children of Sexual Violence Survivors in Conflict Zones* (Bloomfield, CT: Kumarian Press, 2007), 21–39, at 25. Carpenter notes that 'Out of the countless women raped during the conflict, an estimated several hundred children were born in Bosnia-Herzegovina. Some were killed at birth'. Carpenter, ibid., at xiii.

79 Cited in Belma Bećirbašić and Dženana Sačić, 'Invisible Casualties of War' (5 September 2005), available at: https://iwpr.net/global-voices/invisible-casualties-war (accessed 9 January 2016).

80 It is possible that more than three interviewees had given birth as a result of being raped but did not wish to acknowledge or discuss this.

81 John F. Burns, 'Enclave in Bosnia Reported to Fall after U.S. Airdrop' (3 March 1993), available at: www.nytimes.com/1993/03/03/world/enclave-in-bosnia-reported-to-fall-after-us-airdrop.html (accessed 10 February 2016). According to the ICTY, 'On Serbian Orthodox Christmas, 7 January 1993, Bosnian Muslim fighters commanded by [Naser] Orić attacked the Bosnian Serb village of Kravica, causing many casualties. This launched a VRS counter-offensive that eventually captured the villages of Konjević Polje and Cerska'.

other Bosnian Muslims in Cerska, she and her family fled to Srebrenica, and nine months later she gave birth to a son. She wanted to terminate the pregnancy, but conditions in Srebrenica were extremely bad.[82] Having an abortion, therefore, was not an option. When her son was born, she felt nothing towards him, and she admitted that she has never shown him the love and affection that she has given to her other children: 'I have always treated him differently'. She has not told him (or her other children) how he was conceived, but they have never connected with each other. Three years ago, H58's son moved abroad and she no longer has any contact with him.[83]

U78 and her three children – all under the age of 15 – were taken to the Trnopolje camp in north-west BiH in May 1992. They spent three months there and women were regularly raped.[84] When these women returned, they were often bloody and had cigarette marks on their bodies. 'You couldn't ask them what had happened. You didn't know if you would be next'. U78 suffered brutal beatings in the camp and subsequently had to have one of her kidneys removed. She did not speak about the nights that she was raped. In 1993, she gave birth to a son. She has not told him how he was conceived, and she will never tell her children that she was raped.[85] It is a secret that she will carry with her to her grave. Her children now live abroad and all of them have their own trauma. She worries most about her youngest son. He drinks heavily and frequently shouts at his wife and two children. After U78's husband died, her son asked her if this man was in fact his father. He told her that some children at school were claiming that his real father was a '*četnik*'.[86]

*Prosecutor v. Zdravko Tolimir*, IT- 05-88/2-T, ICTY Trial Chamber Judgement (12 December 2012): §174.

82 After Cerska and Konjević Polje fell to the VRS in March 1993, 'large groups of Bosnian Muslims fled to Srebrenica town which swelled to as many as 50,000 to 60,000 people. While advancing on Srebrenica, the VRS destroyed access points to the town's water supplies; food, medicine, and other essentials were also extremely scarce creating terrible living conditions'. Judgement, *Tolimir*, ibid., at §174.

83 Author interview, 10 February 2015.

84 In the *Stakić* trial at the ICTY, the Trial Chamber heard hearsay evidence that women were raped in the Trnopolje camp. According to the judgment, 'the Trial Chamber did hear evidence from an individual who was herself a victim of rape in the camp and confirmed that several women and young girls, including a 13-year-old one, were raped in the camp or taken out at night for this purpose. Thus, the Trial Chamber is satisfied that rapes did occur in the Trnopolje camp'. *Prosecutor v. Milomir Stakić*, IT-97-24-T, ICTY Trial Chamber Judgement (31 July 2003), §244.

85 This is a powerful example of what van Ee and Kleber term 'strategic silences'. According to them, 'A strategic silence protects the children and their mothers'. Elisa van Ee and Rolf J. Kleber, 'Growing Up under a Shadow: Key Issues in Research on and Treatment of Children Born of Rape', *Child Abuse Review* 22 (2013): 386–397, at 394.

86 Author interview, 26 August 2015. During my fieldwork in BiH, I interviewed a young man who was himself born as a result of rape. He explained that he was often taunted at school; children used to tell him 'You aren't one of us', 'You have Serb blood', 'You're a *četnik*'. He became upset and when his adoptive parents found out what was happening, they told him

The stories of U78 and H58 lend support, in different ways, to Daniel-Wrabetz's argument that children conceived as a result of rape are 'secondary victims'. Like their mothers, they too 'may suffer from varying degrees of discrimination, stigmatization and social exclusion'.[87] To construe them as secondary victims, however, is to focus only on the negatives. There can also be 'happy endings', as B46's story illustrates. At the end of 1992, she was on her way to visit her sister who lived close by. It was beginning to get dark, and today she feels angry with herself that she did not set off much earlier. A car pulled up alongside her and five HVO soldiers got out. They took it in turns to rape her and left her naked at the side of the road. When she realized, several months later, that she was pregnant, it was too late for her to have an abortion. A couple of months after giving birth, she began to love her daughter in a way that she had never thought was possible. The child, as she grew up, began to ask more and more questions about her father. If he was killed in the war, as her mother claimed, where was he buried? Why could she not visit his grave? When she was 15 years old, she learnt the truth. B46 told her everything. She recalled that for several months afterwards, the teenager would not look at her and shunned all physical contact. It was as if she was blaming her mother for everything. Over time, however, the situation began to improve. B46 has drawn enormous strength from her husband, who from the outset accepted her daughter as his own, and she stressed that the three of them are a team.[88]

Three months after I met this Bosniak woman, I had the privilege of speaking to her daughter. This young woman articulated how she has spent years working on herself, in order to accept and to come to terms with everything that happened to her and her mother. She has had many problems. When she was growing up, for example, her peers at school often asked her questions about her father; and it continues to irritate her that she is always required to write the name of both her father and mother on official documents. When she does not give the name of her father, this inevitably invites further questions. On one occasion, she was in a history class at secondary school and the teacher asked her to give her father's name. When she could not do so, everyone in the class started to laugh. After this incident, she did not go to school for ten days. Notwithstanding the difficulties and challenges that she has faced in life, and continues to face, she explained that: 'Over time, I have come to realize that the most important thing is that my mother and I are together. We carry the burden of the past together and this makes it easier for both of us'. She emphasized that the two of them are a huge support to each other, and she wanted to make a film about the positive

the story of how his mother had given birth to him. He was nine years old when he found out the truth. He stressed that he does not blame his mother for abandoning him. 'She was psychologically broken'. He was making plans to meet her. Author interview, 11 May 2015.

87 Daniel-Wrabetz, *supra* note 78, at 36.

88 Author interview, 9 December 2014.

relationships that mothers and their children born of rape can have with each other.[89] When I subsequently had the opportunity to observe at first hand this young woman's relationship with her mother, the powerful bond between them was evident. Their story vividly highlights that 'More research is needed on the factors that lead to positive relationships between a rape survivor and her child'.[90]

*****

This chapter has demonstrated that the long-term legacy of the rapes and sexual violence committed during the Bosnian war extends beyond individual survivors. Their families, marital relations and children have also been affected in various ways. The chapter has also shown that while, on one hand, the family unit can be a critical source of support, on the other hand altered family dynamics and new family-related worries can fuel the long-term effects of rape and sexual violence that survivors experience. In other words, legacy issues at the micro and meso levels are tightly intertwined. This book, however, is not only about the long-term effects of rape and sexual violence. It is also about the significance of those effects for transitional justice. The next two chapters seek to show that although there has been important transitional justice work in BiH, it has not sufficiently addressed the long-term consequences of rape and sexual violence – or the needs arising from them. Chapter 5 focuses specifically on criminal trials.

89 Author interview, 4 March 2015.
90 Carpenter, *supra* note 77, at 33.

Chapter 5

# Prosecuting crimes of rape and sexual violence

## Macro developments, micro realities

If, historically, impunity for wartime acts of rape and sexual violence long remained the default position, as discussed in Chapter 1, a new rhetoric of 'no impunity' now dominates international discourse. Speaking in Colombia in 2012, for example, the then UN Special Representative on Sexual Violence in Conflict, Margot Wallström, underlined that 'Failure to hold to account those responsible means that survivors are even less likely to come forward to report these crimes. Impunity must never be an option'.[1] In a similar vein, the Foreword to the International Protocol on the Documentation and Investigation of Sexual Violence in Conflict declares that:

> For decades – if not centuries – there has been a near-total absence of justice for survivors of rape and sexual violence in conflict. We hope this Protocol will be part of a new global effort to shatter this culture of impunity, helping survivors and deterring people from committing these crimes in the first place.[2]

Alongside such discourse, the international landscape has undergone profound architectural change. From the 1990s onwards, there has been a steady growth of international and hybrid courts. Concomitantly, there have been major legal developments in the prosecution of rape and sexual violence in conflict. The first part of this chapter explores some of these developments, to create a contextual

1 Margot Wallström, 'Statement by the Special Representative of the Secretary-General on Sexual Violence in Conflict Margot Wallström' (19 May 2012), available at: www.un.org/sexualviolenceinconflict/wp-content/uploads/2012/07/SRSG-Statement-Colombia-19-May-2012.pdf (accessed 9 December 2015).

2 Foreign and Commonwealth Office, *International Protocol on the Documentation and Investigation of Sexual Violence in Conflict: Basic Standards of Best Practice on the Documentation of Sexual Violence as a Crime under International Law*, 1st edn (London: Foreign and Commonwealth Office, 2014), 4, available at: www.gov.uk/government/uploads/system/uploads/attachment_data/file/319054/PSVI_protocol_web.pdf (accessed 11 February 2016).

backdrop. It is essential, however, not to lose sight of survivors themselves. Consideration must be given to their own role in the fight against impunity, yet, as Stover has underlined, 'little research has been undertaken to understand the experiences, thoughts, or feelings of witnesses as they pass through the judicial process'.[3] The second part of the chapter, therefore, is about the experiential dimensions of criminal trials, from the perspective of survivors of rape and sexual violence in BiH. Of the 79 survivors who participated in this research, 39 had testified in court. Of these, three[4] had testified at the ICTY and the rest had testified in local courts. A further two interviewees were waiting to testify.

By juxtaposing macro developments in the prosecution of rape and sexual violence with the micro level of survivors' actual experiences in court, the aim of this chapter is not to diminish the importance of criminal trials in transitional justice processes. The point, rather, is to caution against an over-reliance on criminal trials and to draw out some of their limitations. The criminal justice process can leave some survivors feeling dissatisfied, bitter and/or used, thereby conceivably fuelling some of the long-term psychological effects of rape and sexual violence. More fundamentally, although criminal trials can potentially provide survivors with legal justice, with answers to some of their questions and with an official acknowledgement that they have been wronged, they do not address survivors' long-term needs – and specifically their everyday practical needs.

## From the top down: criminal trials and international developments

The fight against impunity for rape and sexual violence in conflict is necessarily long and complex, a fact that reflects some of the enormous challenges inherent in prosecuting these crimes – including difficulties of obtaining evidence and finding survivors who are willing to testify. It is estimated, for example, that between 100,000 and 250,000 women were raped during the Rwandan genocide in 1994.[5] In its efforts to investigate and bring to trial some of these crimes, the Office of the Prosecutor (OTP) at the ICTR[6] found that 'Female victims were often reluctant to discuss sexual violence with men, particularly younger men. Some found it difficult to open up to men from a different nationality'.[7]

3 Eric Stover, *The Witnesses: War Crimes and the Promise of Justice in The Hague* (Philadelphia: University of Pennsylvania Press, 2007), 27.
4 One of these three interviewees had testified about the crimes committed in her village, rather than about the crimes specifically committed against her.
5 UN, 'Outreach Programme on the Rwanda Genocide and the United Nations – Background Information on Sexual Violence used as a Tool of War' (n.d.), available at: www.un.org/en/preventgenocide/rwanda/about/bgsexualviolence.shtml (accessed 5 March 2016).
6 The Tribunal closed on 31 December 2015.
7 ICTR, *Prosecution of Sexual Violence: Best Practices Manual for the Investigation and Prosecution of Sexual Violence Crimes in Post-Conflict Regions – Lessons Learned from the Office*

Many survivors were also afraid to testify and concerned about the possible consequences of doing so, including stigmatization, social ostracism and reprisals from the accused's family.[8]

Despite the challenges, there have been major strides forward in the international prosecution of rape and sexual violence. Discussing the work of the ICTY and ICTR, for example, a former president of the Hague Tribunal commented in 2000 that: 'In practical terms, the judgments speak about what was once considered to be unspeakable and, thus, acknowledge the suffering of victims that has traditionally been ignored'.[9] Focusing particularly (although not exclusively) on the ICTY as the institution whose work is most relevant to BiH, this first section examines three important qualitative developments in the international prosecution of rape and sexual violence, namely definitional, gender-sensitive and procedural developments.

### *The evolving definition of rape and the issue of non-consent*

In many national jurisdictions, non-consent is an elemental part of the legal definition of rape. In England and Wales, for example, section 1 of the Sexual Offences Act 2003 states that:

> (1) A person (A) commits an offence [rape] if—
> (a) he intentionally penetrates the vagina, anus or mouth of another person (B) with his penis,
> (b) B does not consent to the penetration, and
> (c) A does not reasonably believe that B consents.
>
> (2) Whether a belief is reasonable is to be determined having regard to all the circumstances, including any steps A has taken to ascertain whether B consents.[10]

In international law, no definition of rape existed until the late 1990s. Rape was defined for the first time in the *Akayesu* trial at the ICTR. The original indictment against Jean-Paul Akayesu – a former teacher who served as the mayor of Taba commune during the Rwandan genocide – did not include charges of sexual violence. After some of the witnesses in the case began to describe acts of rape

*of the Prosecutor for the International Criminal Tribunal for Rwanda* (30 January 2014), §22, available at: http://unictr.unmict.org/sites/unictr.org/files/legal-library/140130_prosecution_of_sexual_violence.pdf (accessed 8 April 2016).

8 Ibid.

9 Gabrielle Kirk McDonald, 'Crimes of Sexual Violence: The Experience of the International Criminal Tribunal', *Columbia Journal of International Law* 39 (2000): 1–18, at 15.

10 Sexual Offences Act (2003), available at: www.legislation.gov.uk/ukpga/2003/42/pdfs/ukpga_20030042_en.pdf (accessed 15 July 2016).

and sexual violence that had occurred,[11] however, the indictment was accordingly amended and the Trial Chamber turned its attention to crucial definitional issues. Underlining that 'rape is a form of aggression and that the central elements of the crime of rape cannot be captured in a mechanical description of objects and body parts',[12] it adopted a broad definition of rape as entailing 'a physical invasion of a sexual nature, committed on a person under circumstances which are coercive'.[13] Similarly defining sexual violence,[14] the Trial Chamber's emphasis on coercive circumstances foregrounded the environment in which these crimes occur during war and armed conflict,[15] rather than the actions or behaviour of a particular victim. Feminists such as Catharine MacKinnon accordingly praised the judgement as having 'built into its rape definition the context of violent inequality common to the crimes the ad hoc tribunals [the ICTR and ICTY] are statutorily authorized to prosecute'.[16]

In the same year, one of the first cases at the ICTY focused, inter alia, on the rape of two Bosnian Serb women in the Čelebići camp in the municipality of Konjic. Convicting Hazim Delić, the deputy camp commander, of rape as an act of torture (a violation of the laws or customs of war and a grave breach of the 1949 Geneva Conventions), the Trial Chamber saw no reason to depart from the *Akayesu* definition of rape.[17] Similarly, in the *Furundžija* trial at the ICTY, which centred on the rape, sexual assault and physical abuse of a Bosnian Muslim woman (Witness A), there was no significant departure from the *Akayesu* definition of rape – except insofar as the Trial Chamber gave greater prominence to the corporeal 'mechanics' of the crime.[18] Consent was not raised as an issue; and even if it had had been, the Trial Chamber made clear that it would have been irrelevant. Witness A was in captivity, and 'any form of captivity vitiates consent'.[19]

11 *Prosecutor v. Jean-Paul Akayesu*, ICTR-96-4-T, ICTR Trial Chamber Judgement (2 September 1998), §416.
12 Ibid., at §687.
13 Ibid., at §688.
14 Ibid.
15 Obote-Odoro underscores that '*Akayesu* considers the reality of wartime violence'. Alex Obote-Odora, 'Rape and Sexual Violence in International Law: ICTR Contribution', *New England Journal of International and Comparative Law* 12 (2005): 135–159, at 151.
16 Catharine A. MacKinnon, 'Defining Rape Internationally: A Comment on Akayesu', *Columbia Journal of Transnational Law* 44 (2006): 940–958, at 955.
17 *Prosecutor v. Zejnil Delalić, Pavo Mucić, Hazim Delić and Esad Landžo*, IT-96-21-T, ICTY Trial Chamber Judgement (16 November 1998), §479.
18 The *Furundžija* Trial Chamber defined rape as: '(i) the sexual penetration, however slight: (a) of the vagina or anus of the victim by the penis of the perpetrator or any other object used by the perpetrator; or (b) of the mouth of the victim by the penis of the perpetrator; (ii) by coercion or force or threat of force against the victim or a third person'. *Prosecutor v. Anto Furundžija*, IT-95-17/1-T, ICTY Trial Chamber Judgement (10 December 1998), §185.
19 Ibid., at §271.

The 'rise' of consent primarily occurred in the ICTY's leading case on rape and sexual violence, in which three (Bosnian Serb) defendants – Dragoljub Kunarac, Radomir Kovač and Zoran Vuković – stood accused of raping Bosnian Muslim women and girls detained in camps and apartments in the eastern Bosnian town of Foča in 1992. The Trial Chamber largely endorsed the *Furundžija* definition of rape, but it emphasized that there are other factors besides force or threat of force which could render an act of sexual penetration '*non-voluntary or non-consensual* on the part of the victim'.[20] For the Trial Chamber in *Kunarac et al.*, thus, the key issue was not whether force had been used or threatened, but rather whether an individual's *sexual autonomy* had been violated[21] – meaning that s/he had not freely consented to the act of sexual penetration or been a voluntary participant.[22] Although the Trial Chamber explicitly included the word 'consent' in its definition of rape,[23] it also effectively circumscribed it by giving precedence to the circumstances in which a person's consent is given.[24] As Grewal argues, 'the Trial Chamber seemed to be explicitly recognizing the importance of taking into account coercive circumstances that may impact on an individual's ability to make free and informed decisions'.[25]

Some commentators maintain that to even discuss the concept of consent in situations of war and armed conflict is inappropriate.[26] Indeed, the *Kunarac et al.* judgement itself makes clear that in certain circumstances, such as captivity and enslavement,[27] the issue of consent becomes irrelevant because an individual cannot exercise autonomy or freedom of choice.[28] The Appeals Chamber has

20 *Prosecutor v. Dragoljub Kunarac, Radomir Kovač and Zoran Vuković*, IT-96-23-T&IT-96-23/1-T, ICTY Trial Chamber Judgement (22 February 2001), §438.

21 Ibid., at §440.

22 Ibid., at §440, §457.

23 Rape is an act of sexual penetration, however slight, that occurs 'without the consent of the victim'. Ibid., at §460.

24 The Trial Chamber stressed that 'Consent for this purpose must be consent given voluntarily, as a result of the victim's free will, assessed in the context of the surrounding circumstances'. Ibid.

25 Kiran Grewal, 'The Protection of Sexual Autonomy under International Criminal Law: The International Criminal Court and the Challenge of Defining Rape', *Journal of International Criminal Justice* 10 (2012): 373–396, at 380.

26 See, for example, Wolfgang Schomburg and Ines Peterson, 'Genuine Consent to Sexual Violence under International Criminal Law', *American Journal of International Law* 101 (2007): 121–140, at 139; Alison Cole, '*Prosecutor v. Gacumbitsi*: The New Definition for Prosecuting Rape under International Law', *International Criminal Law Review* 8 (2008): 55–85, at 75.

27 All three defendants in this case were convicted of rape (as a crime against humanity and as a violation of the laws or customs of war) and sentenced to prison terms of between 12 and 28 years.

28 Judgement, *Kunarac et al.*, *supra* note 20, at §542. The ICTR largely followed the *Kunarac* definition. See, for example, *Prosecutor v. Laurent Semanza*, ICTR-97-20-T, ICTR Trial Chamber Judgement (15 May 2003), §345; *Prosecutor v. Sylvestre Gacumbitsi*, ICTR-2001-64-A, ICTR Appeal Chamber Judgement (7 July 2006), §153. In *Muhimana*, the Trial

reiterated this point.[29] Although this particular body of jurisprudence explicitly includes consent as an element of the crime of rape, the contextualization of consent and the requirement of true/voluntary consent are important conceptual developments that acknowledge situational realities. This, in turn, represents a more holistic approach to rape.

The ICC has gone one step further by effectively de-centring the issue of consent, as highlighted in the 2016 *Bemba* case. What is immediately striking about the judgement is the fact that it contains very few references to consent; and indeed the judges expressly underscored that 'the victim's lack of consent is not a legal element of the crime of rape under the Statute'.[30] Rather, the Trial Chamber focused on the four possible circumstances for rape which are set out in the Elements of Crimes.[31] Only the fourth of these circumstances refers to

Chamber maintained that the *Kunarac* definition was not substantially incompatible with *Akayesu*. It therefore endorsed 'the conceptual definition of rape established in *Akayesu*, which encompasses the elements set out in *Kunarac*'. *Prosecutor v. Mikaeli Muhimana*, ICTR-95-1B-T, ICTR Trial Chamber Judgement (28 April 2005), §551. The SCSL adopted the *Kunarac* approach to consent in the AFRC case; *Prosecutor v. Alex Tamba Brima, Brima Bazzy Kamara and Santigie Borbor Kanu*, SCSL-04-16-T, SCSL Trial Chamber Judgement (20 June 2007), §694. According to Oosterveld, however, 'The [SCSL] Trial Chamber's lack of deeper explanation or examination is disappointing'. Valerie Oosterveld, 'The Special Court for Sierra Leone's Consideration of Gender-Based Violence: Contributing to Transitional Justice?' *Human Rights Review* 10 (2009): 73–98, at 80. In the RUF case at the SCSL, in contrast, the Trial Chamber drew on the definition of rape set out in the ICC's Elements of Crimes and used the terminology of victims being 'incapable' of giving genuine consent. See *Prosecutor v. Issa Hassan Sesay, Morris Kallon and Augustine Gbao*, SCSL-04-15-T, SCSL Trial Chamber Judgement (2 March 2009), §1290, §1577. However, while footnote 16 of the ICC's Elements of Crimes (see note 31) states that 'It is understood that a person may be incapable of giving genuine consent if affected by natural, induced or age-related incapacity', the Trial Chamber in the RUF case opined that this is too restrictive. Judgement, *Sesay et al.*, at §149. Ultimately, therefore, it effectively combined the *Kunarac* definition with the definition contained in the Elements of Crimes, by linking a person's incapacity to give genuine consent with the coercive circumstances that typically prevail in conflict situations. Judgement, *Sesay et al.*, at §147.

29 *Prosecutor v. Dragoljub Kunarac, Radomir Kovač and Zoran Vuković* IT-96-23 & IT-96-23/1-A, ICTY Appeal Chamber Judgement (12 June 2002), §130; Appeal judgement, *Gacumbitsi*, ibid., at §155.

30 *Prosecutor v. Jean-Pierre Bemba Gombo*, ICC-01/05-01/08-3343, ICC Trial Chamber Judgement (2 March 2016), §105.

31 Accompanying the Rome Statute, the Elements of Crimes define rape (as a crime against humanity or as a war crime) as occurring when: '1. The perpetrator invaded the body of a person by conduct resulting in penetration, however slight, of any part of the body of the victim or of the perpetrator with a sexual organ, or of the anal or genital opening of the victim with any object or any other part of the body. 2. The invasion was committed by force, or by threat of force or coercion, such as that caused by fear of violence, duress, detention, psychological oppression or abuse of power, against such person or another person, or by taking advantage of a coercive environment, or the invasion was committed against a person incapable of giving genuine consent'. ICC, *Elements of Crimes* (2002/2010), Article 7(1)(g)-1, Article 8(2)(b)(xxii)-1, available

consent and stipulates that 'the invasion was committed against a person incapable of giving genuine consent'. Crucially, therefore, the Elements of Crimes appear to draw a clear distinction between circumstances and consent, and the *Bemba* judgement reinforces this. It underscores that 'where "force", "threat of force or coercion", or "taking advantage of a coercive environment" is proven, the Chamber considers that the Prosecution does not need to prove the victim's lack of consent'.[32] Hence, a significant way in which the *Bemba* judgement differs from existing international jurisprudence on rape is that it treats circumstances – as set out in the ICC's Elements of Crimes – as important in their own right, rather than in the more limited sense of whether they vitiate consent. This creates the space for a greater focus on the experiential dimensions of rape from the perspective of survivors.[33]

## *Gender-sensitive justice*

*Akayesu* was not only the first case to define rape in international law, but also 'the first case in history that rendered a conviction for either genocide or crimes against humanity through sexual violence'.[34] Although the 1948 Convention on the Prevention and Punishment of the Crime of Genocide[35] does not list rape as a possible *actus reus* of genocide, the *Akayesu* Trial Chamber took the position that rape can constitute an act of genocide if committed with the requisite genocidal intent.[36] Adjudging that this condition was met in Rwanda, it construed the widespread use of rape and sexual violence during the genocide as an integral part of the destruction of the Tutsi ethnic group – 'destruction of the spirit, of the will to live, and of life itself'.[37] Fatou Bensouda, the Prosecutor of the ICC, has thus described the *Akayesu* judgement as constituting '[p]erhaps the most groundbreaking decision advancing gender jurisprudence worldwide'.[38]

at: www.icc-cpi.int/NR/rdonlyres/336923D8-A6AD-40EC-AD7B-45BF9DE73D56/0/ElementsOfCrimesEng.pdf (accessed 2 December 2015).

32 Judgement, *Bemba, supra* note 30, at §106.

33 Janine N. Clark, 'The First Rape Conviction at the ICC: An Analysis of the Bemba Judgement', *Journal of International Criminal Justice* 14 (2016): 667–687.

34 Obote-Odora, *supra* note 15, at 146. Ultimately, the Trial Chamber found Akayesu guilty on nine of the 15 counts laid out in the amended indictment, including rape as both genocide and as a crime against humanity. He was sentenced to life imprisonment and this was upheld on appeal.

35 UN, *Convention on the Prevention and Punishment of the Crime of Genocide* (9 December 1948), available at: https://treaties.un.org/doc/publication/unts/volume%2078/volume-78-i-1021-english.pdf (accessed 9 May 2016).

36 Judgement, *Akayesu, supra* note 11, at §731.

37 Ibid., at §732. See also §508.

38 Fatou Bensouda, '"Gender Justice and the ICC: Progress and Reflections": International Conference: 10 Years Review of the ICC. Justice for All? The International Criminal Court' (14 February 2012), available at: www.icc-cpi.int/NR/rdonlyres/FED13DAF-3916-4E94-9028 123C4D9BB0C9/0/StatementgenderSydeny140212.pdf (accessed 11 May 2016).

The *Akayesu* Trial Chamber powerfully communicated the gravity of rape and sexual violence, and international jurisprudence has continued to convey this message. In *Delalić et al.*, for example, the ICTY confirmed – echoing *Akayesu*[39] – that rape can constitute an act of torture;[40] in *Kunarac et al.*, the trial judges underscored that 'Rape is one of the worst sufferings a human being can inflict upon another';[41] and at the SCSL, the RUF case resulted in 'the first-ever international convictions for the crime against humanity of sexual slavery and of forced marriage (as an inhumane act)'.[42] In that case, the Trial Chamber also referred to sexual violence as an 'act of terrorism'.[43]

International courts have also made some effort to highlight the important reality that rape and sexual violence in conflict affect men as well as women.[44] As defined by the Trial Chamber in the RUF case, for example, one of the constitutive elements of rape is that:

> The Accused invaded the body of a person by conduct resulting in penetration, however slight, of any part of the body of the victim *or of the Accused* with a sexual organ, or of the anal or genital opening of the victim with any object or any other part of the body.[45]

This is highly progressive; it not only acknowledges that a male victim may be penetrated, but also that he may himself be forced to penetrate the body of the perpetrator with his own penis. The ICC's Elements of Crimes similarly allow for this eventuality.[46] The RUF case is also noteworthy because it documents heinous

39 *Akayesu*, *supra* note 11, at §597.

40 Judgement, *Delalić et al.*, *supra* note 17, at §496.

41 Judgement, *Kunarac et al.*, *supra* note 20, at §655.

42 Valerie Oosterveld, 'The Gender Jurisprudence of the Special Court for Sierra Leone: Progress in the Revolutionary United Front Judgements', *Cornell International Law Journal* 44 (2011): 49–74, at 60. The Trial Chamber noted that 'acts which could be classified as sexual slavery have been prosecuted as enslavement in the past. In the *Kunarac* case, for instance… the ICTY Appeals Chamber emphasised that "it finds that enslavement, even if based on sexual exploitation, is a distinct offence from that of rape"'. Judgement, *Sesay et al.*, *supra* note 28, at § 155, citing Appeal Judgement, *Kunarac et al.*, *supra* note 29, at §186.

43 Judgement, *Sesay et al.*, *supra* note 28 at §1345, §1355.

44 See, for example, ICTR *supra* note 7, at §14. Kapur and Muddell, however, note that at the ICTR, 'Prosecutor v. Niyitegeka was the only case in which sexual violence against men was charged in the indictment and resulted in a conviction, but not as sexual violence. Instead, participation in castrating a prominent Tutsi man and displaying his mutilated genitalia on a stake was considered as an "other inhumane act" and as a "crime against humanity" without any reference to its sexual nature'. Amrita Kapur and Kelli Muddell, *When No One Calls it Rape: Addressing Sexual Violence against Men and Boys in Transitional Contexts*, ICTJ (December 2016), 19, available at: www.ictj.org/sites/default/files/ICTJ_Report_SexualViolenceMen_2016.pdf (accessed 9 October 2016). See *Prosecutor v. Eliezer Niyitegeka*, ICTR-96-14-T, ICTR Judgement and Sentence (16 May 2003), §303.

45 Judgement, *Sesay et al.*, *supra* note 28, at §145 (author's emphasis).

46 ICC, *supra* note 31, at Article 7(1)(g)-1(1) and Article 8(2)(b)(xxii)-1(1).

sexual abuses against both men and women in the Sierra Leone civil war. The judgement notes, for example, that 21 male and female civilians were captured in Bomboafuidu in eastern Sierra Leone in early 1998. They were forced to have sex with each other, and 'The sexual violence was combined with sexual mutilations, with the rebels slitting the private parts of several male and female civilians with a knife'.[47] More recently, in the *Bemba* trial at the ICC, Trial Chamber III found Jean-Pierre Bemba Gombo – the leader of the *Mouvement de libération du Congo* (MLC) and the former vice-president of the DRC – responsible, as a superior, for the crimes committed by MLC soldiers in the Central African Republic. He was found guilty, inter alia, of rape as a war crime and as a crime against humanity, and the judgement discusses the suffering of male as well as female victims.[48]

The ICTY was the first international court to prosecute sexual violence against men. Indeed, the Tribunal's very first trial – which focused on crimes committed in camps in north-west BiH – addressed, inter alia, the gruesome sexual mutilation of a male prisoner in the Omarska camp. According to the trial judgement:

> Witness H was threatened with a knife that both his eyes would be cut out if he did not hold Fikret Harambašić's mouth closed to prevent him from screaming; G was then made to lie between the naked Fikret Harambašić's legs and, while the latter struggled, hit and bite his genitals. G then bit off one of Fikret Harambašić's testicles and spat it out and was told he was free to leave… Fikret Harambašić has not been seen or heard of since.[49]

The Trial Chamber concluded that Duško Tadić – a local Serb politician in the town of Kozarac – did not take an active part in this incident. Nevertheless, because he was present on the hangar floor when it occurred,[50] he thereby 'aided and encouraged the group of men actively taking part in the assault'.[51] He was found guilty of aiding and abetting cruel treatment (a violation of the laws or customs of law) and inhumane acts (a crime against humanity). According to the ICTY's website, *Tadić* represents one of its 'landmark cases' on sexual violence.[52] One of the criticisms of the case, however, is that 'neither the indictment nor the judgment acknowledges the sexual nature of the offences, but rather identifies them variously as cruel treatment, an inhumane act, or inhuman act'.[53] This is not

47 Judgement, *Sesay et al.*, *supra* note 28, at §1208.
48 Judgement, *Bemba*, *supra* note 30, at §494.
49 *Prosecutor v. Duško Tadić*, IT-94-1-T, ICTY Trial Chamber Opinion and Judgement (7 May 1997), at §206.
50 Ibid., at §237.
51 *Prosecutor v. Duško Tadić*, IT-94-1-T, ICTY Sentencing Judgement (14 July 1997), at §22. Tadić was sentenced to 20 years' imprisonment for this and other crimes. He was granted early release in July 2008.
52 See www.icty.org/en/in-focus/crimes-sexual-violence/landmark-cases
53 Kapur and, Muddell, *supra* note 44, at 17.

entirely true. The second amended indictment, for example, states that a group of Serb soldiers forced two prisoners, 'G' and 'H', 'to commit oral sexual acts on HARAMBAŠIĆ and forced "G" to sexually mutilate him';[54] and the trial judgement refers to the 'sexual assault on Fikret Harambašić',[55] as well as to 'sexual mutilation'.[56] Yet, it is also the case that this mutilation is discussed in the broader context of 'beatings of great severity and other grievous acts of violence' inflicted on a group of male prisoners.[57] To some extent, this detracts from the serious sexual violence against Harambašić.[58]

Acts of sexual violence were also committed against some of the Serb men detained in the Čelebići camp. Esad Landžo, for example, who was a guard in the camp, 'placed a burning fuse-cord directly against [prisoner] Vukašin Mrkajić's bare skin in the genital area, thereby inflicting serious pain and injury upon him'.[59] He also forced two brothers to perform fellatio on each other.[60] Landžo was not, however, charged with any sexual violence, although the Trial Chamber noted 'the heinous nature of the acts involved and the depravity of mind necessary to conceive of and inflict such forms of suffering'.[61] Vis-à-vis the forced fellatio, the Trial Chamber opined that 'the aforementioned act could constitute rape for which liability could have been found if pleaded in the appropriate manner'.[62] Unfortunately, it failed to elaborate on this point.

The issue of rape arose again in the *Todorović* case. Stevan Todorović, the chief of police and a member of the Serb crisis staff in Bosanski Šamac in the Posavina area of northern BiH, admitted that he kicked and beat Witness A in the genital area; that he instructed Witness A to bite into another man's penis;[63] and that he ordered Witness C and Witness D, and Witness E and Witness F, to perform oral sex on each other.[64] These crimes were initially charged, inter alia, as rape (crime

54 *Prosecutor v. Duško Tadić, Goran Borovnica*, IT-94-1-I, Second Amended Indictment (14 December 1995), §6.
55 Opinion and Judgement, *Tadić, supra* note 49, at §198; see also §222.
56 Ibid., at §237.
57 Opinion and Judgement, *Tadić, supra* note 49, at §726.
58 It should also be noted, however, that 'women's groups criticized the OTP for inappropriately prioritizing charges involving sexual violence crimes against men over those committed against women'. Michelle Jarvis and Kate Vigneswaran, 'Challenges to Successful Outcomes in Sexual Violence Cases', in Serge Brammertz and Michelle Jarvis (eds), *Prosecuting Conflict-Related Sexual Violence at the ICTY* (Oxford: Oxford University Press, 2016), 33–72, at 56.
59 Judgement, *Delalić et al., supra* note 17, at §1039.
60 Ibid., at § 1065. Landžo was convicted of grave breaches of the Geneva Conventions (wilful killing, torture, wilfully causing great suffering or serious injury) and sentenced to 15 years' imprisonment.
61 Ibid., at §1275.
62 Ibid., at §1066.
63 *Prosecutor v. Stevan Todorović*, IT-95–9/1-S, ICTY Trial Chamber Sentencing Judgement (31 July 2001), §38.
64 Ibid., at §§39–40.

against humanity).[65] However, after Todorović pleaded guilty to count one of the indictment – namely persecutions (as a crime against humanity) – the other charges against him were dropped. Count one referred, in part, to 'the murders, sexual assaults and repeated beatings of numerous Bosnian Croats, Bosnian Muslims and other non-Serb civilians detained in various detention camps in and around the Bosanski Šamac municipality'.[66] Within the sentencing judgement, therefore, there is important acknowledgement of the fact that acts of sexual violence against men occurred.[67] Nevertheless, the case would have potentially had a far greater impact if Todorović had been convicted of rape as a crime against humanity.

After initially professing his innocence, Ranko Češić – a member of the Intervention Platoon of the Bosnian Serb Police Reserve Corps at the Brčko police station – pleaded guilty to six counts of crimes against humanity and six counts of violations of the laws or customs of war. Among the crimes that he committed in Brčko, 'Ranko Češić admitted that, on approximately 11 May 1992, he intentionally forced, at gunpoint, two Muslim brothers detained at Luka Camp to perform fellatio on each other in the presence of others'.[68] This was charged as both cruel and degrading treatment (violations of the laws or customs of war) and rape (crime against humanity). The *Furundžija* case made clear that forced oral penetration is sufficient to constitute rape.[69] However, in *Češić*, it was not the defendant himself who orally penetrated the two brothers with his penis, and similarly he did not force them to penetrate him (a scenario which both the SCSL and ICC have envisaged as previously noted). Count 8 of the third amended indictment stated that rape 'includes other forms of sexual violence',[70] but unfortunately this point is not discussed in the judgement. What the judges did make clear, however, is that regardless of whether the victims are male or female, crimes of sexual violence are intrinsically humiliating – and are frequently committed in circumstances that create additional or cumulative humiliation. When Češić forced the two brothers to perform fellatio on each other, for example, he left the office door open to allow several camp guards to watch and laugh,[71] which also

65 *Prosecutor v. Blagoje Simić, Milan Simić, Miroslav Tadić, Stevan Todorović and Simo Zarić*, IT-95–9, Second Amended Indictment (19 November 1998), §44 (count 16), §45 (count 19), §46 (count 22).
66 Ibid., at §34(b).
67 See, for example, Judgement, *Todorović, supra* note 63, at §66.
68 *Prosecutor v. Ranko Češić*, IT-95-10/1-S, ICTY Trial Chamber Sentencing Judgement (11 March 2004), §13.
69 Judgement, *Furundžija, supra* note 18, at §183.
70 *Prosecutor v. Ranko Češić*, IT-95-10/1-PT, Third Amended Indictment (26 November 2002), §15.
71 Judgement, *Češić, supra* note 68, at §14. Češić was sentenced to 18 years' imprisonment. In other cases, similarly, the ICTY has remarked that acts of sexual violence against men

underscores that the line between violence and entertainment can be extremely thin.[72]

The Tribunal's jurisprudence, in short, includes 'a substantial number of documented incidents of sexual violence perpetrated against males'.[73] Cases like *Tadić* and *Češić* critically draw attention to the diverse uses of gender-based violence in situations of war and armed conflict. By highlighting the vulnerability of male bodies and sexual organs, they also complexify the dominant binary narrative of male perpetrators and female victims.[74] The use of rape and sexual violence against men remains an under-researched aspect of the Bosnian war, and feminist scholars and writers have heavily 'emphasized male-on-female sexual violence as the harm that needed to be addressed by the ICTY'.[75] However, the Tribunal's work provides a valuable documentary record that sexual violence against men did occur.

### *Procedural innovations*

When prosecuting rape and sexual violence, one of the major challenges that courts necessarily face is to find witnesses who are willing to testify. De Brouwer, for example, points out that when they appear in court, 'the demanding legal structure may require victims to speak before complete strangers in detail about very intimate and painful experiences'.[76] Political considerations and security

are often deeply humiliating. See, for example, *Prosecutor v. Mladen Naletić and Vinko Martinović*, IT-98-34-T, ICTY Trial Chamber Judgement (31 March 2003), §464.

72 Randall Collins, *Violence: A Micro-Sociological Theory* (Princeton, NJ: Princeton University Press, 2008), 242.

73 Saeeda Verrall, 'The Picture of Sexual Violence in the Former Yugoslavia Conflicts as Reflected in ICTY Judgements', in Serge Brammertz and Michelle Jarvis (eds), *Prosecuting Conflict-Related Sexual Violence at the ICTY* (Oxford: Oxford University Press, 2016), 299–334, at 313. See also *Prosecutor v. Mićo Stanišić and Stojan Župljanin*, IT-08-91-T, ICTY Trial Chamber Judgement, Vol. I (8 March 2013), §1599; *Prosecutor v. Jadranko Prlić, Bruno Stojić, Slobodan Praljak, Milivoj Petković, Valentin Ćorić and Berislav Pušić*, IT-04-74-T, ICTY Trial Chamber Judgement, Vol. II (29 May 2013), §§169–170.

74 See also *Prosecutor v. Pauline Nyiramasuhuko, Arsène Shalom Ntahobali, Sylvain Nsabimana, Alphonse Nteziryayo, Joseph Kanyabashi and Élie Ndayambaje*, ICTR-98-42-T, ICTR Trial Chamber Judgement and Sentence (24 June 2011).

75 Karen Engle, 'Feminism and its (Dis)contents: Criminalizing Wartime Rape in Bosnia and Herzegovina', *American Journal of International Law* 99 (2005): 778–816, at 814. According to MacKinnon, for example, 'Rape is a daily act by men against women; it is always an act of domination by men over women'. Catharine A. MacKinnon, 'Rape, Genocide and Women's Human Rights', in Alexandra Stiglmayer (ed.), *Mass Rape: The War against Women in Bosnia-Herzegovina* (Lincoln, NE: University of Nebraska Press, 1997), 183–196, at 188.

76 Anne-Marie de Brouwer, 'The Importance of Understanding Sexual Violence in Conflict for Investigation and Prosecution Purposes', *Cornell International Law Journal* 48 (2015): 639–666, at 649–650.

concerns may also deter survivors from giving testimony. In the Civil Defence Forces (CDF)[77] case at the SCSL, for example, the original indictment against the defendants did not include any charges of sexual violence. According to Grewal, 'It seems a significant reason for this was that their victims were frequently from among those they were allegedly protecting and this, combined with their hero status, made women very reluctant to come forward and accuse "their own" men'.[78]

International courts have accordingly adopted a number of important and innovative procedures to address some of the concerns that survivors may have about testifying and to try and make the process easier for them. Although it cannot be automatically assumed that every survivor will want his/her identity to be concealed from the public,[79] these courts have put in place a series of protective measures for those who do wish to remain anonymous. Rule 75 of the ICTY's Rules of Procedure and Evidence (RPE), for example, which is divided into 11 subsections, provides for various measures for the protection of victims and witnesses, including the assignment of a pseudonym and the removal of names and other identifying information from the ICTY's public records.[80] Additionally, Rule 79(A) states that 'The Trial Chamber may order that the press and the public be excluded from all or part of the proceedings', on the grounds of public order or morality, the safety and security of a victim/witness or the protection of the interests of justice.[81] The Tribunal's Victims and Witnesses Section (VWS), which is part of the Registry, organizes the necessary protective measures for

77 The CDF was a pro-government militia that fought against the RUF and the AFRC during the civil war in Sierra Leone.

78 Grewal, *supra* note 25, at 71. When it had gathered sufficient evidence of sexual violence committed by the CDF, the Prosecution requested permission to amend the original indictment but this was refused, on the grounds that it would cause undue delays in the trial process. Highly critical of the Majority's decision (Justice Boutet dissented), Kelsall and Stepakoff argue that the judges 'seemed to ignore the genuine fear of reprisals victim-witnesses in the CDF case may have had'. Michelle S. Kelsall and Shanee Stepakoff, ' "When We Wanted to Talk about Rape": Silencing Sexual Violence at the Special Court for Sierra Leone', *International Journal of Transitional Justice* 1 (2007): 355–374, at 361.

79 Jarvis and Vigneswaran – both from the ICTY – emphasize that 'Our experience strongly reinforces the fact that each sexual violence victim has specific requirements and makes individual choices based upon their own personal circumstances'. Jarvis and Vigneswaran, *supra* note 58, at 42.

80 ICTY, *Rules of Procedure and Evidence* (8 July 2015), available at: www.icty.org/x/file/Legal%20Library/Rules_procedure_evidence/IT032Rev50_en.pdf (accessed 8 October 2016).

81 Ibid. The Tribunal's website states that as of June 2015, 'Over a quarter of the total number of witnesses [not just survivors of rape and sexual violence] testified with some type of protective measure. The majority of these witnesses had their testimony conducted in open court with certain steps introduced such as the name being withheld from the public or the audio and visual broadcast of proceedings being distorted to safeguard the identity of the witness'. ICTY, 'Witness Statistics' (30 June 2015), available at: www.icty.org/en/about/registry/witnesses/statistics (accessed 7 August 2016).

individual witnesses. It also provides vital logistical assistance and psycho-social support when they arrive in The Hague.[82]

The Rome Statute similarly contains a number of vital provisions regarding witness support and protection. Article 43(6), for example, requires that the Victim and Witnesses Unit (VWU) 'shall include staff with expertise in trauma, including trauma related to crimes of sexual violence';[83] and Article 68(2) states that 'As an exception to the principle of public hearings provided for in Article 67, the Chambers of the Court may, to protect victims and witnesses or an accused, conduct any part of the proceedings *in camera* or allow the presentation of evidence by electronic or other special means'.[84] It adds that these protective measures 'shall be implemented' in cases involving victims of sexual violence or child victims/witnesses, unless the Court – having regard to all the circumstances and, in particular, the views of the victim or witness – orders otherwise.[85] Once witnesses arrive in The Hague, they receive comprehensive support from the VWU. While a significant part of this consists of psycho-social support, some practical needs are also addressed. For example,

> The VWU provides welcome packages to help ease witnesses' acclimation to the social and physical environment of The Hague. When needed, the packages include a toiletries kit analogous to those provided to travelers by airlines. Items also include a fleece jacket, closed-toe shoes, a blanket and shawls to ease the temperature shock upon arrival in The Hague.[86]

To aid survivors, international courts have also adopted important rules regarding testimony in cases involving rape and sexual violence. Rule 96 of the ICTY's RPE, for example, states, inter alia, that 'no corroboration of the victim's testimony shall be required'.[87] While survivors may of course face tough questions

82 According to a recent report co-authored by staff from the VWS and the University of North Texas, 'As many witnesses report, the fact that most have never testified before in their own home country, not even for traffic violations, puts additional burdens on them to perform well while having no comparable experience on which to draw'. Kimi King, James Meernik, Sara Rubert, Tiago de Smit and Helena V. Schoorl, *Echoes of Testimonies: A Pilot Study into the Long-Term Impact of Bearing Witness before the ICTY* (June 2016), 16, available at: www.icty.org/x/file/About/Registry/Witnesses/Echoes-Full-Report_EN.pdf (accessed 3 September 2016).

83 ICC, *Rome Statute of the International Criminal Court* (17 July 1998), Article 46(3), available at: www.icc-cpi.int/nr/rdonlyres/ea9aeff7-5752-4f84-be94-0a655eb30e16/0/rome_statute_english.pdf (accessed 8 July 2016).

84 Ibid., at Article 68(2).

85 Ibid.

86 Human Rights Centre, UC Berkeley School of Law, *Bearing Witness at the International Criminal Court: An Interview Survey of 109 Witnesses* (June 2009), 22, available at: www.law.berkeley.edu/files/HRC/Bearing-Witness_FINAL(3).pdf (accessed 28 May 2016).

87 ICTY, *supra* note 80. In the aforementioned *Tadić* trial, the Trial Chamber explained that Rule 96 'accords to the testimony of a victim of sexual assault the same presumption of

from defence counsel, the non-corroboration rule helps to ensure that their dignity is protected – and their integrity preserved – during the trial process. To cite Gopalan, Kravetz and Menon, 'At its core, Rule 96 seeks to protect victims from irrelevant and intrusive questioning'.[88] Rule 96 also stipulates that survivors of rape and sexual violence cannot be questioned about their prior sexual history; and it places strict limits on when consent can be invoked as a defence.[89]

Rule 96 of the ICTY's RPE was replicated in the ICTR's RPE.[90] Rule 70 of the ICC's RPE contains similar provisions. There are strict limitations on when consent can be inferred, and subsection (d) stipulates that 'Credibility, character or predisposition to sexual availability of a victim or witness cannot be inferred by reason of the sexual nature of the prior or subsequent conduct of a victim or witness'.[91] Rule 71 of the ICC's RPE further states that 'a Chamber shall not admit evidence of the prior or subsequent sexual conduct of a victim or witness'.[92] The Court's RPE do not specifically provide that no corroboration of testimony is required in cases involving sexual abuses. Rule 63(4), however, specifies that 'a Chamber shall not impose a legal requirement that corroboration is required in order to prove any crime within the jurisdiction of the Court, in particular, crimes of sexual violence'.[93] Interestingly, the RPE of the SCSL, which completed its work in 2013, did not contain either a non-corroboration rule or an express rule on the inadmissibility of evidence regarding a victim's sexual history – omissions which Damgaard has described as 'lamentable'.[94] Rule 96(4) stated simply that 'Credibility, character or predisposition to sexual availability of a victim or witness cannot be inferred by reason of sexual nature of the prior or subsequent conduct of a victim or witness'.[95] Interestingly, Rule 96(4) of the RPE of the Residual

reliability as the testimony of victims of other crimes, something long denied to victims of sexual assault by the common law'. Judgement, *Tadić*, *supra* note 49, at §536.

88 Priya Gopalan, Daniela Kravetz and Aditya Menon, 'Proving Crimes of Sexual Violence', in Serge Brammertz and Michelle Jarvis (eds), *Prosecuting Conflict-Related Sexual Violence at the ICTY* (Oxford: Oxford University Press, 2016), 111–171, at 132.

89 Rule 96(ii) states that 'consent shall not be allowed as a defence if the victim (a) has been subjected to or threatened with or has had reason to fear violence, duress, detention or psychological oppression, Or (b) reasonably believed that if the victim did not submit, another might be so subjected, threatened or put in fear'. ICTY, *supra* note 80.

90 ICTR, *Rules of Procedure and Evidence* (13 May 2015), available at: http://w.unictr.org/sites/unictr.org/files/legal-library/150513-rpe-en-fr.pdf (accessed 20 April 2016).

91 ICC, *Rules of Procedure and Evidence*, 2nd edn (2013), available at: www.icc-cpi.int/icc-docs/PIDS/legal-texts/RulesProcedureEvidenceEng.pdf (accessed 2 February 2016).

92 Ibid.

93 Ibid.

94 Ciara Damgaard, 'The Special Court for Sierra Leone: Challenging the Tradition of Impunity for Gender-Based Crimes', *Nordic Journal of International Law* 73 (2004): 485–503, at 494.

95 SCSL, *Rules of Procedure and Evidence* (31 May 2012), available at: www.rscsl.org/Documents/RPE.pdf (accessed 16 March 2016). Rule 96 of the SCSL's RPE, however, was identical to Rule 70 of the ICC's RPE.

SCSL (RSCSL)[96] goes further. It provides that evidence relating to prior or subsequent sexual conduct 'will only be admissible in exceptional circumstances'; and if such evidence is admitted, 'it may not be the basis for an inference about the credibility, character or predisposition to sexual availability of that victim or witness'.[97] However, there is no explicit rule on non-corroboration.

The first part of this chapter has provided a 'top down' view of criminal trials, by detailing some of the key developments over the last two decades in the international prosecution of rape and sexual violence. While substantial progress has been made at the international level, many survivors will testify in local courts rather than international courts.[98] Moreover, regardless of where they testify, there will always be critical gaps between the strictures of the legal process and survivors' own needs. Accordingly, the second part of this chapter examines the criminal trial process from the 'bottom up', by asking how survivors *experience* the process of testifying in a court of law. It may seem as though the two halves of this chapter are somewhat disconnected from each other, but this is intentional. The juxtaposition of top-down and bottom-up perspectives not only highlights some of the limitations of criminal trials, but also provides important new empirical insights into what it means for survivors to testify.

## The view from below: survivors' experiences of criminal trials

Some of the shortcomings of criminal trials are widely acknowledged within existing scholarship. Among them, legal requirements necessarily take precedence over individual needs;[99] victim-witnesses have little control over their stories within the confines of a courtroom;[100] there is the potential for re-traumatization

96 The purpose of the RSCSL, which was established in 2010, is to carry out the 'residual' functions of the SCSL relating to matters such as witness protection and management of the Court's archives. See www.rscsl.org/.

97 RSCSL, *Rules of Procedure and Evidence* (2 December 2015), available at: www.rscsl.org/Documents/RSCSL-Rules.pdf (accessed 16 March 2016).

98 One reason for this is that international courts are generally temporary bodies. The one exception is the ICC, whose core operating principle is complementarity. Hence, it does not have primacy of jurisdiction over national courts.

99 Marie-Bénédicte Dembour and Emily Haslam, 'Silencing Hearings? Victim-Witnesses at War Crimes Trials', *European Journal of International Law* 15 (2004): 151–177, at 154; Julie Mertus, 'Shouting from the Bottom of the Well: The Impact of International Trials for Wartime Rape on Women's Agency', *International Feminist Journal of Politics* 6 (2004): 110–128, at 118; Stephanie K. Wood, 'A Woman Scorned for the "Least Condemned" War Crime: Precedent and Problems with Prosecuting Rape as a Serious War Crime in the International Criminal Tribunal for Rwanda', *Columbia Journal of Gender and Law* 13 (2004): 274–327, at 308.

100 Binaifer Nowrojee, 'Making the Invisible War Crime Visible: Post-Conflict Justice for Sierra Leone's Rape Victims', *Harvard Human Rights Journal* 18 (2005): 85–105, at 103; Stover, *supra* note 3, at 129; Nicola Henry, 'Witness to Rape: The Limitations and

of those who testify;[101] and the trial process, particularly within international courts, is often 'achingly slow'.[102] It is also crucial, however, to include the views of survivors themselves (and witnesses more generally) in these assessments and analyses of criminal courts. Their viewpoints and experiences add a crucial emic perspective that is frequently missing from legal scholarship. As previously noted, just over 49 per cent of the men and women who participated in this research had testified against their perpetrators, primarily at the State Court of BiH in Sarajevo or in local courts. What follows is a detailed exploration of their 'lived' experiences of testifying.

An interesting macro/micro split quickly emerged within the interview data. Both male and female interviewees overwhelmingly stressed that criminal trials are important as a way of dealing with perpetrators of rape and sexual violence.[103] They frequently argued that when a defendant is found guilty of rape, his crimes thus become public knowledge and he must forever wear the label 'rapist'. This brought some interviewees a certain sense of satisfaction.[104] One interviewee explained that 'When a person is put on trial, people start asking questions, but nobody asks questions if that person just carries on with his life as normal'. She disclosed that the man who had raped her not only remained free, but had also been able to stand as a candidate in local elections in Zvornik.[105]

Potential of International War Crimes Trials for Victims of Wartime Sexual Violence', *International Journal of Transitional Justice* 3 (2009): 114–134, at 126.

101 Kelsall and Stepakoff, *supra* note 78, at 374. It is important to underline, however, that this remains a very grey area. See, for example, King et al. *supra* note 82, at 76.

102 Paul Kirby, 'Ending Sexual Violence in Conflict: The Preventing Sexual Violence Initiative and its Critics', *International Affairs* 91 (2015): 457–472, at 466.

103 The 2003 Criminal Code of BiH does not offer a comprehensive definition of these crimes. Article 172(1) lists a number of acts which, when committed as a part of a widespread or systematic attack on a civilian population, can constitute crimes against humanity. One such act is 'Coercing another by force or by threat of immediate attack upon his life or limb, or the life or limb of a person close to him, to sexual intercourse or an equivalent sexual act (rape), sexual slavery, enforced prostitution, forced pregnancy, enforced sterilisation or any other form of sexual violence of comparable gravity' (Article 172(1)(g)). Article 173(1)(e) further stipulates that rape can constitute a war crime. Criminal Code of Bosnia-Herzegovina (1 March 2003), available at: www.iccnow.org/documents/criminal-code-of-bih.pdf (accessed 19 July 2016). What is immediately striking is that these articles adopt a very narrow definition of force or coercion. They fail to recognize, *pace* cases such as *Kunarac et al.*, that certain circumstances are inherently coercive. While the Criminal Code is applied at the State level, the 1974 Criminal Code of the SFRY is applied in the entities and in Brčko District. The SFRY Criminal Code does not define rape and sexual violence at all. Article 142 ('War Crime against the Civilian Population') simply refers, inter alia, to 'forcible prostitution or rape'. Criminal Code of the SFRY (1 July 1977), available at: www.refworld.org/docid/3ae6b5fe0.html (accessed 19 July 2016).

104 As Nowrojee remarks, 'Public acknowledgment and condemnation of egregious abuses suffered are important first steps in providing recognition and redress to victims of violence'. Nowrojee, *supra* note 100, at 104.

105 Author interview, 22 August 2014.

Another interviewee, who testified at the State Court, explained that society too often blames rape victims for what happened to them, rather than the perpetrators. However, when courts issue a guilty verdict, 'They make it clear that the perpetrators are guilty, not the victims'.[106]

While most interviewees viewed criminal courts as having a vital social (macro) function, they were far more sceptical about the utility of these institutions at an individual (micro) level. Few of them felt that they had gained anything as a result of testifying. One interviewee had been raped in the Vojno camp in Mostar,[107] and subsequently testified against the perpetrators. She recalled that when she entered the courtroom, it was as though a burden had been lifted from her shoulders. This sense of relief, however, was temporary. She stressed that 'When you live in a city where many perpetrators are still free, it isn't easy'; and although she is glad that the men who raped her were prosecuted and convicted, and that the truth thus came out, she also feels that nobody at the court cared about her or her needs.[108]

Overall, many interviewees had not had very positive experiences of testifying, and five issues in particular strongly emerged from the data relating to different stages of the testimony process. During my fieldwork in BiH, I was able to observe several interviewees testify at the State Court and in local courts. The remainder of this chapter draws heavily on the notes that I took. For legal reasons, and because some of the interviewees testified as protected witnesses, no specific information about the trials or the names of the defendants will be given.

### *Lack of adequate preparation and support*

D51 testified at the State Court against the man who forced him to engage in 'sexual acts' with another prisoner in the Batković camp. He described how he began to shake when he entered the courtroom and saw the defendant for the first time in over 20 years. He did not know how he would feel, and he repeatedly emphasized that he would have greatly appreciated some pre-testimony preparation from the court to allow him to put his thoughts in order.

106 Author interview, 7 August 2014.

107 In the trial of *Radić et al.*, the State Court of BiH found that Marko Radić – who was the commander of the First Bijelo Polje Battalion of the Second Brigade HVO – 'contributed to and furthered the functioning of the Vojno prison system in ill-treating and persecuting the Bosnian Muslims by ordering, committing, or otherwise aiding and abetting the commission of various forms of physical, mental and sexual violence, whereby the atmosphere of terror was created'. *Prosecutor v. Marko Radić, Dragan Šunjić, Damir (Emir) Brekalo and Mirko Vračević*, X-KR-05/139, State Court of BiH Trial Chamber Judgement (20 February 2009), 3. Radić received a 25-year prison sentence and his three co-defendants, who also committed various crimes in the Vojno camp, were sentenced to prison terms of between 14 and 21 years.

108 Author interview, 21 April 2015.

He needed more time to prepare because he cannot remember everything after so many years; and he does not want to remember everything. He only spoke out for the first time when he heard that the defendant – who was ultimately convicted – had been arrested. He wanted this man to face justice and to be punished. However, he wishes now that he had remained silent because he felt better before he started talking about Batković. After testifying in court, he is burdened with memories and keeps thinking about the past. Nobody from the State Court has contacted him since he testified. 'Once you have finished testifying, that's it. The court forgets you. You are just used'. He feels that he might have coped better if he had received adequate preparation and known what to expect.[109]

E68 was raped by two HVO soldiers during the summer of 1993. She knew one of them, and this man subsequently committed suicide. Years later, she testified against the second soldier at the State Court. She testified publicly, without protection, and kept telling herself that she needed to be strong; the man who raped her had to pay for what he did. When she arrived at the Court, she was met by a 'nice lady' from the Witness Support Section (WSS). However, the defendant was ultimately acquitted, having successfully convinced the Court that this was a case of mistaken identity. E68 emotionally described how 'When you tell your story without any results, you feel drained and hopeless'. Compounding the situation was the fact that following the trial, she saw the defendant several times in town. She opined that the Court could – and should – have prepared her for the possibility that he might be acquitted. She had never anticipated this outcome.[110]

A psychologist from the State Court's WSS explained that witnesses are typically invited to come to court 30 minutes to an hour before they testify. This is the first time that someone from the WSS will meet them, and it is an opportunity for witnesses to ask questions and to view the courtroom while it is empty. Someone from the WSS can also sit next to a witness during the trial if the individual requests this. Once a witness has testified, s/he will have a short debriefing session. While all of this is important, the psychologist acknowledged that 'The Court is limited in what it can do for victims.[111] It cannot provide psychological help or therapy. If it thinks that a victim isn't coping, it can ask whether that person has family or contact a local NGO to help, but the Court cannot do much'.[112] Nevertheless, it offers more than many local courts.

109 Author interview, 30 January 2015.

110 Author interview, 21 April 2015.

111 Article 31 of the Court's RPE is entitled 'Witness Support'. Rule 31(1) states simply: '[The] Witness Support Office shall provide practical and, when necessary, psychological support to witnesses during testimony before the Court'. State Court of BiH, *Rules of Procedure on the Work of the State Court of BiH* (14 October 2005), available at: www.sudbih.gov.ba/stranica/41/pregled (accessed 9 August 2016).

112 Author interview, 7 August 2014.

D64 testified in a local court, but the defendant was not accused of raping her personally.[113] The prosecution's case was that he had raped one of the women with whom D64 was imprisoned during the first year of the Bosnian war. She had therefore been called as a witness to testify about what she had seen. When she arrived at the court, she spent approximately half an hour with the prosecutor and that was the only preparation that she received prior to testifying. Inside the courtroom, she recounted how one day in 1992, the defendant had pointed at her and instructed her to go with him to his office to clean it. Once inside, he closed the door, lifted up her top and began to fondle her breasts. The female prosecutor asked D64 how she felt when the defendant had touched her and tried to remove her top.[114] 'I could not believe that a man who had a daughter just a few years older than me could do this'. At this point, the defendant looked ashamed and upset.[115] Outside the courtroom, D64 was unsettled and explained that she felt like crying, not because of the stress of testifying but because she had seen that the defendant had tears in his eyes when she mentioned his daughter (who was killed in the war). She felt sorry for him and had not expected to feel any emotion towards this man.[116] She would have liked more preparation prior to testifying and, in particular, the opportunity to speak to a psychologist.

In 2008, the Council of Ministers in BiH adopted a National Strategy for War Crimes Processing, one of the stated aims of which is to '[p]rovide protection, support and equal treatment to all victims and witnesses in the proceedings before all courts in BiH'.[117] At that time, the State Court was the only court in BiH that had a WSS, but this is no longer the case. Since 2012, the United Nations Development Programme (UNDP) in BiH has been running a Victim/Witness Support Service Project in conjunction with, inter alia, the BiH Ministry

113 The men who raped D64 remain free.

114 As courts are interested in the hard facts, this was an unusual question from the prosecutor. On another occasion, I was able to briefly speak to a male prosecutor from another court. Why did he not ask his witnesses how they felt after being raped? His somewhat dismissive response was that 'The court already knows that'.

115 Author's observations from the courtroom.

116 In some cases, victim-witnesses do feel emotions towards defendants, particularly if they knew these individuals before the war. In his research on ICTY witnesses, for example, Stover interviewed a man called Marinko Vladić who testified against Slavko Dokmanović, the president of Vukovar municipality in Croatia who committed suicide while awaiting the verdict of his trial. Vladić had met Dokmanović several times before the war. ' "While I was giving my testimony, I was looking more at [Dokmanović] than the prosecutor. From time to time, [Dokmanović] would nod his head, confirming what I was saying… and I kept thinking, 'Oh, you stupid fool, you and I could have been in a café drinking coffee or sharing a bottle of wine. You don't have to be here as an accused person in this courtroom' " '. Stover, *supra* note 3, at 86.

117 BiH Council of Ministers, *Državna Strategija za Rad na Predmetima Ratnih Zločina* (December 2008), section 1.2(h), available at: http://ft-fbih.pravosudje.ba/vstv/faces/docservlet?p_id_doc=13700 (accessed 18 May 2016). A further aim of the War Crimes Strategy is to resolve all war crimes cases in BiH within 15 years.

of Justice. This has led to the establishment of six witness support offices (WSOs) in district/cantonal courts[118] and prosecutors' offices in Sarajevo, East Sarajevo and Banja Luka.[119] As part of this project, WSOs have also been set up in Una-Sana and Central Bosnia Cantons.[120] While these are important steps forward, significant problems remain. One is that the WSOs are heavily under-resourced. In March 2015, for example, I attended a workshop in Sarajevo, organized by the Forum for Local Democracy, on the issue of support for survivors of rape and sexual violence who testify in court. A psychologist from the WSO of a local cantonal court stressed that the court is limited in what it can do for victim-witnesses. It can pay for their travel expenses to and from the court, but it does not have the resources to provide more than very basic support to victim-witnesses before they testify (and no resources at all to do follow-up work with them). The UNDP has underscored that 'substantial additional investment in the criminal justice and social welfare systems will be required to address all of the deficiencies'.[121]

However, the problems are not only resource-related. During the aforementioned workshop in Sarajevo, a psychologist from another WSO emphasized that prosecutors themselves can be part of the problem. Some prosecutors do not want the court to contact 'their' witnesses, she explained; 'I have heard prosecutors say things like "That's my witness! Don't interfere!"' It is therefore essential that prosecutors receive adequate training in how to deal with survivors of rape and sexual violence.[122] In 2013, for example, two experts from the UK government's Preventing Sexual Violence in Conflict Initiative (PSVI) were deployed to BiH to work with prosecutors and judges dealing with sexual violence cases;[123] and the OSCE has organized a number of trainings.[124] Such activities are an

118 The Federation has cantonal courts and RS has district courts.

119 UNDP, 'Introduction of Victim/Witness Support Services Project: Function of the Project' (n.d.), available at: www.ba.undp.org/content/bosnia_and_herzegovina/en/home/operations/projects/crisis_prevention_and_recovery/introduction-of-victim-witness-support-services-project.html (accessed 7 May 2016).

120 UNDP, 'Witness Support Offices Established in Travnik/Novi Travnik and Bihać' (12 September 2013), available at: www.ba.undp.org/content/bosnia_and_herzegovina/en/home/presscenter/articles/2013/09/12/witness-support-offices-established-in-travnik-novi-travnik-and-biha-.html (accessed 7 May 2016).

121 UNDP, *Capacity Needs Assessment for Enhancing Provision of Victim/Witness Support during the Pre-Investigative Stage of Criminal Proceedings in BiH* (27 January 2014), 21, available at: www.ba.undp.org/content/bosnia_and_herzegovina/en/home/library/crisis_prevention_and_recovery/capacity-needs-assessment-for-enhancing-provision-of-victim-witn/ (accessed 1 August 2016).

122 The ICTR underlined this point in its Best Practices Manual. ICTR, *supra* note 7, at §35.

123 British Embassy Sarajevo, 'UK Experts from Preventing Sexual Violence Initiative Deployed to Bosnia and Herzegovina' (13 November 2013), available at: www.gov.uk/government/world-location-news/uk-experts-from-preventing-sexual-violence-initiative-deployed-to-bosnia-and-herzegovina (accessed 8 June 2016).

124 OSCE, *Combatting Impunity for Conflict-Related Sexual Violence in Bosnia and Herzegovina: Progress and Challenges – An Analysis of Criminal Proceedings before the Courts of the Federation of Bosnia and Herzegovina, Republika Srpska and Brčko District between*

important part of transitional justice and hence they should not be simply one-off events.

### *Witness protection issues*

E30 testified at a local court in BiH more than a decade ago and should have been a protected witness. A couple of days before she was due to testify, however, she saw two policemen standing close to her house. When she later went out to buy some milk, the policemen followed her. The shop assistant told her that the policemen were there to protect her as she was going to court to testify. This quickly became public knowledge within the town and her photograph appeared in the newspaper. The fact that the defendants in the case were Bosnian Muslims created further problems for her when she returned home; some locals told her that she should feel 'ashamed' of having testified against her 'own people'. She insisted that she will never testify in court again. She went through 'hell' and the whole experience re-traumatized her.[125]

There have been many developments since E30 testified. In 2014, for example, BiH adopted a Law on Witness Protection Programme, which states that 'The Head of the Witness Protection Department shall establish and maintain the witness protection programme to protect the safety and welfare of witnesses during and after criminal proceedings'.[126] This Law, however, only applies to the State Court and not to cantonal/district courts.[127] The level of protection that witnesses receive, therefore, hugely varies depending on where they are testifying. This is unacceptable, particularly in cases involving rape and sexual violence. As the Organization for Security and Co-operation in Europe (OSCE) has emphasized, 'The victims of sexual violence merit special attention in the context of witness protection and support. As recognised by the European Court of Human Rights,[128] those victims have heightened interests in privacy because of the stigma attached to their injuries'.[129]

*2004 and 2014* (June 2015), 43, available at: www.osce.org/bih/171906?download=true (accessed 21 July 2016).

125 Author interview, 12 November 2014. After she had testified, E30 visited the NGO that has been helping her for many years. She allowed me to read one of the psychologist's reports. This stated that she suffered 'renewed psychological destabilization and re-traumatization' as a result of testifying in court.

126 BiH, *BiH Witness Protection Programme Law* (2014), Article 4, available at: www.unodc.org/doc/enl/2009/Bosnia_Herzegovina_Witness_Protection_Programme_R09-12.PDF (accessed 8 July 2016).

127 Ibid., at Article 1. In terms of providing information about the sorts of protection that witnesses in the State Court will actually receive, the Law is somewhat 'thin'.

128 See *Martin Bocos-Cuesto v. The Netherlands*, 54789/00, European Court of Human Rights judgement (10 November 2005), §69.

129 OSCE, *Witness Protection and Support in BiH Domestic War Crimes Trials: Obstacles and Recommendations a Year after Adoption of the National Strategy for War Crimes*

Other problems include resource constraints, and the fact that prosecutors often fail to inform their witnesses that they can seek protective measures.[130] Indeed, in one case, I met a prosecutor who repeatedly convinced his witnesses that they did not 'need' to seek protective measures as they had nothing to hide. Standards of professionalism may also be lacking. An interviewee from the NGO *Medica Zenica* explained that 'There have been cases of protected witnesses having their names revealed, and cases of witnesses having to wait in the same area as the perpetrator and his family'.[131] On one occasion, for example, I travelled with K22 to court. She had already testified, but was now back in court to support her friend whose turn it was to give evidence. During a break in the proceedings, everyone left the courtroom and went outside into the corridor. One defendant – who was not being detained in prison – was sitting on a bench with his defence attorney. K22 had to walk straight past him and she was shaking. He was one of the men whom she maintained had raped her in 1992 and she was seized with anger – but also with fear. As this defendant was not in prison, what would she do if he were to come after her?

The European Commission (EC) has emphasized that in BiH, 'a comprehensive witness protection system before and after proceedings is still not in place'.[132] Even in cases where witness protection measures have been implemented, it is important not to lose sight of the long-term implications of being a protected witness. Ć13 testified at the State Court against one of the two men who raped her in 1992 (she knew this man before the war, but she did not know the second man who raped her and she was unable to identify him from photographs). She testified as a protected witness because she did not want people to know what had happened to her and to laugh at her. Although the defendant was convicted, Ć13 feels that she is still waiting for justice. Not only is she angry about the nine-year sentence that her rapist received, but she has been unable to seek damages. As will be discussed in the next chapter, it is extremely difficult for survivors of rape and sexual violence in BiH to secure reparations. They do, however, have the option of seeking damages in a civil court and Ć13 would like to explore this possibility. The problem is that in order to file for damages, she would have to disclose her identity – because civil lawsuits must be filed under a full name[133] –

*Processing – A Report of the Capacity Building and Legacy Implementation Project* (January 2010), 10, available at: www.osce.org/bih/118893?download=true (accessed 8 May 2016).

130 Judge Joanna Korner CMG QC, *Processing of War Crimes at the State Level in Bosnia and Herzegovina* (16 June 2016), 38, available at: www.osce.org/bih/247221?download=true (accessed 6 June 2016).

131 Author interview, 6 August 2014.

132 EC, *Bosnia and Herzegovina Progress Report* (8 October 2014), 14, available at: http://ec.europa.eu/enlargement/pdf/key_documents/2014/20141008-bosnia-and-herzegovina-progress-report_en.pdf (accessed 21 July 2016).

133 Selma Učanbarlić, 'The Need to Reveal Identities of Protected Witnesses' (20 October 2014), available at: www.justice-report.com/en/articles/the-need-to-reveal-identities-of-protected-witnesses (accessed 29 June 2016).

and thus give up her protected status. She is not willing to do this.[134] According to a legal advisor from TRIAL International – formerly TRIAL (Track Impunity Always) – 'Neither civil procedural law nor the applicable legislation related to witness protection in criminal proceedings provide clear guarantees for protection of identity of this category of victims';[135] and this effectively prevents protected witnesses from pursuing damages claims.

### *The difficulties and trauma of actually testifying*

R49 was a protected witness and when she arrived at the State Court, her legs were shaking. She wanted to testify to the best of her ability and she felt that the prosecutor did not allow her to do this because he failed to properly prepare her. Due to her trauma, she has memory problems. If the prosecutor had gone through her statement with her, she would have been more secure in her answers. She felt disappointed with him. She also emphasized, however, that when she entered the courtroom, she experienced a sudden surge of energy: 'When I saw the defendants sitting there, I felt stronger than all of them. They looked old and I no longer felt small and unimportant'. She saw fear in one of the defendant's eyes and she almost felt sorry for him. The man whom she accused of raping her had been her neighbour before the war. He showed no emotion when she spoke. Prior to testifying, she had wanted to tell him that he is a monster. When she saw him in the courtroom, he no longer seemed like a monster. The presiding judge asked her if there was anything else that she would like to say. R49 turned towards the defendant who had raped her, 22 years earlier, and said simply 'You are a very ordinary and weak man'.[136]

N60 was just 14 years old when she was raped on several occasions by five different soldiers. More than 20 years later, she had the opportunity to testify in

134 Author interview, 23 April 2015.

135 Adrijana Hanušić, *Enforcement of Damage Compensation Claims of Victims of War in Criminal Proceedings in Bosnia and Herzegovina: Situation, Challenges and Perspectives*, TRIAL (2015), 16, available at: http://trial.ba/wp-content/uploads/2015/10/ENG_Ostvarivanje-zahtjeva-za-naknadu-%C5%A1tete-%C5%BErtava-ratnih-zlo%C4%8Dina-u-okviru-krivi%C4%8Dnih-postupaka-u-Bosni-i-Hercegovini-%E2%80%93-stanje-problemi-i-perspektive-.pdf (accessed 9 December 2015). A further complication arises from the fact that according to Article 13(1) of the Law on Protection of Witnesses under Threat and Vulnerable Witnesses in BiH, a court may – in 'exceptional circumstances' – decide that a witness's personal details 'shall remain confidential for such period as may be determined to be necessary, but in any event not exceeding thirty years, following upon the day the decision became final'. BiH, *Law on Protection of Witnesses under Threat and Vulnerable Witnesses* (1 March 2003), available at: www.unodc.org/cld/en/legislation/bih/law_on_protection_of_witnesses_under_threat_and_vulnerable_witnesses/chapter_i-iv/article_1-27/law_on_protection_of_witnesses_under_threat_and_vulnerable_witnesses.html (accessed 9 December 2015).

136 Author's observations from the courtroom.

court as a witness for R49 (soldiers had put the two girls together in the same vehicle).[137] She was anxious about going to court; it would have been easier for her to testify four or five years after the events in question. After so many years, she worried that she had forgotten many of the details of what happened. She told the court that she was '1,000 per cent certain' that one of the defendants in the case had raped R49. On cross-examination, the defendant's lawyer repeatedly asked her why she had failed to mention his client in the various statements that she had given to police and prosecutors. N60 was unable to explain this, but stressed that she had named the defendant in a statement that she gave in 1992. The defence counsel did not have a copy of this. When she tried to tell the court that she will never forget what happened to her in 1992, the same defence lawyer was quick to ask her how she had therefore omitted to mention his client in two of her statements.

On the witness stand, N60 became increasingly irritable. Interestingly, the defendant whom she maintained had raped R49 did not wish to cross-examine her. One of the other defendants in the case, however, told the court that he had some questions for the witness. He stood up to begin his cross-examination, looking down at the copious notes that he had made during N60's testimony. She appeared surprised that this man wanted to cross-examine her. Before he had a chance to ask her any questions, however, she told him firmly that she wanted him to look her in the eyes and that she would respond to his questions only if he did so. He promptly informed the presiding judge that he did not have any questions and sat down again.[138] Outside the courtroom, N60 explained that she had felt a huge sense of power when she addressed the defendant: 'I wanted him to look me in the eye, to show me that he wasn't involved in what happened, but he couldn't do that'.[139]

As these examples illustrate, having the opportunity to testify in court can be an empowering experience for survivors.[140] Nevertheless, an individual's

137 The men who raped N60 are still at large.

138 Author's observations from the courtroom.

139 According to *Medica Mondiale*, 'To confront the perpetrator can mean to demonstrate to him, to oneself and the world that he lost his power over you. It can be an act of reclaiming control over one's life, leaving the position of the helpless victim behind'. Medica Mondiale, *"and that it does not happen to anyone anywhere in the world": The Trouble with Rape Trials – Views of Witnesses, Prosecutors and Judges on Prosecuting Sexualized Violence in the War in the Former Yugoslavia* (December 2009), 57, available at: www.medica-mondiale.org/fileadmin/redaktion/5_Service/Mediathek/Dokumente/English/Documentations_studies/medica_mondiale_and_that_it_does_not_happen_to_anyone_anywhere_in_the_world_english_complete_version_dec_2009.pdf (accessed 17 August 2016).

140 Susan Harris Rimmer, 'Sexing the Subject of Transitional Justice', *Australian Feminist Law Journal* 32 (2010): 123–147, at 142. In the criminal trial process, however, those who have suffered rape and sexual violence testify as *victims* and there is a certain expectation that they will appear vulnerable and fragile. Henry, for example, notes that in the *Foča* trial at the ICTY, 'the defense sought to demonstrate that the 16 witnesses who testified to rape

sense of empowerment may oscillate with feelings of disempowerment. N60, for example, felt frustrated that she was not able to ask the defendants any questions.[141] When she tried to do so, the presiding judge interjected. She had wanted to ask one of the defendants how he would feel if someone were to rape his daughter.[142] Other interviewees similarly underlined that the strict question–answer format used in the trial process had prevented them from saying everything that they wished to say. A court's view of what is important necessarily takes precedence over a witness's view because the trial process 'has its own needs'.[143] One particular interviewee, K22, felt aggrieved that she had been able to tell the court only part of her story[144] – and not in her own words. While many survivors choose to testify as protected witnesses, K22 was adamant from the outset that she wanted to testify without protection. 'I want the world to know what happened to me and I want the men who raped me to be humiliated like they humiliated me'.[145]

When the case went to court, the prosecutor argued that the witness's testimony should be given in public. Counsel for the defendants, however, maintained that it should take place in closed session, to protect the defendants' family lives. After conferring on the issue, the judges reached a compromise; the witness would testify in public, but when she discussed the details of what happened to her, the court would go into closed session and the journalists in the public gallery would be asked to leave.[146] After she had given her testimony and left the

were empowered, strong and assertive and were not psychologically traumatized by their experiences of rape. This, they argued, cast doubt on the validity of their testimonies. The suggestion was that these women could not have been raped in the absence of psychoses'. Henry, *supra* note 100, at 132. During my time in BiH, I observed several interviewees testify in court. In one case, the court had been told in advance that the witness was anxious. On the witness stand, however, she was composed and assertive. When she left the courtroom, one of the defence lawyers remarked 'She didn't seem very anxious!' Laughing, the other lawyers nodded in agreement before being reprimanded by the presiding judge.

141 Interviewees frequently expressed a sense of frustration that defendants have the right to cross-examine witnesses, while witnesses do not have an equivalent right to question defendants. They regarded this as a huge injustice.

142 According to the aforementioned report co-authored by the VWS and the University of North Texas, 'many witnesses ask at the end of their testimony if they can make a final statement to the Court. The VWS experience is that these are usually short and that witnesses appreciate it when they are given permission to speak at the end of their testimony'. King et al. *supra* note 82, at 102.

143 Words of an ICTR prosecutor, cited in Jonneke Koomen, '"Without these Women, the Tribunal cannot do Anything": The Politics of Witness Testimony on Sexual Violence at the International Criminal Tribunal for Rwanda', *Signs* 38 (2013): 253–277, at 264.

144 The day before she testified, the prosecutor came to her house to run through everything with her. He kept emphasizing to her that the court would only be interested in a couple of questions: who raped her and how.

145 Author interview, 27 October 2014.

146 Author's observations from the courtroom.

courtroom, K22 expressed anger at the judges' decision: 'Nobody protected me and my family in 1992, and I don't need protection now'.[147]

During a criminal trial process, moreover, many things can happen that create great uncertainty for witnesses. The day before she was due to testify, for example, one interviewee found out that the case had been adjourned, for 'technical reasons'. Further delays, due to the Christmas holiday period and the fact that one of the judges had fallen ill, meant that she did not actually testify until a month later. During this interim period, she felt as though she was in limbo. In another case, two interviewees from the same family travelled to a local court to give testimony. Both of them were extremely anxious and were only able to have a brief meeting with the prosecutor. When they subsequently entered the courtroom, there was no sign of the defendant. His lawyer informed the court that his client was ill and in hospital; he promised to provide the court with medical evidence later that day. It was agreed that the trial should be adjourned. One of the interviewees stood up and asked the judge if she could say something. She did not want the trial to be adjourned for several months; she and her fellow witness wanted to testify as soon as possible to get the experience over with (she later disclosed that her greatest concern was having to tell the court in detail what had happened to her).[148] The trial was adjourned for two months and then subsequently adjourned several more times, due to the defendant's ill-health.

The process of testifying in a court of law can also raise difficult and complex memory issues for survivors. The criminal trial process requires a re-activation of memory; it demands of survivors that they remember – and speak in detail about – traumatic events and experiences that they may have tried to forget. Summarizing some of the findings from her interviews with ten barristers working on domestic rape cases in the UK, for example, Temkin notes that:

> Rape victims often needed to forget what had happened to them in order to cope with their lives and expended much effort in seeking to do so. Where, after a year or so, they had managed to put the experience behind them, it was traumatic then to be forced to recall the event in court and they frequently had a reluctance to talk about it. Their minds sometimes went blank.[149]

In BiH, such problems may be amplified due to the fact that survivors are testifying many years after they were raped. A male interviewee, for example, disclosed that he had testified on several occasions and could not do it anymore. It was

147 As Harris Rimmer points out, 'victims of sexual violence, if they are actually chosen to give testimony at a trial, only get to tell a piece of their story. Further, those experiences remain cloaked in secrecy given that, out of necessity for their protection and safety, the court sessions are often in private'. Harris Rimmer, *supra* note 140, at 142.

148 Author's observations from the courtroom.

149 Jennifer Temkin, 'Prosecuting and Defending Rape: Perspectives from the Bar', *Journal of Law and Society* 27 (2000): 219–248, at 222.

too much and he did not want to keep re-visiting the past.[150] Interviewees also frequently admitted that they struggled with details, and in particular with dates. Many of them thus found it enormously difficult to recount their stories in any sort of chronological order,[151] which could make them vulnerable during cross-examination. To cite Mertus, 'Defense attorneys are not willing to recognize that the trauma of rape often alters the nature and sequencing of the victim's testimony, while not changing the truth of their statements. On the contrary, defense attorneys attempt to pathologize their behavior and undermine their credibility'.[152] In one case, for example, the defence lawyer asked a witness why she had named his client during her testimony, yet had not done so in a statement that she gave to the police in 1999. She maintained that the omission from her statement was a mistake. His rather cutting response was: 'Ok. So you just allow anything to be written'.[153]

### *Post-testimony neglect*

T20 testified at a local court in BiH in 2013. For her, seeing the man who had raped her was extremely difficult, and it felt wrong that she had to stand in the courtroom while he was seated. His defence lawyer was provocative and made her feel as though she herself was on trial. The defendant was convicted but his sentence was less than five years. The experience of testifying set her backwards, and for three months afterwards she was not in a good place psychologically. She has given many statements over the years – to different local courts and to SIPA – and it is too much. 'Each time you give a statement, you have to go back to the past and you can't get on with your life'. For her, what hurts the most is that after she had testified in 2013, nobody from the court ever contacted her to ask how she was feeling.[154] A32 testified as a protected witness at the ICTY (she was called as a

150 Author interview, 24 August 2014.

151 There is also a possible neurophysiological explanation for this. Mason and Lodrick point out that 'The hippocampus is one of the brain structures whose functions are disrupted under threat conditions. Hippocampi are essentially involved in the storage of explicit memory, and they play a central role in the organisation of spatial and temporal information… The effect on brain function, as outlined above, can severely impair the person's ability to recall details of the assault and recall may change over time'. Fiona Mason and Zoe Lodrick, 'Psychological Consequences of Sexual Assault', *Clinical Obstetrics and Gynaecology* 27 (2013): 27–37, at 30. However, interviewees frequently remembered very specific details, including clothing and smells. According to van der Kolk, Hopper and Osterman, 'traumatic memories associated with Posttraumatic Stress Disorder may initially lack narrative elements, even as the trauma is intrusively relived as sounds, smells, bodily sensations and visual images'. Bessel van der Kolk, James W. Hopper and Janet E. Osterman, 'Exploring the Nature of Traumatic Memory: Combining Clinical Knowledge with Laboratory Methods', *Journal of Aggression, Maltreatment and Trauma* 4 (2001): 9–31, at 21.

152 Mertus, *supra* note 99, at 121.

153 Author's observations from the courtroom.

154 Author interview, 18 October 2014.

prosecution witness to give evidence about HVO crimes in her area, but none of the defendants were the men who raped her). The Tribunal looked after her, and most importantly she felt safe. Ultimately, however, she felt used. Once she had testified, there was no follow-up from the Tribunal. She stressed that 'Lawyers are building their careers, but nobody cares about victims and their needs, about whether they have enough to eat or enough money to pay for their medicines'.[155]

Whether interviewees had testified at the ICTY or, more commonly, at the State Court/in local courts, a major theme that emerged from the data was the widespread sense among them of post-testimony abandonment.[156] Many interviewees described feeling 'used' and 'discarded'. As they saw it, they mattered to the courts only when they gave their testimony, and once they returned home they were quickly forgotten about. In a 2014 pilot study conducted by staff from the University of North Texas and the ICTY's VWS, which was designed to explore the long-term effects of giving testimony, 300 former ICTY witnesses were asked, inter alia, what they would change about the proceedings or the process of testifying. Interestingly, 'By almost five to one, interviewees gave more negative (n=157) than positive (n=32) feedback';[157] and one of the commonly cited issues was witnesses' post-testimony needs. For example, 58 interviewees underlined the importance of post-testimony support; and of these, 'thirteen witnesses indicated that they were permanently harmed, and indicated better follow-up contact was needed in the post-testimony period (beyond the routine, regular follow-up calls made by VWS four to six weeks after their return home)'.[158]

Of course, courts do not have the resources or the mandates to provide witnesses with follow-up support and care; they are not social institutions. There are, however, various steps that they should undertake to minimize the possibility of victim-witnesses feeling simply 'cast aside' post testimony. For example, it is imperative that courts refrain from unnecessarily raising expectations, and they can do this by being honest with victim-witnesses about what they can and cannot provide.[159] After conducting interviews with 200 witnesses, for example, the SCSL underlined 'the importance of clearly setting, and continuously reinforcing, realistic expectations regarding what witnesses can expect from their contact with

155 Author interview, 13 November 2014.

156 In his research with witnesses who had testified at the ICTY, Stover found that 'With few exceptions, the witnesses said that no one from the tribunal telephoned or visited them after they testified in The Hague and returned home… Indeed, "abandonment" was the word most used to describe the court's lack of presence after the trial'. Stover, *supra* note 3, at 96.

157 King et al., *supra* note 82, at 112.

158 Ibid., at 113. Some Tribunal staff have themselves acknowledged that 'While all prosecution teams meet with witnesses after their testimony, the OTP could have employed a more consistent and well-enforced protocol regarding follow-up with witnesses after they return home'. Gopalan, Kravetz and Menon, *supra* note 88, at 148.

159 Human Rights Centre, UC Berkeley School of Law, *supra* note 86, at 66.

the court'.[160] Courts should also endeavour to ensure that witnesses – and in particular vulnerable witnesses – feel appreciated and valued. According to Henry, 'Victim and witness support services are vital to ensuring that witnesses understand the contribution they have made to the international criminal justice process [or local justice process]'.[161] Witnesses may not understand this contribution, however, unless it is explicitly communicated to them, and this can be done in different ways. In *Medica Mondiale*'s research, for example, one witness emphasized: '"I can't tell you how much it means when someone calls you and asks how you are doing, whether you need anything. A kind word means a lot"'.[162] A further way in which courts can help to make witnesses feel valued is by keeping them informed of new developments, including the outcome of the case and the appeals process. The ICC's Policy Paper on Gender-Based Crimes highlights this point.[163]

Finally, as will be discussed in Chapter 7, courts should co-operate with local organizations as much as possible, including health institutes and NGOs. This is crucial for ensuring that there are support mechanisms in place for witnesses when they return home. In its Best Practices Manual, for example, the ICTR underlined that 'Each tribunal or court must develop its own organizational framework for ensuring that witnesses receive the medical and counselling services they require'; and it noted that particular attention should be given to the needs of survivors of rape and sexual violence.[164] Relatedly, courts need to provide information to witnesses about the services that are available to them once they return home.[165] Fundamentally, although criminal justice is primarily 'a struggle *against perpetrators* rather than an effort *on behalf of victims*',[166] courts can nevertheless do far more to aid those who testify, and in particular survivors of rape and sexual violence.

*****

160 SCSL, *Best-Practice Recommendations for the Protection and Support of Witnesses* (2008), 20, available at: www.rscsl.org/Documents/WVS%20Best%20Practices.pdf (accessed 11 August 2016).

161 Henry, *supra* note 100, at 120.

162 *Medica Mondiale*, *supra* note 139, at 63.

163 This states that 'The Office [of the Prosecutor] maintains contact with witnesses post-testimony in order to keep them informed of developments in the case, including the sentence, and any appeal'. ICC, *Policy Paper on Sexual and Gender-Based Crimes* (June 2014), §98, available at: www.icc-cpi.int/iccdocs/otp/OTP-Policy-Paper-on-Sexual-and-Gender-Based-Crimes--June-2014.pdf (accessed 13 March 2016).

164 ICTR, *supra* note 7, at §64.

165 According to King et al., 'Efforts should be made to raise awareness among witnesses on the latest developments in the field of trauma treatment and redress and the organizations that can provide them with assistance. Witnesses have a wide range of needs that only one agency cannot easily address'. *Supra* note 82, at 121.

166 Pablo de Greiff, 'Justice and Reparations', in Jon Miller and Rahul Kumar (eds), *Reparations: Interdisciplinary Inquiries* (Oxford: Oxford University Press, 2007), 153–175, at 153.

This chapter has examined international developments in the prosecution of rape and sexual violence alongside survivors' own experiences of testifying. By empirically exploring this often-neglected experiential dimension of criminal trials, it has counter-balanced top-down analyses of courts with a critical bottom-up perspective that provides new insights into the trial process. Quintessentially, the fight against impunity is impossible without the co-operation and testimonies of survivors, and far more attention should therefore be given to their role in this fight – and to the demands that it places on them. Criminal trials, however, are only one form of transitional justice and they cannot do everything. The next chapter is specifically about reparations. As the most 'victim-centred' form of transitional justice, reparations have an important role to play in addressing survivors' long-term needs. In BiH, however, the use of reparations has been limited.

Chapter 6

# Reparations, rape and sexual violence

## Developments and setbacks in Bosnia-Herzegovina

Minow confidently asserts that 'most victims of crime rate their needs to know what happened and why more highly than their desires for compensation or restitution'.[1] This is a remarkably sweeping statement that effectively collectivizes victims as a homogenized group. For individuals who have lost loved-ones in war and armed conflict, finding out what happened and why may indeed be a priority. Nevertheless, it cannot be assumed that the 'need to know' carries the same weight for all victims. Approximately 10 per cent of the female interviewees who participated in this research asked 'why me?' Why were they targeted; could they have done anything differently? More commonly, interviewees expressed the need for legal justice; they wanted their perpetrators to be prosecuted and punished. Yet, what these men and women prioritized above all was some form of socio-economic justice. They repeatedly and consistently emphasized their everyday practical needs – and in particular their needs for healthcare, jobs/an occupation, economic security and general support. These needs illustrate the importance of reparations as a component of transitional justice. As de Greiff argues, reparations represent for victims 'the most tangible manifestation of the efforts of the state to remedy the harms they have suffered'.[2] In the context of conflict-related rape and sexual violence, however, reparations have often been marginalized[3] – and this is largely the case in BiH.

This chapter begins by looking at three key international documents that address the issue of reparations and concretize the concept. Collectively, these documents – one of which is more generalized while the other two are specific to sexual violence – constitute an important normative framework. What ultimately matters, however, is the actual operationalization of reparative

1 Martha Minow, *Between Vengeance and Forgiveness: Facing History after Genocide and Mass Violence* (Boston, MA: Beacon Press, 1998), 103.

2 Pablo de Greiff, 'Justice and Reparations', in Jon Miller and Rahul Kumar (eds), *Reparations: Interdisciplinary Inquiries* (Oxford: Oxford University Press, 2007), 153–175.

3 See Fionnuala Ní Aoláin, Catherine O'Rourke and Aisling Swaine, 'Transforming Reparations for Conflict-Related Sexual Violence: Principles and Practice', *Harvard Human Rights Journal* 28 (2015): 97–146, at 102.

justice.[4] The remaining sections of the chapter examine the limited use of reparations in BiH. They also draw attention to some of the practical challenges associated with this form of transitional justice, and in particular compensation. As Satz remarks, 'Even if compensation is an appropriate response to historical contexts, and even if it can be an important component of repair, there are serious limitations to its usefulness in practice'.[5]

## Victims' right to a remedy

At the international level, it has long been recognized that victims, broadly defined, have a right to a remedy.[6] It is within this normative framework that the UN General Assembly, in December 2005, adopted the Basic Principles and Guidelines on the Right to a Remedy and Reparation for Victims of Gross Violations of International Human Rights Law and Serious Violations of International Humanitarian Law (Basic Principles and Guidelines). Underpinned by cosmopolitanism[7] and the idea of solidarity with all victims, the Basic Principles and Guidelines do not entail new legal obligations. Rather, they 'identify mechanisms, modalities, procedures and methods for the implementation of existing legal obligations under international human rights law and international humanitarian law which are complementary though different as to their norms'.[8]

4 Mani defines reparative justice as 'a response to the complex and shifting realities of societies torn apart by conflict, as well as the varied and often contradictory claims for justice that arise therein'. Rama Mani, 'Rebuilding an Inclusive Political Community after War', *Security Dialogue* 36 (2005): 511–526, at 522.

5 Debra Satz, 'Countering the Wrongs of the Past: The Role of Compensation', in Jon Miller and Rahul Kumar (eds), *Reparations: Interdisciplinary Inquiries* (Oxford: Oxford University Press, 2007), 176–192, at 189.

6 See, for example, UN General Assembly, *Universal Declaration of Human Rights* (10 December 1948), Article 8, available at: www.refworld.org/docid/3ae6b3712c.html (accessed 8 May 2016); UN General Assembly, *International Convention on the Elimination of all Forms of Racial Discrimination* (21 December 1965), Article 6, available at: www.ohchr.org/Documents/ProfessionalInterest/cerd.pdf (accessed 8 May 2016); UN General Assembly, *International Covenant on Civil and Political Rights* (16 December 1966), Article 2(3)(a), available at: /www.ohchr.org/en/professionalinterest/pages/ccpr.aspx (accessed 7 May 2016); UN General Assembly, *Convention against Torture and Other Cruel, Inhuman or Degrading Treatment* (10 December 1984), Article 14, available at: www.ohchr.org/EN/ProfessionalInterest/Pages/CAT.aspx (accessed 7 May 2016).

7 According to Pensky, 'In its simplest sense, cosmopolitan political theory refers to the view that human beings maintain specific moral duties, both positive and negative, to other human beings simply on the basis of the equal basic rights to autonomy shared by all'. Max Pensky, 'Two Cheers for Cosmopolitanism: Cosmopolitan Solidarity as Second-Order Inclusion', *Journal of Social Philosophy* 38 (2007): 165–184, at l67.

8 UN General Assembly, *Basic Principles and Guidelines on the Right to a Remedy and Reparation for Victims of Gross Violations of International Human Rights Law and Serious Violations of International Humanitarian Law* (16 December 2005), Preamble, available at: www.ohchr.org/EN/ProfessionalInterest/Pages/RemedyAndReparation.aspx (accessed 9 May 2016).

In the Basic Principles and Guidelines, 'remedy' is conceptualized as an amalgam of different types of justice. It is emphasized, for example, that 'A victim of a gross violation of international human rights law or of a serious violation of international humanitarian law shall have equal access to an effective judicial remedy as provided for under international law'.[9] Alongside this right to retributive justice, the Basic Principles and Guidelines underline victims' concomitant right to 'Adequate, effective and prompt reparation' for harm suffered.[10] This concept of reparative justice, which closely overlaps with restorative justice,[11] is further disaggregated into five main forms, namely restitution, compensation, rehabilitation, satisfaction and guarantees of non-repetition.[12] This categorization implicitly highlights the importance of a multi-level approach to reparations. To address the harm done to victims, it is essential to provide them with medical and psychological care (rehabilitation);[13] to restore to them lost rights, including human rights and family rights (restitution);[14] and to 'repair' any economically assessable damage, such as physical/mental harm or loss of earnings (compensation).[15] Comprehensive reparative justice, however, needs to go beyond the individual/micro level and include the local/meso and state/macro level. All three levels are inter-related. At the meso and/or macro level, for example, reparative justice can include commemorations and tributes to victims, public apologies and the search for missing persons (satisfaction),[16] as well as increased judicial independence and the provision of human rights training for law enforcement officials and military forces (guarantees of non-repetition).[17]

The Nairobi Declaration on Women and Girls' Right to a Remedy and Reparation (Nairobi Declaration) builds on the Basic Principles and Guidelines. However, it addresses the issue of remedies and reparations through the specific prism of gender-based violence, and particularly sexual violence. Although the purview is restricted to women and girls, there is a recognition that 'the multi-dimensional and long-term consequences of these crimes' extend beyond the direct victims to reach families and communities.[18] This is important because it helps to contextualize the impact of rape and sexual violence, and to thereby reinforce

9 Ibid., at §12.
10 Ibid., at §15.
11 See Margaret U. Walker, 'Restorative Justice and Reparations', *Journal of Social Philosophy* 27 (2006): 377–395.
12 UN General Assembly, *supra* note 8, at §18.
13 Ibid., at §21.
14 Ibid., at §19.
15 Ibid., at §20.
16 Ibid., at §22.
17 Ibid., at §23.
18 *Nairobi Declaration on Women and Girls' Right to a Remedy and Reparation* (March 2007), section 3(E), available at: www.fidh.org/IMG/pdf/NAIROBI_DECLARATIONeng.pdf (accessed 10 May 2016).

the need for more inclusive approaches to transitional justice that broaden the focus beyond direct victims.

In the Nairobi Declaration, reparations are conceptualized as having a critical transformative function.[19] Their role, in short, is not simply to repair wrongs, but also, more elementally, 'to address the political and structural inequalities that negatively shape women's and girls' lives'.[20] While this point is not elaborated on, it reflects the core feminist argument that sexual violence against women in conflict represents a continuation of everyday gender inequalities.[21] As part of its feminist approach to remedies, the Nairobi Declaration also places a strong accent on women's empowerment. Whereas the Basic Guidelines and Principles identify five broad types of reparations, the Nairobi Declaration underscores that women and girls ('or those acting in the best interests of girls') should be empowered 'to determine for themselves what forms of reparation are best suited to their situation'.[22] This is a significant step forward in the direction of more participatory and bottom-up transitional justice.[23] Rejecting top-down approaches wherein important decisions are made on behalf of victims, the Nairobi Declaration promotes the idea that 'those who have seen their human rights violated are best situated to explain what is needed to restore their dignity, heal their wounds, recognise their trauma and compensate for harm suffered'.[24]

Empowerment, in turn, is linked to peace-building. UN Security Council Resolution 1325 was the first in a series of resolutions to focus on women, peace and security and to emphasize the importance of women in the prevention and resolution of conflicts.[25] The Nairobi Declaration, similarly, underscores that women have vital roles to play in 'repairing the social fabric of families, communities and societies'.[26] It thereby promotes bottom-up forms of peace-building that counter dominant externally imposed top-down models based on the

19 Inherent in the notion of 'transformative reparations' is the concern that 'a traditional philosophical and legal standard of justice in reparations, "restoring the status quo ante", can be perverse in the case of women (and other systemically disadvantaged groups)'. Margaret U. Walker, 'Transformative Reparations? A Critical Look at a Current Trend in Thinking about Gender-Just Reparations', *International Journal of Transitional Justice* 10 (2006): 108–125, at 109.

20 Nairobi Declaration, *supra* note 18, at section 3(H).

21 According to Ní Aoláin, O'Rourke and Swaine, for example, 'remedies for sexual violence must take into account the pre-existing structural inequalities that women face as a routine and accepted part of their lives in many societies'. Ní Aoláin, O'Rourke and Swaine, *supra* note 3, at 102.

22 Nairobi Declaration, *supra* note 18, at section 1(D).

23 Female survivors participated in drafting the Nairobi Declaration.

24 Valérie Couillard, 'The Nairobi Declaration: Redefining Reparation for Women Victims of Sexual Violence', *International Journal of Transitional Justice* 1 (2007): 444–453, at 446.

25 UN, *Security Council Resolution 1325*, S/RES/1325 (31 October 2000).

26 Nairobi Declaration, *supra* note 18, at Preamble.

so-called Liberal Peace.[27] More specifically, it promotes the 'potential of reparation programs' to acknowledge the roles of women as peace-builders.[28] In short, if transitional justice practices have 'come to represent one of the cornerstones of the Liberal Peace',[29] the Nairobi Declaration's approach to reparations departs from this.

The UN Secretary-General's Guidance Note on Reparations for Conflict-Related Sexual Violence (Guidance Note) recognizes that men and boys also experience sexual violence in conflict.[30] Hence, while it posits a linkage between gender inequality and sexual violence, it does so in a gender neutral way, noting that 'Sexual violence often results from and perpetuates patterns of pre-existing structural subordination and discrimination for both men and women'.[31] Like the Nairobi Declaration, therefore, the Guidance Note assigns a significant transformative role to reparations, maintaining that they 'have the potential… to assist in overcoming structures of inequality and discrimination'.[32] Although this point is not fully developed or explored, the example of 'women-centred economic compensation' is given to highlight the potential relationship between reparations and women's economic empowerment/autonomy.[33]

Like the Nairobi Declaration, the Guidance Note also places a strong accent on the need for victims to participate, inter alia, in the design and implementation of reparations.[34] However, it also goes further by discussing ways of facilitating accessibility by ensuring, for example, that victims have sufficient information to meaningfully participate.[35] There is also a recognition that measures promoting participation need to take account of cultural and religious sensitivities. Particularly significant in this regard is the acknowledgement of male survivors and of some of the difficulties that they may face in expressing what it is that they want and need from a reparations programme. For example, 'Male victims of sexual violence may experience a feeling of emasculation and of lack of sexual identity as a result of sexual violence and therefore may experience serious difficulties

27 According to Mac Ginty, Liberal Peace is 'the dominant form of peacemaking and peacebuilding favoured by leading states, international organisations and international financial institutions'. Roger Mac Ginty, 'Hybrid Peace: The Interaction between Top-Down and Bottom-Up Peace', *Security Dialogue* 41 (2010): 391–412, at 391.
28 Nairobi Declaration, *supra* note 18, at Preamble.
29 Roddy Brett and Lina Malagon, 'Overcoming the Original Sin of the "Original Condition:" How Reparations may Contribute to Emancipatory Peacebuilding', *Human Rights Review* 14 (2013): 257–271, at 258.
30 UN Secretary General, *Guidance Note of the Secretary General: Reparations for Conflict-Related Sexual Violence* (June 2014), 3, available at: www.ohchr.org/Documents/Press/GuidanceNoteReparationsJune-2014.pdf (accessed 10 May 2016).
31 Ibid., at section A(4), §1.
32 Ibid., at section A(1), §1.
33 Ibid., at section A(4), §2.
34 Ibid., at section A(6).
35 Ibid., at section A(6), §4.

to report'.[36] If the Guidance Note thus addresses some of the gendered obstacles to participation, it further acknowledges that gender is extremely relevant to the types of reparations that may be appropriate in particular cases. As one illustration, if women face considerable obstacles in accessing or keeping money, a one-off compensation payment may not benefit them.[37] As Duggan, Bailey and Guillerot note, moreover, compensation can potentially expose women to new forms of vulnerability.[38]

Taken together, the UN Basic Principles and Guidelines, the Nairobi Declaration and the Guidance Note attest to the growing importance attached to reparations internationally. Concomitantly, the concept of reparative justice has assumed a more concrete and detailed form. These developments are to be welcomed. As Evans argues, 'The right of individuals to receive reparations for serious violations is an indispensable corollary to an effective remedy for the violations suffered'.[39] More specifically, reparations can provide a crucial linkage between the pursuit of justice and on-the-ground needs. In post-war BiH, where so much emphasis has been placed on criminal trials, this linkage remains significantly under-explored. However, the drafting of a Transitional Justice Strategy (TJS) was partly an attempt to address this.

## BiH's TJS

In 2008 and 2009, BiH's Council of Ministers and Ministry for Human Rights and Refugees, in collaboration with the UNDP, organized a series of consultations with, inter alia, representatives of government institutions and victims' associations, to reflect on transitional justice gaps and challenges in BiH. What emerged from these discussions was the need to approach the legacy of the past in a 'new, systemic and inclusive way, through the drafting of a national *Transitional Justice Strategy*'.[40] On 21 January 2010, the Council of Ministers accordingly took the decision to form an expert group tasked with drafting this strategy and

36 Ibid., at section A(6), §4.
37 Ibid., at section B, §7.
38 The authors point out, for example, that 'In Guatemala, female victims have reported being offered money by perpetrators in exchange for dropping legal proceedings. Some victims of SRV [sexual-related violence] in Guatemala are being accused by members in their community of willingly giving sex to the enemy for money'. Colleen Duggan, Claudia Paz y Paz Bailey and Julia Guillerot, 'Reparations for Sexual and Reproductive Violence: Prospects for Achieving Gender Justice in Guatemala and Peru', *International Journal of Transitional Justice* 2 (2008): 192–213, at 210.
39 Christine Evans, *The Right to Reparation in International Law for Victims of Armed Conflict* (Cambridge: Cambridge University Press, 2012), 8.
40 BiH Ministry for Human Rights and Refugees and Ministry of Justice, *Transitional Justice Strategy for Bosnia and Herzegovina 2012–2016* (March 2013), 5, available at: www.nuhanovicfoundation.org/user/file/2013_transitional_justice_strategy_bih_-_new.pdf (accessed 4 December 2015).

an action plan for its implementation; and the Ministry of Justice subsequently created a 15-member Expert Working Group (including representatives of State institutions and of civil society). The drafting process was completed in 2012.

BiH's TJS essentially seeks to ensure that transitional justice processes in BiH are more effective, streamlined and better able to address victims' needs. It does not deal with criminal prosecutions, which are covered elsewhere.[41] Instead, it focuses on the three 'pillars' of fact-finding and truth-telling, reparations and memorials and institutional reforms. For each of these pillars, it describes the current situation in BiH, before proceeding to outline the major changes/reforms that need to be made. The strategic goals that it identifies, however, are often under-developed, due to insufficient reflection on their practical realization. By way of illustration, this section focuses on the TJS's strategic goals relating to compensation and rehabilitation, which are dealt with under the 'Reparations and Memorials' pillar. Although the TJS is a general document that broadly deals with all victims, compensation and rehabilitation are two forms of reparatory justice that emerged from my interviews in BiH as being particularly relevant to survivors' long-term needs.

On the issue of compensation, the TJS notes that because there is no comprehensive approach to compensating war victims in BiH, this necessarily results 'in unequal treatment of different categories of victims and in the complete absence of compensation to some groups of victims, such as victims of torture'.[42] To tackle this, it articulates the strategic goal of ensuring that all victims of violations of international human rights law and international humanitarian law in BiH have a fully protected right to compensation.[43] This is an ambitious objective in a country where the past remains a divisive issue and where the very term 'victim' is inherently contentious and contested. As Bašić comments, 'there has arisen a competition for the victim role after the war'.[44]

41 See, for example, BiH, *Državna Strategija za Rad na Predmetima Ratnih Zločina* (December 2008), available at: www.mpr.gov.ba/web_dokumenti/Drzavna%20strategije%20za%20rad%20na%20predmetima%20RZ.pdf (accessed 2 February 2016). See also BiH, *Bosnia and Herzegovina Justice Sector Reform Strategy* 2014–2018 (May 2015), available at: www.mpr.gov.ba/organizacija_nadleznosti/planiranja_koordinacija/strateska_planiranja/strategija/13%204%20SRSP%20u%20BiH%20-%20EJ.pdf (accessed 2 February 2016).

42 BiH Ministry for Human Rights and Refugees and Ministry of Justice, *supra* note 40, at 53–54.

43 Ibid., at 73.

44 Goran Bašić, 'Constructing "Ideal Victim" Stories of Bosnian War Survivors', *Social Inclusion* 3 (2015): 25–37, at 34. Sullivan et al. note that 'The existing theoretical and correlational work on competitive victimhood suggests that it primarily occurs as a response to the moral social identity threat implied by accusations that one's group has committed illegitimate harm against an outgroup'. Daniel Sullivan, Mark J. Landau, Nyla R. Branscombe and Zachary K. Rothschild, 'Competitive Victimhood as a Response to Accusations of Ingroup Harm Doing', *Journal of Personality and Social Psychology* 102 (2012): 778–795, at 779.

To achieve this particular strategic goal, the TJS calls for the adoption of a framework law to ensure a set of 'minimum standards for the full protection of civilian victims of war and victims of torture'; and further elaboration on these minimum standards is to take place at the entity level (and in Brčko District).[45] There is no doubt that this proposed framework law would be an enormous step forward. It would, for example, hugely benefit victims of torture, of whom there are an estimated 200,000 in BiH.[46] More than 20 years after the Bosnian war ended, these victims still have no legal status.[47] The suggested framework law would similarly be important for ensuring that survivors of war rape and sexual violence have the same right to civilian victim of war status (discussed in the final section) regardless of which entity they live in. While the TJS presents this proposed framework law as the basis for a more equitable of compensation system in BiH, it does so without fully addressing the many obstacles that stand in the way of such a law (from insufficient political will and lack of cross-ethnic agreement to nationalist politics and ongoing denial); and without reflecting on possible ways of tackling or minimizing those obstacles.

Turning to rehabilitation, the TJS's strategic goal is 'To improve the rehabilitation mechanism with a view to overcoming the consequences of the war 1992–1995'.[48] Not only is this extremely vague and imprecise, but it exemplifies the TJS's broad-brush approach to victims. Such an approach is further visible in the three delineated objectives relating to this strategic goal. The first of these objectives is the provision of adequate psycho-social services.[49] The drafters stress that although the TJS adopts a 'comprehensive approach to the provision of psycho-social services to victims of war and other traumatised persons', it also recognizes the need to develop – due to the 'specific nature of their trauma' – a separate policy paper focused on victims of torture and sexual violence.[50] Indeed, at several points throughout the TJS, references are made to victims of gender-based violence and the importance of a 'gender-sensitive approach'.[51] This

45 BiH Ministry for Human Rights and Refugees and Ministry of Justice, *supra* note 40, at 74.
46 Denis Džidić, 'Victims of Torture Want New State Law' (19 November 2012), available at: www.balkaninsight.com/en/article/bosnian-torture-victims-want-new-state-law (accessed 10 December 2015).
47 Agencija Anadolija, '*Bivši logoraši traže donošenje zakona o pravima žrtava torture*' (26 June 2016), available at: www.oslobodjenje.ba/vijesti/bih/bivsi-logorasi-traze-donosenje-zakona-o-pravima-zrtava-torture/173692 (accessed 7 January 2017). In practice, 'Torture victims may achieve their rights and legal interests within the existing legal regulations defining… social welfare and the rights of war veterans, but 78 per cent of the assessed candidates have not achieved those rights because they do not meet the selection criteria'. *Vive Žene*, '"Yesterday's Torture Victims, Today's System Victims. What Shall We Be Tomorrow?"', *Journal of Articles: Rehabilitation of Torture Victims* 4 (2013): 43–58, at 56.
48 BiH Ministry for Human Rights and Refugees and Ministry of Justice, *supra* note 40, at 76.
49 Ibid., at 77.
50 Ibid., at 78.
51 Ibid., at 26.

'gender dimension' of the TJS, however, remains under-developed and appears somewhat 'tagged on'. The TJS would arguably have been a stronger document if it had dealt with different categories of victims separately rather than together. This would have potentially allowed for the formulation and articulation of more nuanced objectives that are better tailored to the needs of particular groups of victims.

Further illustrating this point, the TJS's second specific objective relating to the strategic goal of rehabilitating victims is 'To improve mechanisms for employment and self-employment of victims of war and persons with disabilities for the purpose of their social reintegration and economic independence'.[52] It is unclear why the TJS groups together general victims of war with the more specific category of persons with disabilities, and the fact that it does so is unhelpful. It posits, for example, that facilitating the employment and self-employment of victims of war and people with disabilities 'will result in destigmatisation of these categories of persons and their rehabilitation and social reintegration'.[53] Whether there is indeed a positive correlation between employment and stigma will arguably depend on both the nature of that employment (including the extent to which it creates opportunities for social interaction) and the particular type of stigma in question. The stigma surrounding rape and sexual violence, for example, which often includes elements of reproach and blame,[54] is qualitatively different from disability-related stigma. In the latter case, the roots of stigma may partly lie in perceived difference; those with disabilities are 'not like us'.[55] This critique is not to suggest that employment and rehabilitation are unconnected. As previously discussed in Chapter 3, many of the interviewees who participated in this research stressed that they wanted to have a job, not only to earn money but also to have a new purpose and focus in life. The relationship between employment and rehabilitation, however, needs to be more carefully explored in the context of individual needs. Employment should not be heralded as a generic solution to rehabilitating war victims.

The TJS's third stated objective linked to rehabilitation is 'To ensure a systemic approach to inclusion of victims of war and persons with disabilities in various forms of creative and sporting activities, as specific forms of rehabilitation'.[56] It

52 Ibid., at 79.

53 Ibid., at 80.

54 See, for example, Karen G. Weiss, 'Too Ashamed to Report: Deconstructing the Shame of Sexual Victimization', *Feminist Criminology* 5 (2010): 286–310, at 289.

55 According to a Bosnian researcher from Human Rights Watch, 'Over the last couple of years, I've met hundreds of children and adults in the Western Balkans who have been locked up and hidden away in institutions for the simple fact that they have a disability'. Emina Ćerimović, 'Dispatches: Straight Talk about Disability' (3 December 2015), available at: www.hrw.org/news/2015/12/03/dispatches-straight-talk-about-disability (accessed 16 June 2016).

56 BiH Ministry for Human Rights and Refugees and Ministry of Justice, *supra* note 40, at 80.

goes on to discuss the need to include war victims and persons with disabilities in policymaking processes.[57] Not only is this a completely separate matter from inclusion in sporting and cultural activities, but it is primarily an equal opportunities issue rather than a reparations issue per se. Furthermore, no attention is given to the possible difficulties of including victims of war and persons with disabilities in sport and creative activities. The TJS recognizes, for example, that high levels of trauma exist among citizens in BiH,[58] yet the widespread use of medicines such as sedatives and benzodiazepines can itself obstruct the possible relationship between sport and rehabilitation. Critically, 'side effects related to psychiatric medications, dealing with symptoms, and physical comorbidities' can all constitute barriers to physical exercise in individuals with psychiatric conditions.[59]

Notwithstanding its flaws, the TJS does draw important attention to the fact that war victims in BiH have long-term needs which are not currently being adequately addressed. In relation to those who have suffered gender-based violence, moreover, it emphasizes the need to develop 'a specialized, integrated and multidisciplinary approach, in view of the multidimensional and long-lasting disproportionate effects of these crimes on women, girls, their families and their communities'.[60] Unfortunately, it does not elaborate on what this approach might look like. Five years after it was drafted, however, the TJS has still not been adopted, and this outcome was not unforeseeable. The Strategy was always going to encounter serious challenges in a country where the war remains a profoundly contentious issue;[61] and, as previously noted, it needed to more explicitly deal with some of these challenges in the context of its strategic goals.

The challenges, moreover, are not only of a political nature. They also extend to the economic sphere, reflecting the fact that the implementation of the TJS would have huge financial implications for BiH. The budget estimate contained in the TJS is 16,477,500.00 KM (approximately £7,345,369),[62] a figure that does not include costs relating to reparations programmes, construction of memorials or vetting processes. Those who drafted the TJS insist that BiH has the money to implement it. According to Goran Simić, for example, 'Our society will have to ask itself one day whether it is more important to build a stretch

57 Ibid.
58 Ibid., at 61.
59 Crystal M. Glover, Joelle C. Ferron and Rob Whitley, 'Barriers to Exercise among People with Severe Mental Illnesses', *Psychiatric Rehabilitation Journal* 36 (2013): 45–47, at 46.
60 BiH Ministry for Human Rights and Refugees and Ministry of Justice, *supra* note 40, at 53.
61 According to Laketa and Suleymanova, BiH is an example of a contested nation-building project 'where narratives on the violent past are implicated in political struggles and strategies to control collective and individual memories and emotions'. Sunčana Laketa and Dilyara Suleymanova, 'Enacting the Contested Past: Conflict Narratives in Educational Spaces', *Geographica Helvetica* 75 (2017): 5–16, at 13.
62 BiH Ministry for Human Rights and Refugees and Ministry of Justice, *supra* note 40, at 109.

of road or give a mother who lost four sons and 20 family members a dignified life'.[63] Such arguments problematically reduce complex decision-making to simple black and white, either/or choices. Fundamentally, the process of dealing with the past must take place ***alongside*** the process of building the future. The two are integrally intertwined, and any comprehensive transitional justice strategy should recognize this. Underlining this point, Aleksandra Pandurević, chairwoman of the Human Rights Commission of the State parliament, has criticized the TJS on the grounds that 'There is pressure on Bosnia to take on financial obligations that we cannot fund, unless we want the country to go bankrupt'.[64]

It remains to be seen whether the TJS will ultimately be adopted, though this seems highly unlikely.[65] Even if it is never implemented, it does at least provide an important basis for thinking creatively about transitional justice, and in particular reparations. To date, however, reparations remain a neglected dimension of transitional justice in BiH, and many of the long-term effects of rape and sexual violence remain unaddressed. At the grassroots level, NGOs like *Snaga Žene* and *Medica Zenica* are doing valuable work to rehabilitate survivors of rape and sexual violence, as will be discussed more in the final chapter. At the official level, in contrast, far less is being done to foster reparative justice. Survivors can essentially seek reparations via two main routes, namely a court route and an administrative route. While the former is extremely limited, the latter is a route to social payments rather than reparations per se. Each of these routes will be explored in turn.

## The court route to reparations

In the *Lubanga* case at the ICC, the Appeals Chamber underlined that 'The reparation scheme provided for in the [Rome] Statute is not only one of the Statute's unique features. It is also a key feature. The success of the Court is, to some extent, linked to the success of its system of reparations'.[66] Article 75 of the Rome Statute stipulates that 'The Court may make an order directly against a convicted person specifying appropriate reparations to, or in respect of, victims,

63 Cited in Denis Džidić, 'Bosnian Transitional Strategy Hangs on Political Support' (18 July 2012), available at: www.balkaninsight.com/en/article/bosnian-transitional-justice-strategy-hangs-on-political-support/1431/3 (accessed 7 June 2016).

64 Ibid.

65 In a recent report, Amnesty International notes that 'At the time of the writing, there were no indications that the political commitment for the adoption of this policy document was forthcoming'. Amnesty International, *Bosnia and Herzegovina: Submission to the United Nations Human Rights Committee 119th Session, 6–29 March 2017* (March 2017), 5, available at: www.amnesty.org/en/documents/eur63/5554/2017/en/ (accessed 14 March 2017).

66 *Prosecutor v. Thomas Lubanga Dyilo*, ICC-01/04-01/06-3129, ICC Appeal Judgement, Annex A (3 March 2015), §3.

including restitution, compensation and rehabilitation'.[67] Additionally, Article 79 provides for the establishment of a Trust Fund for Victims (TFV).[68] The TFV has been working with victim communities in the DRC and Uganda since 2008, and the key aim of its diverse programmes is to 'address the harm resulting from the crimes under the jurisdiction of the ICC by assisting victims to return to a dignified and contributory life within their communities'.[69]

In a statement to the UN Security Council in June 2011, the ICTY's then president, Judge Patrick Robinson, underscored the need for the Tribunal to have its own Trust Fund to support victims. Opining that 'The Tribunal cannot, through the rendering of its Judgements alone, bring peace and reconciliation to the region', he further stressed that 'Other remedies should complement the criminal trials if lasting peace is to be achieved, and one such remedy should be adequate assistance to the victims for their suffering'.[70] Such a Fund was never established, and there is limited provision for remedies within the ICTY's Statute.[71] Article 24(3) states that: 'In addition to imprisonment, the Trial Chambers may order the return of any property and proceeds acquired by criminal conduct, including by means of duress, to their rightful owners'.[72] As regards remedies for more serious harms, such as bodily or mental harm, Rule 106 of the Tribunal's RPE specifies, inter alia, that:

(A) The Registrar shall transmit to the competent authorities of the States concerned the judgement finding the accused guilty of a crime which has caused injury to a victim.

67 ICC, *Rome Statute of the International Criminal Court* (17 July 1998), Article 75, available at: www.icc-cpi.int/nr/rdonlyres/ea9aeff7-5752-4f84-be94-0a655eb30e16/0/rome_statute_english.pdf (accessed 8 July 2016)

68 Ibid., at Article 79.

69 See www.trustfundforvictims.org/about-us

70 ICTY, 'Statement by Judge Patrick Robinson, President of the International Criminal Tribunal for the Former Yugoslavia, to the Security Council on 6 June 2011' (6 June 2011), available at: www.icty.org/x/file/Press/Statements%20and%20Speeches/President/110606_pdt_robinson_un_sc.pdf (accessed 7 May 2016). It is interesting that Judge Robinson explicitly linked the issue of reparations with peace and reconciliation. The Supreme Court Chamber of the Extraordinary Chambers in the Courts of Cambodia (ECCC) has taken a far more narrow view of remedies in this regard, underlining that 'the ECCC cannot be overloaded with utopian expectations that would ultimately exceed the attainable goals of transitional justice'. *Prosecutor v. Guek Eav Kaing*, 001/18-07-2007-ECCC/SC, Appeal Judgement (3 February 2012), §655.

71 Liesbeth Ziegveld, 'Victims' Reparations Claims and International Criminal Courts: Incompatible Values?' *Journal of International Criminal Justice* 8 (2010): 79–111, at 87–88.

72 ICTY, *Updated Statute of the International Criminal Tribunal for the Former Yugoslavia* (September 2009), Article 24(3), available at: www.icty.org/x/file/Legal%20Library/Statute/statute_sept09_en.pdf (accessed 3 December 2015). See also ICTR, *Statute: International Criminal Tribunal for Rwanda (ICTR)* (31 January 2010), Article 23(3), available at: http://unictr.unmict.org/en/documents/statute-and-creation (accessed 8 December 2015).

(B) Pursuant to the relevant national legislation, a victim or persons claiming through the victim may bring an action in a national court or other competent body to obtain compensation.[73]

If, as De Brouwer maintains, the Tribunal was concerned about the potentially high number of compensation claims that it might face, Rule 106 was essentially a way of pre-emptively managing this.[74] The reference in Rule 106 to 'national courts', and the fact that it is these courts that are now tasked with prosecuting war crimes cases, gives added salience to the court route to reparations in BiH. In using the term 'court route', this section focuses specifically on the State Court of BiH in Sarajevo. The War Crimes Chamber of the State Court commenced its work in March 2005, and it has been described as 'the most significant national effort in Bosnia and Herzegovina to investigate and prosecute persons allegedly involved in serious violations of international law during the 1992–1995 conflict'.[75] As regards obtaining reparations, however, victims – including individuals who suffered rape and sexual violence during the Bosnian war – face serious hurdles.

### *Reparations challenges*

According to Bosnian law, war victims can submit claims for damages under property law. Article 195 of the Criminal Procedure Code variously states that:

(1) A petition to pursue a claim under property law in criminal proceedings shall be filed with the Prosecutor or Court.
(2) The petition may be submitted no later than the end of the main trial or sentencing hearing before the Court.
(3) The person authorized to submit the petition must state his claim specifically and must submit evidence.
(4) If the authorized person has not filed the petition to pursue his claim under property law in criminal proceedings before the indictment is confirmed, he

73 ICTY, *Rules of Procedure and Evidence* (8 July 2015), Rule 76, available at: www.icty.org/x/file/Legal%20Library/Rules_procedure_evidence/IT032Rev50_en.pdf (accessed 8 October 2016).
74 Anne-Marie De Brouwer, 'Reparation to Victims of Sexual Violence: Possibilities at the International Criminal Court and at the Trust Fund for Victims and their Families', *Leiden Journal of International Law* 20 (2007): 207–237, at 215.
75 Bogdan Ivanišević, *The War Crimes Chamber in Bosnia and Herzegovina: From Hybrid to Domestic Court'*, ICTJ (2008), available at: www.ictj.org/sites/default/files/ICTJ-FormerYugoslavia-Domestic-Court-2008-English.pdf (accessed 8 April 2016). It is also important to emphasize that the majority of information that is available on courts and reparations in BiH specifically pertains to the State Court, which has a useful and well-maintained website. See www.sudbih.gov.ba/

> shall be informed that he may file that petition by the end of the main trial or sentencing hearing.[76]

In reality, however, a number of factors impede war victims from making property claims in criminal proceedings. According to a legal advisor from TRIAL International – previously known as TRIAL (Track Impunity Always) – victims 'are frequently not informed at all or are insufficiently informed by competent authorities about their rights and the manner in which they may obtain [them]'.[77] In one of the trials that I was able to observe at the State Court, several rape survivors were asked before they gave their testimony whether they wanted to pursue a property claim and all of them answered in the affirmative. However, during my subsequent discussions with them, it emerged that they knew little or nothing about making a property claim or what it actually meant; and indeed, two of them believed that a successful claim would give them civilian victim of war status (a completely separate issue that is discussed in the final section).

If survivors do apply for damages, this might affect how the Court perceives them. In the *Baričanin* case, for example, a Bosniak survivor who suffered multiple rapes did not apply for damages, and the Trial Chamber attached considerable weight to this. It adjudged that:

> In support of the truthfulness of her evidence and the intent to testify sufficiently speaks the fact that during the proceedings she filed no property claim, nor did she request any pecuniary compensation for the tragedy survived. This only stands in support of the witness's sincerity.[78]

This is a potentially damaging judgement that sends entirely the wrong message, by problematically conflating the separate issues of truthfulness and exercise of rights. It could thereby contribute to exacerbating a common fear among survivors (which some interviewees expressed) that they will not be believed in court.[79] According to Hanušić, the judgement also reflects, more broadly, the

76 BiH, *Criminal Procedure Code of Bosnia Herzegovina* (24 January 2003), Article 195, available at: www.nuhanovicfoundation.org/user/file/criminal_procedure_code_of_bosnia_and_herzegovina_2003.pdf_-_placed.pdf (accessed 9 June 2016).

77 Adrijana Hanušić, *Enforcement of Damage Compensation Claims of Victim of War in Criminal Proceedings in Bosnia and Herzegovina: Situation, Challenges and Perspectives*, TRIAL (2015), 18, available at: http://trial.ba/wp-content/uploads/2015/10/ENG_Ostvarivanje-zahtjeva-za-naknadu-%C5%A1tete-%C5%BErtava-ratnih-zlo%C4%8Dina-u-okviru-krivi%C4%8Dnih-postupaka-u-Bosni-i-Hercegovini-%E2%80%93-stanje-problemi-i-perspektive-.pdf (accessed 9 December 2015).

78 *Prosecutor v. Saša Baričanin*, S1 1 K004648 11 Kri (X-KR-05/111), State Court of BiH Trial Chamber Judgement (9 November 2011), §230.

79 Gentleman remarks on the paradox that 'Victims of burglary do not have to prove that they have been burgled or to justify their behaviour before the burglary. With rape and sexual assault allegations, victims still find themselves subjected to hostile questioning'. Amelia Gentleman, 'Prosecuting Sexual Assault: "Raped all over again"' (13 April 2013), available

judges' insufficient awareness and knowledge of the 'fundamental rights and needs of victims, and maybe partly even a general stigmatization of victims'.[80]

The actual process of applying for damages, moreover, is typically long and protracted. Article 198(2) of the Criminal Procedure Code of BiH states that:

> In a verdict pronouncing the accused guilty, the Court may award the injured party the entire claim under property law or may award him part of the claim under property law and refer him to a civil action for the remainder. If the data of criminal proceedings do not provide a reliable basis for either a complete or partial award, the Court shall instruct the injured party that he may take civil action to pursue his entire claim under property law.[81]

Article 198(3) further stipulates that 'If the Court renders a verdict acquitting the accused of the charge or dropping the charges or if it decides to discontinue criminal proceedings, it shall instruct the injured party that he may pursue his claim under property law in a civil action'.[82] Even in cases which result in a guilty verdict, however, the State Court has overwhelmingly followed the practice of referring individuals to civil courts.[83] In 2009, for example, the Trial Chamber convicted Milorad Trbić, a former assistant commander within the Zvornik Brigade of the VRS, of genocide and other crimes committed in Srebrenica in 1995. It sentenced him to 30 years' imprisonment. More than 3,000 victims and families of the dead and missing from Srebrenica filed property claims against the defendant but the judges declined to deal with them, seemingly on practical grounds. In accordance with Article 198(2) of the Criminal Procedure Code, the Court referred the victims 'to pursue their property claims by taking civil action, considering that the process of establishing the facts in terms of the amounts of the claims would require a longer time'.[84] Highly critical of the judgement, Clark submits that such reasoning 'might have been more convincing had it not been applied in every single case to date, including those where there was only one applicant seeking compensation'.[85]

at: www.theguardian.com/society/2013/apr/13/rape-sexual-assault-frances-andrade-court (accessed 3 April 2016).

80 Hanušić, *supra* note 77, at 15.

81 BiH, *supra* note 76, at Article 198(2).

82 Ibid., at Article 198(3).

83 Kate Clark, *War Reparations and Litigation: The Case of Bosnia – Report of an International Meeting held at the Law Faculty of the University of Amsterdam 17–18 April 2014 organized by the Nuhanović Foundation* (April 2014),12, available at: www.nuhanovicfoundation.org/user/file/bosniareport-digi.pdf (accessed 1 July 2016).

84 *Prosecutor v. Milorad Trbić*, X-KR-07/386, State Court of BiH Trial Chamber Judgement (16 October 2009), §873.

85 Clark, *supra* note 83, at 12. In 2014, the BiH Constitutional Court quashed the appellate verdict and ordered a re-trial, on the grounds that the State Court had applied the BiH Criminal Code rather than the more lenient SFRY Criminal Code – and had thus violated the defendant's rights under the European Convention of Human Rights. Marija Tausan,

It is also important to underline that not everyone seeking damages will be able to pursue a claim in the civil courts. Firstly, they may not have the financial resources to do so. It has been noted, for example, that 'victims would need a lawyer to represent them in civil claims for compensation and, in almost the totality of cases, they cannot afford it, while free legal aid is not granted to them by the State'.[86] Certainly, almost all of the men and women interviewed for this research described their economic position as 'bad' or 'catastrophic'; and it will be recalled from Chapter 3 that many of them were struggling to afford even essential items such as medicines. Secondly, because survivors of rape and sexual violence frequently testify as protected witnesses, this means that they cannot apply for damages in civil proceedings unless they are prepared to disclose their identity – and thus to potentially jeopardize their personal safety or the safety of their families. The previous chapter introduced interviewee Ć13. She underlined that while she wanted to pursue her right to seek damages, she could not take the risk of losing her status as a protected witness. She described herself as a 'proud woman' and insisted that local people must never know what she had experienced during the war. She also feared possible revenge attacks, including from the defendants' families.[87] How many other survivors are in Ć13's position and unable to apply for damages is unclear as there is no information on this.

Notwithstanding the enormous challenges that confront survivors (and indeed all war victims) in BiH who wish to apply for compensation, the State Court delivered two key judgements in 2015 – against Bosiljko and Ostoja Marković and Slavko Savić respectively. In both cases, it ordered the defendants to pay damages to women who were raped during the war. The high expectations that these two judgements raised at the time,[88] however, have not been met.

'Milorad Trbić's Verdict Quashed' (7 November 2014), available at: www.justice-report.com/en/articles/milorad-trbic-s-verdict-quashed (accessed 3 July 2016). In 2015, following a re-trial, Trbić's sentence was reduced to 20 years.

86 TRIAL (Track Impunity Always), Women's International League for Peace and Freedom, Association of Genocide Victims and Witnesses and Association Movement of Mothers of Srebrenica and Žepa Enclaves, *General Allegation on the Situation in Bosnia and Herzegovina to the Special Rapporteur on Truth, Justice, Reparations and Guarantees of Non-Recurrence* (February 2004), §109, available at: https://trialinternational.org/latest-post/general-allegation-to-the-special-rapporteur-on-truth-justice-and-reparations/ (accessed 25 June 2016). Furthermore, 'Civil litigation regularly results in the dismissal of claims based on statutes of limitations (zastara), forcing survivors – most of whom are already destitute – to pay high court fees'. TRIAL International, *Compensating Survivors in Criminal Proceedings: Perspectives from the Field: A Report by TRIAL International in Bosnia and Herzegovina* (2016), 7, available at: https://trialinternational.org/wp-content/uploads/2016/11/TRIAL-International_compensation-publication_EN_web.pdf (accessed 13 March 2017).

87 Author interview, 23 April 2015.

88 Following the *Marković* judgement, for example, Adrijana Hanušić from TRIAL underlined that 'This is an important moment both for the war crime victim, to whom the compensation will be paid, and for all other victims in Bosnia and Herzegovina and the region, who can now hope that this precedent will pave the road for them to fulfill their right to

### *The Marković and Savić judgements*

On 24 June 2015, the State Court convicted Bosiljko and Ostoja Marković, two Bosnian Serb soldiers, of raping a 14-year-old Bosnian Croat girl (referred to in the judgement as S-4) in Kotor Varoš in June 1992.[89] It sentenced the defendants to ten years' imprisonment each (upheld on appeal) and, exceptionally, it granted S-4's claim under Article 198(2) of the Criminal Procedure Code. She had filed a claim under property law for compensation of the non-pecuniary damage that she suffered as a consequence of being raped during the war, including psychological and physical pain and diminished quality of life. Significantly, this was the first time that anyone had successfully claimed war damages in criminal – as opposed to civil – proceedings in BiH.

Drawing on forensic expert opinion, the judgement discusses in considerable detail some of the multiple ways in which the trauma of being raped had affected S-4, both at the time and in the long term.[90] At the time of the trial, 23 years after she was raped, S-4 was still receiving psychotherapy and needed 'professional medical help to achieve a satisfactory psychological balance'.[91] Concluding that her war trauma had caused 'enormous mental pain and suffering', resulting in 'immeasurable consequences for her life and health'[92] and reducing her quality of life by 12 per cent,[93] the Court decided that S-4 was entitled to compensation of non-pecuniary damages under Article 202 of the Law on Obligations. It ordered the two defendants to jointly pay S-4 a sum of 26,500 KM (£11,878), namely 20,000 KM for 'the suffered mental pain resulting from the violation of personal

compensation through criminal proceedings'. Cited in Lamija Grebo, 'Marković Verdict Paves Way for Right to Compensation' (24 June 2015), available at: www.justice-report.com/en/articles/markovic-verdict-paves-way-for-right-to-compensation (accessed 26 June 2015).

89 The defendants were found guilty of the criminal offence of war crimes against civilians in violation of Article 142(1) of the Criminal Code of the SFRY (CC SFRY). This Code was adopted on 28 September 1976. When BiH became independent, the CC SFRY was adopted as the country's own Criminal Code on 11 April 1992. The judgement notes that 'In Article 142 of the adopted CC SFRY, the legislator provides no definition of the term of rape or inhumane treatment. However, statutory rules relating to torture or inhumane treatment have been well defined by customary international law, as well as by the ICTY's and ICTR's jurisprudence'. *Prosecutor v. Bosiljko Marković and Ostoja Marković*, S1 1 K 012024 14 Kri, State Court of BiH Trial Chamber Judgement (24 June 2015), §208. It concluded that 'the Accused's acts, committed in complicity with the acts undertaken by Predrag Cicmanović [a fellow member of the Koros-Varoš Brigade of the VRS], resulted in the consequences which, by their intensity, duration, and the fact that a minor girl was affected, may qualify as the acts of inhumane treatment. At the same time, pursuant to the existent case law, these acts qualify as the acts of rape'. Judgement, *Marković*, at §210.

90 Ibid., at §237.

91 Ibid., at §238.

92 Ibid.

93 Ibid., at §241.

liberty and rights' and 6,500 KM for the 'mental pain due to diminished quality of life'.[94]

On 29 June 2015, just five days after the *Marković* case was decided, the State Court found Slavko Savić – a former member of the Vogošćanska Light Infantry Brigade of the VRS – guilty of raping a Bosniak woman in Vogošća near Sarajevo in 1993. Savić raped this woman (referred to in the judgement as the 'injured party') twice in 1993. On both occasions, he came to her house, forced her to get into a vehicle with him and subsequently raped her orally and vaginally. Her 11-year-old daughter (Witness E) was present both times when Savić appeared at the house. According to the judgement, 'Witness E described her own feelings at the time when the armed person abducted her mother: she was frozen and in shock'.[95] After the first rape, her mother became pregnant, and she had an abortion after the second rape took place.

Like interviewee Ć13, the 'injured party' in the *Savić* case was a protected witness, and she argued that she was therefore not in a position to pursue a claim for damages in civil law proceedings.[96] She filed a claim under property law instead, seeking 80,000 KM (£35,858).[97] In considering this claim, the Court – as in the *Marković* case – paid close attention to some of the long-term consequences of rape. It noted, for example, that:

> in describing the circumstances of the criminal offense at issue, the injured party stated that she has changed a lot after the incident, withdrew in herself, and that she was more active while her children, who had given her the 'élan',[98] were with her. The witness subsequently 'became depressed' and today feels worthless and hurt, having lost her self-confidence. The witness stated that she is still today being treated at … [it did not name the place] (as confirmed by the medical documentation).[99]

This woman had also experienced problems with alcohol, but was 'currently in the phase of abstinence';[100] and according to a forensic-psychiatric expert witness who examined her, Savić's crimes had diminished her quality of life by 25 per cent.[101] By way of elaboration, the judgement explains that 'the expert witness stated that the speed of the injured party's memorizing, cognitive memory, concentration, and

94 Ibid., at §242.
95 *Prosecutor v. Slavko Savić*, S1 1 K 017213 14 Kri, State Court of BiH Trial Chamber Judgement (29 June 2015), §203.
96 Ibid., at §14.
97 Ibid., at §46.
98 The judgement uses the French spelling of the word, which essentially means 'energy' or 'momentum'.
99 Judgement, *Savić*, *supra* note 95, at §224.
100 Ibid., at §396.
101 Ibid., at §391.

learning has been slowed down and impaired, because … [a condition which the Court did not name] affects the learning ability, wherefore the injured party's primary intellectual and mental abilities are presently diminished'.[102] Sentencing Savić to eight years' imprisonment, the Court also ordered him to pay the injured party 30,000 KM (£13,447), of which 16,000 KM for the mental pain caused by the violation of her liberty or personal rights and 14,000 KM for the suffering caused by her diminished quality of life.[103]

By ordering Savić to pay compensation, the Trial Chamber opined that it had thus 'established a principle of social justice'.[104] It held that 'the purpose of trial must not be merely the repression against the perpetrator, but rather it should seek to completely restore the situation violated by the criminal offense (committed)'.[105] One is left wondering, however, how the judges expected Savić to pay the 30,000 KM. They decided, for example, that it was appropriate to relieve him of the duty to pay court costs, on the basis that 'he is indigent (according to the data in the case record, namely the Defense's evidence), owns no property, that he, his wife and one of his sons are recorded on the list of unemployed persons of the Employment Bureau, while his two other children are regular university students'.[106] They further underlined that as Savić would spend a number of years in prison, he would not be in a position to earn any income.[107]

Bosiljko and Ostoja Marković, similarly, were not required to reimburse the cost of the court proceedings. Not only did Ostoja Marković have a proven disability, but the Trial Chamber also noted 'evidence showing that the Accused are unemployed, and have no steady income, wherefore the payment of the costs would undermine the accused persons' subsistence'.[108] It is unsurprising, therefore, that in both the *Marković* and *Savić* cases, compensation remains unpaid.[109] Nedžla Šehić, a Bosnian lawyer, has insisted that if the men fail to make the

102 Ibid., at §399.
103 Ibid., at §406.
104 Ibid., at §424.
105 Ibid.
106 Ibid., at §425.
107 Ibid., at §426.
108 Judgement, *Marković*, *supra* note 89, at §231.
109 More recently, on 16 March 2016, Adil Vojić and Bekir Mesić were found guilty of the criminal offence of war crimes against civilians – including the rape of a woman in Bihać – and sentenced to seven years' imprisonment each. They were ordered to pay the victim 28,000 KM (£12,387) in compensation. Balkan Transitional Justice, 'Bosnian Soldiers Jailed for Wartime Rape in Bihać' (16 March 2016), available at: www.balkaninsight.com/en/article/bosnian-fighters-sentenced-for-bihac-wartime-rape-03-16-2016 (accessed 20 May 2016). Seven months later, on 6 October 2016, Krsto Dostić was found guilty of at least two rapes of a Bosnian Muslim woman in the town of Foča and sentenced to ten years' imprisonment. While he was relieved of the obligation to pay court costs, he was ordered to pay the victim 40,000 KM (£17,893), namely 15,000 KM for mental pain caused by violation of personal rights and freedoms and 25,000 KM for mental pain caused by diminished quality of life. See State Court of BiH, 'Krsto Dostić Sentenced to 10 Years

necessary payments, she will proceed to file lawsuits against RS.[110] Any such legal action, however, would almost certainly fail. As one commentator points out, RS 'has declared all suits requesting compensation for wartime non-material damage to be obsolete under its statute of limitations'.[111] The State Court does have the possibility of commencing a forced payment procedure, but it can only do so in cases where a defendant has a salary, pension or saleable assets. According to Savić's lawyer, Nevenka Vitomir, 'He does not have this money. So I expect these proceedings to be terminated'.[112]

Interestingly, research conducted by TRIAL International in 2016 has shown that compensation may still be important even if it is never actually paid. The 31 interviewees who participated in the research – including survivors, psychologists and social workers – variously associated compensation with recognition, empowerment and rehabilitation which, they argued, were 'more valuable than monetary reimbursement'.[113] The authors also underline, however, that 'failed enforcement over a *lengthy* time period could chip away at "justice now" and the real progress achieved by the awarding of court-ordered damages'.[114]

of Imprisonment' (6 October 2016), available at: www.sudbih.gov.ba/vijest/krsto-dosti-osuen-na-10-godina-zatvora-20423 (accessed 9 December 2016). The judgements in these two cases are not available.

110 Justice Report, 'Bosnian Rape Victims Struggle for Compensation' (9 September 2016), available at: www.balkaninsight.com/en/article/bosnian-war-rape-victims-struggle-for-compensation-09-09-2016/1440/4 (accessed 10 September 2016).

111 Amer Jahić, 'Bosnia Struggles with Rape Compensation' (14 August 2015), available at: www.balkaninsight.com/en/article/bosnia-struggles-with-war-rape-compensation-08-13-2015 (accessed 7 September 2015). In RS, 'The deadlines applied are 3 years since the date the injured person got to know of the existence of the damage and 5 years since the date the damage occurred. In practice, they are calculated from the date of 19.06.1996, as the date when RS Parliament pronounced the cessation of war and "imminent-danger-of-war situation"'. TRIAL et al., *supra* note 86, at 33, n118. Many victims have therefore been prevented from obtaining damages. Moreover, if they do file a damages claim and fail, they may be ordered to pay court costs. Suljo Topčić, for example, spent 14 months in the Sušica and Batković camps during the Bosnian war. He pursued a damages claim in a court in RS but this was rejected on the grounds that the period for making such a claim had expired. In addition, 'Because he lost, Topčić was ordered to pay 670 euros in court costs, which is now being deducted from his wages when they are paid into his account'. Albina Sorguč, 'Bosnian Courts Deny Compensation to War Prisoners' (8 December 2015), available at: www.justice-report.com/en/articles/bosnian-courts-deny-compensation-to-war-prisoners (accessed 15 December 2015).

112 Cited in Balkan Transitional Justice, 'Bosnian Serb Convict Fails to Compensate Rape Victim' (9 June 2016), available at: www.balkaninsight.com/en/article/bosnian-serb-convict-fails-to-pay-rape-victim-06-09-2016/1443/6 (accessed 9 June 2016).

113 TRIAL International, *supra* note 86, at 25.

114 Ibid., at 26.

## The administrative route to reparations

On 29 May 2015, Croatia's parliament (Sabor) adopted the Law on the Rights of Victims of Sexual Violence during the Armed Aggression against the Republic of Croatia in the Homeland War. This represents an important, albeit delayed, effort to respond to some of the long-term needs of survivors in Croatia.[115] Article 15 of the Law, for example, states that survivors may be entitled, inter alia, to psycho-social support, legal assistance, medical care and rehabilitation, pecuniary compensation and health insurance.[116] There are also significant provisions for financial support. Article 24 stipulates that the beneficiary may be entitled to a one-off compensation payment of 100,000 Croatian Kuna (approximately £11,628), or to an increased pecuniary compensation of 150,000 Croatian Kuna (approximately £17,442); and Article 26 provides that survivors can obtain monthly compensation payments amounting to 73 per cent of the budget base.[117] According to the Commissioner for Human Rights of the Council of Europe:

> Concerning the implementation of the law, as of May 2016, 146 requests for recognition of the status of victim of sexual violence were submitted. Of the 90 requests which were decided upon, 76 were positive, 13 were negative and proceedings were terminated in one case. More than € 900 000 (6 979 131 Croatian kuna) in compensation has been allocated to sexual violence victims in this context.[118]

There have also been important developments in Kosovo. On 20 March 2014, Kosovo's parliament approved amendments (Law no. 04/L-172) to the Law on the Status and the Rights of the Martyrs, Invalids, Veterans, Members of

115 The UNDP has estimated that there are up to 2,000 survivors of conflict-related rape and sexual violence in Croatia. UNDP, *Assessment of the Number of Sexual Violence Victims during the Homeland War on the Territory of the Republic of Croatia and Optimal Forms of Compensation and Support to Victims* (December 2013), 42, available at: www.hr.undp.org/content/dam/croatia/docs/Research%20and%20publications/socialinclusion/UNDP-HR-SEXUAL%20-VIOLENCE%20-IN%20-CONFLICT-RESEARCH-ENG-2014.pdf (accessed 8 August 2015).

116 The Law is only available online in Croatian; see www.zakon.hr/z/794/Zakon-o-pravima-%25C5%25BErtava-seksualnog-nasilja-za-vrijeme-oru%25C5%25BEane-agresije-na-Republiku-Hrvatsku-u-Domovinskom-ratu

117 See Janine N. Clark, 'In from the Margins: Survivors of Wartime Sexual Violence in Croatia and an Early Analysis of the New Law', *Journal of Human Rights Practice* 8 (2016): 128–147.

118 Nils Muižnieks, *Report by Nils Muižnieks: Commissioner for Human Rights of the Council of Europe*, CommDH(2016)31 (5 October 2016), §33, available at: https://rm.coe.int/CoERMPublicCommonSearchServices/DisplayDCTMContent?documentId=09000016806db766 (accessed 8 December 2016).

the Kosovo Liberation Army, Sexual Violence Victims of the War, Civilian Victims and Their Families. These amendments provide for the legal recognition of civilian victims of sexual violence.[119] On 30 December 2015, the parliament further passed Regulation no. 22/2015 on Defining the Procedures for Recognition and Verification of the Status of Sexual Violence Victims during the Kosovo Liberation War; this 'provides the authority for the establishment of the Government Commission on Recognition and Verification of the Status of Sexual Violence Victims During the Kosovo Liberation War'.[120] This Commission (which will comprise members of the government and civil society) is in the process of being established. It is not yet known how exactly it will operate, or how much money survivors will be entitled to receive. However, it is likely to be less than 200 Euros per month, and some survivors may feel that this is not enough to offset the possible risks (including exposure to social stigma) of applying.[121]

While Croatia and Kosovo are just beginning to recognize survivors of conflict-related rape and sexual violence, BiH is considerably further ahead. Survivors have long been able to apply for civilian victim of war status, at least in the Federation. It is important to underline, however, that the monetary payments that civilian victims of war receive are essentially social protection rather than reparations/compensation. To cite TRIAL International, 'the system is geared toward supporting vulnerable groups, not remedying human rights violations'.[122] The fact that social protection is available is nevertheless a step forward, and indeed BiH was the first country in the world to offer survivors monetary monthly payments. In practice, however, many problems exist, and they are compounded by the critical absence of any State-level law on the rights of survivors of rape and sexual violence. This section accordingly deals with the two entities separately.

119 Petrit Collaku, 'Kosovo Plans Benefits for War Rape Victims' (22 June 2015), available at: www.balkaninsight.com/en/article/verification-commission-on-sexual-violence-to-create-during-this-year (accessed 9 June 2016). These amendments were extremely controversial and faced strong opposition from ex-combatants. See Malin Ekerstedt, 'New Hope for Kosovo's Survivors of War Rape' (2 November 2014), available at: http://kvinnatillkvinna.se/en/2014/02/11/new-hope-for-kosovos-survivors-of-war-rape/ (accessed 9 June 2016).

120 UN Women Kosovo, *The Conflict did not Bring us Flowers: The Need for Comprehensive Reparations for Survivors of Conflict-Related Sexual Violence in Kosovo* (July 2016), 30, available at: www.unwomen.org/-/media/headquarters/attachments/sections/library/publications/2016/the-conflict-did-not-bring-us-flowers_eng.pdf?vs=5055 (accessed 9 August 2016).

121 Kristen Chick, 'Ending the Shame of Kosovo's Rape Victims' (22 February 2016), available at: http://foreignpolicy.com/2016/02/22/the-rape-victims-of-kosovo-bosnia-commission/ (accessed 8 August 2016).

122 TRIAL International, *supra* note 86, at 42.

### *Survivors in the Federation*

In the BiH Federation, it is the Law on Principles of Social Protection, Protection of Civil Victims of War and Protection of Families with Children (henceforth the Law) that constitutes the legal basis of civilian victim of war status. Adopted in 1999, Article 54 of the Law defines a civilian victim of war as:

> a person who suffered at least 60 per cent of disability (hereinafter: disabled person), due to injury or wound sustained in:
> 1. abuse or deprivation of liberty through the war situation or immediate war danger
> 2. in war events (bombardment, street fights, ordnance explosion, a stray bullet)
> 3. from the explosion of ordnance after the war ended
> 4. diversionist terrorist actions which endanger the security and order in the Federation of BH.[123]

The requirement of demonstrating a 60 per cent disability is extremely problematic for survivors of rape and sexual violence. In many cases, the injuries that these men and women have suffered are primarily psychological rather than physical.[124] A group of NGOs, led by *Medica Zenica*, accordingly began a campaign calling for changes in the Law with respect to survivors. The campaign was successful and in 2006 the Law was amended. Survivors of rape and sexual violence are now a special category and they are not required, in contrast to other civilian victims of war, to demonstrate a 60 per cent disability.

An interviewee from TRIAL International in Sarajevo opined that 'This amendment to the Law is a big step forward in terms of tackling rape stigma'.[125] However, it is also striking that few survivors have taken advantage of it. To

123 Federation of BiH, *Law on Principles of Social Protection, Protection of Civil Victims of War and Protection of Families with Children* (1999), Article 54, available at www.refworld.org/pdfid/4d30226f2.pdf (accessed 9 November 2015).

124 In BiH, rape primarily took the form of penile (and sometimes digital) penetration. In many conflicts, however, objects such as sticks, guns and bottles are also used to commit rape, thus leaving the victims with serious physical injuries which may lead to death. During the civil wars in Peru and Guatemala in the 1980s and 1990s, for example, 'Women were stripped naked. Sticks and guns were thrust into the vagina and anus of prisoners'. Jean Franco, 'Rape and Human Rights', *PMLA* 121 (2006): 1662–1664, at 1663. Furthermore, in countries such as the DRC, traumatic fistula is a frequent consequence of the rapes committed by armed groups. Mathias Onsrud, Solbjørg Sjøveian, Roger Luhiriri and Dennis Mukwege, 'Sexual Violence-Related Fistulas in the Democratic Republic of Congo', *International Journal of Gynaecology and Obstetrics* 101 (2008): 265–269.

125 Author interview, 11 August 2014.

date, only 830 survivors in the Federation have successfully claimed civilian victim of war status,[126] which is approximately just 4 per cent of the estimated 20,000 men and women who suffered rape and sexual violence during the Bosnian war. There are numerous reasons for the low number of claims. Some survivors no longer live in BiH, and hence they are not eligible to apply for civilian victim of war status. Similarly, anyone who has obtained status will subsequently lose it if they leave BiH for more than three months. Some survivors may be too afraid to apply, concerned that their families would thus find out the truth. Some were killed during the war or have died subsequently. The fact that so few survivors of rape and sexual violence have secured status is also indicative of more fundamental problems. An interviewee from *Medica Zenica* identified two in particular. Firstly, not all survivors are aware that they can apply for civilian victim of war status. Secondly, the process of applying is not always straightforward.[127]

Turning to the first of these problems, among the 52 interviewees who were living in the Federation, 36 had obtained status and two were awaiting a decision on their applications. Of the remaining 16 interviewees, two were ineligible to apply for status as they were combatants during the war and not civilians. Two interviewees had unsuccessfully applied for status. Twelve interviewees, including five living in the same town, knew nothing about civilian victim of war status or that they could apply for it. Many of the survivors interviewed for this research were in contact with NGOs such as *Medica Zenica*, *Snaga Žene*, ŽŽR and *Gerc Sumaja*. As a result, they were informed of their rights and had acted on this knowledge. Those interviewees who were more isolated and who had received little, if any, support from NGOs were the least informed. It is also the case that some NGOs which profess to help survivors are in fact doing little for them. In one location, for example, the head of a local NGO maintained that she was providing a critical service to local women who were raped during the Bosnian war. However, none of the women whom I interviewed in this particular location had civilian victim of war status and none of them appeared to know anything about it. Even when NGOs are helping survivors, their knowledge of the Law may be limited. Interviewee K61, for example, who was introduced in Chapter 4, admitted that a Bosniak soldier had touched her in a sexual way and masturbated on her stomach (she would not say whether he had also raped her).[128] Keen to find out whether she could nevertheless apply for civilian victim of war status, I had to contact three different women's NGOs in order to get the answer.

126 There are no official statistics on the number of survivors who have obtained civilian victim of war status. The figure of 830 was given to me by the heads of two different women's NGOs in BiH in March 2017.

127 Author interview, 6 August 2014.

128 Author interview, 19 March 2015.

The actual process of applying for civilian victim of war status, moreover, presents its own challenges. The first step is for survivors to obtain a document certifying that they were raped. In the Federation, both the *Savez logoraša BiH* (Alliance of Camp Inmates BiH) in Sarajevo and the *Hrvatska udruga logoraša domovinskog rata BiH* (Croatian Association of Camp Inmates of the Homeland War BiH) in Busovača in Central Bosnia Canton can issue the requisite document. Survivors can also visit the NGO ŽŽR in Sarajevo and, since 2014, *Medica Zenica*.[129] Once they have obtained a certificate, survivors must send this, together with relevant supporting documentation (such as medical evidence), to the *Centar za socijalni rad* or Centre for Social Work. The Centre, of which there is one in each of the ten cantons within the Federation, subsequently sends all of the documents to a medical commission consisting of doctors, gynaecologists and psychiatrists. The medical commission will ultimately decide whether an individual should be accorded civilian victim of war status, and the Centre for Social Work will communicate this decision to the applicant. There are two levels of medical commission. If an individual's application for civilian victim of war status is rejected by the first level commission, s/he can request the local court to instruct the second level commission to re-consider the case. According to the head of *Medica Zenica*, the process previously took between six and eight months, whereas now it takes approximately three months (not including appeals against the decision of the first level commission).[130] Although this is an improvement, many problems persist.

Interviewee N21 recalled that she had first sought to obtain civilian victim of war status in 2012 and visited ŽŽR. The organization had insisted, however, that she needed to have two witnesses. Becoming increasingly upset, N21 explained that she had no witnesses. On the two occasions that she was raped, the first time in her apartment, she was alone. A couple of weeks after I interviewed her, a team from *Medica Zenica* visited N21 in her home. They told her that she did not need to have two witnesses and that medical evidence would suffice. Shortly after this, N21 sent all the necessary paperwork to the local Centre for Social Work and subsequently obtained status. For her, however, the process was deeply stressful and emotionally draining.[131] This example – and specifically the contrasting approaches of the two NGOs – also illustrates the fact that 'The

129 The head of *Medica Zenica* explained that she spent a great deal of time at the Federal Ministry, stressing the importance of giving survivors a choice. Author interview, 6 February 2015. According to Helms, Hasečić 'had been instrumental in putting her group forward as the only organization that could verify claims. When I pressed her on how this could be done with certainty, she confidently stated that she and her members "knew who the victims were"'. Elissa Helms, *Innocence and Victimhood: Gender, Nation and Women's Activism in Postwar Bosnia-Herzegovina* (Madison, WI: University of Wisconsin Press, 2013), 211–212.

130 Author interview, 6 February 2015.

131 Author interview, 26 October 2014.

procedures to be recognised as victims of sexual violence... are not always applied homogeneously'.[132]

In north-west BiH, interviewee A39 obtained a certificate from the Alliance of Camp Survivors BiH in Sarajevo, confirming that she was raped. She gave all of her documents to the relevant Centre for Social Work, but the medical commission rejected her case on the grounds that there was not enough evidence of rape. A39 has since made several visits to the Centre for Social Work, asking for help, but she has been told that she now needs to obtain a certificate from ŽŽR. She refuses to do so. She already has a certificate and Sarajevo is a significant distance from where she lives, particularly now that she has a baby to look after. She was unwilling to travel there for a second time. She also maintained that she did not want the women at ŽŽR deciding whether or not she was raped.[133]

Interviewee P17 had also been unsuccessful in her attempts to gain civilian victim of war status. A Bosnian Croat, she described how she was raped during the Bosnian war by members of her own ethnic group and, subsequently, by men from a Bosnian Muslim paramilitary group. The Croatian Association of Camp Inmates of the Homeland War had issued her with the requisite certificate and this should have been sufficient. The local Centre for Social Work, however, was refusing to accept the document, maintaining that she must have a certificate from ŽŽR. P17 had accordingly visited Hasečić's organization, but the latter had taken the decision not to issue a certificate. Although it had provided a written explanation for this, P17 was convinced that the real reason was political; as an organization run by Bosnian Muslims, ŽŽR had no interest in acknowledging that Bosniak forces also committed rape.[134] A couple of weeks after I interviewed her, P17 informed me that she was planning to go on hunger strike, as a way of drawing attention to her situation. Although she did not follow through on this, she became increasingly depressed over the following

132 TRIAL (Track Impunity Always), Association of Women-Victims of War, Centre of Legal Assistance for Women Zenica, Citizens Association *Budućnost Modriča, Forum Žene Bratunac*, Foundation of Local Democracy, Foundation United Women Banja Luka, *Izvor-Prijedor, Medica Zenica, Naš Glas* Association, Section of Women Victims of War in Republika Srpska, Sehara Association, *Snaga Žene, Vive Žene*, Women's International League for Peace and Freedom, Women's Section of the Association of Concentration Camp Torture Survivors Canton Sarajevo, *Follow-up Report on the Implementation by Bosnia and Herzegovina of the Recommendations Issued by the Committee on the Elimination of Discrimination against Women in July 2013* (July 2015), §48, available at: http://tbinternet.ohchr.org/Treaties/CEDAW/Shared%20Documents/BIH/INT_CEDAW_NGS_BIH_21073_E.pdf (accessed 8 May 2016).

133 Author interview, 30 November 2014. Like several other interviewees, A39 maintained that ŽŽR has become heavily politicized and that Hasečić (a survivor from Višegrad) only cares about women from her own area. Other interviewees, in contrast, maintained that they would have never obtained civilian victim of war status without Hasečić's help and support.

134 Author interview, 13 October 2014.

months and felt unjustly victimized. She proceeded to initiate legal proceedings, petitioning the local court to order the cantonal Centre for Social Work to accept her certificate from the Croatian Association of Camp Inmates of the Homeland War. When I left BiH in October 2015, she was still awaiting a decision from the court.

Even when civilian victim of war status is obtained, further problems can arise. A major issue is the critical disconnect that exists between the rights that civilian victims of war have on paper and the rights that they actually have in practice. According to the aforementioned Law on Principles of Social Protection, Protection of Civil Victims of War and Protection of Families with Children, survivors of rape and sexual violence who secure civilian victim of war status should receive a monthly social payment (currently 586 KM or £262),[135] as well as, inter alia, psycho-social and legal help, priority in relation to social housing and jobs and assistance in preparing for work (including rehabilitation and educational opportunities). Some interviewees complained, however, that the money that they receive each month is often paid late.

Furthermore, because many of the rights stipulated in the Law depend on cantonal laws, they are rarely implemented in practice.[136] For example, while the Law states that civilian victims of war should be given priority in the job market, this right can only be translated into practice at the cantonal level – and none of the cantonal laws recognize this right.[137] The lack of sensitization among some professionals, moreover, means that there is sometimes a lack of sympathy for survivors seeking to realize their wider set of rights. *Medica Zenica* notes that some female survivors have received comments such as '"What do you want?! You get money every month!", "It is easy for you getting money from the State!" and "What you went through is nothing, so what if you were raped, you weren't killed!"'.[138]

Notwithstanding the problems that exist in the Federation, the situation is substantially worse in RS. BiH's Assistant Minister of Human Rights and Refugees rightly emphasized that 'When it comes to human rights, there should not be any differences between the entities'.[139] In reality, however, the lack of a State-level law means that significant inter-entity differences exist, to the considerable detriment of survivors in RS.[140]

135 Irina Terzić, *Položaj Žrtava Ratnog Seksualnog Nasilja u Bosni i Hercegovini* (2016), 10, available at: http://zenskamreza.ba/site/wp-content/uploads/2016/03/Istra%C5%BEiva%C4%8Dki-rad_Irina-Terzic_11.3.pdf (accessed 19 July 2016).

136 Medica Zenica, *Ja sam Hrabra i Snažna, ali ipak Hoću svoju Prava!* (Zenica: Medica, 2014), 6. Copy on file with the author, at 15.

137 Terzić, *supra* note 135, at 7.

138 Medica Zenica, *supra* note 136, at 23.

139 Author interview, 13 August 2014.

140 Amnesty International, *supra* note 65, at 10.

### *Survivors in RS*

The Law on Civilian Victims of War RS requires that civilian victims of war must have at least a 60 per cent disability, as assessed by a medical commission.[141] Unlike in the Federation, survivors of rape and sexual violence are not treated as a special category and hence are not exempted from this disability requirement.[142] The Law also states that applications for civilian victim of war status needed to be submitted within five years of sustaining the relevant disability;[143] and the final deadline for the submission of applications was 31 December 2007.[144] These restrictive timeframes mean that survivors living in RS are no longer able to apply for civilian victim of war status or to realize their rights as set out in the Law, including a monthly social payment,[145] healthcare, rehabilitation and an allowance for family members unable to work.[146] According to a psychologist at *Vive Žene* in Tuzla, 'There is no help for rape victims in RS unless their husbands were killed or went missing during the war'.[147]

Of the 13 Serb interviewees living in RS, only one had obtained civilian victim of war status – and only after surmounting various hurdles. The relevant medical commission initially rejected K22's case on the grounds that she did not have sufficient evidence of a disability. A local district court, however, ruled in her favour, concluding that the medical commission had not taken account of all her circumstances. It therefore ordered the commission to re-consider its decision. Although K22 was subsequently awarded civilian victim of war status, she stressed that she will not be satisfied until all of her children also have status.[148] They had been detained (in a house) with her and had their own war trauma. One of them had obtained status, but the other two had not; the medical commission had quantified their level of disability at 30 per cent and 40 per cent respectively. For a second time, K22 petitioned the local district court. It ruled in her favour, but the medical commission again reached the decision that K22's

141 RS, *Zakon o Zaštiti Civilnih Žrtava Rata* (15 March 2010), Article 2, available at: www.udas.rs.ba/wp-content/uploads/2010/03/zakon_o_zastiti_civilnih_zrtava_rata.pdf (accessed 8 September 2014).
142 Amnesty International notes that 'The assessment of bodily damage was conducted by health commissions on the basis of the Rulebook on criteria for estimation of military disabilities, which does not refer to psychological damage'. Amnesty International, *When Everyone is Silent: Reparations for Survivors of Wartime Rape in Republika Srpska in Bosnia and Herzegovina* (1 October 2012), 8–9, available at: www.amnesty.nl/sites/default/files/public/wheneveryoneissilent.pdf (accessed 5 May 2014).
143 RS, *supra* note 141, at Article 33.
144 Ibid., at Article 34.
145 The amount of money paid depends on the applicant's particular disability. Ibid., at Article 9. Typically between 100 KM (£44) and 350 KM (£155) per month, the payments are substantially lower than those in the Federation. Terzić, *supra* note 135, at 10.
146 Ibid., at Article 9.
147 Author interview, 21 August 2014.
148 Author interview, 27 October 2014.

children did not meet the 60 per cent disability threshold. Several months later, this middle-aged woman suffered a mild heart attack. She attributed this to the combined stress of fighting to secure civilian victim of war status for her children and testifying in court.

N60, also a Serb living in RS, was just 14 years old when she was raped in 1992. She applied for civilian victim of war status in 2007, but the medical commission ruled that there was no evidence of any disability. She explained that she had appealed against the decision of the first level medical commission, and that she had been waiting 'years' for a decision from the second level commission. However, she seemed confused about this and could not provide any dates. As neither she nor her husband had a job, N60 was regularly travelling to Germany for several months at a time to earn money for her family. She expressed anger towards the RS government. If she had been able to secure civilian victim of war status, she would not need to find work abroad and be separated from her children.[149]

Some Bosniaks living in RS also have difficulties. For example, as it is no longer possible to apply for civilian victim of war status in RS, H58 applied in the Federation. Her application was successful, but this means that she must travel from her home in RS to the Federation (a two-hour bus journey) every time that she is ill and needs medical treatment. Although she must pay for certain medications in the Federation, she can receive some free medical care. This is not the case in RS, where she is required to pay for everything. This sexagenarian stressed that her life would be considerably easier if she could apply for and obtain civilian victim of war status in the entity in which she lives.[150]

Survivors living in Brčko District have also had fewer rights than survivors in the Federation, although this may be starting to change. As a result of amendments to the Decision on the Protection on Civilian Victims of War in 2012, survivors of rape and sexual violence could only obtain civilian victim of war status if they had a final court judgement against their perpetrators.[151] This requirement effectively barred many survivors from applying for status. According to the Office of the High Representative (OHR), 'As a consequence of the application of this decision, many civilian victims who live in the Brčko District have moved to the Federation or registered their place of residence there in order to be recognized as victims of war and to be entitled to benefits'.[152] However, following further

149 Author interview, 5 March 2015.

150 Author interview, 10 February 2015.

151 Skupština Brčko Distrikta BiH, *Odluka o Zaštiti Civilnih Žrtava Rata* (8 August 2012), Article 13(1)(c), available at: http://skupstinabd.ba/2-registar/ba/Odluke/2012%20prethodni%20mandat/619.%2071.%20redovna%20sjednica%20-%20Odluka%20o%20zas+titi%20civilnih%20z+rtava%20rata%20BOS.pdf (accessed 8 November 2015).

152 Office of the High Representative, *48th Report of the High Representative for Implementation of the Peace Agreement on Bosnia and Herzegovina to the Secretary-General of the United Nations* (9 November 2015), §17, available at: www.ohr.int/?p=63204 (accessed 8 May

amendments in June 2015, individuals wishing to apply for status are no longer required to have a court judgement. Instead, they 'will now have to go through special procedures before committees of experts and court experts to see their status as civilian victims of war duly recognised'.[153] This is a welcome development.[154] Ultimately, however, what is needed is a State-level law to ensure that all survivors of rape and sexual violence in BiH – regardless of where they live – have the same rights and the same opportunities to realize those rights. Such a law would also contribute to building cross-ethnic solidarity among survivors in BiH; interviewees living in RS frequently expressed anger and resentment that they do not have the same rights as those living in the Federation. Such sentiments, while understandable, impede the potential relationship – emphasized in the aforementioned Nairobi Declaration – between reparations and peace-building.

*****

Notwithstanding the importance of reparations, they have not been a significant part of transitional justice in BiH. While the authors of the TJS sought, in part, to redress this, the Strategy is in many respects an idealistic document that does not sufficiently grapple with the practical challenges of implementation. Recent judgements from the State Court, namely *Marković* and *Savić* (and also *Vojić/Mesić* and *Dostić*) similarly promise more than they are likely to deliver, thus highlighting the ease with which reparative justice can be derailed. The fact that some survivors can at least obtain civilian victim of war status and receive a monthly social payment is a positive development. Regrettably, this is offset by the operationalization of non-harmonized entity laws that place some survivors in a stronger position than others. While this must be rectified, the long-term needs of survivors ultimately require more than just a law or a strategy. What is needed is a new, more holistic approach to transitional justice that comprehensively addresses the long-term effects of rape and sexual violence – and the long-term needs that result from these. The final chapter reflects on what this approach might look like in practice.

2016). The OHR is an ad hoc institution that was set up under the Dayton Peace Accords to oversee implementation of particular (civilian) aspects of the peace agreement.

153 TRIAL et al., *supra* note 132, at §47.

154 Amnesty International notes that 'The current provisions are less restrictive and recognize psychological injury as a ground for the status, but require a certificate that the victim suffered sexual violence and a medical proof of permanent psychological harm issued by an independent expert commission'. Amnesty International, *supra* note 65, at 9.

Chapter 7

# Transitional justice and survivors' long-term needs

## Mapping and operationalizing a new holistic approach

A recent report by the UK's Select Committee on Sexual Violence in Conflict assertively states that individuals who commit sexual violence in conflict 'must be left in no doubt that they cannot evade justice'.[1] The rhetoric of no impunity, however, is used in conjunction with a wider insistence on the need to cultivate a '*comprehensive and survivor-focused approach*'.[2] The development of such an approach remains a paramount challenge and it points to the critical importance of exploring more holistic ways of doing transitional justice. In the introduction to this book, Boraine's conceptualization of holism was discussed. For him, holism is quintessentially an amalgamation of different forms and dimensions of transitional justice, and more particularly a fusion of the five 'key pillars' of accountability, truth recovery, reconciliation, institutional reform and reparations.[3] This research, in contrast, maintains that a more systematic approach to holism is required.

Ontologically, holism is not simply about combining retributive, restorative and reparative justice. More fundamentally, it is about how we actually *do* transitional justice – and what we want it to do. A crucial starting point is the issue of legacy. As this book defines it, the term holistic transitional justice signifies an expanded approach to dealing with the legacy of past human rights abuses, and specifically rape and sexual violence. Crucial to this expanded approach are three core dimensions of holism that were identified in the introduction, namely a temporal, a socio-economic and a gender dimension. This final chapter focuses on the operationalization of these dimensions, and thus on the practical realization of more holistic and legacy-inclusive ways of dealing with the past. To

1 House of Lords Select Committee on Sexual Violence in Conflict, *Sexual Violence in Conflict: A War Crime*, Report of Session 2015–2016 (12 April 2016), 4, available at: www.publications.parliament.uk/pa/ld201516/ldselect/ldsvc/123/123.pdf (accessed 3 November 2016).

2 Ibid., at 64. Emphasis in the original.

3 Alexander L. Boraine, 'Transitional Justice: A Holistic Interpretation', *Journal of International Affairs* 60 (2006): 17–28, at 19–24.

emphasize the wider importance of holistic transitional justice, it extends the purview beyond BiH.

## A temporal dimension of holistic transitional justice

Lambourne has used the word holism in relation to peace-building. For her, a holistic approach to peace-building 'implies a commitment to establishing the security, legal, political, economic, structural, cultural and psychosocial conditions necessary to promote a culture of peace in place of a culture of violence'.[4] In other words, holistic peace-building is a long-term approach and investment. As an extension of this, Lambourne has developed a transformative model of transitional justice that accentuates transformation rather than simply transition.[5] As she theorizes it, 'Transformative justice not only deals with the past but also establishes conditions and structures in order to ensure justice in the present and the future, creating a longer-term vision and commitment than suggested by the term "transitional justice" '.[6] It is precisely this longer-term vision that is frequently missing from transitional justice processes; the past is often addressed in a temporally bounded way that makes little provision for long-term needs.

This book's conceptualization of holistic transitional justice is similarly transformative. Fundamentally, if transitional justice is to address the long-term legacy of rape and sexual violence, or indeed the enduring legacy of violence more generally, it needs to operate in a longitudinal way, with the main emphasis on 'justice' – broadly defined – rather than transition. In other words, a critical widening of the temporal parameters of transitional justice is required. Goodin has introduced the concept of 'temporal justice'. According to him, 'Control over one's time, the capacity to spend it as one wishes, is another important resource; and its distribution raises another important aspect of justice'.[7] He is concerned with discretionary time, or with the amount of time that people have once they have undertaken essential activities such as securing a minimum income, cooking, eating and sleeping.[8] If individuals are in a position where they must focus their attention and energy on meeting their elemental everyday needs, they will thus have little discretionary time. While none of the survivors who participated in this research talked about needing discretionary time, the general concept

4 Wendy Lambourne, 'Transformative Justice, Reconciliation and Peacebuilding', in Susanne Buckley-Zistel, Teresa Koloma Beck, Christian Braun and Friederike Mieth (eds), *Transitional Justice Theories* (Abingdon: Routledge, 2014), 19–39, at 22.

5 Ibid., at 19.

6 Wendy Lambourne, 'Transitional Justice and Peacebuilding after Mass Violence', *International Journal of Transitional Justice* 3 (2009) 28–48, at 45. See also Paul Gready and Simon Robins, 'From Transitional to Transformative Justice: A New Agenda for Practice', *International Journal of Transitional Justice* 8 (2014): 339–361.

7 Robert E. Goodin, 'Temporal Justice', *Journal of Social Policy* 39 (2010): 1–9, at 1.

8 Ibid., at 2.

of 'temporal justice' is a useful one that underscores the pivotal relationship between justice and time. Essentially, a holistic approach to transitional justice needs to include what Crawford has termed 'victim-sensitive temporalization',[9] by addressing the temporal legacy of rape and sexual violence and resultant needs.

This section explores two important ways in which the temporal boundaries of transitional justice can be broadened. Firstly, transitional justice processes should entail follow-up work with survivors. In BiH, the heavy emphasis on criminal prosecutions, combined with the prevailing international discourse of 'no impunity', underscores the particular importance of follow-up work by courts. Secondly, there is a critical need for local NGOs to be more involved in transitional justice practice.

### *A temporal broadening via follow-up work*

One of the key themes that emerged from the interview data was survivors' need for support. They wanted support from the State, institutions and society in general; and as was discussed in Chapter 5, those who had testified in court (just under 50 per cent) expressed a need for greater support both during the trial process and, in particular, afterwards. Although criminal courts are primarily focused on perpetrators, there is potentially more that they could do to provide post-testimony support, in particular to survivors of rape and sexual violence. A critical prerequisite for this is a temporal broadening of their mandates to include follow-up work.

On 22 December 2010, the UN Security Council established the UN Mechanism for International Criminal Tribunals (the Mechanism), 'to perform a number of essential functions' of the ICTR and ICTY following the completion of their mandates.[10] The ICTR branch in Arusha began its work on 1 July 2012, and the ICTY branch in The Hague followed suit exactly a year later. The Mechanism has a number of ad hoc functions, which include the tracking and prosecution of remaining fugitives (only relevant to the Arusha branch), appeals proceedings and trials for contempt of court and false testimony. It also has several continuing functions, one of which is the protection of victims and witnesses.[11] Article 20 of the Mechanism's Statute states simply that: 'The Mechanism shall provide in its Rules of Procedure and Evidence for the protection of victims and witnesses in relation to the ICTY, the ICTR, and the Mechanism'.[12] It adds that 'Such protection measures shall include, but shall

9 Adam Crawford, 'Temporality in Restorative Justice: On Time, Timing and Time-Consciousness', *Theoretical Criminology* 19 (2015): 470–490, at 482.

10 See www.unmict.org/en/about

11 See www.unmict.org/en/about/functions

12 UN, *Statute of the International Residual Mechanism for Criminal Tribunals* (22 December 2010), Article 20, available at: www.unmict.org/sites/default/files/documents/101222_sc_res1966_statute_en.pdf (accessed 3 July 2016).

not be limited to, the conduct of in camera proceedings and the protection of the victim's identity'.[13] The RPE, in contrast, are more expansive in discussing the types of protection that the Mechanism might offer. Specifically, Rule 32 stipulates that:

(A) There shall be set up under the authority of the Registrar a Victims and Witnesses Section consisting of qualified staff to:
  (i) recommend protective measures for victims and witnesses in accordance with Article 20 of the Statute; and
  (ii) provide counselling and support for them, in particular in cases of rape and sexual assault.

(B) A gender sensitive approach to victims and witnesses protective and support measures should be adopted.[14]

There is clearly a longitudinal dimension to victim/witness protection. If protective measures have been put in place, the need for these measures does not simply end once an individual has testified. It is unclear from Rule 32 whether there is a similar longer-term dimension to the counselling and support that will be provided. Like the ICTR and ICTY, the Mechanism is an ad hoc body.[15] It is also a much smaller institution, 'whose functions and size will diminish over time'.[16] Nevertheless, there is a strong case for arguing that the Mechanism's residual functions should include, where possible, follow-up work with and continuing support for victims and witnesses, as part of a temporal expansion of international criminal justice. Indeed, it would seem that some level of expansion is already occurring. Both branches of the Mechanism, for example, have a Witness Support and Protection Unit (WISP), and Article 6(1) of the Policy for the Provision of Support and Protection Services to Victims and Witnesses (adopted on 26 June 2012) states that 'WISP shall provide witness support and protection services, in application of principles

13 Ibid.

14 Mechanism for International Criminal Tribunals, *Rules of Procedure and Evidence* (26 September 2016), Rule 32, available at: www.unmict.org/sites/default/files/documents/160926-rules-rev2-en.pdf (accessed 17 July 2017).

15 According to UN Security Council Resolution 1966, the Security Council 'Decides that the Mechanism shall operate for an initial period of four years from the first commencement date referred to in paragraph 1, and to review the progress of the work of the Mechanism, including in completing its functions, before the end of this initial period and every two years thereafter, and further *decides* that the Mechanism shall continue to operate for subsequent periods of two years following each such review, unless the Security Council decides otherwise'. UN, *Security Council Resolution 1966*, S/RES/1966 (22 December 2010), §17.

16 Ibid., at Preamble.

common to both branches prior to, during and after testimony'.[17] Article 10(1) of the Policy further underlines that 'Establishing and maintaining contact with witnesses are main objectives of the Mechanism's mandate which WISP shall carry out. Such contact shall not cease upon the completion of the witnesses' testimony'.[18]

In his 2016 assessment and progress report, Judge Theodor Meron, the president of the Mechanism, provides some practical illustrations of the Mechanism's sustained contact with victims and witnesses. He notes, for example, that:

> The Arusha branch provides ongoing support services to witnesses. Witnesses residing in Rwanda continue to receive medical and psychosocial services, particularly those witnesses experiencing psychotrauma or living with HIV/AIDS, many of whom contracted the virus as a result of crimes committed against them during the genocide.[19]

Such developments are neither completely new nor specific to the Mechanism. The Rwanda branch of the WISP Unit, for example, is supported by the Kigali Field Office. This was established in 2004 to offer essential support to ICTR witnesses; and according to the Mechanism's website, 'In its first year, the Kigali Field Office provided treatment to 211 victims and witnesses, and in the seven years of its existence it has provided an estimated 35,000 consultations'.[20] Moreover, in its Best Practices Manual for the Investigation and Prosecution of Sexual Violence Crimes, the ICTR emphasized that 'many victims will continue to need ongoing medical and psychological support long after legal proceedings

17 Mechanism for International Tribunals, *Policy for the Provision of Support and Protection Services to Victims and Witnesses* (26 June 2012), Article 6(1), available at: www.unmict.org/sites/default/files/documents/mict_witness_support_policy_en.pdf (accessed 5 July 2016).

18 Ibid., at Article 10(1). In 2010, the government of Sierra Leone and the UN signed an Agreement on the Establishment of a Residual Special Court for Sierra Leone (RSCSL). The RSCSL commenced its work in 2013. Based in The Hague, it has a sub-office in Freetown for witness protection and support. Rule 34(A)(ii) of the Court's RPE states that staff working on witness protection and support shall, inter alia, 'Provide them [victims and witnesses] with adequate protective measures and security arrangements and develop long- and short-term plans for their protection and support'. According to Rule 34(A)(iii), the Court should also ensure that victims and witnesses 'receive relevant support, counselling and other appropriate assistance, including medical assistance, physical and psychological rehabilitation, especially in cases of rape, sexual assault and crimes against children'. RSCSL, *Rules of Procedure and Evidence* (as amended on 2 December 2015), available at: www.rscsl.org/Documents/RSCSL-Rules.pdf (accessed 5 July 2016).

19 Theodor Meron, 'Letter Dated 17 May 2016 from the President of the International Residual Mechanism for Criminal Tribunals Addressed to the President of the Security Council' (17 May 2016), §40, available at: www.unmict.org/sites/default/files/documents/160517_progress_report_en.pdf (accessed 28 July 2016).

20 See www.unmict.org/en/about/functions/witnesses

have concluded. Many will also require financial and socio-economic support if they are to rebuild their lives and become fully-integrated members of society'.[21]

These examples of follow-up work are extremely positive and such work should continue. The fact, however, that courts are primarily perpetrator-centred institutions, with specific mandates and limited resources, necessarily raises questions about the level of follow-up work that is either feasible or practical. The pilot study *Echoes of Testimonies*, which was referred to in Chapter 5, highlights this point. Undertaken by the ICTY's VWS in collaboration with staff from the University of North Texas, and based on a representative sample of 300 ICTY witnesses from across the former Yugoslavia, the study underlines that the VWS does not have resources to provide witnesses with long-term therapy – and indeed this is not part of the Tribunal's mandate'.[22] While this is true, post-testimony follow-up work and support could entail something as simple as periodic contact. The authors of the pilot study found, for example, that:

> Numerous and intense – sometimes positive and sometimes negative – reactions during the participant recruitment calls gave the VWS staff members reason to believe that post-testimony contact fulfilled a need of the witnesses to share their thoughts and feelings about their experiences. Similar reactions occurred during the in-person meetings in which it seemed that many interviewees had been waiting for an opportunity to finally provide feedback.[23]

Those who have suffered severe trauma are often encouraged to speak about their experiences. It is also important that they are given the opportunity to talk about their experiences of testifying. Some of the survivors who participated in this research, for example, had never imagined that their perpetrators would face justice. Those whom I accompanied to court felt an intense mixture of emotions immediately after testifying – relief, anger, sadness, pity, emptiness – and needed to speak about how they felt. Yet, they also needed time to process these emotions and to talk about the experience of testifying several months on. Two months after she had taken the witness stand at the State Court, for example, one interviewee disclosed that she kept re-playing her testimony in her mind and thinking about what she would have liked to say to the defendants had she

21 ICTR, *Prosecution of Sexual Violence – Best Practices Manual for the Investigation and Prosecution of Sexual Violence Crimes in Post-Conflict Regions: Lessons Learned from the Office of the Prosecutor for the International Criminal Tribunal for Rwanda* (30 January 2014), §252, available at: http://w.unictr.org/sites/unictr.org/files/legal-library/140130_prosecution_of_sexual_violence.pdf (accessed 8 April 2016).

22 Kimi King, James Meernik, Sara Rubert, Tiago de Smit and Helena V. Schoorl, *Echoes of Testimonies: A Pilot Study into the Long-Term Impact of Bearing Witness before the ICTY* (June 2016), 16, available at: www.icty.org/x/file/About/Registry/Witnesses/Echoes-Full-Report_EN.pdf (accessed 3 September 2016).

23 Ibid., at 123.

been given the opportunity. Some interviewees insisted that their experiences of testifying in court had been so distressing that they would never testify again. In such cases, post-testimony contact and support from the courts is especially important and necessary. Judges and prosecutors, moreover, can learn from those who testify in their courtrooms about how to conduct the proceedings with sufficient sensitivity.

Koss draws a crucial distinction between 'justice needs' (including the need for acknowledgement of wrongdoing) and 'survival needs', such as physical health, mental health and economic priorities.[24] Courts have the key role to play in addressing these 'justice needs', and follow-up work with survivors is a critical part of this. However, survivors also have a host of concrete and practical needs that extend far beyond more abstract needs for legal justice. Finding a balance between 'justice needs' and 'survival needs' is a significant challenge, and transitional justice work in BiH has primarily concentrated on the former. Based on Boraine's aforementioned conceptualization of holistic transitional justice, the fusion of retributive, restorative and, in particular, reparative justice would appear to offer the optimal route to realizing a synthesis of symbolic and more practical forms of justice. Such a synthesis, however, can potentially also be achieved through new partnerships. Although courts themselves are not equipped to address the long-term needs of survivors, or indeed any witnesses, greater collaboration with local organizations and NGOs would enable a more comprehensive and long-term approach to dealing with the legacy of rape and sexual violence. These local partnerships constitute a second important temporal aspect of holistic transitional justice.

### *A temporal broadening via local partnerships*

In its Convention on Combatting and Preventing Violence against Women and Domestic Violence (Istanbul Convention), the Council of Europe underlines the importance of NGOs. Article 9 of the Convention states that 'Parties shall recognise, encourage and support, at all levels, the work of relevant non-governmental organisations and of civil society active in combating violence against women and establish effective co-operation with these organisations'.[25] In the context of rape and sexual violence, however, the significance of NGOs extends beyond prevention. Scholars have examined some of the diverse ways in which NGOs may participate in international law and court proceedings,[26] including as *amici*

24 Mary P. Koss, 'Restoring Rape Survivors: Justice, Advocacy and a Call to Action', *Annals of the New York Academy of Sciences* 1087 (2006): 206–234, at 208–209.

25 Council of Europe, *Council of Europe Convention on Preventing and Combating Violence against Women and Domestic Violence* (12 April 2011), Article 9, available at: https://rm.coe.int/CoERMPublicCommonSearchServices/DisplayDCTMContent?documentId=090000168046031c (accessed 1 August 2016).

26 See, for example, Jacqueline Peel, 'Giving the Public a Voice in the Protection of the Global Environment: Avenues for Participation by NGOs in Dispute Resolution at the European

*curiae* and 'norm entrepreneurs'.[27] What has received far less attention is the fact that NGOs also have a vital role to play in working alongside international and domestic criminal courts to deliver a more needs-based justice to survivors of war rape and sexual violence.

Transitional justice currently operates in a strongly top-down and institutional way.[28] Kent, for example, laments that 'Legal and quasi-legal institutions are too easily seen as holding the capacity to resolve complex legacies of conflict, as providing a solution to trauma arising from it, or as the obvious safeguard against future violence'.[29] If these institutions, and particularly criminal courts, engage with local organizations and NGOs on the ground, this can inject an important bottom-up dimension into transitional justice practice. This, in turn, is crucial for enabling a better 'fit' between the process of addressing past human rights abuses and the concrete needs to which those abuses give rise, both in the short term and the long term. In its aforementioned report, the UK Select Committee on Sexual Violence in Conflict makes precisely this point. It observes, inter alia, that:

> Local and grassroots organisations are well placed to assess the needs of victims and survivors of sexual violence in conflict. They may be in place before, during and after a conflict. Such organisations are also more attuned to the local context and have greater access than international organisations that might be present for a limited period only. They can also play a critical role when state agents are either unable or unwilling to provide the necessary support.[30]

The ICTY's Outreach Office has engaged with local NGOs, and indeed it claims that 'Communicating with victims' representatives and NGOs from the former

Court of Justice and World Trade Organization', *Colorado Journal of International Environmental Law and Policy* 12 (2001): 47–76; Donald J. Kochan, 'The Political Economy of the Production of Customary International Law: The Role of Non-Governmental Organizations in U.S. Courts', *Berkeley Journal of International Law* 22 (2004): 240–278; Steve Charnovitz, 'Nongovernmental Organizations and International Law', *American Journal of International Law* 100 (2006): 348–372.

27 Heidi Nichols Haddad, 'After the Norm Cascade: NGO Mission Expansion and the Coalition for the International Criminal Court', *Global Governance* 19 (2013): 187–206, at 200. The ICTJ, for example, notes that 'Since 2003, civil society groups in Argentina have led a vigorous push to hold criminals accountable for the human rights abuses perpetrated during military rule – which has ultimately resulted in a new wave of trials of high-ranking officers'. See www.ictj.org/our-work/regions-and-countries/argentina

28 Simon Robins, 'Towards Victim-Centred Transitional Justice: Understanding the Needs of Families of the Disappeared in Postconflict Nepal', *International Journal of Transitional Justice* 5 (2011): 75–98, at 75.

29 Lia Kent, 'Transitional Justice in Law, History and Anthropology', *Australian Feminist Law Journal* 42 (2016): 1–11, at 11.

30 House of Lords Select Committee on Sexual Violence in Conflict, *supra* note 1, at 89.

Yugoslavia is at the core of Outreach's work'.[31] Primarily, the Outreach Office has sought to work with NGOs to ensure that key information about the Tribunal and its legacy is effectively transmitted and disseminated to communities on the ground. Through co-ordination meetings, seminars and presentations, it has engaged with NGO representatives, local community leaders and the heads of victims' groups to ensure 'a continuous flow of information'.[32] Such work is both valuable and necessary. The Tribunal's ultimate legacy will remain limited if communities on the ground do not sufficiently understand its work[33] or are only able to see its flaws. It is essential, however, that institutional legacy concerns do not detract from the concrete everyday needs of survivors. Hence, courts should not only work with NGOs as a way of disseminating information about their work. As part of a temporal broadening, their engagement with NGOs should have as its central focus the long-term needs of those who have testified. Addressing these needs requires a division of labour, and institutional forms of transitional justice are not enough.

Some courts and tribunals have themselves acknowledged the importance of having local partners. Rule 34(B) of the SCSL's RPE, for example, stated that, where appropriate, staff working with victims and witnesses should co-operate with NGOs and inter-governmental organizations.[34] Similarly, in its Best Practices Manual for the Investigation and Prosecution of Sexual Violence Crimes, the ICTR underlined that 'From an early stage, the prosecution, in particular, and tribunal, in general, should coordinate the provision of medical and psychological services with outside entities'.[35] It further noted that NGOs and other service providers may be able to offer medical and related support to survivors of rape and sexual violence on a long-term basis.[36]

In the pilot study *Echoes of Testimonies*, the ICTY's VWS outlines some of the work that it has undertaken to build relationships and networks with relevant professionals and organizations across the former Yugoslavia. In 2004, for example, and with funding from the EC, it organized a series of conferences. These conferences 'were designed to better inform health and welfare professionals about the role and function of the ICTY VWS, and to include psychiatrists, medical

31 ICTY, *ICTY Outreach Programme: Annual Report 2013* (2014), 23, available at: www.icty.org/x/file/Outreach/annual_reports/annual_report_2013_en.pdf (accessed 9 July 2016).
32 ICTY, *ICTY Annual Outreach Report 2011* (2012), 20, available at: www.icty.org/x/file/Outreach/annual_reports/annual_report_2011_en.pdf (accessed 9 July 2016).
33 As part of a previous research project focused on BiH, Croatia and Kosovo, I found that communities were generally poorly informed about the ICTY and that significant knowledge gaps exist. Janine N. Clark, *International Trials and Reconciliation: Assessing the Legacy of the International Criminal Tribunal for the former Yugoslavia* (Abingdon: Routledge, 2014, 2015).
34 SCSL, *Rules of Procedure and Evidence* (last amended 31 May 2012), available at: www.rscsl.org/Documents/RPE.pdf (accessed 8 June 2016).
35 ICTR, *supra* note 21, at §248.
36 Ibid.

doctors, psychologists and social workers from public and private sectors'.[37] More importantly, the Tribunal's Field Office in Sarajevo has referred various categories of victims to these support networks, to ensure that they receive the assistance they need.[38] Unfortunately, there is little information available regarding the results of these referrals or the operationalization of the networks in practice.

It is important not to idealize the role of NGOs.[39] It must also be acknowledged that these organizations have their own limitations. They cannot reach out to everyone, they have finite resources and their very existence is dependent on their ability to attract donors and secure funding. Nevertheless, if their activities were to be more closely aligned with the work of international and in particular local courts, and with institutional transitional justice processes more broadly, this could potentially give them greater financial security. They could thus develop their own activities within the framework of, and with reference to, an overarching transitional justice project aimed at collaboratively addressing long-term needs.

This transitional justice endeavour should also entail greater co-operation between NGOs and governments/states.[40] Within extant scholarship on transitional justice and civil society, the principal emphasis is on the advocacy role of NGOs; they can apply strong pressure on states to deliver justice, accountability and truth. In the aftermath of the post-election violence in Kenya in 2007 and 2008, for example, civil society groups demanded peace and justice and they exerted pressure on the government by, inter alia, 'providing data and briefings to representatives of the UN, the AU [African Union] and the European Union'.[41] In Uruguay, civil society groups played a key role in overturning the country's 1986 Expiry Law, which had critically hindered the fight against impunity for human rights violations committed during the period of military dictatorship (1973–1985);[42] and in neighbouring Argentina, 'The weekly marches of

37 King et al., *supra* note 22, at 18.

38 Ibid.

39 See, for example, Roberto Bellioni, 'Civil Society and Peacebuilding in Bosnia and Herzegovina', *Journal of Peace Research* 38 (2001): 163–180.

40 BiH's Human Rights Ombudsman, for example, has emphasized that: 'The state should identify established models of non-governmental organizations for rehabilitation (shelter) and provide assistance and support to women-survivors of rape and other forms of sexual violence, and establish institutional networks to support victims and witnesses, and ensure necessary funding and other services to maintain this support system'. Institution of Human Rights Ombudsman of BiH, *Universal Periodical Review on the Situation of Human Rights in Bosnia and Herzegovina – II Cycle* (March 2014), §6.2.7, available at: www.ombudsmen.gov.ba/documents/obmudsmen_doc2014042915344347eng.pdf (accessed 3 August 2016).

41 Thomas Obel Hansen and Chandra Lekha Sriram, 'Fighting for Justice (and Survival): Kenyan Civil Society Accountability Strategies and Their Enemies', *International Journal of Transitional Justice* 9 (2015): 407–427, at 420.

42 Jo-Marie Burt, Gabriela Fried Amilivia and Francesca Lessa, 'Civil Society and the Resurgent Struggle against Impunity in Uruguay 1986–2012', *International Journal of Transitional Justice* 7 (2013): 306–327, at 308.

the mothers and grandmothers [who have formed their own organizations] in Buenos Aires' Plaza de Mayo ... have become emblematic of forceful demands for justice'.[43]

Backer, in contrast, is more interested in the different types of possible relationships that may exist between NGOs and governments in a transitional justice context. His theoretical model identifies six possible relationship 'scenarios', from 'strength and symbiosis' to 'hands off the wheel'.[44] The first of these scenarios emphasizes collaboration between government and civil society; and according to Backer, it represents an 'ideal' which transitional justice processes 'typically fail to achieve'.[45] His use of the word 'ideal', however, detracts from the utility of such collaboration. The late Antonio Cassese, the first president of the ICTY, once described the Tribunal as 'a giant without arms and legs' that needs 'artificial limbs to walk and work'.[46] It is state authorities, he explained, that constitute these official limbs.[47] By way of analogy, it can be argued that in the field of transitional justice, NGOs partly constitute the eyes and ears of governments. They can provide politicians and policymakers with crucial information about communities, individuals and long-term needs. It will be recalled from the previous chapter, for example, that BiH's Council of Ministers formed a 15-member expert group to draft a TJS, the members of which included civil society representatives. If states, governments and civil society co-operate and work together on transitional justice issues, this will help to create a symbiosis between the process of dealing with past human rights abuses and the needs that exist because of those abuses.

In the previous chapter, it was emphasized that the absence of a State-level law on civilian victims of war means that survivors of rape and sexual violence have different rights depending on whether they live in the Federation or in RS. The differences, however, are not only inter-entity but also intra-entity. In BiH, the main NGOs that work with survivors are based in the Federation and they are concentrated in the largest cities, namely Sarajevo, Zenica and Tuzla. Outside of these areas, available support for survivors is extremely varied and, in many cases, almost non-existent. While Crocker is right to accentuate that 'Civil society is not... without its limitations',[48] a more co-ordinated approach to transitional

43 Francesca Lessa, Tricia D. Olsen, Leigh A. Payne, Gabriel Pereira and Andrew G. Reiter, 'Overcoming Impunity: Pathways to Accountability in Latin America', *International Journal of Transitional Justice* 8 (2014): 75–98, at 77.

44 David Backer, 'Civil Society and Transitional Justice: Possibilities, Patterns and Prospects', *Journal of Human Rights* 2 (2003): 297–313, at 307.

45 Ibid., at 306.

46 Antonio Cassese, 'On the Current Trends towards Criminal Prosecution and Punishment of Breaches of International Humanitarian Law', *European Journal of International Law* 9 (1998): 2–17, at 13.

47 Ibid.

48 David Crocker, 'Transitional Justice and International Civil Society: Toward a Normative Framework', *Constellations: An International Journal of Critical and Democratic Theory* 5 (1998): 492–517, at 507.

justice involving closer collaboration between NGOs and governments/state institutions would help to identify where the main support gaps exist and what can be done to address these.

Although civil society has an important role to play in transitional justice and in facilitating a temporal broadening that allows for a greater focus on long-term needs, the voices of survivors must also be heard. In October 2014, I attended an event in Sarajevo about women civilian victims of war in the Federation and their rights (as they exist on paper). NGO leaders and representatives constituted the overwhelming majority of participants. I travelled to the event with, and sat next to, an NGO leader (X) who was herself raped during the Bosnian war. At one point during the morning's discussions, Y, the head of a Sarajevo-based women's NGO, described rape survivors as her '*zanimanje*' (occupation). X immediately took offence, and during the subsequent coffee break she expressed deep anger that someone had referred to her and her fellow survivors in this way. She felt that the word 'occupation' trivialized their lives and problems.

During my time in BiH, I participated in a number of seminars and talks focused on survivors of rape and sexual violence, and it was striking how in most cases no more than one or two actual survivors were present. NGO leaders and representatives in BiH frequently come together to speak about survivors and their problems, but there is often little opportunity for survivors themselves to contribute to these discussions. Indeed, a number of interviewees explicitly argued that they resented NGOs speaking on their behalf and in their name.[49] Interviewee E30 maintained that 'Many of these organizations only "care" about us when they are writing their projects'.[50] Civil society has a core role to play in helping to operationalize a more temporally expanded transitional justice, but not if survivors – and war victims more generally – perceive NGOs as simply 'following the money'.[51]

There have been calls for more participatory approaches to transitional justice that allow those affected by human rights abuses to make crucial decisions and to have a voice.[52] Lundy and McGovern, for example, maintain that local communities should be involved in every stage of a transitional justice process,

49 This is a broader issue that is not specific to BiH. Kent, for example, notes that in East Timor, 'Civil society leaders have also begun to acknowledge that NGOs have tended to "speak on behalf of" victims rather than strengthening victims' political voice and, in this sense, have replicated government's mistakes by purporting to understand their best interests'. Lia Kent, 'Local Memory Practices in East Timor: Disrupting Transitional Justice Narratives', *International Journal of Transitional Justice* 5 (2011): 434–455, at 452.

50 Author interview, 12 November 2014.

51 Ezekiel Pajibo, 'Civil Society and Transitional Justice in Liberia: A Practitioner's Reflection from the Field', *International Journal of Transitional Justice* 1 (2007): 287–296, at 293.

52 In 2008, for example, Colombia adopted Law 1257. Known as the Gender Equality Law, this legislation sets out some of the key services to which survivors of rape and sexual violence are entitled, including state counselling and legal advice. Significantly, 'The constructive framework that this law offers is as a result of collaboration with women's groups who have worked on the different elements and the design of this law'. ABColombia, Sisma

including 'conception, design, decision-making, and management'.[53] It will be recalled from the previous chapter that both the Nairobi Declaration on Women and Girls' Right to a Remedy and Reparation (Nairobi Declaration) and the UN Secretary-General's Guidance Note on Reparations for Conflict-Related Sexual Violence (Guidance Note) similarly underscore this participatory element. The concept of participation, moreover, necessarily extends to the work of NGOs. Fundamentally, their discussions and activities should include the direct participation of survivors (who can also support each other). They cannot only talk *about* survivors but also need to talk *with* them. According to Jacqueline Mutere, a rape survivor in Kenya who founded the organization Grace Agenda,[54] 'We really believe in having the survivor's voice at every table, because it will always give you a perception that you may not otherwise hear'.[55] In other words, the concept of partnership within transitional justice needs to operate not only between NGOs and courts, and between NGOs and governments/states, but also between NGOs and survivors.

## A socio-economic dimension of holistic transitional justice

While this research focuses on the long-term needs of survivors, its purpose is not to portray these men and women simply as individuals who need help and support. The holistic approach to transitional justice that it advocates seeks precisely to empower survivors. The Preamble of UN Security Council Resolution 1325, for example, reaffirms 'the important role of women in the prevention and resolution of conflicts and in peace-building'; and it stresses 'the importance of their equal participation and full involvement in all efforts for the maintenance and promotion of peace and security'.[56] It is difficult, however, to envisage how female survivors might assume a peace-building role if their basic everyday needs – or 'survival needs'[57] – remain unmet.[58] Mani's concept of reparative justice similarly emphasizes a critical nexus between

Mujer and U.S. Office on Colombia, *Colombia: Women, Conflict-Related Sexual Violence and the Peace Process* (November 2013), 17, available at: www.abcolombia.org.uk/downloads/ABColombia_Conflict_related_sexual_violence_report.pdf (accessed 6 May 2016).

53 Ibid., at 266. See also Lambourne, *supra* note 6, at 48.

54 See www.graceagenda.co.ke/aboutus.html

55 Berkley Center for Religion, Peace and World Affairs, 'A Discussion with Jacqueline Mutere, Founder and Director of Grace Agenda' (3 June 2015), available at: https://berkleycenter.georgetown.edu/interviews/a-discussion-with-jaqueline-mutere-founder-and-director-of-grace-agenda (accessed 31 May 2016).

56 UN, *Security Council Resolution 1325*, S/RES/1325 (31 October 2000), Preamble.

57 Koss, *supra* note 24.

58 Emphasizing this point, Rees and Chinkin assert that 'without access to their economic and social entitlements, survivors of and witnesses to wartime atrocities are less likely to be able participate in court proceedings, or truth commissions, thereby denying access to justice and sustaining perpetrator impunity'. Madeleine Rees and Christine Chinkin, 'Exposing the Gendered Myth of Post Conflict Transition: The Transformative Power of

needs and agency. According to her, 'while reparative justice places the needs and trauma of victims at the centre of its concerns, it does not trap them in a passive role and in their past suffering, but rather helps them build a "bridge" towards their future and seeks to reintegrate them actively into society'.[59] These examples point to an important socio-economic dimension of holistic transitional justice. Turning firstly to the economic part of this, transitional justice can help to build the 'bridge' which Mani refers to if it is combined with development. Although development is discussed in this chapter as part of a socio-economic dimension of holistic transitional justice, it necessarily overlaps with the temporal dimension of holism expounded in the previous section.

### *An economic dimension: transitional justice and development*

War crimes and systematic human rights abuses can have a profound impact on communities. As de Greiff remarks, 'non-victims often have the sense that after what happened to the victims, *no one* can be safe, no one can really know what to expect. The end result is a generalized weakening of agency, trust and social capital, not only for victims but for society as a whole'.[60] This, in turn, can adversely affect development. When people live in fear, when trust has been broken, when insecurity prevails, the scope for development may be severely restricted. Indeed, it can be argued that 'Conflict and violence represent "development in reverse," generating costs that adversely affect countries and communities for decades'.[61]

If violence has implications for development, some scholars and practitioners have also pointed to important linkages between development and transitional justice. De Greiff, for example, regards transitional justice as a potential catalyst for development. Holding perpetrators to account and providing redress to victims are critical processes for allowing societies to move forward. From this perspective, thus, 'justice is a part of development rather than outside it' and 'an instrumental contribution to the attainment of conditions that are needed for development'.[62] If one may facilitate the other, Duthie notes that transitional justice and development, broadly defined, may also share the same long-term

Economic and Social Rights', *New York University Journal of International Law and Politics* 48 (2016): 1211–1226, at 1219.

59 Rama Mani, 'Rebuilding an Inclusive Political Community after War', *Security Dialogue* 36 (2005): 511–526, at 523.

60 Pablo de Greiff, *Transitional Justice and Development* (2009), 15, available at: www.developmentideas.info/website/wp-content/uploads/Ch24_TransitionalJustice_PablodeGreiff_2013.pdf (accessed 7 April 2016).

61 Small Arms Survey, *Insecurity and Violence in the Post-2015 Development Agenda* (September 2013), 2, available at: www.genevadeclaration.org/fileadmin/docs/MDG_Process/UNDP%20AVR%20post%202015%20Paper_withSASLogo_FIN.pdf (accessed 11 February 2016).

62 De Greiff, *supra* note 60, at 28.

goals, including the rule of law, good governance and peace.[63] Further illuminating a vital nexus between transitional justice and development, there have been calls for transitional justice processes to address socio-economic crimes and structural injustices.[64] Arbour, a former chief prosecutor at the ICTY, was one of the first to advocate this position. According to her, transitional justice 'must reach to, but also beyond the crimes and abuses committed during the conflict which led to the transition, into the human rights violations that pre-existed the conflict and caused, or contributed to it'.[65]

This research adopts a more forward-looking approach. Transitional justice should not only be about dealing with the past in the hope of building a better future. At the grassroots level, it also needs to be about helping people to build a better future *for themselves*. What is required, therefore, is a greater emphasis not simply on development, but more specifically on human development. The term 'human development', which was briefly introduced in Chapter 3, was first used by the UNDP in 1990 in its Human Development Report. According to this, 'Human development is a process of enlarging people's choices. The most critical ones are to lead a long and healthy life, to be educated and to enjoy a decent standard of living'.[66] In other words, the concept emphasizes the human dimension of development, by 'bringing the lives of people to the forefront'.[67]

The basic idea of human development is rooted in Sen's work on capabilities. According to him, the concept of capability is critically linked to opportunity, and, more precisely, 'the opportunity to achieve valuable combinations of human functionings – what a person is able to do or be'.[68] Inherent in the idea of capability, thus, is the notion of choice. In Sen's words, 'A capability reflects the alternative combinations of functionings from which the

63 Roger Duthie, 'Towards a Development-Sensitive Approach to Transitional Justice', *International Journal of Transitional Justice* 2 (2008): 292–309, at 294.

64 See, for example, Christopher J. Colvin, 'Purity and Planning: Shared Logics of Transitional Justice and Development', *International Journal of Transitional Justice* 2 (2008): 412–425; Zinaida Miller, 'Effects of Invisibility: In Search of the "Economic" in Transitional Justice', *International Journal of Transitional Justice* 2 (2008): 266–291; Rosemary Nagy, 'Transitional Justice as Global Project: Critical Reflections', *Third World Quarterly* 29 (2008): 275–289; Tafadzwa Pasipanodya, 'A Deeper Justice: Economic and Social Justice as Transitional Justice in Nepal', *International Journal of Transitional Justice* 2 (2008): 378–397; Yvette Selim and Tim Murithi, 'Transitional Justice and Development: Partners for Sustainable Peace in Africa?' *Journal of Peacebuilding and Development* 6 (2011): 58–72.

65 Louise Arbour, 'Economic and Social Justice for Societies in Transition', *New York University Journal of International Law and Politics* 40 (2007): 1–28, at 3.

66 UNDP, *Human Development Report 1990* (1990), iii, available at: http://hdr.undp.org/sites/default/files/reports/219/hdr_1990_en_complete_nostats.pdf (accessed 9 September 2016).

67 Ibid., at 1.

68 Amartya Sen, 'Human Rights and Capabilities', *Journal of Human Development* 6 (2005): 151–166, at 153.

person can choose one combination'.[69] In BiH, many survivors do not have these choices. Some are psychologically broken and unable to envisage different ways of living. Some of the older interviewees, in particular, variously claimed: 'I will never be the person I was', 'I no longer experience any joy or pleasure in life', 'I see no purpose in life anymore'.[70] In contrast, some interviewees – and especially those who were still young – could imagine different ways of living and they wanted to change their lives for the better. Yet, often they did not know how to or where to begin; they saw only obstacles and hurdles ahead of them.

Like Sen, Nussbaum has also discussed the concept of capabilities. The central focus of her capabilities approach is the notion of human dignity. Human dignity, in turn, is associated with 10 fundamental capabilities which are 'part of a minimum account of social justice'.[71] Everyone, she maintains, is entitled to 'a decent minimum level' of these capabilities,[72] which include bodily health, bodily integrity and affiliation.[73] These capabilities, and their realization, constitute critical markers of social justice.[74] For Nussbaum, moreover, the concept of social justice has a critical gender dimension linked to women's entitlements.[75] According to her, it is the combination of poverty with gender inequality that results in 'an acute failure of central human capabilities'.[76] This argument can be modified by shifting the focus from gender to transitional justice. Quintessentially, if the legacy of rape and sexual violence is addressed in a way that neglects survivors' long-term needs, this will often have a negative impact on human capabilities and on the realization of 'thick' justice that extends beyond the legal sphere.

69 Ibid., at 154.
70 Based on a review of existing research, Neville and Heppner point out that 'Generally, it appears that older rape survivors have a more difficult psychological adjustment than do younger rape survivors'. Helen A. Neville and Mary J. Heppner, 'Contextualizing Rape: Reviewing Sequelae and Proposing a Culturally Inclusive Ecological Model of Sexual Assault Recovery', *Applied and Preventive Psychology* 8 (1999): 41–62, at 50.
71 Martha C. Nussbaum, 'Capabilities as Fundamental Entitlements: Sen and Social Justice', *Feminist Economics* 9 (2003): 33–59, at 40.
72 Martha C. Nussbaum, 'Human Rights and Human Capabilities', *Harvard Human Rights Journal* 20 (2007): 21–24, at 21.
73 Ibid., at 23–24. One aspect of this affiliation is 'Having the social bases of self-respect and non-humiliation; being able to be treated as a dignified being whose worth is equal to that of others. This entails provisions of non-discrimination on the basis of race, sex, sexual orientation, ethnicity, caste, religion, national origin'. Ibid., at 23–24.
74 Nussbaum, *supra* note 71, at 40.
75 Nussbaum explains that: 'I adopt a "principle of each person's capability", based on a "principle of each person as end". Women have all too often been treated as the supporters of the ends of others, rather than as ends in their own right; thus, this principle has particular critical force with regard to women's lives'. Martha C. Nussbaum, 'Women's Capabilities and Social Justice', *Journal of Human Development* 1 (2000): 219–247, at 223.
76 Martha C. Nussbaum, *Women and Human Development: The Capabilities Approach* (Cambridge: University of Cambridge Press, 2000), 3.

The process of fostering and strengthening human capabilities, as part of a more developmental approach to transitional justice, is not simply about responding to individual needs. It is also about empowering men and women to address their own needs. In discussing their current lives, interviewees in BiH consistently reverted to the theme of employment. If they had a job, they maintained, they would have far fewer financial worries and would be able to think about the future rather than the past. However, none of them were optimistic about their economic prospects. As previously noted, there is high unemployment in BiH (at around 27 per cent), although there has been some reported improvement.[77] In addition to stressing the importance of jobs, interviewees also emphasized their need to have an occupation; they wanted something to do and to have a clear focus in life. While transitional justice is not about creating jobs, it can assist in giving people a new sense of meaning and direction. This further highlights the importance of NGOs in transitional justice work, and particularly in the delivery of reparative justice. It will be recalled from Chapter 6 that reparations are not only about the payment of compensation. One of the five forms of reparations which the UN General Assembly has identified is rehabilitation, defined as including 'medical and psychological care as well as legal and social services'.[78] More broadly, rehabilitation can be understood as a process of fostering human capabilities, giving people choices and providing them with a renewed sense of purpose.[79]

To illustrate this point, as previously noted I closely worked with the NGO *Snaga Žene* during my fieldwork in BiH. The organization's core mission is to rehabilitate female survivors of rape and sexual violence (and more recently a group of male survivors) through the provision of occupational and horticultural therapy. It developed this model more than a decade ago through its work with women in Srebrenica who lost husbands and sons in the 1995 genocide. Sixty per cent of BiH's population live in rural areas,[80] and it is common for people to have their own plots of land (see figure 7.1). Covering diverse areas of northern and

77 World Bank, 'Moderate Growth Improves Job Prospects in Bosnia and Herzegovina' (27 September 2016), available at: www.worldbank.org/en/news/press-release/2016/09/27/moderate-growth-improves-jobs-prospects-in-bosnia-and-herzegovina (accessed 4 December 2016).

78 UN General Assembly, *Basic Principles and Guidelines on the Right to a Remedy and Reparation for Victims of Gross Violations of International Human Rights Law and Serious Violations of International Humanitarian Law* (16 December 2005), §21, available at: www.ohchr.org/EN/ProfessionalInterest/Pages/RemedyAndReparation.aspx (accessed 9 May 2016).

79 Lee et al. maintain that 'purposefulness is a critical component in recovery and rehabilitation'. Joshua Y Lee, Emily A. Ready, Eric N. Davis and Philip C. Doyle, 'Purposefulness as a Critical Factor in Functioning, Disability and Health', *Clinical Rehabilitation* (2016): 1–16, at 2 (DOI: 10.1177/0269215516672274).

80 Simon Davies, 'Life in Rural Bosnia: Anguish, Idyll or Something In Between?' (21 July 2015), available at: www.brookings.edu/blog/future-development/2015/07/21/life-in-rural-bosnia-anguish-idyll-or-something-in-between/ (accessed 29 August 2016).

north-east BiH, as well as parts of central BiH and Herzegovina, *Snaga Žene* provides survivors (from all three ethnic groups) with seeds, *plastenici* (a type of greenhouse), medicinal herbs such as lavender, bees, agricultural tools and, most recently, solar-powered fruit drying machines. It seeks not only to give survivors a new sense of purpose and pride, but also to economically empower them.[81] The results are impressive. In October 2014, I visited an area of central BiH where the economy is particularly stagnant and spoke to a group of survivors, all of whom stressed that they wanted opportunities to be creative, to engage in something constructive and to improve their lives. Two months later, I returned to the town with the head of *Snaga Žene*, to introduce her to the women and to discuss their needs. The NGO is now working with this group of survivors and regularly visits them. With the support of *Snaga Žene*, the women have gone on to establish their own organization and they supplement their low incomes by selling what they make, including soaps, honey, and macerated oils (see figures 7.2 and 7.3). From the time of my first visit in October 2014 to my final visit in October 2015, the difference in these women was significant. They were more confident, positive and had a newfound energy.[82]

Providing survivors with opportunities to re-build their lives and to gain a new sense of direction are important elements of a holistic and more development-oriented approach to transitional justice. What this research has consistently stressed, however, is that rape and sexual violence are ricochet crimes that do not only affect the lives of survivors themselves. They also affect families and, as Chapter 2 explored, communities. How families and communities respond to survivors, moreover, can strongly influence the long-term effects of rape and sexual violence.[83] Accordingly, an individualist approach to transitional justice that focuses only on direct victims is too narrow. Rather, as part of a more holistic way of addressing the past, there needs to be a far greater emphasis on some of the wider social and contextual effects of rape and sexual violence.

81 The work that *Medica Zenica* is doing is also extremely important in this regard. See http://medicazenica.org/uk/index.php?option=com_content&view=article&id=56&Itemid=50

82 In northern Uganda, the NGO *Warocho Kwan Wwawa* (Renovate Our Lives) is doing similar work to *Snaga Žene*. Set up by the UK-based charity Send a Cow, *Warocho Kwan Wwawa* works with children who were abducted by the LRA, many of whom were raped in the context of forced marriages to LRA commanders. The NGO enables these formerly abducted children to earn a living by engaging in dairy farming and selling milk. In addition, *Warocho Kwan Wwawa* 'has contracts to make uniforms for two primary schools'. Nathalie Bonney, 'Life after Kony: How Uganda's Women are Rebuilding their Lives' (2 August 2016), available at: www.theguardian.com/world/2016/aug/02/life-after-joseph-kony-uganda-women-rebuilding-lives-child-soldiers (accessed 9 September 2016).

83 Rebecca Campbell, Emily Dworkin and Gianinna Cabral, 'An Ecological Model of the Impact of Sexual Assault on Women's Mental Health', *Trauma, Violence and Abuse* 10 (2009): 225–246, at 226.

*Figure 7.1* Rural Bosnia

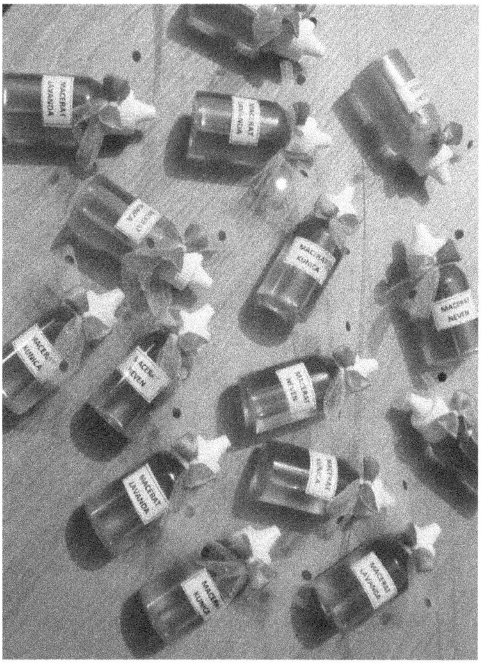


*Figure 7.2* Macerated oils made by an interviewee

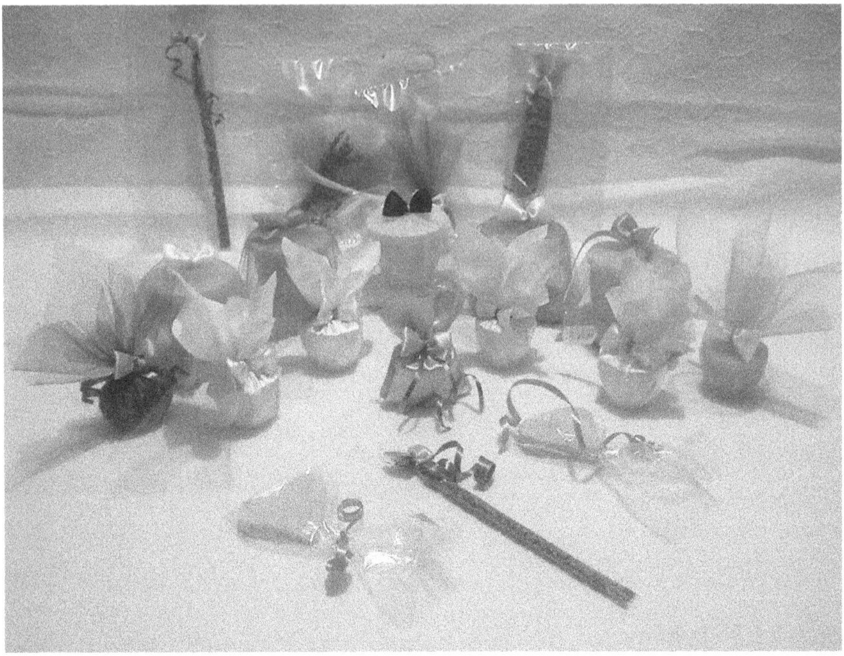

*Figure 7.3* Soaps and lavender gifts made by an interviewee

### ***A social dimension: transitional justice and the social ecology of violence***

The concept of ecology emphasizes the complex interactions between individuals and their environments.[84] In ecological models, these interactions are represented visually in the form of several concentric circles depicting '*a nested arrangement of structures, each contained within the next*'.[85] Individual behaviours are thus situated within a broader social context of inter-locking and multivariate influences, from the micro to the macro levels. Ecological models have been widely used in research on trauma, including rape trauma, and adjustment/recovery.[86]

84 Urie Bronfenbrenner, *The Ecology of Human Development: Experiments by Nature and Design* (Cambridge, MA: Harvard University Press, 1979).

85 Urie Bronfenbrenner, 'Toward an Experimental Ecology of Human Development', *American Psychologist* 32 (1977): 513–531, at 514. Emphasis in the original.

86 See, for example, Mary R. Harvey, 'An Ecological View of Psychological Trauma and Trauma Recovery', *Journal of Traumatic Stress* 9 (1996): 3–23; *idem*, 'Towards an Ecological Understanding of Resilience in Trauma Survivors: Implications for Theory, Research and Practice', *Journal of Aggression, Maltreatment and Trauma* 14 (2007): 9–32; Neville and Heppner, *supra* note 70; Campbell, Dworkin and Cabral, *supra* note 83; Kenneth E. Miller and Andrew Rasmussen, 'The Mental Health of Civilians Displaced by Armed Conflict: An Ecological Model of Refugee Distress', *Epidemiology and Psychic Sciences* 26 (2017): 129–138.

However, there has been little attention to ecology within the field of transitional justice. This is regrettable. As David and Choi underscore, 'To employ the best possible mechanisms of redressing victims, one must consider changes and interventions beyond the individual level, as an individual is to return to his community, rejoin society, and reenter the polity'.[87] In the context of this research, one particular issue that powerfully highlights the relevance of ecology is rape stigma, and transitional justice has a role to play in tackling this stigma.

### *Addressing rape stigma*

In the trial of the Slavko Savić at the State Court of BiH, which was discussed in the previous chapter, the defendant was found guilty of raping a Bosniak woman in Vogošća in 1993. During the trial, Witness B, the woman's sibling, spoke about the sense of shame that both she and her sister felt as a result of Savić's actions. According to the judgement:

> Witness B's foregoing statement undoubtedly speaks about the patriarchal environment in which the injured party and witness B were brought up, and to a certain extent about the embedded feeling of guilt for being raped. This is, most probably, due to the view commonly accepted within the small environment where they were brought up that a woman herself 'must have provoked the rape' or that 'she herself is guilty for being raped'. This also speaks, to a certain extent, about the injured party's motives to report the incident only subsequently.[88]

Many of the female interviewees who participated in this research, and particularly the older women, often spoke about their war experiences in similar terms as Witness B.[89] Even though the majority of them acknowledged that they themselves were not to blame for what had happened to them during the war, they consistently referred to rape as something deeply shameful and disgraceful. Such views partly reflect wider societal attitudes. In her work on the Holocaust, Danieli has identified what she calls the '*conspiracy of silence* between Holocaust survivors and society... including mental health, justice, and other professionals'.[90]

87 Roman David and Susanne Y.P. Choi, 'Victims on Transitional Justice: Lessons from the Reparation of Human Rights Abuses in the Czech Republic', *Human Rights Quarterly* 27 (2005): 392–435, at 430–431. See also Naomi Cahn, 'Beyond Retribution and Impunity: Responding to War Crimes of Sexual Violence', *Stanford Journal of Civil Rights and Civil Liberties* 1 (2005): 217–270, at 221–222.

88 *Prosecutor v. Slavko Savić*, S1 1 K 017213 14 Kri, State Court of BiH Trial Chamber Judgement (29 June 2015), §314.

89 Male interviewees did not describe their experiences as shameful. As previously noted, however, they rarely expressed feelings or emotions in relation to their war trauma.

90 According to Danieli, 'After liberation, as during the war, survivors of the Holocaust encountered a pervasive societal reaction consisting of indifference, avoidance, repression

This silence, she maintains, 'has proven detrimental to the survivors' familial and sociocultural reintegration by intensifying their already profound sense of isolation, loneliness, and mistrust of society'.[91] A similar 'conspiracy of silence' exists in BiH. As in many cultures, rape and sexual violence are not readily or openly spoken about, and this has contributed to the creation of an ecological context in which some survivors feel socially marginalized and neglected. According to Durkalić, 'Women who survived wartime rape [in BiH] find no understanding within their communities or the wider society, which fails to comprehend that the women are not guilty for what happened to them'.[92]

Certainly, some of the female interviewees had experienced blame and reproach from members of their community.[93] In north-east BiH, for example, E11 maintained that she cannot talk to her neighbours about what she went through in 1992. According to them, she should have left the area when the war started, and so she herself is to blame for everything that happened to her.[94] Interestingly, some female interviewees had experienced problems with other women within the community. Interviewee Č18 explained that before the war, she was friends with a fellow Bosniak living in an adjacent house. Today, the two women no longer communicate and Č18 tries to avoid her neighbour as much as possible. In her words, 'She has told me that I should feel ashamed that I was raped, and she blames me for staying in Brčko District when the war started'.[95] Č18 was not in a position to leave the area when the war began due to her husband's ill-health. Interviewee B10, a Bosniak, revealed that her female Serb neighbour had accused her of having 'willingly slept' with Serb soldiers.[96] Female suffering in conflict can contribute to creating bonds of solidarity between women who have gone through similar experiences.[97] Such solidarity may be more elusive, however, when women have experienced different types of trauma; and particularly in cases involving rape and sexual violence, the stigma attached to these crimes can foster intra-female divides.[98]

and denial of their Holocaust experiences. Like other victims, survivors' war accounts were too horrifying for most people to listen to or believe'. Yael Danieli, 'Introduction: History and Conceptual Foundations', in Yael Danieli (ed.), *International Handbook of Multigenerational Legacies of Trauma* (New York: Plenum Press, 1998), 1–20, at 4.

91 Yael Danieli, 'Massive Trauma and the Healing Role of Reparative Justice', *Journal of Traumatic Stress* 22 (2009): 351–357, at 351.

92 Masha Durkalić, *My Voice Echoes…* (Sarajevo: CURE Foundation, 2015), 49–50, available at: http://fondacijacure.org/uploads/my%20voice2%20final%20print%20poslano.pdf (accessed 12 September 2016).

93 In contrast, none of them male interviewees mentioned this.

94 Author interview, 28 August 2014.

95 Author interview, 16 October 2014.

96 Author interview, 27 August 2014.

97 See, for example, Brett Schmoll, 'Solidarity and Silence in the Spanish Civil War', *Journal of Spanish Cultural Studies* 15 (2014): 475–498.

98 During the civil war in Bangladesh in 1971, thousands of women were raped. While the government publicly declared that these women should be regarded as '*birangonas*' or

Fundamentally, acts of rape and sexual violence may trigger a 'chain of harmful reactions from surrounding (and often loved) people, such as partners, family members, and villagers'.[99] These reactions, in turn, can greatly compound the suffering of survivors. While the stigma that often surrounds rape and sexual violence is widely acknowledged, far less attention has been given to the possible role of transitional justice in addressing it. Criminal courts, for example, could help to tackle stigma and prejudicial attitudes through their outreach work. The ICC has made special efforts to communicate with women, as highlighted by its Women's Outreach Programme,[100] but outreach work needs to extend beyond a focus on court proceedings. It should also engage communities in discussions about the importance of prosecuting rape and sexual violence, the impact of these crimes on survivors' lives and the support that male and female survivors need. OTPs can also contribute to fostering greater social support and understanding for survivors, and the ICC's Policy Paper on Sexual and Gender-Based Crimes acknowledges this point. It states that as part of the Court's policy to integrate a gender perspective into its work, the OTP's public information activities 'will include creating and seizing opportunities to highlight the impact of sexual and gender-based crimes and increase awareness and contribute to the prevention of future crimes'.[101] As possible platforms for doing so, it identifies public events, media/social media campaigns, media programmes and documentary projects.[102]

It is not only criminal courts, however, that have a necessary role to play in fighting the stigma attached to rape and sexual violence. Reparations are also

heroines, Mookherjee notes that many of them remained socially ostracized. According to her, '[t]his highlights the unease and ambiguity surrounding the issue of transgression of "female virtue" in Bangladesh'. Nayanika Mookherjee, 'Gendered Embodiments: Mapping the Body-Politic of the Raped Woman and the Nation in Bangladesh', *Feminist Review* 88 (2008): 36–53, at 40. It is women themselves, moreover, who may be especially critical of such 'transgressions'.

99 Ruth Rubio-Marín, 'Reparations for Conflict-Related Sexual and Reproductive Violence: A Decalogue', *William & Mary Journal of Women and the Law* 19 (2012): 69–104, at 75.

100 ICC, *Outreach Report 2008: Public Information and Documentation Section/Outreach Unit* (2008), 20, available at: www.icc-cpi.int/iccdocs/PIDS/publications/OUR2008Eng.pdf (accessed 20 September 2016). In the course of nine meetings in Uganda between October 2009 and October 2010, '2,459 women were reached, in comparison with 836 directly engaged during ten meetings organised in 2009. There has also been a marked increase in the number of women attending general village/town hall meetings, which were previously almost exclusively attended by men'. ICC, *Outreach Report 2010: Public Information and Documentation Section/Outreach Unit* (2010), 10, available at: www.icc-cpi.int/iccdocs/PIDS/publications/OUR2010Eng.pdf (accessed 20 September 2016).

101 ICC, *Policy Paper on Sexual and Gender-Based Crimes* (June 2014), §111, available at: www.icc-cpi.int/iccdocs/otp/OTP-Policy-Paper-on-Sexual-and-Gender-Based-Crimes--June-2014.pdf (accessed 8 September 2016).

102 Ibid.

important in this regard. As discussed in Chapter 6, both the Nairobi Declaration and the UN Secretary-General's Guidance Note underline the idea that reparations should be 'transformative'. For such transformation, what is needed is an ecological approach to reparations that situates individual survivors within the broader context of their environments. As Rubio-Marín argues, 'the aspiration of having reparations which are transformative can only be adequately fulfilled when reparations manage to contribute meaningfully to subvert the system of meanings underlying the stigmatization of victims of SRV [sexual and reproductive violence]'.[103] There are a number of potential ways in which reparations could challenge and problematize these meanings. Two in particular will be considered, the first of which is memorials.

The UN has identified 'Commemorations and tributes to the victims' as an example of 'satisfaction' – one of the five forms of reparations set out in the Basic Principles and Guidelines on the Right to a Remedy and Reparation for Victims of Gross Violations of International Human Rights Law and Serious Violations of International Humanitarian Law (UN Basic Principles and Guidelines).[104] Within transitional justice practice, however, memorials are commonly under-utilized. Furthermore, memorial landscapes are often deeply gendered.[105] In BiH, where the process of memorialization is highly politicized,[106] there are numerous memorials honouring former soldiers and combatants. There are also memorials – like the Potočari Memorial Centre – commemorating civilian victims. In contrast, there are no memorials specifically dedicated to women and their experiences. Logan and Reeves use the term 'difficult heritage' to refer to the ways in which 'sites representing painful and/or shameful episodes in a national or local community's history' are remembered and commemorated – or indeed forgotten.[107] In BiH, rape and sexual violence are elements of BiH's 'difficult heritage' that are noticeably absent from the memorial landscape.

The creation of memorials honouring survivors – male and female – of rape and sexual violence could contribute to tackling some of the stigma surrounding these crimes, both in BiH and further afield. Such memorials would represent a form of 'counter-monument'[108] that challenges traditional memorial styles.

103 Rubio-Marín, *supra* note 99, at 76.

104 UN General Assembly, *supra* note 78, at §22(g).

105 See, for example, Sara McDowell, 'Commemorating Dead "Men": Gendering the Past and Present in Post-Conflict Northern Ireland', *Gender, Place and Culture* 15 (2008): 335–354.

106 Džana Brkanić, 'Bosnian War Memorials become Political Battleground' (8 August 2016), available at: www.balkaninsight.com/en/article/bosnian-war-memorials-become-political-battleground-08-08-2016 (accessed 11 October 2016).

107 William Logan and Keir Reeves, 'Introduction: Remembering Places of Pain and Shame', in William Logan and Keir Reeves (eds), *Places of Pain and "Shame": Dealing with Difficult Heritage* (Abingdon: Routledge, 2009), 1–14, at 1.

108 James E. Young, 'Germany's Memorial Question: Memory, Counter-Memory, and the End of the Monument', *The South Atlantic Quarterly* 96 (1997): 854–880.

According to Luger, a counter-monument 'might remember in public crimes that are typically both committed and remembered in private'.[109] 'Counter-monuments' to survivors of rape and sexual violence would symbolically bridge this private/public divide, putting into the public arena crimes that are often considered as 'private' and deeply shameful. They would therefore help to convey the message that survivors are not to be shunned and hidden from view, and that they and their experiences are an integral and legitimate part of public remembering. The 'Thinking of You' exhibition in Kosovo, which will be discussed in the Conclusion, is a poignant example of this. In keeping with the aforementioned Nairobi Declaration's strong emphasis on empowerment, survivors themselves could be involved in the design of such memorials (or at least consulted). Indeed, many of the female interviewees who participated in this research were engaged in a range of creative activities, including painting, craft-making, knitting and crocheting (see figures 7.4 and 7.5).

*Figure 7.4* Knitting and sewing work by survivors in Tuzla

109 Moberley Luger, 'Remounting, Remembering: Gendered Memorials and Colleen Wagner's *The Monument*', *English Studies in Canada* 35 (2009): 71–93, at 86.

*Figure 7.5* An interviewee's artwork

Turning to a second example of how reparations could be used to tackle rape stigma, 'guarantees of non-repetition' are another of the five types of reparations identified in the UN Basic Guidelines and Principles. Examples of these guarantees include ensuring adequate civilian control of military and security forces and strengthening judicial independence.[110] As previously noted, the UN Basic Guidelines and Principles have a general application to all victims of violence. Specifically in relation to survivors of rape and sexual violence, however, the notion of non-repetition is relevant not only to the actual occurrence of these crimes, but also to the stigma that is so often conjoined to them. In other words, the non-repetition of stigma should be one of the goals of transitional justice (including reparations),[111] which in turn points to the critical importance of education. Relatively little attention has been given to education within the field of transitional scholarship, and existing scholarship has tended to mainly focus on the teaching of history and design of history textbooks.[112] However,

110 UN General Assembly, *supra* note 78, at §2 (a) and (c).

111 Indeed, a recent report published by the ICTJ underlines that 'education itself can be part of a transitional justice approach, especially one committed to guarantees of non-recurrence'. Clara Ramírez-Barat and Roger Duthie, *Educational and Transitional Justice: Opportunities and Challenges for Peacebuilding*, ICTJ (November 2015), 6, available at: www.ictj.org/sites/default/files/ICTJ-UNICEF-Report-EducationTJ-2015.pdf (accessed 7 December 2016).

112 See, for example, Elizabeth A. Cole, 'Transitional Justice and the Reform of History Education', *International Journal of Transitional Justice* 1 (2007): 115–137; Alan McCully, 'What Role for History Teaching in the Transitional Justice Process in Deeply Divided Societies?' in Irene Nakou and Isabel Barca (eds), *Contemporary Public Debates over History*

the relationship between education and transitional justice is not only about how the past is taught. It is also about using education to positively influence harmful social attitudes that can hinder the realization of core transitional justice goals, such as peace and reconciliation. As Ramírez-Barat and Duthie underline, 'Once the conflict or repression comes to an end, education can be an important vehicle for remembering the past, facilitating the transmission of memory, and contributing to the promotion of peace'.[113]

In partnership with *Snaga Žene*, I am currently undertaking a schools-based project which involves the delivery of a series of interactive discussions in high schools across BiH on the subject of rape and sexual violence in conflict.[114] To avoid the discussions becoming an ethnically driven debate about who did what to whom during the Bosnian war, the focus is on the global issue of rape and sexual violence in conflict, from Myanmar and Colombia to the DRC and Sierra Leone. The students, aged 17 and 18, are asked to reflect on some of the reasons why rape and sexual violence are used in war and armed conflict, to consider some of the short- and long-term effects of these crimes on survivors (male and female) and to think critically about rape stigma. Through the discussion of these issues in a 'neutral' international context, the students are thus encouraged to give more thought to survivors in BiH. The ultimate aim of the project, which complements the ICTY's Youth Outreach Programme,[115] is to utilize education in a novel way to help create a more socially supportive environment for Bosnian survivors of rape and sexual violence. The final phase of the project will involve the development of a new school subject covering gender-based violence, citizenship and transitional justice, with the goal of introducing this into Bosnian high schools.[116] If, as Swartz argues, it is 'an important task of researchers to locate themselves within the research and to explicitly reflect on how personal subjectivities affect (even transform) research and research relationships',[117]

*Education* (Charlotte, NC: Information Age Publishing, 2010), 169–184. For a more diversified approach to the relationship between education and transitional justice, see Clara Ramírez-Barat and Roger Duthie (eds), *Transitional Justice and Education: Learning Peace* (New York: Social Science Research Council, 2017).

113 Ramírez-Barat and Duthie, *supra* note 111, at 5.

114 The project is funded by the Economic and Social Research Council through its Impact Acceleration Account scheme.

115 According to the ICTY's former head of outreach and communications, the Youth Outreach Programme – which is mainly targeted at high school students – includes lectures and discussions that are 'aimed at stimulating the young people's interest in the issues of justice and accountability and the tribunal's contribution to both'. Nerma Jelačić, 'Building a Legacy: The Youth Outreach Program at the ICTY', in Clara Ramírez-Barat and Roger Duthie (eds), *Transitional Justice and Education: Learning Peace* (New York: Social Science Research Council, 2017), 261–289, at 267.

116 See www.birmingham.ac.uk/schools/law/news/2016/11/clark-battlefield-classroom.aspx

117 Sharlene Swartz, '"Going Deep" and "Giving Back": Strategies for Exceeding Ethical Expectations when Researching amongst Vulnerable Youth', *Qualitative Research* 11 (2011): 47–68, at 54.

we can also use the research process to empower those on the ground to help drive positive change.

The relationship between education and transitional justice, however, is not confined to school environments. As part of the process of working towards 'non repetition', and thereby diluting the potency of rape stigma, community events should be organized to encourage open and reflective discussion on the issue of rape and sexual violence. Jones et al., for example, emphasize 'a need for broader community education programmes that address the stigma that surrounds sexual violence and the hyper-masculinity that leaves women and girls vulnerable in so many post-conflict areas'.[118] Another possible way of encouraging such debate and discussion is through a greater use of what Bickford has termed 'unofficial truth projects'.[119] One example is the Women's Court that took place in Sarajevo in May 2015. The initiative of the Women in Black in Belgrade, the Women's Court provided 36 women from across the former Yugoslavia with an opportunity to tell their own war and post-war stories in their own words, without any interruptions. Four of the women spoke about rape and sexual violence. By standing up in front of a large audience, they conveyed the powerful message that rape has not destroyed them, that they have no reason to feel ashamed and that nobody has the right to judge or criticize them. One of them concluded her story with the words: 'A part of my childhood was taken away from me, but I will not give up on the present and future.'[120]

### *Family needs*

Rape stigma is both a community (meso) and a societal (macro) issue. These dialectically interwoven layers reflect and influence each other. For many of the female interviewees who took part in this research, however, the main locus of negative attitudes towards them was their own family – a substratum of the meso level – and in particular their husbands.[121] It will be recalled from Chapter 4 that few interviewees had received support and understanding from their husbands, and some of them were continuing to hide the truth from their spouses. Contributing to these difficult marital relations was the fact that husbands often had their own war trauma.

118 Nicola Jones, Janice Cooper, Elizabeth Presler-Marshall and David Walker, *The Fallout of Rape as a Weapon of War: The Life-Long and Intergenerational Impacts of Sexual Violence in Conflict* (June 2014), 5, available at: www.odi.org/sites/odi.org.uk/files/odi-assets/publications-opinion-files/8990.pdf (accessed 8 July 2016).

119 Louis Bickford, 'Unofficial Truth Projects', *Human Rights Quarterly* 29 (2007): 994–1035.

120 Janine N. Clark, 'Transitional Justice as Recognition: An Analysis of the Women's Court in Sarajevo', *International Journal of Transitional Justice* 10 (2016): 67–87, at 81.

121 As discussed in Chapter 4, none of the male interviewees spoke about family/marital problems or about needing to conceal their war experiences from their wives.

Situations of war and armed conflict call for, and legitimize, the expression of militarized forms of masculinity.[122] When men continue to use violence in post-conflict societies, this is often interpreted as evidence of 'compromised masculinity'.[123] In some countries, programmes have accordingly been designed to allow violent men 'to develop positive ideas about what it is to be a man and about masculinities in their society, and empowering them to adopt these new values in their thoughts and practices'.[124] Examples include the Rwanda Men's Resource Centre,[125] the Men's Programme *Humqadam* in Pakistan[126] and the 'One Man Can' campaign in Sudan.[127] While such initiatives are important and necessary, the focus on masculinity – and more specifically on 'correcting' masculinity – should not detract from men's own needs.

During my fieldwork in BiH, I did not have an opportunity to speak to any of the interviewees' husbands (with one exception, which was discussed in Chapter 4). From the information that these women disclosed about their marital relations, however, it was clear that husbands were struggling to deal with what had happened to their wives (and sometimes also to themselves). They needed help to come to terms with this and to be able to give their wives support. This reinforces the argument that a holistic approach to transitional justice entails more than just a focus on the long-term needs of survivors themselves. It also requires attention to the refracted needs of those around them. Hamber maintains that 'Overly stressing the needs of "men" at the expense of considering the place of masculinity in transitional justice and a web of gendered relationships could have negative results, such as the spawning of inwardly focused men's movements around transitional justice processes'.[128] The point, however, is not to stress these needs in isolation, but rather to view them in the context of a wider

122 According to Masters, 'militarized masculinity is intimately linked to specific processes of militarization (the making of "man" into "soldier")'. Christina Masters, 'Bodies of Technology: Cyborg Soldiers and Militarized Masculinities', *International Feminist Journal of Politics* 7 (2005): 112–132, at 117.

123 Colleen Duggan, 'Foreword', in Ruth Rubio-Marín (ed.), *What Happened to the Women? Gender and Reparations for Human Rights Violations* (New York: Social Science Research Council, 2006), 15–18, at 18.

124 Tu-Anh Hoang, Trang Thu Quach and Tam Thanh Tram, '"Because I am a Man, I Should be Gentle to my Wife and Children": Positive Masculinity to Stop Gender-Based Violence in a Coastal District in Vietnam', *Gender and Development* 21 (2013): 81–96, at 82.

125 UN Women, 'In Rwanda, Men Work to Change Attitudes and Confront Gender-Based Violence' (21 November 2013), available at: www.unwomen.org/en/news/stories/2013/11/in-rwanda-men-work-to-change-attitudes-and-confront-violence (accessed 6 May 2016).

126 See www.rozan.org/?q=article/mens-program-humqadam

127 See www.genderjustice.org.za/publication/sonkes-one-man-can-campaign-supports-peace building-and-gender-equality-in-sudan/

128 Brandon Hamber, 'Masculinity and Transitional Justice: An Exploratory Essay', *International Journal of Transitional Justice* 1 (2007): 375–390, at 387.

needs-matrix. The unmet needs of husbands will often impact on the needs of their wives.

Although transitional justice processes primarily give attention to those who have directly experienced human rights abuses, there is nevertheless some recognition of the fact that such abuses (and not only rape and sexual violence) can also affect families. According to the UN Basic Principles and Guidelines, for example, 'Where appropriate, and in accordance with domestic law, the term "victim" also includes the immediate family or dependants of the direct victim'.[129] Similarly, in the context of discussing the creation of a Trust Fund for Victims, the Rome Statute states that this Fund 'shall be established... for the benefit of victims of crimes within the jurisdiction of the Court, and of the families of such victims'.[130] The ongoing challenge is to translate the recognition of these wider ripple effects into practical policies. It is particularly important that long-term support is offered, where possible, to survivors of rape and sexual violence and their families.[131] In the DRC, for example, the NGO *Synergie des Femmes pour les Victimes des Violences Sexuelles* provides mediation to families affected by sexual violence, to help them to collectively work through and come to terms with their trauma.[132] While rape stigma is a potential obstacle to such work, this further reinforces the importance of holism. Quintessentially, work with families should take place alongside broader efforts to tackle stigma and social prejudices towards survivors.

## A gender dimension of transitional justice

Policy discourse on rape and sexual violence in conflict is typically 'gendered' in a way that leaves salient gaps in the resulting meta narrative. If sexual violence 'is ostensibly a gender-neutral term that refers to violence of a sexual nature against either women or men',[133] in practice it overwhelmingly refers to violence committed against women by men. Hence, just as female perpetrators are heavily neglected,[134] so too, concomitantly, are male survivors. In its 2005 Guidelines for Gender-Based Violence Interventions in Humanitarian Settings, the Inter-Agency Standing Committee (IASC) acknowledged that 'Men and boys are also

129 UN General Assembly, *supra* note 78, at Article 8.

130 ICC, *Rome Statute of the International Criminal Court* (17 July 1998), Article 79(1), available at: www.icc-cpi.int/nr/rdonlyres/ea9aeff7-5752-4f84-be94-0a655eb30e16/0/rome_statute_english.pdf

131 ICTR, *supra* note 21, at §251.

132 Synergie des Femmes pour les Victimes des Violences Sexuelles, *Rapport Annuel d'Activitiés* (2012), available at: http://donordirectaction.org/wp-content/uploads/2013/12/annualreport2012.pdf (accessed 9 October 2016).

133 Kirsten Campbell, 'The Gender of Transitional Justice: Law, Sexual Violence and the International Criminal Tribunal for the Former Yugoslavia', *International Journal of Transitional Justice* 1 (2007): 411–432, at 416.

134 See, however, Susanne Buckley-Zistel, 'Redressing Sexual Violence in Transitional Justice and the Labelling of Women as "Victims"', in Thorsten Bonacker and Christoph Safferling

vulnerable to sexual violence, particularly when they are subjected to torture and/or detention'.[135] As Dolan notes, however, 'this is immediately qualified by the statement that "[n]evertheless, the majority of survivors/victims of sexual violence are females"'.[136] Dolan has thus called for an 'ethos of gender inclusivity',[137] and this 'ethos' needs to be injected into transitional justice. In this regard, the concept of masculinity offers a useful starting point.

Hamber has highlighted the 'marginal nature of the concept of masculinity in transitional justice studies'.[138] What is also striking, however, is that discussions of masculinity within existing transitional justice scholarship rarely consider male victims/survivors. More commonly, masculinity is simply used as a lens for looking at and understanding violence against women. Cahn and Ní Aoláin, for example, maintain that 'An emphasis on the relationship between masculinities and violence in conflicted and postconflict societies permits us to identify a much broader array of enabling phenomena resulting in women's experiences of systematic violence'.[139] Theidon, for her part, suggests that both DDR [disarmament, demobilization and reintegration] programmes and transitional justice work could usefully benefit from 'exploring the ways in which militarized men are produced and militarized masculinities are performed';[140] and part of the performativity of militarized masculinity is precisely the use of violence – often against women. What strongly stands out from existing scholarship on

(eds), *Victims in Transitional Justice* (The Hague: T.C.M. Asser Press, 2013): 91–100, at 98; Dara K. Cohen, 'Female Combatants and the Perpetration of Violence: Wartime Rape in the Sierra Leone Civil War', *World Politics* 65 (2013): 383–415, at 404. In a recent book, Sjoberg notes that 'Discussions of wartime sexual violence that do mention women perpetrators are few and far between, and many of them sensationalize those women'. Laura Sjoberg, *Women as Wartime Rapists: Beyond Sensation and Stereotyping* (New York: New York University Press, 2016), 2.

135 IASC, *Guidelines for Gender-Based Violence Interventions in Humanitarian Settings: Focusing on Prevention of and Response to Sexual Violence in Emergencies* (September 2005), 4, available at: www.unhcr.org/453492294.pdf (accessed 21 November 2016). The 2015 Guidelines give greater attention to male survivors. IASC, *Guidelines for Integrating Gender-Based Violence Interventions in Humanitarian Action: Reducing Risk, Promoting Resilience and Aiding Recovery* (2015), 153, available at: http://gbvguidelines.org/wp-content/uploads/2015/09/2015-IASC-Gender-based-Violence-Guidelines_lo-res.pdf (accessed 21 November 2016).

136 Chris Dolan, 'Letting Go of the Gender Binary: Charting New Pathways for Humanitarian Interventions on Gender-Based Violence', *International Review of the Red Cross* 96 (2013): 485–501.

137 Ibid., at 486.

138 Brandon Hamber, 'There is a Crack in Everything: Problematising Masculinities, Peacebuilding and Transitional Justice', *Human Rights Review* 17 (2016): 9–34, at 10.

139 Naomi Cahn and Fionnuala Ní Aoláin, 'Hirsch Lecture: Gender, Masculinities and Transition in Conflicted Societies', *New England Law Review* 44 (2009): 1–23, at 11.

140 Kimberly Theidon, 'Reconstructing Masculinities: The Disarmament, Demobilization and Reintegration of Former Combatants in Colombia', *Human Rights Quarterly* 31 (2009): 1–34, at 33.

masculinity and transitional justice, thus, is that the concept of masculinity 'has become swamped with discussions about how it relates to perpetuating certain harms'.[141] This 'violation-centric'[142] approach not only marginalizes male survivors, but it also neglects the relationship between male suffering and masculinity.

Masculinity enters the discourse on male rape and sexual violence only to the extent that these crimes are frequently theorized and understood as constituting an attack on masculinity.[143] Yet, this is a reductionist approach not only to masculinity, but also to male survivors' individual experiences of rape and sexual violence. None of the male survivors who participated in this research described feeling 'less of a man' as a result of their experiences, although it is also important to reiterate that these men were far less forthcoming than female interviewees and rarely spoke in affective terms. What did clearly emerge from the data, however, is that the men felt that they needed to deal with what had happened to them in a 'masculine' way, by being strong, finding their own ways to cope and concealing their emotions. If masculinity is defined as 'the widespread social norms and expectations of what it means to be a man, or the multiple ways of "doing male" ',[144] it is significant that male interviewees – including those who were no longer of working age – particularly stressed the importance of having a job. The emphasis that they placed on employment can be viewed as partly reflecting a deeper underlying desire to 'do male' and to 'perform' masculinity.[145] It is striking, for example, that one interviewee, now retired, had returned to his pre-war job as a driver as soon as he was freed from the Ljubiški camp in Herzegovina. Another interviewee had immediately joined the ABiH upon his release from the Batković camp. For these men, having a job was also a return to 'normality'. Unlike the female interviewees, all of them had worked prior to the war.

Christian et al.'s study of male survivors in the DRC, which was discussed in Chapter 2, highlights similar themes. If the men in the study did express a sense of diminished and impugned masculinity, the mental and psychological effects of rape had further impaired their sense of masculine self by rendering them unable to work. In cases where their wives thus needed to become the family's main breadwinner, this frequently caused intra-marital tensions and conflict.[146]

141 Hamber, *supra* note 138, at 25.

142 Ibid.

143 See, for example, Sandesh Sivakumaran, 'Sexual Violence against Men in Armed Conflict', *European Journal of International Law* 18(2007): 253–276, at 267; Cahn and Ní Aoláin, *supra* note 139, at 121; Valerie K. Vojdik, 'Sexual Violence against Men and Women in War: A Masculinities Approach', *Nevada Law Journal* 13 (2009): 923–952, at 927.

144 Brandon Hamber, 'Masculinity and Transitional Justice: An Exploratory Essay', *International Journal of Transitional Justice* 1 (2007): 375–390, at 739.

145 Judith Butler, 'Performative Acts and Gender Constitution: An Essay in Phenomenology and Feminist Theory', *Theatre Journal* 40 (1988): 519–531.

146 Mervyn Christian, Octave Safari, Paul Ramazani, Gilbert Burnham and Nancy Glass, 'Sexual and Gender Based Violence against Men in the Democratic Republic of Congo: Effects

What strongly emerges from Christian et al.'s research, therefore, is that rape and sexual violence can deeply affect not only the way in which male survivors perceive themselves, but also the gender roles that they perform. This, by extension, necessarily has a wider impact on their families and their communities.[147]

These examples point to an important angle of enquiry vis-à-vis the relationship between masculinity and the long-terms needs of male survivors of rape and sexual violence. Fundamentally, to what extent does masculinity – or rather survivors' own ideas about masculinity and what it means to be a 'real' man – impact on long-term needs? How do unmet long-term needs affect survivors' sense of masculinity? And how can transitional justice processes contribute to addressing male survivors' needs? Reparations are particularly important in this regard, and more specifically rehabilitation. In the case of male survivors, the practical operationalization of rehabilitation should have a strong masculinity-based focus through the development of, for example, micro-finance schemes and programmes offering skills training.

According to Hamber, 'Many feminists have been reluctant to engage in the debate about masculinity because of the potential for the notion of masculinity being equated with men's needs at the expense of those of women and a proper power analysis'.[148] The notion of holism, however, is about inclusivity rather than either/or choices. By definition, therefore, a gendered holistic approach to transitional justice requires that the experiences and needs of both male and female survivors are taken seriously and not differentiated in terms of their importance. Greater attention to masculinity, and to utilizing transitional justice processes to facilitate the 're-performativity' of masculinity, is not about overshadowing female survivors, but rather about bringing male survivors in from the margins.

*****

This chapter has mapped out a new holistic approach to transitional justice. Specifically, it has both identified and explored possible ways of operationalizing three particular dimensions of holism. Firstly, emphasizing a temporal dimension of holism and the concomitant imperative of broadening the temporal parameters within which transitional justice operates, it has discussed the importance of follow-up work with survivors and the critical need for transitional justice institutions to work closely and develop partnerships with local NGOs. Secondly, it has underlined a socio-economic dimension of holism, drawing attention to some of the economic and wider social consequences of rape and sexual violence. For the practical realization of this socio-economic dimension, it has stressed the relationship between transitional justice and development, reflected on how transitional

on Survivors, their Family and the Community', *Medicine, Conflict and Survival* 27 (2011): 227–246, at 238.

147 Ibid., at 238–239.

148 Hamber, *supra* note 138, at 12.

justice processes could be used to tackle rape stigma and argued that transitional justice needs to look beyond individuals to consider the broader impact of rape and sexual violence on survivors' families and communities. Finally, it has sought to demonstrate that there is a critical gender dimension of holism, which can be operationalized through greater attention and care within transitional justice practice towards male survivors. One criticism of this three-pronged holistic approach might be that it is asking transitional justice to do too much. In a discussion specifically on reparations, for example, Rubio-Marín and de Greiff warn that 'a price is always paid for comprehensiveness'.[149] However, transitional justice has ambitious goals; and these goals – in particular justice and reconciliation – will remain largely chimeric if the basic long-term needs of survivors of rape and sexual violence are left unaddressed.

149 Ruth Rubio-Marín and Pablo de Greiff, 'Women and Reparations', *International Journal of Transitional Justice* 1 (2007): 318–337, at 328.

# Conclusion

## Final reflections

In June 2015, the Kosovo-born artist Alketa Xhafa-Mripa created a unique exhibition inside the city stadium in Priština. Her aim was to draw attention to the thousands of women who suffered rape and sexual violence during the war in Kosovo at the end of the 1990s. In her words, 'I started questioning the silence, how we could not hear their voices during and after the war and thought about how to portray the women in contemporary art'.[1] The exhibition consisted of 5,000 dresses hung on a latticework of washing lines. Freshly washed and clean, the dresses symbolically conveyed the powerful message that survivors of rape and sexual violence in Kosovo are similarly unsoiled and unstained. Aptly named 'Thinking of You', Xhafa-Mripa's exhibition drew attention to these survivors and created a space for visitors to think about them. This added to its uniqueness. How often do we think about survivors of war rape and sexual violence many years on? How much thought do we give to where they are now and how they live their lives? Notwithstanding the wealth of existing scholarship on conflict-related rape and sexual violence, little attention has been given to the long-term effects of these crimes. This book's key aim was specifically to address this gap through the adoption of a *longue durée* perspective. More than 20 years after the Bosnian war ended, it has empirically explored a pivotal 'life-trauma dialectic',[2] by looking at how the trauma of rape and sexual violence continues to affect and shape the lives of survivors today.

While the long-term effects of these crimes are significant and consequential in their own right, they also have important implications for transitional justice and how it is done. If transitional justice is quintessentially about dealing with the legacy of the past, the concept of 'legacy' must be expanded to include the long-term legacy of rape and sexual violence. In other words, the ethos of 'Thinking of

1 Mark Tran, 'Dresses on Washing Lines Pay Tribute to Kosovo Survivors of Sexual Violence' (11 June 2015), available at: www.theguardian.com/world/2015/jun/11/kosovo-sexual-violence-survivors-art-dresses (accessed 9 January 2017).

2 Paul Valent, *From Survivor to Fulfillment: A Framework for the Life-Trauma Dialectic* (Philadelphia, PA: Brunner/Mazel, 1998).

You' must be translated into the discourse and practice of transitional justice. As a crucial starting point, more attention must be given to the individual stories of survivors. According to Porter, 'The reason for placing a high priority on stories is because stories occur in the local, particular, mundane, and everyday lives of individuals, yet they are rarely discussed in conventional literature on transitional justice'.[3] This is problematic. While transitional justice focuses on 'extraordinary' crimes, it is in the 'local, particular, mundane, and everyday lives of individuals' that the long-term consequences of these crimes are most pronounced.

## Long-term legacies

Based on semi-structured interviews with 79 survivors of war rape and sexual violence in BiH, this book has shown that these men and women are still profoundly affected by their war trauma in numerous ways. It is fully anticipated that some readers, and particularly feminist scholars, will criticize this study on the grounds that it places too much emphasis on the *suffering* of survivors and on the traumatology of rape and sexual violence. The research, however, was precisely about the long-term effects on survivors of the rapes and sexual violence committed during the Bosnian war, and few of the interviewees had positive stories to tell. They talked about the problems that they face today, from psychological and medical problems to relationship difficulties and economic insecurity. A small number of them, moreover, revealed that they no longer see any purpose in life; they wished that their rapists had killed them. These are realities that cannot be glossed over or ignored. Yet, this does not mean that we need to portray survivors as weak and passive, or that exploring their ongoing problems effectively traps them into a perpetual victim role. According to Burstow, symptoms of trauma 'are best theorized as survival skills. Correspondingly, traumatized people are most adequately conceptualized as competent practitioners of their lives, none of which means that they do not get stuck or that help is inappropriate'.[4] All of the interviewees were survivors and many of them expressed the view that regardless of what they had gone through, 'life goes on'. Even those who now struggled to find any joy or happiness in life were coping in their own individual ways; they were still alive and they still found a reason to get up every morning.

The very fact that interviewees were able to tell their stories, often in considerable detail, itself attests to their remarkable strength. Their story-telling also manifested their agency. They chose which parts of their story they would share and how they would recount them (chronologically, episodically, diachronically, synchronically). Creating a space for survivors to tell their stories, and in their

3 Elizabeth Porter, 'Gendered Narratives: Stories and Silences in Transitional Justice', *Human Rights Review* 17 (2016): 35–50, at 37.

4 Bonnie Burstow, 'Toward a Radical Understanding of Trauma and Trauma Work', *Violence against Women* 19 (2003): 1293–1317, at 1305–1306.

own words, is an agency-enabling approach.[5] It is the silencing of these stories that suppresses agency.[6] More broadly, this book has sought to demonstrate that victimhood and agency can comfortably co-exist. It is not the case that the former supplants or negates the latter. Stringer notes that 'Even among feminists who in other moments are interested in polysemy and resignification, there is consensus that the words "victim", "victimhood" and "victimization" are incurably connotative of passivity, helplessness, dependence and innocence'.[7] Yet, victimhood is not a singular notion that can be reductively compressed, nor is it a spatially exclusionary idea that denies 'other spaces' – and more specifically 'spaces of actualization'[8] wherein new identities are formed. As Skjelsbaek's work has shown, victims can re-define their social identities 'in the post-conflict socio-political space'.[9]

The individuals who participated in this research were in one sense victims, by virtue of what they had experienced. Victimhood, however, was not the sum total of their identities. As Bryson points out, 'For many individuals... victimhood is but one element of their identity. They may be victims when talking about the shot that punctured their mobility, but they are empowered when talking about other aspects of their lives including, in some cases, profoundly courageous peace building work'.[10] All of the interviewees talked about the multiple ways in which their war trauma continues to affect their lives. Nevertheless, the majority were resolute that they would not be destroyed by what had happened to them, however difficult life was. Three of them were running NGOs; one had established a lavender business; one had written a book; some had spoken publicly about their experiences. Their trauma was part of them and they lived with it, but it did not define who they were. Ultimately, therefore, the individuals who participated in this research can be described as *victim-survivors*, a term which encapsulates the inter-relationship between victimhood and agency.

5 Erin K. Baines, '"Today, I Want to Speak Out the Truth": Victim Agency, Responsibility and Transitional Justice', *International Political Sociology* 9 (2015): 316–332, at 317.
6 Vis-à-vis Srebrenica, for example, Helms points to the existence of a 'notable silence'. In her words, 'The main focus was on the murder of so many men. Rape, which had been part of the abuse and terror inflicted by the invading Serbs during the fall of the enclave, was never a subject associated with Srebrenica'. Elissa Helms, *Innocence and Victimhood: Gender, Nation and Women's Activism in Post-War Bosnia-Herzegovina* (Madison, WI: University of Wisconsin Press, 2013), 200. This silencing has constrained the agency of women who suffered rape and sexual violence in and around Srebrenica. They remain voiceless.
7 Rebecca Stringer, *Knowing Victims: Feminism, Agency and Victim Politics in Neoliberal Times* (Hove: Routledge, 2014), 5.
8 Daniel Hjorth, 'Creating Space for Play/Invention – Concepts of Space and Organizational Entrepreneurship', *Entrepreneurship and Regional Development* 6 (2004): 413–432, at 421.
9 Inger Skjelsbaek, *The Political Psychology of War Rape: Studies from Bosnia and Herzegovina* (Abingdon: Routledge, 2012), 44–45.
10 Anna Bryson, 'Victims, Violence and Voice: Transitional Justice, Oral History and Dealing with the Past', *Hastings International and Comparative Law Review* 39 (2016): 299–353, at 340.

This book has also demonstrated that many survivors suffered multiple traumas during the Bosnian war, including forced displacement, beatings and the loss of loved-ones. It has thus introduced and discussed the idea of 'entangled traumas', to emphasize that rape trauma does not exist in a vacuum. This is important for contextualizing the idea of victimization. According to Helms, for example, 'giving in to the idea that a raped woman's life has been ruined by this form of victimization accepts the notion that the female social being must be defined by who has had access to her body'.[11] Focusing solely on this bodily aspect of victimization, however, neglects broader webs or constellations of trauma that are often intertwined with rape trauma. The reality that trauma is a layered phenomenon[12] complexifies the very notion of victimhood because survivors are often simultaneously dealing with different dimensions of victimhood. This further problematizes the equation of victimhood with passivity and lack of agency. In the very act of navigating through their layers of trauma, survivors are exhibiting agency.

This book, however, is not only solely about survivors. It has also sought to explore the wider effects of rape and sexual violence on survivors' families. According to the 'rape as a weapon of war' discourse, rape destroys communities. Diken and Laustsen, for example, argue that 'Strategic rape attacks not only the victim but also aims to dissolve the social structure of the attacked group. It taints its ethnic stock. Rape destroys communities by transforming women into abjects'.[13] More specifically, rape and sexual violence harm communities by harming families, but this family dimension remains under-researched. When it is addressed, family impact is typically approached through the prism of marital relations, as highlighted by some of the studies discussed in Chapter 2. This book has looked at some of the ways in which rape and sexual violence in BiH affected interviewees' conjugal relations. In so doing, it has sought to transcend the 'dichotomy of the public/private divide',[14] by illuminating how 'public' rapes affect 'private' relations. It has also examined the intra-marriage effects of combined marital traumas, noting that some survivors' husbands were expressing their own trauma through domestic violence. Additionally, this research has discussed the impact of rape and sexual violence on interviewees' relations with their children, including children born of rape. As an extension of this, it has shown that the long-term ricochet effects of these crimes can include the transgenerational transmission of trauma. While this theme arose more prominently from interviews with female survivors, two of the 13 male interviewees expressed concern that their own trauma might be affecting their children.

11 Helms, *supra* note 6, at 239.
12 Burstow, *supra* note 4, at 1309.
13 Bülent Diken and Cartsen Bagge Laustsen, 'Becoming Abject: Rape as a Weapon of War', *Body and Society* 11 (2005): 111–128, at 117.
14 Aisling Swaine, 'Beyond Strategic Rape and Beyond the Public and Private: Violence against Women in Armed Conflict', *Human Rights Quarterly* 37 (2015): 755–786, at 785–786.

Rape and sexual violence have multiple long-term effects (often interlaced with additional traumas), and these effects have critical implications for transitional justice. Using transitional justice as its overarching framework, this book has endeavoured to show that the concept of 'justice' is ultimately hollow if it is approached in a temporally curtailed way that neglects the long-term legacy of rape and sexual violence. It is erroneous, therefore, to reductively view survivors simply as individuals in need. Their stories are crucial for enabling a deeper understanding of the longevity of rape trauma and its consequences, and this understanding is a prerequisite for the development of more holistic ways of doing transitional justice that expand the concept of legacy. Drumbl has commented on 'the fuzziness about what exactly transitional justice should concern itself with'.[15] This research has aimed to reduce this 'fuzziness' by arguing specifically that transitional justice should take account of long-term effects and long-term needs.

## Legacy and holistic transitional justice

Outside of transitional justice, the concept of legacy is primarily discussed in a sporting context. Leopkey and Parent, for example, note that 'The growing importance of legacy within sport events has resulted in a heightened interest in the concept of legacy by various Olympic Games stakeholders, especially the International Olympic Committee (IOC), host cities, and governments who have financed the Games'.[16] In relation to major sporting events, moreover, the term 'mega-event legacy' is often used.[17] Transitional justice processes such as criminal trials and TRCs can themselves be viewed as 'mega-events', and this helps to explain why so much attention is given to their legacies. The example of the ICTY is a case in point. Since 2010, the Tribunal has organized a series of conferences focused on its legacy both internationally and within the former Yugoslavia.[18] South Africa's TRC during the 1990s is another prominent example.[19] A purely institutional-focused approach to legacy, however, is too narrow. More is required.

15 Mark A. Drumbl, 'Transitional Justice Moments', *International Journal of Transitional Justice* 10 (2016): 203–210, at 210.
16 Becca Leopkey and Milena M. Parent, 'Olympic Games Legacy: From General Benefits to Sustainable Long-Term Legacy', *International Journal of the History of Sport* 29 (2012): 924–943, at 924.
17 Holger Preuss, 'The Conceptualisation and Measurement of Mega Sport Event Legacies', *Journal of Sport and Tourism* 12 (2007): 207–228; Eva Kassens-Noor, Mark Wilson, Sven Müller, Brij Maharaj and Laura Huntoon, 'Towards a Mega-Event Legacy Framework', *Leisure Studies* 34 (2015): 665–671; Caitlin Pentifallo and Robert VanWynsberghe, 'Mega-Event Impact Assessment and Policy Attribution: Embedded Case Study, Social Housing and the 2010 Winter Olympic Games', *Journal of Policy Research in Tourism, Leisure and Events* 7 (2015): 266–281.
18 See, for example, www.icty.org/en/outreach/legacy-conferences
19 See, for example, Mahmood Mamdani, 'Amnesty or Impunity? A Preliminary Critique of the Report of the Truth and Reconciliation Commission of South Africa (TRC)', *Diacritics* 32

Kassens-Noor et al. suggest a linkage between mega-events and urban development. They argue that 'For event planners in potential host cities, the goal should be turning mega-events into efficient development vehicles that serve public purposes, so that legacies are conceived as furthering existing planning objectives'.[20] In the context of transitional justice, similarly, there is an important link between legacy and development. Using Preuss' idea of a 'legacy cube', which emphasizes the multi-dimensional legacies of mega sporting events,[21] a critical legacy dimension of transitional justice, holistically defined, is the legacy of crimes themselves – and the extent to which this legacy is addressed. Dealing with this long-term dimension of legacy necessarily brings to the forefront the relationship between justice and time. Discussing the notion of complementarity, Akhavan observes that 'The ICC often arrives on the scene as the ambulance and trauma surgeon, while a national system, as next of kin, must nurse the patient back to health at home in a prolonged convalescence'. For him, therefore, achieving the right balance between time and justice 'is at the root of an effective system of complementarity'.[22] It is also at the root of transitional justice more broadly. The process of dealing with the legacy of past human rights abuses does not require only an ambulance and trauma surgeon. It also requires long-term care. Without this, recovery will be compromised.

In outlining a new holistic approach to transitional justice, therefore, this book has emphasized – as one of the key dimensions of holism – the need for a widening of the temporal parameters within which transitional justice currently operates. Some scholars have similarly recognized this imperative. Balint, Evans and McMillan, for example, are concerned that transitional justice processes do not take account of long-term injustices, and specifically injustices linked to colonialism. Critical of the 'artificiality of the temporal framework that currently shapes transitional justice, stymying its ability to recognize and redress long-term harm',[23] they insist that the purview of transitional justice needs to extend further back in time.[24] What this book has argued, in contrast, is that transitional justice should be more forward looking, in recognition of how the long-term legacy of

(2004): 33–59; Jay A. Vora and Erika Vora, 'The Effectiveness of South Africa's Truth and Reconciliation Commission: Perceptions of Xhosa, Afrikaner, and English South Africans', *Journal of Black Studies* 34 (2004): 301–322; James L. Gibson, 'The Contributions of Truth to Reconciliation: Lessons from South Africa', *Journal of Conflict Resolution* 50 (2006): 409–432.

20 Kassens-Noor et al., *supra* note 17, at 669.

21 Preuss, *supra* note 17, at 211.

22 Payam Akhavan, 'Complementary Conundrums: The ICC Clock in Transitional Times', *Journal of International Criminal Justice* 14 (2016): 1043–1059, at 1044.

23 Jennifer Balint, Julie Evans and Nesam McMillan, 'Rethinking Transitional Justice, Redressing Indigenous Harm: A New Conceptual Approach', *International Journal of Transitional Justice* 8 (2014): 194–216, at 212.

24 Ibid.

rape and sexual violence extends into the present and future. In short, the concept of 'transition' should not define or circumscribe the temporal boundaries of transitional justice. The term 'transitional' conveys the idea of something transitory and passing. In contrast, the achievement of 'justice' – holistically defined and extending beyond simply legal justice – demands a long-term commitment.

Nickson and Braithwaite posit the need to 'broaden our conception of justice, then deepen it, then lengthen it'.[25] For them, 'lengthening' means 'transitional justice that is no longer transitional because the justice institutions created in the aftermath of the conflict survive all victims of the conflict'.[26] What this research has underscored is the imperative need for a 'lengthening' of the support that is offered to survivors of war rape and sexual violence. There is certainly an institutional dimension to this. Chapter 7 stressed the need for follow-up work by transitional justice institutions, and in particular criminal courts. What it also underlined, more broadly, is the importance of local partnerships between transitional justice institutions and local NGOs (and between states and NGOs). These are critical temporal components of holistic transitional justice.

Some scholars have utilized the term 'post-transitional justice', to stress that important transitional justice developments can occur outside of a 'transition' period. The example of Spain is a case in point. Aguilar, for example, points out that there has been significant transitional justice in the country 'in spite of the agreements reached during the transition aimed at avoiding discussion of the past in the political arena, and even in spite of the fact that the 1977 Amnesty Law is still operative'.[27] In her view, therefore, 'This proves not only that transitional justice measures can be transformed over time, but also that their content can be reinterpreted even while they are still in force'.[28] Similarly focusing on Spain, Golob argues that the country is a 'pioneer' in the sense that it has shown the way 'for pacted democracies to pursue justice after, and apart from, the transition moment', thereby highlighting a shift towards '"post-transitional justice" politics'.[29] Of course, in many cases – BiH included – there will be no clear dividing line between transitional justice and post-transitional justice; where does one end and the other begin? However, the delineation of transitional justice into transitional and post-transitional justice phases is significant because it represents a temporally expanded approach to transitional justice as an ongoing process. Hence, the concept of post-transitional justice necessarily overlaps with holistic transitional justice. The latter partly entails a temporal over-reaching into a

25 Ray Nickson and John Braithwaite, 'Deeper, Broader, Longer Transitional Justice', *European Journal of Criminology* 11 (2014): 445–463, at 445.

26 Ibid., at 454.

27 Paloma Aguilar, 'Transitional or Post-Transitional Justice? Recent Developments in the Spanish Case', *South European Society and Politics* 13 (2008): 417–433, at 430.

28 Ibid.

29 Stephanie R. Golob, 'Volver: The Return of/to Transitional Justice Politics in Spain', *Journal of Spanish Cultural Studies* 9 (2008): 127–141, at 128.

post-transitional justice phase, and this is crucial for ensuring that the long-term legacy of rape and sexual violence is addressed and monitored.

Developing a holistic approach to transitional justice, as this book has conceptualized it, is not only about altering temporal parameters. It is also about understanding 'legacy' in the sense of who is affected by rape and sexual violence – and how. This research has identified and sought to operationalize a critical socio-economic dimension of holistic transitional justice, to draw attention to the fact that rape and sexual violence can affect all aspects of an individual's life. To address economic effects, it has stressed the importance of development – which overlaps with a temporal dimension of holism – and more particularly human development. In relation to social effects, it has sought to show that individualistic approaches to transitional justice are discordant with the wider ricochet effects of these crimes. Shroff notes that 'At the heart of holism, there is an awareness of the unity and mutual interrelation of all things and events'.[30] Attention to these mutual interrelations is similarly needed within transitional justice, in particular through a greater emphasis on families and communities.

Alongside temporal and socio-economic dimensions of holistic transitional justice, this research has also identified and discussed a crucial gender dimension. Although it must be acknowledged that only a small number of men participated in this research, one of the book's aims was to draw attention to male survivors in BiH and to the wider reality of rape and sexual violence against men in conflict. It has argued that transitional justice processes should give more attention to the experiences and needs of male survivors, and it has particularly underlined the theme of masculinity. Crucially, masculinity is not only relevant to understanding why men commit acts of violence, but also to understanding how men experience rape and sexual violence and how they deal with their trauma. Particularly significant is the unexplored relationship between masculinity and male survivors' long-term needs, which is also central to the operationalization of a gender dimension of holistic transitional justice. One of the challenges is to develop ways of doing transitional justice that enable male survivors to regain a sense of masculinity, and rehabilitation (as a component of reparative justice) is especially important in this regard.

Through its exploration of some of the long-term effects of rape and sexual violence in BiH, and its emphasis on the need for a holistic approach to transitional justice that addresses these effects, this research is ultimately calling for an 'ethics of care' to be introduced into transitional justice discourse and practice. Justice and care are often portrayed as competing values.[31] Botes,

30 Farah M. Shroff, 'Conceptualizing Holism in International Interdisciplinary Critical Perspective: Toward a Framework for Understanding Holistic Health', *Social Theory and Health* 9 (2011): 244–255, at 245.

31 Tatek Abebe and Sharon Bessell, 'Advancing Ethical Research with Children: Critical Reflections on Ethical Guidelines', *Children's Geographies* 12 (2014): 126–133, at 130.

for example, argues that 'The ethics of justice is characterized by fairness and equality, rational decision-making based on universal rules and principles, and autonomous, impartial and objective decision-making'.[32] In contrast, 'the ethics of care is characterized by caring, involvement and the maintenance of harmonious relationships from a need-centred, holistic and contextual point of view'.[33] If one appears 'hard' while the other is 'soft', they are in no way polar opposites. The process of dealing with the past cannot be solely about the narrow pursuit of an amorphous and decontextualized notion of 'justice'. Nor can it be divorced from the long-term effects of crimes and the needs to which they give rise. The recognition of an ethics of care towards survivors (and victims more generally) draws attention to these aspects of 'legacy' and concretizes the meaning of 'justice'.

## Wider implications

Unlike *jus ad bellum* (the reasons for going to war) and *jus in bello* (the way in which wars are fought), *jus post bellum* (justice after war) is 'the least developed part of just war theory'.[34] This is unsurprising; it reflects a long-standing neglect of the aftermath of war.[35] The situation is now changing and far more attention is being given to *jus post bellum.*[36] Criminal trials and legal accountability are frequently viewed as key elements of *jus post bellum.* Orend, for example, maintains that 'Individuals who play a prominent role during wartime must be held accountable for their actions and what they bring about'.[37] Trials, in turn,

32 Annatjie Botes, 'A Comparison between the Ethics of Justice and the Ethics of Care', *JAN: Informing Policy and Practice Worldwide through Research and Scholarship* 32 (2000): 1071–1075, at 1074.

33 Ibid.

34 Michael Walzer, *Just and Unjust Wars: A Moral Argument with Historical Illustrations*, 3rd edn (New York: Basic Books, 2000), 288.

35 Robert E. Williams Jr. and Dan Caldwell, '*Jus Post Bellum*: Just War Theory and the Principles of Just Peace', *International Studies Perspectives* 7 (2006): 309–320, at 313.

36 See, for example, Brian Orend, '*Jus Post Bellum*', *Journal of Social Philosophy* 31 (2000): 117–137; *idem*, '*Jus Post Bellum*: The Perspective of a Just-War Theorist', *Leiden Journal of International Law* 20 (2007): 571–591; Carsten Stahn, '*Jus Post Bellum*: Mapping the Discipline(s)', *American University International Law Review* 32 (2007): 311–347; Mark Evans, 'Moral Responsibilities and the Conflicting Demands of *Jus Post Bellum*', *Ethics and International Affairs* 23 (2009): 147–164; Larry May, '*Jus Post Bellum* Proportionality and the Fog of War', *European Journal of International Affairs* 24 (2014): 315–333; Carsten Stahn, Jennifer S. Easterday and Jens Iverson (eds), *Jus Post Bellum: Mapping the Normative Foundations* (Oxford: Oxford University Press, 2014).

37 Brian Orend, 'Justice after War', *Ethics and International Affairs* 16 (2002): 43–56, at 53. See also Davida E. Kellogg, '*Jus Post Bellum*: The Importance of War Crimes Trials', *Parameters* 32 (2002): 87–99, at 93; Gary J. Bass, 'Jus Post Bellum', *Philosophy and Public Affairs* 32 (2004): 384–412, at 406; Major Richard P. DiMeglio, 'The Evolution of the Just War Tradition: Defining *Jus Post Bellum*', *Military Law Review* 186 (2005): 116–163, at

are seen as important for addressing violations of *jus ad bellum* and *jus in bello*.[38] Beyond this strong accent on criminal trials, there is a lack of consensus on what exactly *jus post bellum* entails and requires. Highlighting this point, Bellamy notes that 'Minimalists envisage *jus post bellum* as a series of restraints on what it is permissible for victors to do once the war is over. By contrast, maximalists argue that victors acquire certain additional responsibilities that must be fulfilled for the war as a whole to be considered just'.[39] This focus on the 'victors', however, is problematic because conflicts end in a variety of different ways and in many cases there is no clear victor.[40] Even if military victories are more common in intra-state than in inter-state conflicts, 'the majority of intrastate conflicts end without any decisive outcome'.[41] Reducing *jus post bellum* to the responsibilities and duties of the 'victors', moreover, leads to an over-emphasis on regimes and States to the detriment of local communities.

Conceptually, there have been efforts to counter-balance this top-down focus. Österdahl and van Zadel, for example, propose that when it comes to *jus post bellum*, we should aim for a set of minimum goals. These could include 'non-discrimination between civilians and combatants with regard to rights; discrimination between civilians and combatants with regard to obligations; fair, transparent and impartial trials for all prosecuted individuals; human rights applicable to all individuals; and rights to economic support for all families with children'.[42] However, precisely because every conflict is different, the authors also posit that communities could develop – beyond this set of minimum goals – their own 'tailor-made' *jus post bellum*. This adds a crucial bottom-up dimension, allowing communities themselves to define what post-war 'justice' means.[43]

This research goes a step further and argues that *jus post bellum* should include providing those who have suffered during war with justice. 'Justice', in this regard, is not simply about prosecuting violations of *jus ad bellum* and *jus in bello*. As Bellamy rightly insists, 'the justice of the peace should be assessed independently of the war'.[44] This 'justice of the peace', in turn, points to crucial interconnections between *jus post bellum* and transitional justice, which some

154; Inger Österdahl and Esther van Zadel, 'What Will *Jus Post Bellum* Mean? Of New Wine and Old Bottles', *Journal of Conflict and Security Law* 14 (2009): 175–207, at 178.

38 Bass, ibid., at 404; DiMeglio, ibid., at 154.

39 Alex J. Bellamy, 'The Responsibilities of Victory: *Jus Post Bellum* and the Just War', *Review of International Studies* 34 (2008): 601–625, at 602.

40 Virginia Page Fortna, 'Where Have All the Victories Gone? Peacekeeping and War Outcomes', Prepared for Presentation at the Annual Meetings of the American Political Science Association, Toronto (6 September 2009), available at: www.columbia.edu/~vpf4/victories%20Sept%202009.pdf (accessed 3 January 2017).

41 Joakim Kreutz, 'How and When Armed Conflicts End: Introducing the UCDP Conflict Termination Dataset', *Journal of Peace Research* 47 (2010): 243–250, at 246.

42 Österdahl and van Zadel, *supra* note 37, at 192.

43 Ibid.

44 Bellamy, *supra* note 39, at 622.

scholars have already begun to explore.[45] Many of the six conditions of *jus post bellum* that May identifies,[46] for example – and in particular retribution, reconciliation, restitution and reparations – are dimensions of transitional justice. For May, transitional justice is needed to realize the type of peace that is ultimately sought in *jus post bellum* – a 'just peace'.[47] This book similarly works back from transitional justice, but in a different way. By developing a holistic approach to transitional justice that is focused on the longevity of legacy, it has concretized the concept of 'justice' and shown why justice for survivors – and indeed for victims more broadly – is a necessary and legitimate normative element of *jus post bellum*.

It is clear, thus, that this book conceptualizes holistic transitional justice as a cross-cultural approach to dealing with the past that is not geographically or culturally circumscribed. It is an approach, in short, that has a wider relevance and application beyond BiH. This does not mean, however, that an acontextual 'cookie cutter' approach to transitional justice is being advocated. Discussing legal reform, Alkon comments that:

> The Cookie Cutter Syndrome is an approach that fails to look at the individual differences of the specific countries receiving rule of law development assistance. Instead, the Cookie Cutter approach is for aid providers to treat each nation as unformed dough, onto which the Cookie Cutter of a Western legal system is applied.[48]

To continue the analogy, this book is arguing that individual countries need to cut their own cookies from the dough of holistic transitional justice. Hence, the holistic approach to transitional justice that it has outlined should be viewed as a meta model. Ehrig, Küster and Taentzer note that in system modelling theory, 'a meta model is designed which defines the abstract syntax of the language in a declarative way. Instantiation of the meta model then yields a concrete model'.[49] In other words, country-specific applications of holistic transitional justice will

45 See, for example, Larry May and Elizabeth Edenberg (eds), *Jus Post Bellum and Transitional Justice* (New York: Cambridge University Press, 2013); Ruti Teitel, 'Rethinking *Jus Post Bellum* in an Age of Global Transitional Justice: Engaging with Larry May and Michael Walzer', *European Journal of International Law* 24 (2013): 335–342; Stahn, Easterday and Iverson, *supra* note 36.

46 Larry May, '*Jus Post Bellum*, Grotius and Meionexia', in Carsten Stahn, Jennifer S. Easterday and Jens Iverson (eds), *Jus Post Bellum: Mapping the Normative Foundations* (Oxford: Oxford University Press, 2014), 15–25, at 16–18.

47 Ibid., at 25.

48 Cynthia Alkon, 'The Cookie Cutter Syndrome: Legal Reform Assistance under Post-Communist Democratization Programs', *Journal of Dispute Resolution* 2002 (2002): 327–365, at 328.

49 Karsten Ehrig, Jochen M. Küster and Gabriele Taentzer, 'Generating Instance Models from Meta Models', *Software and Systems Modeling* 8 (2009): 479–500, at 479.

create the crucial 'instance models' of the meta model. More specifically, the three key dimensions of holistic transitional justice that this research has identified – namely temporal, socio-economic and gender dimensions – lend themselves to crucial variations or 'instances' of the meta model.

To take an example, this research has discussed possible ways of extending the temporal parameters of transitional justice and has emphasized the importance of follow-up work with survivors. Such work is likely to be least problematic at the international level. At the national level, in contrast, country-specific variables will influence the operationalization of this temporal dimension of transitional justice. As one illustration, the recent peace agreement between the Colombian government and the Revolutionary Armed Forces of Colombia (Farc) has created an important new opening for transitional justice within the country.[50] Concomitantly, however, amnesty provisions within the peace accord and the 52-year duration of the conflict between the Colombian government and the Farc are two potential factors that could heavily circumscribe the possibilities for follow-up work with survivors.[51] Similarly, the scope for follow-up work with survivors may be extremely limited in countries, such as Bangladesh, where the tardiness of transitional justice efforts may affect the number of individuals who are willing and/or able to participate in them.[52] For these reasons, therefore, there can be no template approach to holistic transitional justice and what exactly it should look like.

This research has also underlined the indispensable role of local NGOs in operationalizing temporally expanded transitional justice, and it has emphasized the need for transitional justice institutions to work closely with NGOs as a form of capacity-building. The example of Kenya illustrates the importance of these partnerships. The crimes committed during the post-election violence between December 2007 and February 2008 included an estimated 900 cases of rape

50 Sibylla Brodzinsky, 'Colombia Signs Historic Peace Deal with Farc' (24 November 2016), available at: www.theguardian.com/world/2016/nov/24/colombia-signs-historic-peace-deal-with-farc-rebels (accessed 21 December 2016).

51 The use of rape and sexual violence within the Colombian conflict has not received significant attention. In a 2009 report, Oxfam underlined that 'It is impossible… to quantify, even as an approximation, the actual number of women who are or have been victims of some form of sexual violence in the 50 years of the armed conflict. Nevertheless, testimony that has been collected and the stories told by women who live in areas occupied by armed actors and by the victims of forced displacement indicate that sexual violence is much more frequent than generally believed, than reported by the media or than suggested by official statistics and registries'. Oxfam, *Sexual Violence in Colombia: Instrument of War* (9 September 2009), 12–13, available at: www.oxfam.org/sites/www.oxfam.org/files/bp-sexual-violence-colombia.pdf (accessed 4 January 2017).

52 Biyojeta Das, 'Bangladesh Rape Victims Say War Crimes Overlooked' (4 September 2011), available at: http://womensenews.org/2011/09/bangladesh-rape-victims-say-war-crimes-overlooked/ (accessed 17 September 2016).

and sexual violence.[53] In the aftermath of this violence, several transitional justice initiatives were adopted, including the establishment of a Truth, Justice and Reconciliation Commission (TJRC). The Commission, however, which submitted its report to President Kenyatta in May 2013, has been criticized. According to Bosire and Lynch, 'as ownership of the TJRC shifted away from prominent human rights organizations, the TJRC increasingly became a technical exercise consisting of public hearings, witness statements, lawsuits and report chapters, divorced from popular and CSO [civil society organization] political debate and interests'.[54] This example highlights the fact that NGOs will often need to be proactive in developing partnerships with transitional justice institutions, in order to avoid being sidelined. In other words, the dynamics of these partnerships will substantially vary from country to country.

Drumbl has criticized the 'catch-all nature of what constitutes transitional justice' and the concomitant 'push towards professionalized homogeneity and the triumph of the checklist, manual and boilerplate'.[55] Similarly eschewing a 'checklist approach', this book has ultimately developed a heuristic frame – based on fieldwork in BiH – that can be adapted to local and country-specific realities. There is nothing to be gained from a prescriptive approach to transitional justice. In contrast, there is much to be gained from exploring possible ways of operationalizing transitional justice to ensure that long-term effects and needs are addressed. This book's conceptualization and delineation of a holistic approach to transitional justice offers an important starting point.

## Suggestions for further research

The long-term effects of rape and sexual violence in conflict remain heavily under-explored. Further research – and especially qualitative research – on the legacy of these crimes is therefore essential. To simply acknowledge that rape and sexual violence can leave in their wake a myriad of long-term effects is not sufficient. Through the adoption of a narrative approach and the use of vignettes, this book has sought precisely to emphasize that the long-term effects of these crimes develop in the context of individual lives, which themselves unfold within a broader social context. Accordingly, further detailed studies are needed, focused on different post-conflict societies. Multi-country comparative studies will also be important for illuminating more generic, as well as culturally specific, long-term effects. Backer and Kulkarni stress that 'Transitional justice measures aim to serve interests of people in conflict-affected societies – or are frequently justified

53 Human Rights Watch, *"I Just Sit and Wait to Die": Reparations for Survivors of Kenya's 2007–2008 Post-Election Sexual Violence* (4 February 2016), 4, available at: www.hrw.org/sites/default/files/report_pdf/kenya0216_web.pdf (accessed 29 December 2016).

54 Lydiah K. Bosire and Gabrielle Lynch, 'Kenya's Search for Truth and Justice: The Role of Civil Society', *International Journal of Transitional Justice* 8 (2014): 256–276, at 276.

55 Drumbl, *supra* note 15, at 210.

by such claims'.[56] In their view, thus, 'collecting data from and about individuals ought to be fundamental to advancing knowledge, developing policy, and honing practice in this field'.[57] Collecting data about the durable effects of rape and sexual violence should also be a critical part of this endeavour.

This data collection will be important for further developing the idea of holistic transitional justice. Future research should examine possible ways of operationalizing holistic justice in diverse post-conflict societies, with a particular emphasis on the temporal, socio-economic and gender dimensions which this book has identified. Such research will help to generate crucial 'instance models' that focus attention on the transformative dynamics of locality and context. Further empirical studies are also necessary for identifying possible additional dimensions of holism that build on this research. While these dimensions should be broad enough to work at a meta level, the requirement of practical operationalization means that they should be empirically informed. As Shaw and Waldorf underline, 'The reality with which we have to begin – and without which transitional justice cannot be effective or legitimate – is that of a nuanced understanding of what justice, redress and social construction look like from place-based standpoints'.[58]

While this research has developed the concept of holistic transitional justice specifically in relation to the long-term effects of rape and sexual violence, all of the crimes with which transitional justice is concerned – from disappearances and abductions to mass killings and systematic persecution – have long-term effects. A broader exploration of long-term effects accordingly constitutes a further fruitful avenue for future research. To cite van der Merwe and Lykes, 'If we are serious about ensuring that transitional justice contributes to human rights, social justice and democracy, we need to demand that advocates, researchers and activists situate their work within a longer-term framework – and embrace their work as longer-term teachers and agents of transformation'.[59] Such long-term-focused research can provide the empirical basis for developing an extended holistic approach to transitional justice that has a wider application beyond survivors of rape and sexual violence. Of course, there will be many overlaps. In discussing a socio-economic dimension of holistic transitional justice, for example, this research has partly stressed the significance of development. A greater developmental focus within transitional justice would have generic benefits that are not

56 David Backer and Anupma Kulkarni, 'Humanizing Transitional Justice: Reflections on the Role of Survey Research in Studying Violent Conflict and its Aftermath', *Transitional Justice Review* 1 (2016): 187–232, at 188.

57 Ibid.

58 Rosalind Shaw and Lars Waldorf, 'Introduction: Localizing Transitional Justice', in Rosalind Shaw and Lars Waldorf, with Pierre Hazan (eds), *Localizing Transitional Justice: Interventions and Priorities after Mass Violence* (Stanford, CA: Stanford University Press, 2010), 3–26, at 6.

59 Hugo van der Merwe and M. Brinton Lykes, 'Transitional Justice Processes as Teachable Moments', *International Journal of Transitional Justice* 10 (2016): 361–365, at 364.

tied to particular crimes. The gender dimension of holism that this research has discussed, in contrast, would be less relevant in cases that do not involve acts of rape and sexual violence. In other words, there will be crime-specific variations, and these variations could be conceptualized as constituting 'instance models' alongside cultural and country-specific variations.

*****

Marija was the first survivor whom this book introduced. She smoked heavily and her hands trembled when she spoke about the war. Nevertheless, she said that it had helped her to talk to someone and to tell her story; to be listened to and not judged. Like so many survivors in BiH, she felt forgotten and neglected. While there is a deep sense of research fatigue in BiH, and while my critics in the field insisted that I should not speak to survivors, ultimately I wrote this book to try and ensure that people like Marija are not forgotten. By sharing the stories of some of the men and women who suffered rape and sexual violence during the Bosnian war and exploring how these crimes continue to affect their lives today, more than two decades on, this book has endeavoured to convey the same message as Xhafa-Mripa's aforementioned exhibition in Kosovo: Thinking of You.

# Index

As 'Bosnia-Herzegovina' and 'rape and sexual violence' are the main subjects of the book, index entries for these headings have been kept to a minimum and readers are advised to search under more specific topics.

Note: page numbers in *italic* type refer to Tables; those in **bold** type refer to Figures.


Abdić, Fikret 45, 46, 86
ABiH (Army of Bosnia-Herzegovina): sexual violence crimes by 45, 86, 102, 112, 115
Abu Ghraib 48
accountability, in transitional justice 9, 185
AFRC (Armed Forces Revolutionary Council), Sierra Leone 53
agency: and victimhood 221; and vulnerability 4
Akayesu, Jean-Paul 126–127, 130–131
Akhavan, Payam 224
Allen, Beverly 64
Alliance of Camp Inmates BiH *(Savez logoraša BiH)* 17, 180
Amnesty International 10–11, 43, 47
apologies, in transitional justice 7
APWB (Autonomous Province of Western Bosnia) 45
Arbour, Louise 11, 199
Argentina 194–195
Arkan (Ražnatović, Željko) 1
Armed Forces Revolutionary Council (AFRC) 53
Army of Bosnia-Herzegovina (ABiH): sexual violence crimes by 45, 86, 102, 112, 115
art therapy 87n44
Askin, Kelly D. 30, 33
Austrian women survivors of World War II rape and sexual violence 55–56
*Autonomaši* 45, 46, 86, 104, 118
Autonomous Province of Western Bosnia (APWB) 45

Bangladesh 26, 206n98, 230
*Baričanin* case, State Court of BiH 168–169
Basic Principles and Guidelines on the Right to a Remedy and Reparation for Victims of Gross Violations of International Human Rights Law and Serious Violations of International Humanitarian Law 22, 156–157, 160, 210, 214
Bassiouni, M. Cherif 39, 40
Batković camp 105, 117, 141, 216
Bemba Gombo, Jean-Pierre 25, 53–54, 129–130, 132
Bensouda, Fatou 130
BiH (Bosnia-Herzegovina): Criminal Code, 2003 140n103; Criminal Procedure Code 167–168, 169, 171; ethnic diversity 37–38; independence 38; National Strategy for War Crimes Processing 143; research fatigue 16; *Transitional Justice Strategy* 22, 160–165, 195; unemployment 87–98
Boraine, Alexander L. 9, 185, 191
Bosnia-Herzegovina *see* BiH (Bosnia-Herzegovina)

Bosnian Croats 38; camps run by 43; sexual violence crimes by 43, 44; survivors of rape and sexual violence *18*, 19
Bosnian Muslims (Bosniaks): camps run by 43; population in BiH 37–38; rape and sexual violence crimes against *18*, 19, 21, 45–46, 64–65, 66–67, 68–70, 72–74; sexual violence crimes by 43, 44
Bosnian Serbs *18*, 19, 38; *see also* Serbs
Bosnian Spring 98
Bosnian war, background to 35–38
Bourke, Joanna 28, 48
Brčko 43, 183–184
Breza camp 43
Brnjić, Marijan 43n130
*Budućnost* 80n14
Burgess, Ann W. 54
Burma (Myanmar) 24, 211

cancer 90–92
capability 199–200
Caparde 41
Carpenter, R. Charli 119–120
Cassese, Antonio 195
castration 47, 48
Čelebići camp 41, 43, 53, 127, 133
Čelopek camp 41
Central African Republic 53–54, 132
Centre for Social Work *(Centar za socijalni rad)* 179, 180, 181
*Ćešić* case, ICTY 134–135
childhood sexual abuse: long-term effects of 51n3; resilience of adult survivors 5
children born of war rape 3, 5, 21, 68, 69, 119–123; *see also* pregnancy, resulting from rape
children of survivors, impact of trauma on 5, 21, 61, 114–119, 222
Chinkin, Christine 31, 54
circumcision 47
civil society: and follow-up work 191–197, 225, 230–231
civil wars, public health effects of 91–92
civilian victim of war status 16, 17, 22, 92, 95–97, 95n83, 95n84, 96n88, 114, 162, 176, 177–181, 182–184; *see also* reparations in BiH (Bosnia-Herzegovina)
Colombia 196n52, 211, 230
'comfort women' 26, 31–32
community education, and transitional justice 212
complementarity 224
Congo *see* DRC (Democratic Republic of Congo)
consensual sex, in the Bosnian war 3
consent issues 126–130
Convention on Combatting and Preventing Violence against Women and Domestic Violence (Istanbul Convention) 191
Convention on the Prevention and Punishment of the Crime of Genocide, 1948 65n74, 130
Cookie Cutter Syndrome 229
Copelon, Rhonda 3, 31, 64
Council of Europe: Convention on Combatting and Preventing Violence against Women and Domestic Violence (Istanbul Convention) 191
Council of Ministers, BiH 160–161, 195
counter-memorials 208–209
craft activities 109, **209**
Crawford, Adam 187
creative activities 209, **209**, **210**
crimes against humanity, recognition of rape and sexual violence in conflict as 34, 131, 132, 134
Criminal Code of BiH, 2003 140n103
Criminal Procedure Code, BiH 167–168, 169, 171
Croat women: rape and sexual violence crimes against 68–70; *see also* Bosnian Croat women
Croatia: independence 36, 37, 38; legislation for survivors of rape and sexual violence 25; reparations 175; Serb minority 37
Croatian Association of Camp Inmates of the Homeland War BiH *(Hrvatska udruga logoraša domovinskog rata BiH)* 179, 180, 181
Croatian Defence Council *see* HVO (Croatian Defence Council)
Croatian Defence Force (HOS), sexual violence crimes by 77–78
Croatian Spring 36

DDR (disarmament, demobilization and reintegration) programmes 215
De Greiff, Pablo 155, 198, 218

Decision on the Protection of Civilian Victims of War (Brčko District) 183–184
Defining the Procedures for Recognition and Verification of the Status of Sexual Violence Victims during the Kosovo Liberation War 176
Degni-Ségui, René 56
*Delalić* case, ICTY 53, 127, 131
Delić, Hazim 53, 127, 131
Democratic Republic of Congo *see* DRC (Democratic Republic of Congo)
development, and transitional justice 198–202, **203**, **204**, 224, 226, 232–233
diabetes 21, 76, 79, 90, 92–93, 111
disarmament, demobilization and reintegration (DDR) programmes 215
dissociation, and trauma 81
Dolan, Chris 215
domestic violence 5, 13, 21, 80n14, 82, 112–113
domino theory 37
Dostić, Krsto 173n109
Douglas, Raymond, M. 108
DRC (Democratic Republic of Congo) 132, 214; declaration to combat sexual violence in war 25; rape and sexual violence crimes 53–54, 57–61, 89–90, 101, 109n38, 177n124, 211, 216–217; reparations 166
Dretelj camp 41, 78
Drmeljevo camp 45
Drumbl, Mark A. 223, 231
Duić, Tomislav 83, 84

EC (European Commission) 146
ecological models 204–205
education, and transitional justice 210–212
employment/unemployment 21, 76, 97–98, 201–202
empowerment approach to research 15–16
Engle, Karen 4, 41, 43
entangled traumas 21, 75, 82–88, **88**, 100, 119, 222
ethical issues in research 14–17
ethics of care 226–227
European Commission (EC) 146
European Court of Human Rights 145
'exceptional' warfare violence against women 5

family honour, in the Hague Conventions 29
family relationships of survivors of rape and sexual violence in BiH 21, 71–72, 101–114, 212–214, 218, 222
fellatio, forced 2, 17, 70, 78, 110, 133–135, 172
Filipovič, Zlata 35
Foča 41–42, 43, 128
follow-up work with survivors by criminal courts 187–191, 225
forced fellatio 2, 17, 70, 78, 110, 133–135, 172
forced marriage 61
forced pregnancy 2
forced prostitution 2, 34
forced sterilization 2
Fourth Geneva Convention 32–33
*Furundžija* case, ICTY 127, 128, 134

gender dimension of holistic transitional justice 13–14, 22, 185, 214–217, 218, 226, 233
Geneva Conventions 32–33, 127; Additional Protocols 33–34
genocide: definition 65n74; genocidal rape in BiH 64–65; recognition of rape and sexual violence in conflict as 34, 130–131
*Gerc Sumaja* 178
Global Summit to End Sexual Violence in Conflict 25, 47
Government Commission on Recognition and Verification of the Status of Sexual Violence Victims during the Kosovo Liberation War 176
Guatemala 25, 160n38, 177n124
Guidance Note of the Secretary-General: Reparations for Conflict-Related Sexual Violence 22, 159–160, 197, 208
Guidelines for Gender-Based Violence Interventions in Humanitarian Settings, IASC (International Agency Standing Committee) 214–215
gynaecological problems, survivors of rape and sexual violence in BiH 79, 89

Hague Conventions 29–30
Hamber, Brandon 213, 215, 217
Hanušić, Adrijana 168–169, 170n88
Harambašić, Fikret 48, 132, 133
Hasečić, Bakira (*Žena Žrtva Rata*) 66–67
health problems of rape and sexual violence survivors in BiH 21, 75–76, 79, 88–95
Helms, Elissa 67, 119, 222
Henry, Nicola 153
HIV/AIDS: infection following rape 57, 59
holistic transitional justice 9–10, 185–186, 224, 229, 232; gender dimension 13–14, 22, 185, 214–217, 218, 226, 233; and legacy 223–227; socio-economic dimension 11–12, 22, 185, 197–202, **203**, **204**, 204–214, **209**, **210**, 217–218, 226; temporal dimension 10–11, 22, 185, 186–197, 217, 224–226, 230
Holocaust survivors 116, 205–206
Holstrom, Lynda 54
honour, women's 66; and the Geneva Conventions 32–33
horticultural therapy 201–202, **203**, **204**
HOS (Croatian Defence Force), sexual violence crimes by 77–78
HPV (human papilloma virus) 91–92
*Hrvatska udruga logoraša domovinskog rata BiH* (Croatian Association of Camp Inmates of the Homeland War BiH) 179, 180, 181
human development 199–200; *see also* development
human papilloma virus (HPV) 91–92
human security 97
husbands, effect of wife's rape and sexual violence on 57, 59, 70, 73, 77, 79, 82, 83, 97, 102–114, 212–214; combined marital trauma 110–14; sexual relations 106–110; South Kivu 62; supportive 67; unsupportive 21, 101; wife blaming 104–107
HVO (Croatian Defence Council) 52, 77n6; sexual violence crimes by 43–44, 77, 83–84, 86, 105, 107, 122, 142, 152; *see also Vatreni konji* (Fire Horses)
IASC (International Agency Standing Committee), Guidelines for Gender-Based Violence Interventions in Humanitarian Settings 214–215
ICC (International Criminal Court) 224; *Bemba* case 25, 53–54, 129–130, 132; definition of rape 129–130; definition of sexual violence in Rome Statute 2; Elements of Crimes 129–130, 131; *Lubanga* case 165–166; Policy Paper on Sexual and Gender-Based Crimes 207; TFV (Trust Fund for Victims) 166, 214; VWU (Victims and Witnesses Unit) 137; Women's Outreach Programme 207; *see also* Rome Statue of the ICC (International Criminal Court)
ICTR (International Criminal Tribunal for Rwanda) 125; *Akayesu* trial 126–127, 130–131; Best Practices Manual for Investigation and Prosecution of Sexual Violence Crimes 153, 189–190, 193; *see also* UN Mechanism for International Criminal Tribunals
ICTY (International Criminal Tribunal for the former Yugoslavia) 195, 223; *Češić* case 134–135; *Delalić* case 131; *Furundžija* case 127, 128, 134; *Kunarac et el* case 43, 128–129, 131; non-corroboration rule 138; outreach office 192–193; post-testimony neglect 151–152; *Prlić et al.* case 43–44, 78n7; prosecutions for sexual violence crimes 41–42, 43, 44, 86n39, 86n40, 125, 127–129, 128–129; and reparations 166–167; RPE (Rules of Procedure and Evidence) 136, 137–138, 166–167; and sexual violence against men 132–135; *Tadić* case 48, 132–133, 135; *Todorović* case 133–134; VWS (Victims and Witnesses Section) 136–137, 152, 190, 193–194; Youth Outreach Programme 211; *see also* UN Mechanism for International Criminal Tribunals
*In the Land of Blood and Honey* 66–67
Independent State of Croatia (NDH) 37
institutional reform in transitional justice 9, 185

International Agency Standing Committee (IASC), Guidelines for Gender-Based Violence Interventions in Humanitarian Settings 214–215
International Criminal Court *see* ICC (International Criminal Court)
International Criminal Tribunal for the former Yugoslavia *see* ICTY (International Criminal Tribunal for the former Yugoslavia)
International Criminal Tribunal for Rwanda *see* ICTR (International Criminal Tribunal for Rwanda)
International Military Tribunal for the Far East (Tokyo Tribunal) 31–32
International Protocol on the Documentation and Investigation of Sexual Violence in Warfare 124
intersectionality 60
Iraqi prisoners, sexual abuse of 48
Islamic State 24
Istanbul Convention (Convention on Combatting and Preventing Violence against Women and Domestic Violence) 191
Izetbegović, Alija 38

Japanese army, World War II 26
JNA (Yugoslav National Army) 36–37, 52
Jolie, Angelina 66–67
*jus ad bellum* 227, 228
*jus in bello* 32, 227, 228
*jus post bellum* 22–23, 227–229

Karadžić, Radovan 38, 105n17
Kelly, Jocelyn T. 59
Kenya 194, 197, 230–231
Konjic camp 43, 52
Kosovo: reparations 175–176
Kovač, Radomir 41
Kraljević, Blaž 77n6
*Kunarac et el* case, ICTY 43, 128–129, 131

Lambourne, Wendy 186
Landžo, Esad 133
Law on Civilian Victims of War, Republika Srpska (RS) 181
Law on the Principles of Social Protection, Protection of Civil War Victims and Protection of Families with Children, BiH Federation 177, 181
Law on the Rights of Victims of Sexual Violence during the Armed Aggression against the Republic of Croatia in the Homeland War 175
Law on the Status and the Rights of Martyrs, Invalids, Veterans, Members of the Kosovo Liberation Army, Sexual Violence Victims of War, Civilian Victims and their Families 175–176
Law on Witness Protection Programme 145
legacy: and development 224; and holistic transitional justice 223–227; long-term 220–223; and transitional justice 7–9, 13, 219; *see also* long-term effects of rape and sexual violence in BiH
'legacy cube' 224
LGBTI (lesbian, gay, bisexual, transsexual, intersex) community: prejudice against in BiH 65n73
Liberia 53
Lieber Code, US 29, 30
Ljubuški prison 84, 216
long-term effects of rape and sexual violence in BiH 20–21, 22–23, 68–74, 75–76, 172; entangled traumas 21, 75, 82–88, **88**, 100, 119, 222; further research 231–233; male survivors 217; physical health issues 21, 75–76, 79, 88–95; previous studies of 68–74; psychological effects 75, 76–82, 100; socio-economic issues 76, 95–99, 100
long-term effects of rape and sexual violence in conflict 20–21, 51–63; multi-dimensional effects 56–61; multi-layered effects 61–63
Lora camp 83–84, 110
LRA (Lord's Resistance Army) 61
*Lubanga* case, ICC (International Criminal Court) 165–166
Luka camp 41, 111

MacKinnon, Catharine 3, 64, 127
Mani, Rama 197–198
Manjoo, Rashida 102n7, 105
*Marković* case, State Court of BiH 170, 171–172, 173–174, 184

masculinity 14, 213, 215–217, 226
mass graves 85n36
May, Larry 229
Maya Q'eqchi' community, Guatemala 25
McEvoy, Kieran 113
*Medica Mondiale* 21, 73–74, 79n10, 81–82, 104, 107, 114, 153
*Medica Zenica* 21, 73–74, 79n10, 81–82, 104, 107, 114, 146, 165, 177, 178, 179, 181
medicines 81–82, 164; cost of in BiH 76, 79, 94–95
mega-events, and legacy 223–224
memorialization 208–209
memory issues of survivors of rape and sexual violence 150–151
Men of Hope, Uganda 109
men, rape and sexual violence against 2, 13–14, 42, 226; RUF case 131–132; South Kivu 62–63; and transitional justice 214–217; UN Secretary-General's Guidance Note on Reparations for Conflict-Related Sexual Violence 159–160
men, rape and sexual violence against in BiH 17–19, *18*, 70–71; family relationships 21; lack of support for 80n14, 83n29; sexual relations 108–109
Men's Programme *Humqadam*, Pakistan 213
Meron, Theodor 189
Mertus, Julie 81, 151
methodology and fieldwork 14–20, *18*
'militarized masculinity' 14
Milošević, Slobodan 36–37
Ministry of Justice, BiH 143–144, 160, 161
Minow, Martha 155
MLC *(Mouvement de libération du Congo)* 53–54, 132
Mozambique 51
Myanmar 24, 211

Nairobi Declaration on Women's and Girls' Right to a Remedy and Reparation 22, 157–159, 160, 184, 197, 208, 209
narrative approach 76
National Strategy for War Crimes Processing, BiH 143
NDH (Independent State of Croatia) 37
Nepek camp 45
NGOs: and follow-up work with survivors 191–197, 225, 230–231; hostility to research 16
NÍ Aoláin, Fionnuala 7, 215
Nikolić, Dragan 86n39
Nolan, Aoife 12
non-consent issues 126–130
Nuremburg military tribunal 30–31
Nussbaum, Martha C. 200

occupational therapy 201–202, **203**, **204**
Omarska camp 41, 48, 132
'One Man Can', Sudan 213
oral sex, forced 2, 17, 70, 78, 110, 133–135, 172
'ordinary' everyday violence against women 5, 13
OSCE (Organization for Security and Co-operation in Europe) 145
outreach office, ICTY 11, 21–22, 35, 52–53, 126, 192–193

peace-building: and holism 186; women's role in 158–159, 197
Peru 177n124
Pham, Phuong 7
Policy Paper on Sexual and Gender-Based Crimes, ICC (International Criminal Court) 207
Porter, Holly E. 61–62
post-transitional justice 225–226
post-traumatic stress disorder *see* PTSD (post-traumatic stress disorder)
pregnancy, resulting from rape 68–69, 119–123; *see also* children born of war rape
Preventing Rape and Sexual Violence in Conflict Initiative (PSVI) 144
prison contexts, male rape in 48
privatization in BiH 98
*Prlić et al.* case, ICTY 43–44, 78n7
prosecutions of rape and sexual violence crimes 124–125; international developments 125–139; procedural innovations 135–139
prosecutions of rape and sexual violence crimes in BiH 9–10, 21–22, 41–42, 43, 44, 63–64, 86n39, 86n40;

survivors' experiences of 22, 53, 139–153
prosecutors: training on dealing with rape and sexual violence survivors 144–145
protected witness status 141, 145, 146, 147, 149, 151–152, 170, 172
PSVI (Preventing Rape and Sexual Violence in Conflict Initiative) 144
psychotherapy/counselling: survivors of rape and sexual violence in BiH 81–82
PTSD (post-traumatic stress disorder): Austrian women survivors of World War II rape and sexual violence 55–56; and diabetes 92–93; survivors of rape and sexual violence in BiH 73, 77, 79, 81, 92
Pupavac, Vanessa 6
purposive sampling 19

Radić, Marko 141n107
rape: as an act of torture 127, 131; as a crime against humanity 34, 131, 132, 134; definition issues 126–130, 129n31; as genocide 34, 130–131; terminology 2–3; as terrorism 131
rape and sexual violence in BiH 1–2, 3, 20, 26, 34–35, 38, 39–42; age profile of victims 40–41; early studies of 63–68; inter-ethnic rapes 44, 45–46; by non-Serb forces 42–44; scale of 39–40, 65; *see also* long-term effects of rape and sexual violence in BiH; men, rape and sexual violence against; prosecutions of rape and sexual violence crimes in BiH; rape stigma; rape trauma; survivors of rape and sexual violence in BiH
rape and sexual violence in conflict 6, 20; 'recovery' from 82; 'social imprint' of 2; changing international context 28–35; historical overview 24–35; international recognition of 34; long-term effects of 20–21, 51–63; motivations for 27–28; multi-dimensional effects of 56–61; multi-layered effects of 61–63; non-consent 126–130; as a war crime 132;as a weapon of war 222
rape myths 105
'Rape of Nanking' 26, 31
rape stigma 58–59, 163, 205–212, 218
rape trauma 54–55, 60, 82, 104, 107, 171, 204, 222, 223
Ražnatović, Željko (Arkan) 1
re-traumatization 15, 139–140
RECOM (regional fact-finding commission) 10
reconciliation, in transitional justice 9, 185
Red Army, World War II 26
rehabilitation 162–164, 201–202, **203**, **204**; male survivors 217
reparations 9, 10, 22, 146, 155–160, 185, 207–208, 210, 218; Croatia 175; Kosovo 175–176; male survivors 217
reparations in BiH (Bosnia-Herzegovina) 22, 155, 156, 167–168, 201; administrative route to 22, 176–184; BiH's *Transitional Justice Strategy* 160–165; Brčko District 183–184; court route to 22, 165–174; Federation 176–181, 195; RS (Republika Srpska) 181–184, 195
reparative justice 197–198
research fatigue 16
resilience 4–5, 73–74
restorative justice 9, 10
retributive justice 9, 10
Revolutionary United Front (RUF), Sierra Leone 53
Rome Statue of the ICC (International Criminal Court): definition of sexual violence 2; and reparations 165–166; witness support and protection 137; *see also* ICC (International Criminal Court)
RPF (Rwandan Patriotic Front) 58
RS (Republika Srpska) 38, 195; reparations 181–184, 195
RSCSL (Residual Special Court of Sierra Leone) 138–139, 189n18; *see also* SCSL (Special Court of Sierra Leone)
Rubio-Marín, Ruth 208, 218
RUF (Revolutionary United Front), Sierra Leone 53
Russian military, World War II 31
Rwanda: rape and sexual violence in 1994 genocide 3, 27, 56–58, 125–126, 126–127; *see also* ICTR (International Criminal Tribunal for Rwanda); UN Mechanism for International Criminal Tribunals

Rwanda Men's Resource Centre 213
Rwandan Patriotic Front (RPF) 58

*Savez logoraša BiH* (Alliance of Camp Inmates BiH) 17, 180
*Savić* case, State Court of BiH 170, 172–174, 184, 205
Scarce, Michael L. 108
Schwartz, Stephen 64n74
Scorpions (*Škorpioni*) 106
SCSL (Special Court of Sierra Leone) 152–153; AFRC (Armed Forces Revolutionary Council) case 53; CDF (Civil Defence Forces) case 136; RPE (Rules of Procedure and Evidence) 138–139, 193; RUF case 131–132; *see also* RSCSL ( Residual Special Court of Sierra Leone)
Select Committee on Sexual Violence in Conflict, UK 185, 192
Sen, Amartya 199–200
Sepur Zarco trial, Guatemala 25
Serbs: camps 43; rape and sexual violence crimes against 43; sexual violence crimes by 43, 44, 64–65; *see also* Bosnian Serbs; Croatian Serbs
sexual intercourse, painful 79, 79n10, 107
sexual mutilation 47, 48, 132
Sexual Offences Act 2003 (England and Wales) 126
sexual slavery 2; Guatemala 25; Yazidi community 24; *see also* comfort women
sexual violence 3–7; definition of in Rome Statue of the ICC (International Criminal Court) 2; terminology 2; *see also* rape and sexual violence
SFRY - Socialist Federal Republic of Yugoslavia (Yugoslavia) 35–36
Sierra Leone: rapes and sexual violence in civil war 26–27, 53, 131–132, 211; *see also* RSCSL (Residual Special Court of Sierra Leone); SCSL (Special Court of Sierra Leone)
Sikkink, Kathryn 22
Simić, Goran 164–165
Simić, Olivera 3
SIPA (State Investigation and Protection Agency) 114
Sivakumaran, Sandesh 14
Skjelsbaek, Inger 67, 71–73, 221
Slovenia 36–37, 38
*Snaga Žene* 17, 19, 98–99, 165, 178, 202, 211
snowball sampling 19
socio-economic conditions of survivors of rape and sexual violence in BiH 21, 201–202
socio-economic dimension of holistic transitional justice 11–12, 22, 185, 197–202, **203**, **204**, 204–214, **209**, **210**, 217–218, 226
South Africa: TRC (Truth and Reconciliation Commission) 223
South Kivu: rape and sexual violence 62–63
South Sudan 24, 27
Spain 225
Special Court of Sierra Leone *see* SCSL (Special Court of Sierra Leone)
sports events, legacy of 223
Srebrenica 85n35, 121
Sri Lanka 28
State Court of BiH: *Baričanin* case 168–169; *Dostić* case 173n109; *Marković* case 170, 171–172, 173–174, 184; *Savić* case 170, 172–174, 184, 205; *Trbić* case 169
State Investigation and Protection Agency (SIPA) 114
stigma *see* rape stigma
STIs (sexually transmitted infections) 57, 59
Stover, Eric 125, 143n116, 152n156
stress: and cancer 91; and endocrine abnormalities 93; of health problems 94–95; *see also* PTSD (post-traumatic stress disorder)
structural violence against women 5, 13, 60
suicidal thoughts 81
survivors of rape and sexual violence: ethical issues in research 14–16; follow-up work with 187–191, 225–226, 230; further research 231–233; memory issues 150–151; temporal dimension of holistic transitional justice 11; *see also* long-term effects of rape and sexual violence in conflict; prosecutions of rape and sexual violence crimes
survivors of rape and sexual violence in BiH: children, relationships with

114–119, 222; ethical issues in research 15–17; ethnicity *18*, 19; family relationships 21, 71–72, 101–114, 212–214, 218, 222; interviewee profiles 17–20, *18*; and resilience 5; socio-economic conditions 21, 201–202; terminology 3–4; *see also* long-term effects of rape and sexual violence in BiH; prosecutions of rape and sexual violence crimes in BiH; rehabilitation; reparations/reparative justice in BiH (Bosnia-Herzegovina)
Sušica camp 41, 86
*Synergie des Femmes pour les Victimes des Violences Sexuelles* 132, 214

*Tadić* case, ICTY 48, 132–133, 135
Tamil Tigers, Sri Lanka 28
Teitel, Ruti G. 7
temporal dimension of holistic transitional justice 10–11, 22, 185, 186–197, 217, 225–227, 230
'temporal justice' 186–187
terrorism, rape as 131
TFV (Trust Fund for Victims), ICC 166, 214
Theidon, Kimberly 14, 215
'Thinking of You' exhibition (Xhafa-Mripa), Kosovo 209, 219–220, 233
Tito, Josip Broz 35–36
TJRC (Truth, Justice and Reconciliation Committee), Kenya 231
*Todorović* case, ICTY 133–134
Tokyo Tribunal (International Military Tribunal for the Far East) 31–32
torture: rape as 127, 131; reparations for victims 161, 162
transgenerational transmission of trauma 21, 61, 101, 114, 116–119
transitional justice 6–7, 223; in BiH (Bosnia-Herzegovina) 9–10, 21–23; and development 198–202, **203**, **204**, 224, 226, 232–233; ecological models 204–205; and education 210–212; ethics of care 226–227; and gender 13–14; 'hierarchies of victimhood' within 113; legacy issues 7–9, 13, 219; and social justice 11–12; temporal dimension 10–11; transformative model of 186; *see also* holistic transitional justice
*Transitional Justice Strategy*, BiH 22, 160–165, 195
trauma: rape trauma 54–55, 60, 82, 104, 107, 171, 204, 222, 223; transgenerational transmission of 21, 61, 101, 114, 116–119; *see also* PTSD (post-traumatic stress disorder)
traumatic fistula 89, 177n124
*Trbić* case, State Court of BiH 169
TRIAL International 147, 168, 170n88, 174, 176
Trnopolje camp 41, 121
truth recovery in transitional justice 9, 185
Truth, Justice and Reconciliation Committee (TJRC), Kenya 231
Tuđman, Franjo 36, 37

Uganda 82, 202; formerly abducted girls 61; rape and sexual violence 60n48, 61–62, 89, 109; reparations 166
Ukraine 24
UN Commission of Experts 39, 40–41, 42–43, 44, 47
UN General Assembly, Basic Principles and Guidelines on the Right to a Remedy and Reparation for Victims of Gross Violation of International Human Rights Law and Serious Violations of International Humanitarian Law 22, 156–157, 160, 210, 214
UN Mechanism for International Criminal Tribunals 187–190
UN Secretary-General's Guidance Note on Reparations for Conflict-Related Sexual Violence 22, 159–160, 197, 208
UN Security Council: *Report of the Secretary-General on Conflict-Related Sexual Violence* 2; Resolution 1325 47, 158, 197; Resolution 1820 47; Resolution 2106 47; Resolution 780 39; Resolution 819 85n35; UN Mechanism for International Criminal Tribunals 187–190
UNDP (United Nations Development Programme) 143–144, 160; Human Development Report 199
unemployment/employment 21, 76, 97–98, 201–202, **203**, **204**
Uruguay 194

US: and comfort women 32; Lieber Code 29, 30; rapes and sexual violence in the Vietnam war 26
*Ustaše* 37, 78n7

vaginismus 79n10
van der Merwe, Hugo 232
*Vatreni konji* (Fire Horses): sexual violence crimes by 43, 44; *see also* HVO (Croatian Defence Council)
Velika Kladuša 45, 46
vetting systems in transitional justice 7
victim and witness protection 136–139; experiences of survivors of rape and sexual violence in BiH 142, 143–144, 145–147, 152–153, 190–191; protected witness status 141, 145, 146, 147, 149, 151–152, 170, 172; UN Mechanism for International Criminal Tribunals 188–189
*victim-survivors* 221
Victim/Witness Support Service Project 143–144
victimhood, and agency 221
Victims and Witnesses Section (VWS), ICTY 136–137, 152, 190, 193–194
Victims and Witnesses Section (VWS), UN Mechanism for International Criminal Tribunals 188
victims, terminology 3
Vietnam war 26
Viktor Bubanji camp 41, 103
Vinck, Patrick 7
violence: social ecology of 204–214, **209**, **210**; *see also* rape and sexual violence; sexual violence
*Vive Žene* 182
Vojno camp 141
von Hagenbach, Peter 29
vulnerability, and agency 4
VWS (Victims and Witnesses Section), ICTY 136–137, 152, 190, 193–194
VWS (Victims and Witnesses Section), UN Mechanism for International Criminal Tribunals 188

Waldorf, Lars 12, 232
Wallström, Margot 124
war crimes, recognition of rape and sexual violence in conflict as 34
Weinstein, Harvey M. 7
wife blaming 104–107
WISP (Witness Support and Protection Unit), UN Mechanism for International Criminal Tribunals 188–189
witness support offices (WSOs) 144
Witness Support Section (WSS), State Court of BiH 142, 143
witnesses: protected 141, 145, 146, 147, 149, 151–152, 170, 172; *see also* victim and witness protection in criminal prosecutions
women: ordinary everyday violence 5, 13; participation in war crimes 83, 83n30; as peace-builders 158–159, 197; portrayal of as victims 3, 13;structural violence against 5, 13, 60
Women's Court 9, 212
Women's Outreach Programme, ICC (International Criminal Court) 207
World War II: post-war military tribunals 30–32; rape and sexual violence 26–27, 30–32; sexual trauma following 55–56
WSOs (witness support offices) 144
WSS (Witness Support Section), State Court of BiH 142, 143

Xhafa-Mripa, Alketa 209, 219–220, 233

Yazidi community 24
Youth Outreach Programme, ICTY 211
Yugoslav National Army (JNA) 36–37, 52
Yugoslavia (SFRY: Socialist Federal Republic of Yugoslavia) 35–36

Žarkov, Dubravka 3
*Žena Žrtva Rata* 66, 114, 178, 179, 180

For Product Safety Concerns and Information please contact our EU
representative GPSR@taylorandfrancis.com
Taylor & Francis Verlag GmbH, Kaufingerstraße 24, 80331 München, Germany

www.ingramcontent.com/pod-product-compliance
Ingram Content Group UK Ltd.
Pitfield, Milton Keynes, MK11 3LW, UK
UKHW020010200926
475702UK00014B/1805
* 9 7 8 0 3 6 7 1 9 1 7 8 8 *